The Lost Sheep in Philosophy of Religion

Contemporary research in philosophy of religion is dominated by traditional problems such as the nature of evil, arguments against theism, issues of foreknowledge and freedom, the divine attributes, and religious pluralism. This volume instead focuses on unrepresented and underrepresented issues in the discipline. The essays address how issues like race, sexual orientation, gender identity, disability, feminist and pantheist conceptions of the divine, and non-human animals connect to existing issues in philosophy of religion. By staking out new avenues for future research, this book will be of interest to a wide range of scholars in analytic philosophy of religion and analytic philosophical theology.

Blake Hereth is a PhD Candidate in philosophy at the University of Washington. Ze has defended animal immortality in *Heaven and Philosophy* (2018), animal universalism in *Paradise Understood: New Philosophical Essays on Heaven* (2017), and afterlife justice for transgender persons in *Hinder Them Not: Centering Marginalized Voices in Analytic Theology* (forthcoming).

Kevin Timpe holds the William H. Jellema Chair in Christian Philosophy at Calvin College. His books include *Disability and Inclusive Communities* (2018), the *Routledge Companion to Free Will* (2017), and *Free Will and Theism* (2016). In addition to philosophy of religion, Timpe's scholarly work focuses on philosophy of disability, metaphysics, and virtue ethics.

Routledge Studies in the Philosophy of Religion

Galileo and the Conflict between Religion and Science
Gregory W. Dawes

The Arguments of Aquinas
A Philosophical View
J. J. MacIntosh

Philosophical Approaches to Demonology
Edited by Benjamin W. McCraw and Robert Arp

Eighteenth-Century Dissent and Cambridge Platonism
Reconceiving the Philosophy of Religion
Louise Hickman

Systematic Atheology
Atheism's Reasoning with Theology
John R. Shook

Does God Matter?
Essays on the Axiological Consequences of Theism
Edited by Klaas J. Kraay

Religious Ethics and Constructivism
A Metaethical Inquiry
Edited by Kevin Jung

Philosophical Essays Against Open Theism
Edited by Benjamin H. Arbour

The Lost Sheep in Philosophy of Religion
New Perspectives on Disability, Gender, Race, and Animals
Edited by Blake Hereth and Kevin Timpe

For more information about this series, please visit: www.routledge.com/Routledge-Studies-in-the-Philosophy-of-Religion/book-series/SE0427

The Lost Sheep in Philosophy of Religion

New Perspectives on Disability, Gender, Race, and Animals

Edited by Blake Hereth and Kevin Timpe

NEW YORK AND LONDON

First published 2020
by Routledge
52 Vanderbilt Avenue, New York, NY 10017

and by Routledge
2 Park Square, Milton Park, Abingdon, Oxon OX14 4RN

Routledge is an imprint of the Taylor & Francis Group, an informa business

© 2020 Taylor & Francis

The right of the editors to be identified as the authors of the editorial material, and of the authors for their individual chapters, has been asserted in accordance with sections 77 and 78 of the Copyright, Designs and Patents Act 1988.

All rights reserved. No part of this book may be reprinted or reproduced or utilised in any form or by any electronic, mechanical, or other means, now known or hereafter invented, including photocopying and recording, or in any information storage or retrieval system, without permission in writing from the publishers.

Trademark notice: Product or corporate names may be trademarks or registered trademarks, and are used only for identification and explanation without intent to infringe.

Library of Congress Cataloging-in-Publication Data
A catalog record for this book has been requested

ISBN: 978-0-367-07747-1 (hbk)
ISBN: 978-0-429-02253-1 (ebk)

Typeset in Sabon
by Apex CoVantage, LLC

To Benjamin, Jameson, Margaret, Mary, Sadie, and Kona, children of God who shame the wise—

To everyone whose voice has been silenced, whose dignity has been downtrodden:

> *He prayeth best, who loveth best*
> *All things both great and small;*
> *For the dear God who loveth us,*
> *He made and loveth all.*
> —Samuel Taylor Coleridge,
> "The Rime of the Ancient Mariner"

Contents

Acknowledgments	x
Foreword	xii
NICHOLAS WOLTERSTORFF	
Introduction	1
KEVIN TIMPE AND BLAKE HERETH	

SECTION I
Methodology   29

1 Philosophy of Religion From the Margins: A Theoretical Analysis and Focus Group Study — HELEN DE CRUZ   31

2 That We May Be Whole: Doing Philosophy of Religion With the Whole Self — MICHELLE PANCHUK   55

SECTION II
Religious Epistemology and Experience   77

3 Epistemic Injustice and Religious Experience — KIRK LOUGHEED   79

4 Smelling God: Olfaction as Religious Experience — JOSHUA COCKAYNE   97

5 'Not My People': Jewish-Christian Ethics and Divine Reversals in Response to Injustice — JOSHUA BLANCHARD   120

SECTION III
Non-Human Animals — 139

6 Eschatology for Creeping Things (and Other Animals) — 141
   DUSTIN CRUMMETT

7 Exploring Theological Zoology: Might Non-Human Animals Be Spiritual (but Not Religious)? — 163
   FAITH GLAVEY PAWL

8 Animal Gods — 183
   BLAKE HERETH

SECTION IV
Disability — 209

9 The Resurrection of the Minority Body: Physical Disability in the Life of Heaven — 211
   DAVID EFIRD

10 Disabled Beatitude — 241
   KEVIN TIMPE

11 When Personhood Goes Wrong in Ethics and Philosophical Theology: Disability, Ableism, and (Modern) Personhood — 264
   SCOTT M. WILLIAMS

SECTION V
Sex, Gender, and Race — 291

12 Marriage, Reproduction, and the Incarnation: What Could Jesus Do? — 293
   ERIC T. YANG AND STEPHEN T. DAVIS

13 A Transfeminist Critique of Mormon Theologies of Gender — 312
   KELLI D. POTTER

14 Heavenly (Gendered) Bodies? Gender Persistence in the Resurrection and Its Implications — 328
   HILARY YANCEY

15 Limbo, Hiddenness, and the Beatific Vision (and
   Procreation, for Some, in the Life to Come) 347
   DAVID WORSLEY

16 Religious Racial Formation Theory and Its Metaphysics:
   A Research Program in the Philosophy of Religion 365
   SAMEER YADAV

   Contributors 391
   Index 394

Acknowledgments

This volume was conceived in the summer of 2016, growing from dissatisfaction with the state of contemporary philosophy of religion. While both of us had complained publicly and privately about this, the further step of *doing* something about it was a step into the darkness. Each of us had worked to change philosophy of religion in small ways—Kevin with disability, Blake with non-human animals—but these efforts were piecemeal and unlikely to solicit widespread attention. So, in October 2016, Blake contacted Kevin about the possibility of a volume that would not only cover underrepresented topics, but one that would also actively seek to promote work done by philosophers from underrepresented groups.

The ideas in this book are due principally to the imagination of the contributors. When the call for papers was released, we invited contributors to write about underrepresented topics in philosophy of religion. We were pleased and thrilled to see a smattering of philosophical questions that, until now, have oft been under-discussed or outright ignored by the larger sub-discipline. Despite our inability to include all of the fascinating abstracts sent to us, we can report that the boundaries of contemporary philosophy of religion are expanding in exciting ways. This is good because, as we observe in our introduction, philosophy of religion is something of an 'occupied' territory and the 'occupiers' are not especially diverse. The field therefore reflects a relatively narrow set of interests. Fortunately, that is changing thanks to essays like the ones in this volume. We're thankful especially to philosophers from underrepresented groups who are willing to introduce new and important issues motivated by their own historically marginalized experiences. This volume is a testament to the fact that when queer philosophers, philosophers of color, disabled philosophers, women philosophers, and non-Christian philosophers work together, great things can happen.

Special thanks are owed, too, to our Routledge editor, Andrew Weckenmann, who enthusiastically embraced our project, and to Allie Simmons, who shepherded the volume to its final conclusion. Our project coincided with three similar projects: a special issue of *Res Philosophica* edited by Jon Jacobs, the 2018 Logos Workshop in Philosophical Theology at the

University of Notre Dame led by Michelle Panchuk and Mike Rea, and the volume that resulted from that same workshop. Each of these projects embraces the work we undertake in this volume, and we benefited greatly from the partnerships. So we extend our thanks to Jon, Michelle, and Mike for supporting what could have been seen as a competing project. Much of our work was also inspired by the late Marilyn McCord Adams, whose tireless work in defense of LGBTQ+ persons and their interests has been for many of us the very hand of God in the world. Finally, we are grateful for our partners, Rebekah and Allison, who were wellsprings of good ideas for this book and without whom the volume would not exist. Their courage, love, and desire to see philosophy of religion change for the better can't be overestimated.

Blake Hereth and Kevin Timpe
April 2019
Seattle, WA

Foreword

As most readers of this volume will know, over the past 50 years there has been a remarkable resurgence of philosophy of religion within the analytic tradition of philosophy—less so within the contemporary continental tradition. The essays in this collection constitute an expansive and venturesome contribution to that resurgence, taking it in distinctly new directions.

The flourishing of analytic philosophy of religion has not suffered from lack of critics, critics both hostile to the movement and critics sympathetic to it. In their introduction to *The Lost Sheep*, the editors, in order to explain the particular contribution that the essays make to the movement, offer a very helpful survey of the sorts of criticisms that have been lodged against the movement.

Some of those opposed to the movement make no secret of the fact that it is religion they deplore. Others are opposed not to religion but to analytic philosophy. They dislike it for its dry, 'lifeless' style, finding the style especially inappropriate for discussing religion. Others disapprove of the fact that analytic philosophers, rather than discussing religion as such, have focused most of their attention on one particular religion, namely, the Christian religion. It's not really philosophy of *religion*. And yet others are critical of the fact that, rather often, participants in the movement do not discuss the topic at hand 'objectively' but write in defense of some component of their own religious thought or practice. It's not 'real' philosophy, these critics say, but apologetics. One wonders whether these critics would launch the same criticism against the writings of contemporary naturalists—or against the writings of the so-called *new atheists*, Richard Dawkins, Daniel Dennett, and Sam Harris—that it's not 'real' philosophy but apologetics.

Those who have no problem with analytic philosophy of religion as such but are critical of the way in which it has developed generally find it too narrow in various respects. The editors share this criticism, as do I.

A criticism that those working in ancillary fields—religious studies, theology, biblical studies—often lodge against the movement is that analytic philosophers are ignorant or dismissive of work in their fields, sometimes arrogantly so, with the result that learning from developments in those fields is foreclosed. Others lament the fact that most analytic philosophers of religion focus their attention on theistic religions, especially the Christian religion, rather than bringing religions in general into the discussion. Others regret the narrow range of participants in the movement; the great majority of participants are white males. And many of those sympathetic to the movement lament the narrow range of topics that have been discussed. Philosophical theology and the epistemology of religious belief have garnered far and way most of the attention. This present volume is an important contribution to correcting those last two types of narrowness: the narrow range of participants and the narrow range of topics.

The religion of some people is pinched, consisting of little more than some beliefs about God, some beliefs about the afterlife, and a couple of moral maxims, such as do unto others as you would have them do unto you. But if we look at the religions of human beings in general, what we see is that, in thought and practice, religious people engage, in distinctly religious ways, the totality of what we human beings care about: plants, animals, the environment, disabled persons, youth, old age, sickness, health, morality, violence, love, justice, certain books, certain images, certain places, birth, death, sex, marriage—on and on. And what we see is that it is not just white males who are religious but human beings of all sorts. The signal contribution of this volume is that, with great philosophical imagination, the authors engage religiously a good many of the vast array of things that we human beings care about, and that the racial, ethnic, and gender identity of the authors is diverse.

As I was reading the essays, two contrasting images came to mind: one, the image of formerly peering at religion through cracks between the boards along with men like me; the other, the image of now looking at religion through doors thrown wide open with people quite different from me.

Nicholas Wolterstorff

Introduction

Kevin Timpe and Blake Hereth

The 'Standard Story'

According to a fairly standard story, philosophy of religion and philosophical theology are flourishing as subspecialties.[1] As one proponent of this standard story puts it: "Never since the late Middle Ages has philosophical theology so flourished as it has during the past 30 years" (Wolterstorff 2009, 155; see also Swinburne 2005; Hasker 2019). The present flourishing was made possible by the collapse of logical positivism and empiricist and Popperian requirements of falsifiability in the middle of the 20th century. This collapse was then followed by an increase in theistic, as opposed to naturalistic, philosophy of religion.[2] During the 'metaphysical turn' of the 1970s, analytic philosophy of religion began a period of proliferation. Initially, this renewed interest focused largely on religious language, religious epistemology, and natural theology (including not only arguments for existence of God but also competing accounts of the nature of the traditional divine attributes). Then, beginning in approximately the mid-1980s, philosophy of religion broadened out in a number of ways. It underwent diversification, both in terms of topics and in terms of methodology. (As we'll see below, this diversification wasn't as robust as many think it should be. *The Lost Sheep* seeks to make philosophy of religion even more diverse than it has been, by welcoming into the fold topics and perspectives that previously have been marginalized.) Paul Draper and Ryan Nichols think that evidence of the standard story is easy to find, including the interest of students of all levels and the quantity of articles, journals, books, and conferences devoted to philosophy of religion (Draper and Nichols 2013, 420f.). The flourishing of philosophy of religion has even led Alvin Plantinga to admit that specifically Christian philosophy of religion, which as discussed below is the vast majority of contemporary philosophy of religion, now faces the potential danger of "triumphalism" (Plantinga 2011, 268).

While the standard story holds sway as a description of philosophy of religion in the later decades of the 20th century and the opening of the 21st, it is not uniformly endorsed. John Loftus, for instance, thinks that it fails. Instead of flourishing, Loftus thinks that philosophy of religion is in a 'crisis.' What exactly, one might ask, is the nature of this crisis?

> There is no longer any debate about what the truth is among intellectually honest individuals. Faith-based reasoning is not a virtue. Faith as a method is unreliable. It should no longer be tolerated as a justification for anything. . . . We can no longer take obfuscationist philosophy used in defense of the Christian delusion or any other religion seriously.
>
> (Loftus 2016, 113)[3]

Though it's not inevitable, Loftus thinks it's only a matter of time before the curtain is pulled back and the philosophical wizard is revealed for a theological charlatan. Loftus's reasoning for this conclusion, in our view, leaves much to be desired. But he isn't alone in rejecting the standard story. Graham Oppy, for instance also rejects it, though his rejection of it is more measured than Loftus's excessive rhetoric (see Oppy 2019).

Criticisms of Contemporary Philosophy of Religion

Even if, unlike Loftus, one thinks that the standard story is true—or true enough as a general characterization of an academic field and its practitioners—one could still think that the standard story is problematic as a view about what philosophy of religion ought to be.[4] Philosophy of religion, after all, is not without its critics.

Among these critics is Nick Trakakis, who argues against analytic philosophy of religion in his provocatively titled book, *The End of Philosophy of Religion*. Analytic philosophy, Trakakis argues, is in a "deep crisis" (Trakakis 2008, 113).[5] It appears "'colorless' and monotonous, even mournful and melancholic in its endlessly futile attempts to render everything rationally comprehensible" (Trakakis 2008, 1). Whereas philosophy ought to, like religion, connect with the "existential and lived dimension" (Trakakis 2008, 115) of life, too often analytic analyses and arguments "quickly become convoluted and technical" (Trakakis 2008, 49). Trying to capture the lived experience of religion in analytic prose renders the material sterile, controlled, and constrained. The overly objective approach, inherited from analytic philosophy's modeling itself on the supposed objective and neutral approach of science, "cannot come to terms with the mysterious transcendent reality that is disclosed in religious practice" (Trakakis 2008, 2; see also Westphal 1973). Trakakis's book's title is prescriptive rather than descriptive. Unlike Loftus, he doesn't seem to think that philosophy of religion is floundering. But it should end, at least as practiced in its current form:

> This kind of philosophy may not, as a matter of historical fact, have come to an end, but a growing awareness of the unduly narrow

ends that can be pursued under its banner, as well as the personal and political dangers involved in the pursuit of such ends, is leading to widespread calls for an end to be finally put to this approach to philosophy.

(Trakakis 2008, 1)

The analytic approach to philosophy is especially problematic in philosophy of religion given that "philosophy of religion is the last place one would expect to find such a disconnect between life and thought, between the lived praxis of faith in the philosophical pursuit of wisdom (philo*sophia*)" (Trakakis 2008, 2). Philosophy of religion needs to recognize this disconnect and work to take back engagement with the lived experiences rooted in their wider socioeconomic environment of religious believers (Trakakis 2008, 118).

In an extended review, Timothy Knepper compares to *The End of Philosophy of Religion* to a "Hollywood blockbuster [that] fails to deliver on a provocative title" (Knepper 2014, 123). Knepper agrees that analytic philosophy of religion of the sort that Trakakis is calling for the end of is problematic, primarily because of

> the simple fact that philosophy of religion is significantly out of step with, and therefore has very little offer to, one of its parent fields, religious studies. . . . Philosophy of religion can look more like philosophical theology—not a (relatively) religiously neutral examination of reason-giving in the religions of the world, but an overt apologetic for (or against) the reasonableness or value of some particular kind of religion.
>
> (Knepper 2014, 123)[6]

Philosophy of religion, Knepper goes on to argue, is strangely silent when it should be contributing to "cultural-historical diversity among the human acts of religious reason-giving about which it inquires . . . [including fostering] diversity of race, gender, class, and creed among its inquiring community" (Knepper 2014, 123). We return to the issue of diversity below.

Perhaps unsurprisingly given that what you hold in your hands is a book in the philosophy of religion, we don't find the above objections to philosophy of religion, either individually or collectively, to be unanswerable. However, our goal in the present book isn't to argue for why philosophy of religion is worth doing. We think arguing for such is a worthy goal, but not our present goal. While we think that philosophy of religion is worth doing, we agree with some of its critics that, even if it ought to continue, certain features of philosophy of religion need to change.

Some think that philosophy of religion is not just problematic in detail, but in whole. What is called 'philosophy of religion' isn't, since it's not really engaged in philosophical inquiry at all. John Schellenberg illustrates this suspicion about specifically Christian philosophy of religion in the following passage:

> What Plantinga and Co. are doing is not really philosophy at all, as I have mostly been assuming so far, but rather theology or theological apologetics, on behalf of the Christian community as they understand it, using the tools of philosophy.
> (Schellenberg 2009, 100; see also Schellenberg 2019)

And Greg Dawes levels a similar objection:

> While the arguments put forward by many Christian philosophers are serious arguments, there is something less than serious about the spirit in which they are being offered. There is a direction in which those arguments will not be permitted to go. Arguments that support the faith will be seriously entertained; those that apparently undermine the faith must be countered, at any cost. Philosophy, to use the traditional phrase, is merely a 'handmaid' of theology. There is, to my mind, something frivolous about a philosophy of this sort.
> (Dawes 2014; for discussion and criticism of this more general suspicion of philosophy of religion, see Taliaferro and Dressen 2013)

This sort of objection is most often raised against specifically natural theology. We agree that some of the natural theology that is published by Christian philosophers is theologically or apologetically motivated philosophical inquiry. But we don't think that natural theology is the only proper task in philosophy of religion. As Scott MacDonald has argued, "even if strict natural theology represents an appropriately philosophical manner of reflection on theological matters, it is a mistake to think of it as the only sort of theological reflection open to philosophers" (Macdonald 2009, 20f). Whereas one task of philosophy is justification, another appropriate task is what MacDonald calls clarification. The philosopher of religion engaged in clarification is

> not primarily concerned with the epistemic justification of [a particular view]. She is concerned instead with understanding, developing, systematizing, and explaining it. It is possible for her to do all these things without raising the issue of its truth or her justification for holding it. The fact is that a very large part of philosophy has nothing directly to do with the truth or justification of certain theories or propositions. . . . Clarification of theological matters is a legitimate task for the philosopher. Philosophers have not only a justificatory but also a clarificatory role to play in theology. Moreover, given that the nature of clarificatory activities is such that one can engage in them without regard to the epistemic status of the theories one

> takes up, it follows that there can be no epistemic restrictions of any sort on the kinds of issues open to philosophical clarification. . . . When the philosopher takes up these kinds of issues with the aim of articulating and developing them, probing their internal coherence, joint consistency, and systematic connections, and exploring their relations to other theological and nontheological doctrines, she will be engaged in appropriately philosophical reflection on specifically Christian theological matters.
>
> (Macdonald 2009, 24f.)[7]

So, if the task is primarily of the clarification of religious belief rather than a justification for it, we don't see an author's commitment to a particular religious tradition (or even opposition to religious belief altogether) as an insurmountable obstacle. It is true that clarification in philosophy of religion should be understood as conditional in nature, where that conditional is 'if a particular religious tradition or doctrine is taken to be true. . . .' Granted, this requires accepting theological evidence within the philosophical approach in question. But we don't see this as ultimately problematic so long as it's done transparently.

The Need to Diversify in Light of Narrowness

Much more problematic, in our view, is a set of objections to contemporary philosophy of religion which hold that the field is too restricted in one or more ways. Here we'll mention four, though we don't think that these are exhaustive. The first, already hinted at in the comments from Knepper but also found in Schilbrack, is that philosophy of religion is too narrow in terms of its engagement with cognate disciplines like religious studies, comparative religion, biblical studies, and historical theology. It's this narrowness that leads scholars in these other areas to disengage from, or never engage with, analytic philosophy of religion. Harriet Harris and Christopher Insole, for instance, write that

> theologians are very resistant to engaging in the kind of reflection that analytical philosophers of religion employ. . . . We should not assume that this is due to a sense of threat from philosophy. On the contrary, it is often because philosophers seem to theologians to take an inappropriate approach to the Bible, to religious phenomena[,] or to articles of faith.
>
> (Harris and Insole 2005, 17)

Doing either theology or religious studies well requires engagement with sources, disciplines, and approaches that do not easily lend themselves to analytic analysis. Few analytic philosophers of religion have professional training in these areas. Speaking specifically of Christian philosophers of religion (and, as we'll see shortly, they're almost all Christian), Alan Torrance writes that the philosopher of religion

> is obliged to engage with a book that is full of metaphor, rhetorical plays, and the semantic shifting of everyday concepts, not to mention the kind of counter-intuitive claims and hermeneutical dilemmas that would cause most analytic philosophers to turn to drink. This makes it tempting for theologians to allow the theism of natural theology to condition the distinctively historical character of knowledge of God as we find it presented in the philosophically counter-intuitive testimony of the Old and New Testaments.
> (Torrance 2013, 31)

Related here are the claims that philosophers of religion often take problematic, and in some cases naïve, approaches to revealed texts and other theological sources (see Cortez 2013) or that they're insufficiently attentive to the historical nature of the religious faith that they're seeking to engage. Thomas McCall, for instance, says that philosophers working on religious issues are sometimes "naive with respect to the history of doctrine," particularly an awareness of and sensitivity to the social and intellectual context of those doctrines (McCall 2015, 27; see also Simmons 2019, 199).

What it would take to pay attention to religious studies, historical theology, and religious hermeneutics is an even more daunting task when one considers the second way in which contemporary analytic philosophy of religion is too narrow, and that's in terms of the sort of religions (or, in most part, *religion*) that it seeks to engage. We noted how Knepper thinks that contemporary philosophy of religion fails to be sufficiently diverse:

> the object of inquiry in any philosophy of religion that has something to offer to the academic study of religion must be religiously diverse—not the religious reason giving of some one religion or type of religion but the religious reason-giving of all religions in so far as this is possible. . . . For philosophers of religion hardly understand anything about human acts of religious reason—given in general their diversities, patterns, deployments, genealogies—if they limit their inquiry to a small subset of the whole. First, philosophers of religion risk mistaking part for the whole.
> (Knepper 2014, 125–126)

And the part it has in mind that is too often mistaken for the whole is hardly a shock: Christian theism.[8] Knepper isn't the only one to raise this criticism about the overly Christian focus of analytic philosophy of religion. Moti Mizrahi recently writes that analytic philosophy of religion "does not pay much attention to religions other than Christianity, even monotheistic religions other than Christianity, such as Judaism and Islam" (Mizrahi 2019, 3; see also De Cruz and De Smedt 2017; Draper and Nichols 2013; Frankenberry 2004). Knepper notes that in three recent edited collections on philosophy of religion (Peterson and VanArragon 2004; Nagasawa and Wielenberg 2008; Kvanvig 2009), only two of the 88 total entries devote significant attention to religions other than Christianity or Judaism (Knepper 2014, 10 footnote 12; see also Loewen 2015). Even books with entries on Hinduism, Buddhism, and African or Chinese religions, like the *Routledge Companion to Philosophy of Religion* or Blackwell's *A Companion to Philosophy of Religion*, are typically overly Christian-centric in terms of the specific topics explored at length (e.g., chapters on resurrection but not reincarnation, or chapters on divine command theory that engage almost exclusively Christian authors despite a robust history of the same issues in Muslim theology). J. Aaron Simmons describes the non-Christian and especially non-theistic perspectives in much philosophy of religion, where these perspectives are found, as usually nothing more than "an add-on to the book . . . rather than a constitutive aspect of the various questions being asked throughout" (Simmons 2019, 199). As Knepper again notes, "given that they are collections in the philosophy of *religion*, their lack of diversity with respect to religious-philosophical commitments is more conspicuous" (Knepper 2014, 10, footnote 12; see also Oppy 2014, 118; Schilbrack 2014; Simmons 2019).

The second kind of narrowness that one finds in the contemporary philosophy of religion can be found in the diversity, or lack thereof, of those who are doing the contemporary work in philosophy of religion. In addition to, as discussed above, being overwhelmingly Christian,[9] the field of philosophy of religion is overwhelmingly male and even more overwhelmingly white (see Knepper 2014, 10, footnote 12).[10] Contemporary analytic philosophy in general has begun paying more attention to diversity. But philosophy of religion seems to lag behind this general trend. This lack of diversity should not be ignored. Knepper thinks that being unaware of the lack of diversity is more troubling than the lack of diversity (Knepper 2014, 133).

Contemporary philosophy of religion as a whole is also overly cognitive. This isn't to say that the focus on the rationality of religious beliefs or particular religious doctrines is problematic, nor that any particular author working on these issues is at fault for doing so. Rather, the point is one about the overarching pattern that leaves out important religious practices (see Cottingham 2014, especially ch. 1 and 7). Merold Westphal writes that "the primacy of [the] theoretical reasonable" needs to be challenged, as does the "corollary that our chief end is to collect a pocket full of true propositions about God" (Westphal 2019, 79). Philosophy of religion has been criticized along these lines for tending toward a hyper-intellectualism that doesn't sufficiently connect with, for instance, religions' commitment to spiritual formation, worship, and other practices (for an articulation of and reply to this worry, see Crisp 2017, 165; for related discussions see Wolterstorff 2018; Ebels-Duggan 2019; Simmons 2019).

We take the preceding paragraphs to sufficiently establish a number of ways in which contemporary philosophy of religion is too narrow, even though we think the case for that conclusion is sufficiently obvious for those familiar with the discipline. What might not be as obvious is *why* that narrowness is problematic, if in fact it is. As indicated earlier, we don't think that it's problematic for, say, a white male to write about how a particularly philosophical issue, say the contemporary free will debates, relates to Christian eschatological doctrines. What we think is problematic is the distribution of (or lack thereof) a wide range of authors writing on a maximal spread of religious topics, engaging with a wide variety of religious traditions and related scholarly fields. Harriet A. Harris argues that

> the narrow focused and rigour promoted by analytical philosophy reduces the ambition of philosophers of religion. It clips our wings by restricting itself to it what Basil Mitchell . . . calls 'minute philosophy,' philosophy that stays with these topics that can be treated with exemplary clarity into rigour.
>
> (Harris 2005, 101)

Similarly, Eleonore Stump has drawn our attention to the ways that "philosophy in the Anglo-American tradition has tended to leave to one side the messy and complicated issues involved in relations among persons" (Stump 2010, 25). While she agrees with Harris that the focus on rigor restricts its focus to those topics where such rigor can be pursued, she thinks it's misleadingly imprecise to locate the problem simply in such narrowness:

> Its cognitive *hemianopia* is its problem. Its intellectual vision is included or secured for the right half of the cognitive field, especially for the part in reality that include the complex, nuanced thought, behavior, and relations of persons. The deficit will perhaps be undetectable in work on modal logic or philosophy of mathematics, but in any issues where the interactions of persons make a difference [like religion] it is more likely to be in evidence.
>
> (Stump 2010, 25)[11]

Even if the standard story about philosophy of philosophy of religion in the 20th century that we began with is true, things have changed dramatically in the past 50 or 60 years. As J. Aaron Simmons puts it, "today contemporary Christian philosophy is no longer the excluded community within the philosophical mainstream, but instead is now in the position of potentially excluding those who don't fit into its own self-conception—either of proper Christianity or proper philosophy" (Simmons 2019, 200).

If, as Draper and Nichols argue, group membership can create bias (Draper and Nichols 2013, 430), one way to try and reduce that bias is to increase the range of views held by the group.

Given these forms of narrowness, we think philosophy of religion would benefit from widening or diversification in a number of ways—by bringing more sheep into the fold. Fortunately, that seems to be happening. We understand the present volume to be part of a larger effort to diversify philosophy of religion in light of these forms of narrowness. Specifically, our volume seeks to direct attention to both underrepresented topics and persons within philosophy of religion. In terms of topics, there's been an almost exclusive focus on what Amber Leigh Griffioen has called 'proper philosophy of religion,' relegating 'anti-orthodox philosophy of religion' to the fringe.[12] The contemporary scene within philosophy of religion is dominated by classic problems in the discipline such as problems of evil and other arguments against theism, issues of foreknowledge and freedom, the divine attributes, and religious pluralism. We think these traditional issues are important and note our support of further work on them. Nevertheless, these are not the only topics of importance. Other important topics have been left unrepresented or underrepresented in the contemporary literature. "[I]t may be that the primary threat to Christian philosophy today does not come from particular notions of anti-realism or naturalism, but instead from the emergence of potential hegemonic privilege and hermeneutic amnesia within contemporary Christian philosophy itself" (Simmons 2019, 196). This privilege also relates to a need to focus on authors from historically underrepresented groups.[13] Despite our efforts to help philosophy of religion diversify, we admit that even in this book there are kinds of diversity that are still not present. Methodologically, our volume prioritizes what is often referred to as analytic philosophy. And even though it's specifically a work in analytic philosophy of religion, it is nevertheless perhaps too limited in terms of its theological assumptions (or, to put the point a slightly different way, perhaps too little explicit attention is paid to those assumptions). Our list of contributors is also too heavily American/European, and thus interacting almost exclusively with Western theological traditions (and especially the Christian tradition). Our book isn't intended to do everything that is needed. In fact, no single volume could do all that needs to be done. Nevertheless, it's intended to be a part of this larger trajectory that we endorse. We must start somewhere.

The Present Volume

This brings us to what we *do* cover in this volume. The volume is divided into five sections. The first section addresses philosophical methodology within philosophy of religion and philosophical theology. The second section is about religious epistemology and experience. The third and fourth sections cover the place of non-human animals and disability in philosophical theology, respectively. The fifth and final section address issues of sex (including reproduction), gender, and race.

In Chapter 1, Helen De Cruz leads off by exploring how intersectionality affects the practice of philosophy of religion, which is obviously related to the issue of narrowness of perspectives mentioned above. To do this, De Cruz conducted a study with 12 people in two focus groups, all of whom are academic philosophers of religion. Drawing from the APA's Directory of Philosophers from Underrepresented Groups, De Cruz selected philosophers whose identities are in some way marginalized within academic philosophy generally and philosophy of religion more specifically. Those identities include Jewish, Muslim, Mormon, queer, trans*, woman, Latinx, African American, and Asian American from the United States, the United Kingdom, Israel, and Germany. Her focus group studies show not only that personal life experiences sparked interest and provided continued motivation to work in philosophy of religion, but also that the participants experienced significant *exclusion* within philosophy of religion. For example, some religious minorities report that they modify their presentations for a predominantly Christian audience. As De Cruz argues, the underrepresentation problem in philosophy of religion affects not only those who are underrepresented. It can also serve to explain why the sociological borders of philosophy of religion have failed to expand.

Michelle Panchuk's chapter takes its cues from De Cruz's empirical work and charts an expanded vision for philosophy of religion. Whereas traditional philosophy of religion has, like most of philosophy, shown a strong preference (if not a mandate) for a purportedly 'objective' methodology in which the philosopher is fully dispassionate and uninvested, Panchuk argues such an approach isn't feasible. In fact, that practice routinely privileges cisgender, heterosexual, middle-class, able-bodied, white, Christian, and male points of view. She draws on feminist theories of epistemic oppression to show how implicit attitudes and epistemically exclusionary practices harm both communities and the quest for philosophical knowledge. For example, philosophical discussions of race and gender often mention historical abuses of these groups, and 'solutions' proposed to these practices are often highly politicized. When, for example, a philosopher of religion who is also African American defends their view on how these wrongs should be righted, only to have their views subjected to further doctrinal tests from a predominantly white audience, they risk appearing as biased or emotionally invested if they defend their oppressed status or a theological proposal for relieving it. In other words, they appear as if they (but not their interlocutors) are *failing* to occupy the dispassionate view from nowhere. Panchuk writes (56),

If those who are not cisgender, straight, able-bodied, white, Christian men are more likely to be seen as not occupying that view, as especially emotional and especially biased, then it follows that members of underrepresented groups in the profession are most likely to be in a position where they feel the need to smother their own testimony.

In order for philosophy of religion to progress, it must include more non-dominant voices. Panchuk recommends making room for those voices by changing how philosophy is done. Instead of privileging an objective view from nowhere, we should recognize that this is unachievable by fallible beings who can scarcely escape their own epistemic positioning. Not only should we show epistemic humility in the face of our finitude, we should actively *embrace* non-dominant perspectives and assign a higher credence to them than we would otherwise. We should do this because the epistemic condition of those in privileged groups tends to *lessen* their knowledge by depriving them of other valuable perspectives. By widening the epistemic 'in-group,' we widen the knowledge that comes with it. Thus, Panchuk argues we should do philosophy "with the whole self" (73).

In Chapter 3, Kirk Lougheed opens the section on religious epistemology and experience. Despite considerable work on the epistemology of religious experience (Alston 1991; Moser 2008), issues of epistemic injustice have received comparatively little attention. Lougheed's chapter works to begin filling that gap. Following Miranda Fricker (2007), Lougheed contends that testimonial injustice "occurs when a testifier is given less credibility in her report about proposition P than is (epistemically) deserved" due to her inclusion in "a certain social group" (80). Women, for example, are members of a particular social group and their testimony often receives less credibility than it deserves, as Panchuk has already observed. This not only empowers members of dominant social groups, but *harms* those of less dominant (including oppressed) groups. Similarly, hermeneutical injustice occurs "when someone lacks the conceptual resources to fully understand her experiences because of the social group to which she belongs" (82). Lougheed then introduces readers to religious experience. He argues that intuitive knowledge is both possible in the context of religious experience and counts as evidence for religious beliefs. Using two fictional examples of otherwise credible persons whose history includes religious experiences, Lougheed claims that it would be presumptively irrational *not* to trust them.

Lougheed then invites us to consider common epistemic practices in the educated West. Theists, or at least those who claim a history of religious experience, often have their testimony rebuffed in those contexts. He cites Christopher Hitchens, Daniel Dennett, and Richard Dawkins as examples of persons who are *dismissive*—indeed, often *preemptively* dismissive—of religious persons and their testimonies. These individuals have their testimonies dismissed *because* they are members of a particular social group. Yet these individuals are often otherwise credible. Without a defeater for their testimony, Lougheed argues, the New Atheists and others are committing epistemic injustices. Moreover, Lougheed argues that even if someone is justified in believing that naturalism is true, which precludes the possibility of certain kinds of veridical religious experience, the general credibility of those who testify to having religious experiences is still *evidence* for the propositions supported by those experiences and should be treated as such. The tendency to dismiss testimony of religious experience out of hand fails to treat such experience as evidence.

The next chapter, by Joshua Cockayne, advocates a particular and oft-ignored kind of religious experience: olfaction. Contemporary accounts of religious experience prioritize seeing and hearing (Alston 1991; James 1902); Cockayne's chapter reveals a rich history of the use of smell in religious experience. As Cockayne observes, accounting for smell is an important feature of any exhaustive epistemology of religious experience since it includes experiences from social groups whose testimonies often receive little uptake in many religious settings. As an example, he cites the testimony of an autistic individual who expressed excitement at the prospect of smelling Jesus—a prospect others found surprising. After reviewing both ancient and contemporary views of the place of olfaction within religious experience, Cockayne draws on work by Adam Green (2009) to argue that "ordinary sense perception (seeing, hearing, touching, tasting, and, indeed, smelling) should be thought of as providing opportunities for indirect, but non-metaphorical experiences of God" (98). As a model of this, Cockayne applies N. Russell Hanson's (2002) and Michael Rea's (2018) accounts of *seeing-as*. According to Cockayne, even if a person's background beliefs and other cognitive states incline them to interpret certain experiences as perceptions of God, this can and does 'count' as an indirect, non-metaphorical experience of God. He argues:

> An ultrasound technician, in virtue of her training, sees a blob on a screen as the leg of an unborn child. . . . Just as the training of the ultrasound technician means that her various background beliefs and other cognitive states incline her to have certain experiences *as* perceptions of arms and legs of fetuses, a person with the relevant cognitive states might perceive an internal sense, an audible voice, or a beautiful sunset as an experience *as* perceptions of God.
>
> (113)

The technician's experience of the fetus, while indirect, is clearly non-metaphorical. She does not experience the blob as a metaphor for a fetus in the same way that someone might experience a crown as a metaphor for Queen Elizabeth II. Similarly, the smell of incense during Mass might serve not simply as a metaphor for God, but an indirect experience of God, even if the experiencing subject's background beliefs and experiences play a role in how they perceive the incense. As Cockayne argues, "one benefit of this account is that it leaves room for the kind of subjectivity (or subject dependency) of religious experience" (115). It's also inclusive of more kinds of religious experience, as the example with the autistic's comments about smell shows.

In Chapter 5, Joshua Blanchard offers a Jewish perspective on 'divine reversals': cases in which God appears to take the side of 'the enemy' in response to injustices committed against them. This runs counter to the typical theme of God standing alongside the Israelites in battle and in their quest for the Promised Land. The Hebrew Scriptures, however, clearly show both possibilities. For example, God appears to promise land to the Israelites only to side *against* them in battle and deliver the land to the Babylonians. The lesson, Blanchard claims, is that "correctness about doctrine and morals can be pulled apart from not just divine favor but also real relationship and covenantal standing, even divine favor and standing *with respect to those very matters that one is correct about*" (131), which has interesting implications in a number of places in contemporary philosophy of religion in addition to debates over political and theological Zionism. In the debate about Christian sexual ethics, for example, even if a conservative position is true, it might also be true "that, *for the time being* and even for quite a while, God not only permits but sanctifies alternative models that serve the underlying values" for human love and sexuality in the first place (133). To illustrate: if God's plan for love and sexuality includes, as an essential goal, that love persist despite trials and tribulations, then oppression against gay love might result in God *legitimating* that love for a time. Although far from settling these issues, Blanchard's essay poses the unsettling possibility that even the theologically clearheaded might be confronted with a God who sides against them in cases where they are "failing to live in ways that reflect the values that undergird the very idea that one is right about" (135). Perhaps this is why, as some have argued, it is not enough to be right but to be 'right about being right' or to be 'right in the right way.' Blanchard's conclusion could thus put constraints on how we ought to engage in philosophy of religion.

Even a cursory glance at the major issues in contemporary philosophy of religion and philosophical theology reveals an anthropocentric bias. Humans are at the forefront our research. Non-human animals (hereafter 'animals,' even though this shouldn't be taken to imply that humans are not animals) have been discussed only at the periphery, particularly with respect to the problem of evil. The two major contemporary philosophical monographs on animals, for example, have focused exclusively on the problem of evil (Murray 2008; Dougherty 2014). Fortunately, animals are the subject of increased attention. Dustin Crummett's chapter, "Eschatology for Creeping Things (and Other Animals)," introduces the book's section on animals. This paper builds on Crummett's prior work on animals within philosophy of religion (Crummett 2017), where he argued that traditional philosophers of religion have ignored the suffering of insects, which (controversially) he argues have a morally relevant kind of well-being. In this chapter, Crummett reviews six arguments for animal universalism, the thesis that all animals with interests will receive eternal, infinitely good afterlives. According to the Beneficence Argument, which Crummett defends, moral agents (including God) have a presumptive obligation to benefit others, especially when there's no moral cost to doing so. Since providing animals with eternal, infinitely good afterlives would benefit them, God is obligated to save them from death and bring them to heaven (or someplace just as good). This is Crummett's primary, original contribution to the defense of animal universalism.

Crummett then considers a handful of other arguments, arguing that most of them are either implausible or are insufficiently attentive to the diversity of animals such that the argument doesn't establish animal *universalism*. For example, he argues that the Harm Avoidance Argument (Graves, Hereth, and John 2017) fails because it's unclear that all animals are harmed by their premature deaths. Crummett also argues that the Compensation Argument, according to which God is obligated to bring all animals to heaven because they have suffered unjustly in the world (Murray 2008; Hereth 2018), fails to establish animal universalism. The argument fails, he argues, because God is obligated *only* to provide enough of a good afterlife to suffering animals that their earthly harms are sufficiently compensated. Eternal, infinitely good afterlives go beyond that, so they aren't required. Despite what Crummett believes are the failings of these arguments, he argues that both his Beneficence Argument and two other arguments—the Divine Love Argument and a modified Relationship Argument—jointly make a powerful case for animal universalism.

In Chapter 7, Faith Glavey Pawl explores the possibility that animals might share human awareness of the divine. To show this, she reviews the long history of theists, particularly Christian theists, who have held that humans are aware of God's existence and attributes. She considers two models for thinking about human awareness of God: propositional knowledge and what Eleonore Stump calls "Franciscan knowledge" (Stump 2010). We acquire perceptual knowledge in cases where we have direct, presentational knowledge of something, such as a chair or the presence of a person in the room. But we have Franciscan knowledge, or knowledge of persons, when we have knowledge-by-acquaintance. Pawl uses Frank Jackson's famous example of Mary, the color-blind scientist, to illustrate this kind of knowledge:

> If poor Mary had been locked in a prison with only third-person descriptions of other people for her whole life, but had never had a face-to-face contact with anyone, she would not know anyone *as*

a person. No amount of propositional knowledge gained from biographical sources could suffice for Mary to know her own mother in the way she would know her if she were to encounter her face to face. (166)

After exploring reasons for skepticism of animal awareness of God, Pawl defends an argument from analogy. She argues,

1. The God of Christian theism is personal and desires to be known and loved by God's creatures.
2. Loving and knowing God both require some awareness of God.
3. Humans are able to know and love God because God has endowed them with capacities that allow them to be aware of God (or God's activity in the world), and because God communicates Godself to them in ways suited to their capacities.
4. There are animal analogs of those human capacities which are tied to awareness of God.
(C) Thus, we should expect that animals endowed with such capacities can have awareness of God.

(173)

Animals, therefore, likely have Franciscan knowledge of God—a knowledge of God's person. This is distinct from, and does not entail, that animals have propositional knowledge of God, since they may not understand propositions at all any more than young human children do. Yet young human children know their parents in some sense. Pawl then defends a further claim: that animals who are aware of God might direct praise to God. "Why *not* think," she asks, "that sentient creatures, especially ones with rich capacities for social cognition, can relate to God in a way that involves their capacities for social connection?" (175). She concludes with some applications of animal knowledge of and communion with God, one of the most interesting of which is her contention that some of the contemporary literature on the problem of animal suffering is lacking in speculative depth: "But if I am right that some animals are capable of experiencing communion with God in *this* life," then perhaps "we can come up with better stories" about animal suffering (179).

The concluding entry on animals is Blake Hereth's "Animal Gods." Hereth defends the view that some non-human animals *are* divine, and warns that if zootheism is true "then a lack of attention to non-human animals within philosophical theology is not only a glaring omission but an *impious* one," since it reflects an improper exclusion of divine individuals (183). Ze distinguishes zootheism from zoomorphism, the view that some divine person(s) appear as animals (as Zeus did), and zoolatry, where some animals are worshipped or worthy of worship irrespective of their divinity status. Hereth proceeds to endorse Anselmian theism, or perfect being theology, according to which God is maximally perfect. Ze then offers two arguments for an Anselmian-motivated zootheist view: the Power Argument and the Incarnation Argument. According to the former, God's moral perfection entails maximal fairness which is a presumption of shared power among those with interests, including animals. If a divine person exists but no animal is a divine person, then divine persons have decisive power over animal interests, which is less than maximally fair. Thus, either there are no divine persons or there are divine animals. Thus, if theism is true, then zootheism is true. Hereth concludes this argument by remarking that "it's not enough for [divine animals] to exist *contingently* within the Godhead, for contingent membership in the Godhead is contingent power in the Godhead and contingent power is contingent maximal fairness" (189). Thus, according to Hereth, "animal members must enjoy *necessary* membership in the Godhead and share eternally in the Godhead's power" (189).

The second argument Hereth gives for zootheism, the Incarnation Argument, aligns with the one popular strand of thinking about the Christian Incarnation that God became incarnate principally to share in human suffering to demonstrate their love and solidarity with us (Anselm 1998; Swinburne 1994; McCord Adams 2008). Hereth also approvingly cites black liberation theologian James Cone (2018, 128), that God incarnates principally to identify with the suffering of the oppressed, and reviews recent attempts to argue that this includes suffering alongside animals (Creegan 2013, 60; Clough 2013, 81–82). Ze argues that these thinkers are mistaken to reject animal incarnations, and that there's something problematic about a God who takes on the flesh of humans to share in their suffering but declines to incarnate as the animals that humans routinely oppress. Hereth argues that just "as the world needs not only a white savior but a *black* savior, so also the world needs not only a human savior but an *animal* savior" (197). Having motivated an animal incarnation, ze reviews three ways this might occur, defending one. On the Appearance View, God merely appears as an animal without becoming one. On the Transformation View, preincarnate God isn't an animal but becomes one. And on the Preexistence View, God was always an animal but comes to join the earthly world in its suffering. Hereth rejects both the Appearance View and the Transformation View in favor of the Preexistence View, which ze argues entails zootheism. Thus, if the Incarnation Argument succeeds, then zootheism is established.

The next three chapters engage issues related to disability in philosophy of religion. The first two chapters in this section seek to show disability too needs to be given a more prominent place in philosophy of religion. Leading off is David Efird's "The Resurrection of the Minority Body: Physical Disability in the Life of Heaven." Assuming the traditional account of the resurrection of the body in Christian theology, Efird argues that there are no reasons that all physical disabilities would need to be eliminated in heaven, what Efird calls 'the elimination view,' despite the history of Christian reflection on the topic typically assuming that the elimination view is true. Efird begins by drawing on the work of Elizabeth Barnes, who argues that physical disabilities are 'mere-differences' rather than 'bad-differences.' While there may be some physical disabilities that involve 'bad-difference'—Efird suggests that disabilities that involve so much pain that they prevent a person from experiencing God in the ways involved in heaven—it's not the case that all physical disabilities involve 'bad-difference.' Since not all physical disabilities detract from a person's well-being, there's no reason that they would need to be removed for the perfection of human flourishing in heaven.

On Efird's view, God has no reason to need to eliminate all physical disabilities for the life in the world to come. They could be, as he puts it, "minority bodies in heaven" (213). While disability might shape a person's practical identity, the existence of acquired disabilities shows that not all disabilities are part of a person's metaphysical (or numerical) identity. But Efird also thinks that God wouldn't retain all physical disabilities, even if they involve positive and not just neutral differences, unilaterally. Efird favors what he calls 'the optionality view' in which God gives those who have physical disabilities in their early lives the option of retaining or eliminating those disabilities in their heavenly lives. Efird gives three reasons why a person could reasonably choose to retain their physical disability, including as a sign of their love for and union with God despite the trials of their early life.

Kevin Timpe's contribution also looks at the presence of disability in heaven. Elsewhere, Timpe has argued, like Efird does in the present volume, that there could be 'mere-difference' disabilities in heaven (Timpe 2020). Since our theological beliefs about disability can shape religious communities' behavior toward individuals with disabilities, the view that disabilities can't be present in heaven sometimes contributes to religious communities not fully welcoming and valuing disabled individuals at present. Here, in "Disabled Beatitude," Timpe examines positive reasons for thinking that there not only *can be* but *will be* disabilities present in the beatific vision. Theologians Nancy Eiesland and Amos Yong have argued that the Incarnation, and particularly the retained scars Jesus had in the resurrection, support that there will be disabilities in heaven. Timpe argues, however, that their arguments only support that the marks of disability will be present, and that the presence of the marks of disability doesn't entail that the disabilities are still present. Instead, Timpe finds other reasons to affirm heavenly disability. Though not decisive, the social nature of disability identity and disability pride suggest certain corporate goods that could contribute to the goodness of heaven. He then suggests that there are goods related to a number of specific disabilities (e.g., Williams syndrome and autism) that could contribute positively to the goodness of heaven. He also considers some general features of human embodiment that God had good reason to instill in creation but which also make disability possible. There are numerous kinds of human diversity that plausibly contribute to the goodness of creation; thinking that of those kinds of diversity disability can't contribute to the perfection of heaven is rooted in normate biases that presume all disabilities involve bad-difference.

The closing chapter for the section on disability is Scott Williams's "When Personhood Goes Wrong in Ethics and Philosophical Theology: Disability, Ableism, and (Modern) Personhood." Williams's essay is as much an exploration of *how* conceptions of personhood go wrong as *when* they go wrong. He carefully reviews the history of moral philosophers, particularly John Locke, Immanuel Kant, and Mary Anne Warren, whose views on personhood exclude those with profound cognitive disability. Such views, argues Williams, are "obviously and deeply morally disturbing" (272), though he concedes that some might regard the exclusion of fetuses as less obviously problematic than the exclusion of the cognitively disabled. He then offers two arguments against these conceptions of personhood, the first of which he calls the Moral Shift Argument: if modern conceptions of moral personhood are true, then profoundly cognitively disabled human beings aren't equal members of the moral community, which is false. Williams thinks this argument has gained traction in recent years and has been defended at length by philosophers like Eva Feder Kittay (2016). The reason for excluding the cognitively disabled is grounded in a putatively 'moral' preference for non-disabled lives, and that preference, so Williams and Kittay argue, is a preference for 'normal' (i.e., non-disabled) human lives, which is objectionable. Williams's second argument, which he calls the Argument against Exclusive Moral Personhood, is more complex than the first. In it, he argues that Warren (and, one assumes, all those who agree with her assessment or who advocate similar positions) has a good reason for the exclusive association of modern personhood with direct moral status only if her conception of a person is self-evident. But it's *not* self-evident. There's no fine-grained analysis of personhood, making her conception neither clear nor distinct. Furthermore, the modern conception of personhood is at best a relatively recent minority position (277).

After defending these two arguments at length, Williams contends that philosophy of religion is rife with Warren-type views of personhood. Developments in Social Trinitarianism in the 19th and 20th centuries, for example, create models of personhood on which "incommunicable mental powers (e.g., intellect and will)" and "incommunicable mental acts, including higher-order cognitive acts" are essential to personhood, thereby excluding those incapable of performing higher-order cognitive acts (285). It's here, in Williams's view, that philosophy of religion has taken bad cues from contemporary ethics. Can talk of personhood be saved, in Williams's view? The answer, he thinks, is 'no': "Personhood, modern or Boethian, is bad for ethics and unnecessary for conciliar Christian theology" (288). We should disavow it.

In addition to bringing philosophy of religion into greater interaction with non-human animals and disability, this volume also seeks to engage issues related to sex and gender. In Chapter 12, Stephen T. Davis and Eric T. Yang raise a provocative and underexplored question within philosophical theology: "Marriage, Reproduction, and the Incarnation: What Could Jesus Do?" Despite popular-level speculation about whether Jesus ever married or reproduced, the topic has attracted surprisingly little philosophical attention. Davis and Yang distinguish between two questions at the outset. The first is whether it's *morally impermissible* for an incarnate God to marry, have sex, or reproduce. The second is whether it's *overall unfitting* for an incarnate God to do this. As they point out, surprisingly, "no academic scholar has offered an argument for the moral impermissibility of Christ" marrying or procreating (294). Davis and Yang defend the view that although Christ marrying or procreating while incarnate passes the permissibility test, it would fail the overall fittingness test. 'Fittingness,' in the relevant sense, is a matter of whether engaging in a behavior "would bring about a greater number of desired effects" (302). Actions that satisfy this condition are overall fitting, and actions that fail to satisfy the condition aren't overall fitting. The likely effects of Christ marrying, having sex, or reproducing include idolatrously elevated statuses for Christ's partner and children and a denigration of "those who are single or without children" (305). These effects are not only negative, but have such a negative valence that they tip the scales of fittingness toward overall unfitting. Davis and Yang argue that because God will do what is overall fitting, it follows that in the Incarnation God wouldn't marry, have sex, or reproduce, even though such actions would be permissible for God.

The next chapter, by Kelli D. Potter, critiques Mormon theologies of gender through a transfeminist lens. She points out that Mormonism is theologically and philosophically interesting due to its materialist commitments about the nature of God, who is claimed to be embodied. A further commitment of Mormon theology, clarified in "The Family: A Proclamation to the World" (1995), is that gender "is an essential characteristic of individual premortal, mortal, and eternal identity and purpose" (316). Each human being, on this view, has exactly one definite gender and has both essentially and eternally. Potter argues that this view is central to orthodox Mormon theology because it underpins their view that "[h]uman beings are Gods in embryo and part of being a God is being in a procreative, heterosexual, and eternal marriage" (317). If one's gender could change, or if there could be non-binary genders, this view would be undermined since then some marriages would be either non-heterosexual or only temporarily heterosexual. The implications, she argues, are clear:

> Moreover, a member of the church that was assigned 'female' at birth might come out as a trans man and petition to be ordained

to the priesthood. This is very dangerous because it threatens the LDS Church's patriarchal system of governance. It seems clear that the LDS commitments to patriarchy, heteronormativity, and cisnormativity are intertwined. The latter two are a necessary condition for maintaining the patriarchy, which gives cishet men the power to control the direction of the church.

(317)

But, Potter argues, the possibility of trans persons doesn't undermine the theology of the Proclamation. The fact that a person can be embodied as male, for example, doesn't entail that their spirit isn't female. This possibility has not escaped the attention of Mormon theologians; but Potter argues that their 'solutions' are implausible. They could claim, for example, that there *can't* be a mismatch between one's gender and one's biological sex. The fact that such an obvious reply hasn't been given is indicative, she argues, that "the homophobic and sexist tail is wagging the theological dog" (319). The problem, Potter contends, is not "whether to accept or reject the language of the Proclamation," but rather "whether there is a non-arbitrary rationale for interpreting it in an anti-trans manner" (325).

In Chapter 14, Hilary Yancey defends the view that gender will persist in any just afterlife. She pits herself at odds with some philosophers, such as Sally Haslanger (2000, 2012), who defend the view that just societies can't contain women or men as genders. What gender presently is, on Haslanger's view, is a way of being marked for privilege or subordination due to particular bodily features—typically the ones used for reproduction. Yancey locates her project within philosophical theology by asking whether *resurrected* persons will be gendered. Contrary to Haslanger and others, Yancey argues that it's a *requirement* of justice that resurrected persons sometimes be gendered. First, she argues that gendered oppression is both real, systemic, and severe. Persons are wronged because of their gender. This is an uncontroversial commitment between Yancey and Haslanger. Second, the victims of identity prejudice must bear their gendered properties when they receive the moral rectification they are due, since "they must be capable of recognizing themselves as the participants in the injustices that they suffered, so as to fully experience the restoration of justice" (335). Yancey's defense of this claim is further supported by the fact that if sexists were forced to make amends with their victims but knew their victims were no longer gendered, they could view their good deeds as not being directed to women but to genderless persons—an outcome consistent with their normative sexist ends. Yancey concludes her chapter with an examination of whether gender is accidental or essential, exploring how resurrection justice works under either possibility.

David Worsley's chapter "Limbo, Hiddenness, and the Beatific Vision (and Procreation, for Some, in the Life to Come)" continues the volume's engagement with eschatological issues in philosophy of religion. Worsley engaged with previous work by Timpe (2015) which provides a philosophical argument for limbo as an alternative eschatological option in addition to heaven and hell. (The limbo advocated by Timpe is importantly different than the limbo often found in Catholic theology.) Worsley follows Eleonore Stump and argues that persons must exercise higher-order desires to cooperate with God so that God can remove the stain of original sin, in order to be fit for admittance into heaven. However, Worsley also thinks that the stain of original sin, apart from the guilt of unrepented mortal sin, isn't sufficient for deserving hell. Limbo is offered as an option precisely for those who die with the stain of original sin but without unrepented moral sin. Since some individuals die without *any* higher-order desires, it might appear that they are all consigned to limbo for the eschaton. But this appearance, Worsley argues, is misleading. He argues that *everyone* will eventually leave limbo because God will grant each 'Limbonian' the higher-order desires necessary to gain entrance either to heaven or hell. However, to preserve creaturely freedom, it's also necessary on Worsley's view that "God must remain (at least partially) hidden, such that [they] are not determined to desire divine union" (351). We ought to expect a certain degree of divine hiddenness not only in the present life, but in limbo. The Beatific Vision, for all its wonderfulness, entails *full* knowledge of God, and such knowledge would exclude rational reasons for choosing against God. Worsley then raises two other theological implications of limbo, so understood. The first is that given the possibility of redemption for limbonians and the centrality of the incarnation is securing the possibility of redemption, we have reason to think there could be another incarnation in limbo. Second, if incarnation requires an incarnational birth, we also have reason to think endorse the possibility of procreation in heaven. Thus, procreation is possible in limbo.

The volume closes with a call for philosophy of religion, and specifically Christian philosophy of religion, to address issues related to race. Sameer Yadav begins "Religious Racial Formation Theory and Its Metaphysics: A Research Program in the Philosophy of Religion" by arguing that "if we are going to understand and evaluate the merits of an intersection between Christian group identity and various forms of racism, what is needed is a research program" (365). But the resources for developing such a research program are "strewn across the landscape of many distinct academic disciplines, lacking any integrated framework that might coordinate them" (365). Rather than offering a substantive theory of the intersection between race and the Christian religion, Yadav seek to gather these three distinct disciplinary contributions—sociohistorical, philosophical, and normative-theological—into a single integrated explanatory framework (366). He accordingly seeks to provides what Nathaniel Goldberg calls a "conceptual cartography" by which to understand a religious racial formation theory (366). Such a theory, however, can't be determinate apart from a specification of its underlying metaphysic that determines what social categories like 'Christianity' and 'race' are. Philosophers of religion thus need not only to engage in social ontology but also explore how approaches to social reality have historically led to the racist attitudes that infect so much Christian, and particularly white evangelical, culture. Yadav's chapter illustrates the need for interdisciplinary work that the criticisms of much extant philosophy of religion, as discussed above, call for.

As mentioned above, these essays merely contribute to the task of expanding the current exploratory boundaries within analytic philosophy of religion and philosophical theology. More is certainly needed, and we commend further work on both these and other topics. There is much growing to be done, but development must begin somewhere. Our hope is that this volume, and the essays within it, are in service to a larger movement within religious philosophy that amplifies issues and voices that have been historically both unheard or misheard.[14]

Notes

1. One of use has endorsed the standard story elsewhere; see Speak and Timpe 2016; Timpe 2009.
2. J. Aaron Simmons suggests that the rise of philosophy of religion also correlates with the increased political and cultural capital of evangelicalism, particularly in the American context.
3. Though not fans of contemporary philosophy of religion, Paul Draper and Ryan Nichols claim that attempts to end philosophy of religion are "misguided" and "arguably . . . pathological" (2013, 438). More on their objections to contemporary philosophy of religion below.
4. This is the view of Schellenberg 2019; Moser 2019, who seem to endorse the standard story but think the developments at the heart of that story have not been beneficial.
5. To be fair, Trakakis aims his critique at what he thinks are the excesses of philosophy of religion, not philosophy of religion per se. There is, in his view, a proper role for analytic philosophy of religion to play.
6. In the conclusion, Knepper continues:

   > If philosophy of religion is supposed to be philosophy *about* religion, then neither continental nor analytic philosophy of religion is philosophy of religion. Rather, they are, at best, philosophies of narrow subsets of religion (religionized postmodernism and Christian theism, respectively); at worse, theological efforts at understanding and defending those subsets (that more closely resemble philosophical or apologetic theology).
   >
   > (2014, 144)

7. Compare clarification to what Gary Gutting refers to as

   > the process of persuasive elaboration[:] . . . a matter of working with a set of ideas or claims and developing them . . . all for the sake of showing

their interest and power. In short, it's a matter of showing what we can *do* with certain ideas.

(Gutting 2009, 89)

8. There are, of course, exceptions such as Harrison 2010; Oppy 2019; Kapitan 2009. But these are, as the saying goes, the exceptions than prove the rule.
9. "Exacerbating the problem at the group level is the fact that the vast majority of philosophers in English-speaking world who specialize in philosophy religion are theists—remarkably, just over 70 percent according to recent studies" (Draper and Nichols 2013, 440; citing De Cruz 2012; Bourget and Chalmers 2009). Dissenting here, Paul Moser argues that Christian philosophy isn't Christian enough, with practitioners of supposedly Christian philosophy tending to

> omit the crucified Christ, as an actual person, from their philosophy, despite the indispensable role of the term 'Christ' in the term 'Christian'. . . . We find no definitive role for the crucified Christ as God's supreme mediator and Savior for humans and their 'advice' [obviously a reference to Plantinga]. So, we seem to be left with some kind of 'mere theism' that falls short of being 'Christian.'
>
> (Moser 2019, 210)

10. Notice that the literature we've cited thus far, which we take represents a representative sampling of contemporary philosophy of religion, is written by scholars who are overwhelmingly male and even more uniformly white. And this is to say nothing of their sexual orientation, gender identity, disability status, etc.
11. Stump's own preferred method to correcting this cognitive *hemianopia* is to rediscover narrative.
12. Personal communication. In using this terminology, Griffioen is reporting the way that many in the discipline view the boundaries of 'properness,' not defending that use.
13. In her contribution to this volume Helen De Cruz talks about the need to specifically commission minority perspectives in philosophy of religion; we put together our contributors to do just this.
14. We are grateful for helpful comments from and discussions with Michelle Panchuk and Aaron Simmons about this introduction.

References

Alston, William P. *Perceiving God: The Epistemology of Religious Experience*. Ithaca: Cornell University Press, 1991.

Anselm of Canterbury. "Why God Became Man." In *Anselm of Canterbury: The Major Works*, edited by Brian Davies and G. R. Evans. New York: Oxford University Press, 1998.

Bourget, David and David Chalmers. "Correlations with: AOS Philosophy of Religion." *The PhilPapers Surveys*, 2009. http://philpapers.org/surves/linear_most_with.pl?A=profile%3AAOS%3APhilosophy%20of%20Religion.

The Church of Jesus Christ of Latter-Day Saints. "The Family: A Proclamation to the World." 1995. Accessed August 30, 2018. www.lds.org/topics/family-proclamation.

Clough, David L. *On Animals: Volume 1: Systematic Theology*. New York: Bloomsbury T&T Clark, 2013.

Cone, James H. *A Black Theology of Liberation*. New York: Orbis Books, 2018.
Cortez, Marc. "As Much as Possible: Essentially Contested Concepts and Analytic Theology: A Response to William J. Abraham." *Journal of Analytic Theology* 1 (2013): 17–24.
Cottingham, John. *Philosophy of Religion: Towards a More Humane Approach*. Cambridge: Cambridge University Press, 2014.
Creegan, Nicola Hoggard. *Animal Suffering and the Problem of Evil*. New York: Oxford University Press, 2013.
Crisp, Oliver. "Analytic Theology as Systematic Theology." *Open Theology* 3.1 (2017): 156–166.
Crummett, Dustin. "The Problem of Evil and the Suffering of Creeping Things." *International Journal for Philosophy of Religion* 82.1 (2017): 71–88.
Dawes, Greg. "On Theism and Explanation." Interview by Richard Marshall, *3:AM Magazine*, 2014. www.3ammagazine.com/3am/on-theism-and-explanation/.
De Cruz, Helen. "Confirmation Bias or Expertise? The Prevalence of Theism in Philosophy of Religion." 2012. http://prosblogion.ektopos.com/archives/2012/02/one-of-thestri.html.
De Cruz, Helen and Johan De Smedt. "Intuitions and Arguments: Cognitive Foundations of Argumentation in Natural Theology." *European Journal for Philosophy of Religion* 9 (2017): 57–82.
Dougherty, Trent. *The Problem of Animal Pain: A Theodicy for All Creatures Great and Small*. New York: Palgrave Macmillan, 2014.
Draper, Paul and Ryan Nichols. "Diagnosing Bias in Philosophy of Religion." *The Monist* 96.3 (2013): 420–446.
Ebels-Duggan, Kyla. "Christian Philosophy and the Christian Life." In *Christian Philosophy: Conceptions, Continuations, and Challenges*, edited by J. Aaron Simmons, 55–72. Oxford: Oxford University Press, 2019.
Frankenberry, Nancy. "Feminist Approaches." In *Feminist Philosophy of Religion: Critical Readings*, edited by Pamela Sue Anderson and Beverley Clack, 3–23. New York: Routledge, 2004.
Fricker, Miranda. *Epistemic Injustice: Power and the Ethics of Knowing*. Oxford: Oxford University Press, 2007.
Graves, Shawn, Blake Hereth, and Tyler M. John. "In Defense of Animal Universalism." In *Paradise Understood: New Philosophical Essays About Heaven*, edited by T. Ryan Byerly and Eric J. Silverman, 161–192. New York: Oxford University Press, 2017.
Green, Adam. "Reading the Mind of God (Without Hebrew Lessons): Alston, Shared Attention, and Mystical Experience." *Religious Studies* 45.4 (2009): 455–470.
Gutting, Gary. 2009. *What Philosophers Know: Case Studies in Recent Analytic Philosophy*. Cambridge: Cambridge University Press.
Hanson, N. Russell. 2002. "Seeing and Seeing As." In *Philosophy of Science, Contemporary Readings*, edited by Yuri Balashov and Alex Rosenberg, 331–339. London and New York: Routledge, 2002.
Harris, Harriet A. "Does Analytical Philosophy Clip Our Wings? Reformed Epistemology as a Test Case." In *Faith and Philosophical Analysis: The Impact of Analytical Philosophy on the Philosophy of Religion*, edited by Harriet A. Harris and Christopher J. Insole, 100–118. Aldershot: Ashgate, 2005.

Harris, Harriet A. and Christopher J. Insole. "Verdicts on Analytical Philosophy of Religion." In *Faith and Philosophical Analysis: The Impact of Analytical Philosophy on the Philosophy of Religion*, edited by Harriet A. Harris and Christopher J. Insole, 1–20. Aldershot: Ashgate, 2005.

Hasker, William. "Responding to Challenges." In *Christian Philosophy: Conceptions, Continuations, and Challenges*, edited by J. Aaron Simmons, 286–303. Oxford: Oxford University Press, 2019.

Haslanger, Sally. "Gender and Race: (What) Are They? (What) Do We Want Them to Be?" *Nous* 34.1 (2000): 31–55.

Haslanger, Sally. *Resisting Reality: Social Construction and Social Critique*. Oxford: Oxford University Press, 2012.

Harrison, Victoria S. "Philosophy of Religion, Fictionalism, and Religious Diversity." *International Journal for Philosophy of Religion* 68 (2010): 43–58.

Hereth, Blake. "Two Arguments for Animal Immortality." In *Heaven and Philosophy*, edited by Simon Cushing, 171–200. Lanham, MD: Lexington, 2018.

James, William. *Varieties of Religious Experience*. London: Longmans, Green, and Co., 1902.

Kapitan, Tomis. "Evaluating Religion." In *Oxford Studies in Philosophy of Religion: Volume 2*, edited by Jonathan L. Kvanvig, 80–104. Oxford: Oxford University Press, 2009.

Kittay, Eva Feder. "Deadly Medicine: Project T4, Mental Disability, and Racism." *Res Philosophica* 93.4 (2016): 715–741.

Knepper, Timothy D. "The End of Philosophy of Religion?" *Journal of the American Academy of Religion* 82.1 (2014): 120–149.

Kvanvig, Jon, ed. *Oxford Studies in Philosophy of Religion*, vol. 2. Oxford: Oxford University Press, 2009.

Loftus, John W. *Unapologetic: Why Philosophy of Religion Must End*. Durham: Pitschstone Publishing, 2016.

Loewen, Nathan R.B. "Prolegomena to Any Future Mashups with the Philosophy of Religion." *The Journal for Cultural and Religious Theory* 14.2 (2015).

McCall, Thomas. *An Invitation to Analytic Christian Theology*. Downers Grove: IVP Academic, 2015.

McCord Adams, Marilyn. *Christ and Horrors: The Coherence of Christology*. Cambridge: Cambridge University Press, 2008.

Macdonald, Scott. "What Is Philosophical Theology?" In *Arguing About Religion*, edited by Kevin Timpe, 17–29. New York: Routledge, 2009.

Mizrahi, Moti. "If Analytic Philosophy of Religion Is Sick, Can It Be Cured?" *Religious Studies* (2019): 1–20.

Moser, Paul. *The Elusive God: Reorienting Religious Epistemology*. Cambridge: Cambridge University Press, 2008.

Moser, Paul. "Christian Philosophy and Christ Crucified: Fragmentary Theory in Scandalous Power." In *Christian Philosophy: Conceptions, Continuations, and Challenges*, edited by J. Aaron Simmons, 209–228. Oxford: Oxford University Press, 2019.

Murray, Michael J. *Nature Red in Tooth and Claw: Theism and the Problem of Animal Suffering*. New York: Oxford University Press, 2008.

Nagasawa, Yujin and Erik J. Wielenberg, eds. *New Waves in Philosophy of Religion*. New York: Palgrave Macmillan, 2008.

Oppy, Graham. *Reinventing Philosophy of Religion: An Opinionated Introduction.* New York: Palgrave Macmillan, 2014.
Oppy, Graham. "Christian Philosophy and Christ Crucified: Fragmentary Theory in Scandalous Power." In *Christian Philosophy: Conceptions, Continuations, and Challenges*, edited by J. Aaron Simmons, 244–259. Oxford: Oxford University Press, 2019.
Peterson, Michael J. and Raymond J. VanArragon, eds. *Contemporary Debates in Philosophy of Religion.* Malden, MA: Blackwell, 2004.
Plantinga, Alvin. "Response to Nick Wolterstorff." *Faith and Philosophy* 28.3 (2011): 267–268.
Rea, Michael C. *The Hiddenness of God.* Oxford: Oxford University Press, 2018.
Schellenberg, J. L. "Philosophy of Religion: A State of the Subject Report." The Canadian Theological Society's Inaugural Jay Newman Memorial Lecture in Philosophy of Religion. *Toronto Journal of Theology* 25 (2009): 95–110.
Schellenberg, J. L. "Is Plantinga-Style Christian Philosophy Really Philosophy?" In *Christian Philosophy: Conceptions, Continuations, and Challenges*, edited by J. Aaron Simmons, 229–243. Oxford: Oxford University Press, 2019.
Schilbrack, Kevin. *Philosophy and the Study of Religions: A Manifesto.* Malden, MA: Wiley-Blackwell, 2014.
Simmons, J. Aaron. "The Strategies of Christian Philosophy." In *Christian Philosophy: Conceptions, Continuations, and Challenges*, edited by J. Aaron Simmons, 187–208. Oxford: Oxford University Press, 2019.
Speak, Daniel and Kevin Timpe. "Introduction." In *Free Will and Theism: Connections, Contingencies, and Concerns*, edited by Kevin Timpe and Daniel Speak, 1–26. Oxford: Oxford University Press, 2016.
Stump, Eleonore. *Wandering in Darkness.* Oxford: Oxford University Press, 2010.
Swinburne, Richard. *The Christian God.* Oxford: Clarendon Press, 1994.
Swinburne, Richard. "The Value and Christian Roots of Analytical Philosophy of Religion." In *Faith and Philosophical Analysis*, edited by Harriet A. Harris and Christopher J. Insole, 33–45. Burlington, VT: Ashgate, 2005.
Taliaferro, Charles and Austin Dressen. "Praise and Blame in Philosophy of Religion." *Toronto Journal of Theology* 29.2 (2013): 227–244.
Timpe, Kevin. "Introduction." In *Metaphysics and God: Essays in Honor of Eleonore Stump*, edited by Kevin Timpe, xvii–xxv. New York: Routledge, 2009.
———. "An Argument for Limbo." *Journal of Ethics* 19 (2015): 277–292.
———. "Defiant Afterlife." In *Marginalized Identities, Peripheral Theologies: Expanding Conversations in Analytic Theology*, edited by Michelle Panchuk and Michael Rea. Oxford: Oxford University Press, 2020.
Torrance, Alan J. "Analytic Theology and the Reconciled Mind: The Significance of History." *Journal of Analytic Theology* 1.1 (2013): 3–44.
Trakakis, Nick. *The End of Philosophy of Religion.* London: Continuum, 2008.
Westphal, Merold. "Prolegomena to Any Future Philosophy of Religion Which Will Be Able to Come Forth as Prophecy." *International Journal for Philosophy of Religion* 4.3 (1973): 129–150.
———. "Taking Plantinga Seriously: Advice to Christian Philosophers." In *Christian Philosophy: Conceptions, Continuations, and Challenges*, edited by J. Aaron Simmons, 73–82. Oxford: Oxford University Press, 2019.

Wolterstorff, Nicholas. "How Philosophical Theology Became Possible Within the Analytic Tradition of Philosophy." In *Analytic Theology: New Essays in the Philosophy of Theology*, edited by Oliver D. Crisp and Michael C. Rea, 155–168. Oxford: Oxford University Press, 2009.

———. *Acting Liturgically: Philosophical Reflections on Religious Practice*. Oxford: Oxford University Press, 2018.

Section I
Methodology

1 Philosophy of Religion From the Margins
A Theoretical Analysis and Focus Group Study

Helen De Cruz

Introduction: Philosophical Practice From the Margins

How do our personal life experiences and position in society affect our philosophical practice? This paper examines how being a minority in philosophy might affect the practice of philosophy of religion. I use the concept of intersectionality as a guiding methodological principle. Intersectionality moves away from a single-axis way of thinking about identity to a matrix level analysis. Rather than considering, say, gender, as a homogeneous identity, intersectionality encourages us to think about how different aspects of someone's identity might intersect with each other, for instance, gender, religious belief, and ethnicity. Such social identities are crucial in patterns of power relationships, in particular, dominance, oppression, and discrimination. For example, women of color experience forms of violence that are a result of intersecting patterns of sexism and racism that are not clearly reducible to either their gender or ethnicity (Crenshaw 1991). Intersectional invisibility refers to the inability to recognize people who are multiply disadvantaged in this way (Purdie-Vaughns and Eibach 2008). Intersectionality has become a crucial concept in critical social science, but its uptake in other fields, such as philosophy or psychology, has been slow (Bowleg 2017).

Although the term 'intersectionality' was first coined by Kimberlé Crenshaw (1989), members of minorities, including black feminist activists and civil rights activists, have long before recognized the complex ways in which multiple aspects of their identity intersect. Philosophers often conceive of themselves as being able to produce a view from nowhere, that is, a view that is not informed by the way they are societally positioned, but that somehow abstracts away from their situation in life. This position is exemplified by Descartes (1637 [2000], 51), who locked himself up in a stove-heated room, saying this made him "completely free to converse with myself among my own thoughts." Descartes believed that philosophy was best conducted by a single man "of good sense," rather than being the product of accumulated wisdom. However, this epistemic individualism has come increasingly under fire. Experimental philosophers have found that philosophers are subject to biases and framing effects to the same extent as non-philosophers, including on problems and questions they have expertise in. A vivid example is the observation that philosophy PhD holders' endorsement of the doctrine of double effect is influenced by the order in which trolley scenarios are presented to them (switch first, or push first) (Schwitzgebel and Cushman 2015).

Social epistemologists have drawn attention to such factors as belief polarization and confirmation bias, which philosophers are not immune to (e.g., Kelly 2008). Philosophy at Western academic institutions is predominantly conducted by individuals who are white, male, and from privileged socioeconomic backgrounds. They are not only numerically in the majority, but also occupy the most prestigious positions such as being tenured at philosophy departments that are top-ranked in the Philosophical Gourmet Report (De Cruz 2018a). Their work is cited more, receives more attention in philosophical syllabi, and tends to be published in prestigious journals. Women and people of color are underrepresented in the most prestigious general and specialist journals, even relative to their numbers in the profession (Botts et al. 2014; Wilhelm, Conklin, and Hassoun 2018).

Philosophy has a *culture of justification*: a routine question for philosophical work that does not fit core domains (such as epistemology, philosophy of language, or philosophy of mind) is not just whether it is good philosophy, but whether it is philosophy at all. Justifying norms, such as perceived rigor, are used to adjudicate whether work counts as philosophy. Minorities in philosophy do not recognize themselves in such justifying norms, or the ways they are applied (Dotson 2013). Given that minorities in philosophy frequently work in domains that are not regarded as core, such as non-Western philosophy, feminist philosophy, or philosophy of race, personal identity can intersect with one's philosophical practice in complex ways: minorities not only face barriers in finding employment or getting published, but are also constantly required to justify the merits of their philosophical work.

I here present a case study of philosophy of religion from the margins. How do philosophers of religion who don't belong to majority religious traditions, or who are not male or white (or an intersection of these) conduct their work? This is a small, exploratory study that uses two focus group discussions. Participants have identities that are underrepresented in philosophy. The "Being Minority in Philosophy of Religion" section examines which minority positions, and their intersections, might be relevant in the philosophy of religion. The next section explains the methodology of the study. "Key Findings" presents and summarizes its key findings, using transcribed excerpts from the discussions as illustrations. The last section examines the implications of this research for the practice of philosophy of religion.

Being a Minority in Philosophy of Religion

Philosophy of religion examines a wide range of topics such as the existence and attributes of God, arguments for atheism, the significance of religious experience, and questions that are specific to given religious traditions, such as the nature of the Trinity, or whether there is free will in heaven. In Western academic departments, philosophers of religion tend to be mainly white, male, and Christian. There are an estimated 61 to 73% theists in philosophy of religion, the vast majority of whom are Christians. By contrast, in philosophy as a whole there are only an estimated 11 to 25% theists (Bourget and Chalmers 2014; De Cruz 2018b). Several authors, for example Kevin Schilbrack (2014), have criticized philosophy of religion for its narrow focus on traditional Christian theism, and its lack of openness to other religious traditions. There is an enduring worry that because of its focus on Christianity and the predominance of theists in the discipline, philosophy of religion is more partisan and less open to criticism than other philosophical disciplines (Draper and Nichols 2013).

What is less acknowledged is how patterns of dominance and oppression caused by the intersection of different identities, such as gender, race, and sexual orientation, might shape this field. Feminist authors in philosophy of religion, such as Sarah Coakley and Pamela Sue Anderson, have recognized that philosophy of religion may be influenced by the gender of its practitioners. Topics such as sacrifice (Anderson 2000) and the epistemic significance of religious experience (Coakley 2009) are not immune to gender dynamics. Coakley (2009), for example, argues that recent work in analytic philosophy of religion has shifted to topics traditionally associated with the feminine, such as trust and private experience, and is now engaging with female mystics such as Teresa of Ávila. At the same time, she contends that the male authors who were and are primarily engaged in this work, e.g., William Alston and Alvin Plantinga, refrain from a serious engagement with the work of these female mystics, perhaps because there are "elements of their witness that will not quite fit the laudable epistemic purposes that these philosophers intend" (Coakley 2009, 284), such as the explicit, sensual imagery of divine union.

This intersectionality of gender and religious authority has been recognized by authors in the past. For instance, mystics such as Teresa of Ávila (1577 [1921]) and Hadewijch (13th century [1996]) explicitly mentioned their gender in relationship to their authority as mystics. Teresa of Ávila (1577 [1921], 18), at the outset of her *Interior Castle*, was adamant that she does not presume to write for anyone but fellow Carmelite nuns, "Thus I am writing only to my sisters; the idea that any one else could benefit by what I say would be absurd." Given the limited religious authority of women in the 16th-century Roman Catholic Church (which continues to this day, as women are barred from holding positions such as priest, bishop, and so on), Teresa deliberately restricted her religious and epistemic authority to fellow nuns. By contrast, Hadewijch, a 13th-century mystic from Brabant, negotiated the lack of perceived religious authority of women in a different way. She detailed a series of visions where she is the bride of Christ. Through this rich bridal imagery, and by enumerating her virtues (such as discernment, reason, and wisdom; see vision 12 in particular), she also claimed religious authority: she was able to speak with authority about the visions she experienced, because she was God's bride, and exhibited virtues (including epistemic virtues, such as reason and wisdom) to be up to the task of communicating these visions to a wider audience.

Gender can intersect with other dimensions, giving rise to intersectional invisibility. For most identities, men are regarded as the prototype. The percentage of women faculty at US doctoral-granting philosophy departments is estimated at about 25% (Schwitzgebel and Jennings 2017). The prototypical philosopher is a white man (e.g., Aristotle, Descartes, and Kant). Philosophers, more so than scholars in other humanities, tend to think that being a good philosopher requires an innate brilliance that cannot be taught. Brilliance is a gendered trait, far more associated with men than with women, as well as a racialized trait, associated more with white people than with people of color (Leslie et al. 2015). The historic and current low representation of women in philosophy, as well as stereotypes about brilliance, could thus give rise to intersectional invisibility of women philosophers. Religion adds an intriguing dimension to the mix because of ideas about gender and (epistemic) authority that prevail in many religious traditions. There are no official statistics for how many women specialize in the philosophy of religion, but estimates put this as lower than the percentage of women in philosophy in general, perhaps as low as 10% (Van Dyke 2015). It is not unusual, being a woman in philosophy of religion, to be the only (invited) speaker at a conference, or even the only female member in the audience.

My working hypothesis is that religious background, gender, and race have an influence on how authors engage in philosophy of religion. The philosophy of religion is suitable for such an analysis because, like academia in general, philosophy is dominated by prestige hierarchies and status relationships that are traditionally tied to class (with upper-class and middle-class academics having clear advantages in terms of economic, social, and cultural capital), and to gender. It is also tied to race, with white students and academics having better access to prestigious universities for their undergraduate and graduate studies compared to non-whites, in ways that have large downstream effects (De Cruz 2018a).

Methodology

Focus Groups in Experimental Philosophy

I use the method of a focus group study to examine how minority status affects the practice of philosophers of religion. Focus groups are informal discussions between about six and eight participants, and rarely over 12 people (Wilkinson 1999). It is a qualitative method that is used for initial exploratory research, or for phenomenological research questions, which probe participants' lived, subjective experiences. As James Andow (2016) notes, qualitative methods are not something experimental philosophers tend to use; in particular, focus group studies remain relatively under-explored as a research method. The exception is bioethics, where focus group studies are sometimes used to look at first-personal accounts of patients, e.g., about how laypeople—children and adults—think about the storage and use of biological tissue samples from minors for research (Hens et al. 2011). Surveys with multiple-choice answers are still the most frequent method used in experimental philosophy. For instance, Cova et al. (2018), in their large-scale replication study of experimental philosophical work carried out between 2003 and 2015, note that "many experimental philosophy studies are simple surveys that can be relatively quickly and inexpensively administered." This is only slowly changing, with methods such as fMRI, eye-tracking, and qualitative surveys in experimental philosophical work (Alexander 2012).

Focus groups are useful to understand how personal factors might shape philosophical practice. They feature interactive discussion between members of demographics a researcher is interested in, and thus are more ecologically valid compared to closed surveys. To explore minority status in philosophical practice, focus groups can be useful because they avoid the decontextualization that is typical of many other research methods (Wilkinson 1999). Other qualitative methods such as open survey questionnaires still isolate research participants, and offer a decontextualized, pre-set context in which they have to answer questions. This does not allow for new themes to emerge through discussion with peers. Focus groups, by contrast, recognize the collective and interpersonal nature of philosophical work. Bringing philosophers from minorities together in groups may help bring out experiences of disadvantage or epistemic injustice, and more broadly, could bring out more vividly the ways in which philosophers are socially situated. Thus, I selected the focus group study as the most suitable method to carry out this research. My aim is to provide a first analysis of the question of how personal identity, including intersecting minority identities, may affect the practice of philosophy of religion.

Participants and Procedures

I recruited a total of 12 participants spread over two focus groups in the course of March 2018. Participants were academic philosophers of religion, at the following levels: advanced graduate student, postdoc, visiting assistant professor, assistant professor, and associate professor. Thus all participants ranged from early to mid-career. Because I was interested in minorities for this study, I invited philosophers of religion who were listed on the UP Directory,[1] a website that publicizes information about philosophers who have identities that are traditionally underrepresented in philosophy, and who write or teach in English (listed members add themselves, and any self-identifications, to this list). As I was also interested in speaking to participants who have identities that are not listed in the UP, such as being Jewish, or being Muslim (these are minorities in philosophy of religion, but not areas of interest to the UP Directory), I additionally recruited participants with such self-identifications through my knowledge of the field, as well as participants not in the UP Directory who have publicly self-identified as being members of religious minorities. The number of focus groups in this study is smaller than in usual focus group studies, both because of the exploratory nature of the study and the highly specific demographic, namely academic philosophers of religion.

My participants self-identify with one or more of the following categories: Christian (among others, Roman Catholic, fundamentalist, evangelical, Eastern Orthodox), atheist, agnostic, Jewish, Muslim, cultural Mormon, queer, trans*, woman, man, Latinx, African American, Asian American, and white. This obviously does not cover the full range of intersectional identities in philosophy of religion, but it provides a starting point for an initial exploratory analysis. Each participant received an invitation email with an information and consent sheet. All the names used in this study are pseudonyms and some identifying information has been removed.

Because of the geographic spread of the participants, living in various states in the United States, United Kingdom, Israel, and Germany, it was necessary to conduct the focus group study online. I used Zoom Pro (a videoconferencing software package that allows for audio and video recording), and video-recorded each focus group discussion. I used an open-ended interview protocol to guide discussion (see Appendix for details on the protocol). Focus group studies are unlike ordinary interviews, in that the interview questions are used as starting points for interactive discussion. In both groups, we did end up having quite some interactive discussion, but nevertheless adhered roughly to the order of questions. Each discussion lasted about two hours.

Data Analysis

A professional transcriber used the recorded video files to transcribe each of the focus group discussions. She used intelligent verbatim, a transcription style that preserves the text verbatim, but increases legibility by omitting fillers (such as "ehm," "you know"), false starts, and repetitions. However, it does not correct grammatical mistakes or slang and thus largely preserves the original spoken text. I checked the transcription for accuracy, taking care that philosophical terminology was correctly transcribed (the transcriber has an academic background but is not a philosopher).

I coded each transcribed discussion using NVivo, a software package for analyzing qualitative research. This allows detailed analysis whereby data[2] can be flexibly divided into segments or units (nodes and cases) that reflect specific thoughts, attitudes, and experiences of participants. The same piece of text can be simultaneously coded in several categories. Because the present study is exploratory, the categories were only compiled after the discussions were completed. Data from across both focus groups was collated using NVivo to examine whether a picture of intersectional issues in the philosophy of religion emerged. This was indeed the case. The next section will present my key findings.

Key Findings

As will be shown in detail in this section, the main themes that came out of the focus group discussion do not neatly fit into the six open-ended interview questions. This is not unusual given that focus groups are interactive, and group dynamics give rise to new topics that are not part of the original set of questions. The main emerging themes can be summarized as follows:

1. In both focus groups, participants frequently mentioned how their personal life experiences sparked their interest or provided continued motivation to work in philosophy of religion.
2. Participants experienced exclusion, and found exclusion of certain voices in the profession (especially non-Western philosophers, philosophers of color, women) harmful. They tried to rectify this in their research and particularly in their teaching, but experienced challenges to achieve this.
3. Participants reflected on how intersectional identity affected their ability to be regarded as authorities in their field, and how they felt compelled (especially as religious minorities in a mainly Christian field) to modify their testimony to fit their audience.
4. The topic of underrepresentation of women in philosophy of religion was discussed in detail, with participants from various backgrounds exploring how in certain contexts (e.g., Orthodox Judaism, fundamentalist Christianity, Shia Islam) intra-religious factors further exacerbate this underrepresentation.
5. Harm, both abstractly as explored in the problem of evil, or in concrete forms of harm done in religious communities, affected participants' views and influenced their philosophical practice. This was particularly discussed in the second focus group.
6. Participants reflected on the specialization of philosophy of religion in academic philosophy, and on the whole found their department and colleagues supportive. They did not think it posed a major obstacle, but the majority received explicit advice not to specialize in it as graduate students.

Each of these key findings will be introduced by a brief description in bullet point style.

I will also provide excerpts of transcripts of what participants said as illustrations.

Key Finding 1: Personal Life Experiences

- The common perception across both focus groups is that life experiences profoundly shape participants' practice in philosophy of religion. All participants had a religious background, including the atheists and agnostics.
- Participants mentioned their home religious environment more frequently than their college education or inspirational teachers, although these also played a role.
- When recounting anecdotes, discussants primarily focused on social religious encounters. For example, Sophia (associate professor, US) mentioned how she tried to convert an agnostic to Mormonism during her missionary work in Portugal, but to her surprise, the potential convert returned to Catholicism. This instilled in Sophia an enduring fascination for religious disagreement and diversity. David, a Jewish postdoc (Israel) had Christian friends from a comprehensive public school pray for him in the hope of converting him to Christianity. He was not particularly religious at this time, and the prayers appeared to work, as he became a religious Jew. This "wasn't quite what they were hoping for."
- Personal experiences with religion were not uniformly positive (this will be explored separately in subsection Key Finding 5).

Many participants had a traditional religious background. For example, Kai, a US graduate student, shares with several other discussants a religious background in the Deep South:

> I think I got into philosophy of religion because I was raised in this really religious background in the Deep South. I was queer and closeted and knew that all sort of claims were being made about people like me and that just got me naturally interested in whether or not what they were saying was true. So when I got into college, I started taking some philosophy courses, became a philosophy major, and then just continued my interest in philosophy of religion.

Anne, an atheist assistant professor (US) with specializations in Hume and philosophy of religion, mentions her Roman Catholic background, which got her into religion. As a Roman Catholic aged 13, she was required to go through confirmation.

> It caused a lot of trouble, and when I was picking my confirmation name I actually got into a big argument with the bishop . . . but

> I really was very skeptical about the whole thing, a precocious child and very skeptical. I was skeptical of Santa Claus when I was five. And so after confirmation, basically my dad just said, "If she doesn't want to, she doesn't have to go to church again, she can stay home with me." I never really thought that much about it, it was never a big deal and when I was in undergrad. I just randomly took an intro to philosophy class just to fulfill some requirement, within the little philosophy of religion unit, and I realized that a lot of the same sort of things that I had been thinking back when I was 13 were real things that people in the world had thought about and written about and things like that. So that just got me super interested in philosophy, and becoming a philosophy major and it came from this place of skepticism and confusion and I think that's actually partially what attracted me to Hume is his skeptical questioning.

Not only did a religious background contribute to participants' initial interest in the field, it also provided motivation, and philosophical work interacted with personal beliefs in complex ways. A typical example is Chris, an associate professor (US), who discussed the relationship between his personal religious views and his work on the nature of faith:

> One respect in which my personal beliefs led to the work that I'm doing, it was for me the loss of the religious faith and my being troubled by that initially and wanting to reconnect with and understand the value of what I had that led to some of the questions that I'm now talking about in philosophy of religion. But also I think that the work that I've done in philosophy of religion has helped me get some peace about my own agnosticism. I feel that I have a better understanding of what was important to me about my earlier religious practice and I've been able to rejoin a religious community and focus on those things—like going to church again, for example, and I feel like I've been able to do that wholeheartedly and find it valuable in part because I have a better understanding of things through working through some of these issues.

Key Finding 2: Patterns of Religious Exclusion

- Participants thought some voices were excluded or marginalized, particularly from women, people of color, and people from religious minorities.
- Participants made efforts to try to diversify their syllabus, but experienced challenges doing this. Their difficulties were caused in part by student expectations, but also by lack of resources. There was a clear sense of not knowing where to begin in creating a more diverse syllabus (especially in the first focus group).
- Personal experiences of racism, sexism, and other forms of exclusion were mentioned.

For Chris, who is African American, the experience of racism and exclusion led him to drift away from religion, which he only gradually got back into, in part due to his philosophical work:

> I grew up in a religious household, and I went to a school that would now be described as fundamentalist Christian, and in that community I grew accustomed to wrestling with some of the questions that are traditionally addressed in philosophy of religion. I remember talking about Pascal's Wager in classes and things like that. So that interest persisted through college, but there were also many respects in which I did not at all identify with the community that I went to high school and junior high with. People were politically much more conservative than I was. Demographically it was very white but also a very racist environment and it didn't take long for me, once I was in a new environment in college, to very quickly drift away from that aspect of my past and I lost the religious beliefs and commitments that I had.

Throughout both focus group discussions, participants talked about marginalization of minority voices. They made efforts to be more inclusive in their pedagogy, but this was taxing. As Simba (who is white), a visiting assistant professor (US) put it:

> I don't know what skin color Maimonides or Gersonides or Avicenna had. I'm close to clueless. Some of my syllabi have listed only white authors, even only American authors. But others have more ethnic, racial, or national representativeness. Others are more representative in gender. None is representative in both ethnicity and gender.

Raúl, associate professor (US), found his efforts to make his philosophy of religion course more diverse challenged by student expectations and lack of diversity in anthologies:

> All these older anthologies frame the debate precisely in those terms: atheism versus something like Christian theism, when there's many other options in between, not just in between, but elsewhere. I think pedagogically you can see the tension, but there's also a sense of students, at least in my classes, that students in my courses, that that's the kind of debate they want to hear about, though. Many of our students come from Christian backgrounds and raise questions about religious belief or God or the supernatural, that's how they think of it and they frame their questions more or less in the traditional atheism versus theism debate on that. For better, for worse, it's a useful opportunity to introduce your students to philosophical issues by way of their own interest. But those interests are narrowly framed.

When not relying on anthologies, making a diverse philosophy of religion syllabus is also challenging because of the amount of extra work involved. As Catherine, assistant professor (US), said:

> It takes more work to create a philosophy of religion class that doesn't just stick to that narrative, because, as you [Raúl] said, most of the text books, especially the older ones, just assume that framing and most of us are overworked anyway and we have to choose our books really early and all of these pressures push us towards the path of least resistance and that path is often framed in atheism versus Christian theism. In my feminist philosophy class last semester I did a module on religion and bringing together a piece on feminist Islamic thought, feminist Jewish thought and feminist Christian thought, and then white Christian feminist thought and black Christian feminist thought, or womanist thought. It took an extraordinary amount of work to get a coherent set of papers that I could teach in the module that would be three weeks long in a class and so I understand why people don't do this. It was hard work for me and this is an area I specialize in! For people who don't specialize in it, I think it's going to take a lot of work to get out of this pattern of framing.

Key Finding 3: Epistemic Authority, Religious Constraints, and Epistemic Injustice

- Philosophers who were part of minority religious traditions in both focus groups found that intersectional identity, both of themselves and others, impacted the ability of philosophers of religion to be authorities in their field.
- Participants who were part of religious minorities were mindful to shape their testimony in ways that became more palatable to the majority culture in philosophy of religion.
- Participants found the dichotomy between classic theism and atheistic naturalism in their field stifling and unhelpful. This was also the case for atheists, such as Anne, who felt that philosophy of religion conferences often were "hostile and in opposition. You're on Team Theism or Team Atheism."

In traditional religious contexts, epistemic and religious authority are intertwined; religious officials (such as rabbi, imam, or priest) have purported expert knowledge of a particular religious tradition. The topic of how one can have epistemic authority, as a philosopher of religion and as someone writing from the perspective of religious minority, came up spontaneously during both focus group discussions. Zahra, a Muslim (Shia) assistant professor (US), worried that writing about Islam in a critical voice would lead to further marginalization of Muslims in the US, as her criticism might not be used for constructive work within the Shia tradition, but by outsiders to further control that population:

> On a personal level, one of the things that has bothered me for a very long time is: How do minorities within religion question an already minority religion without further ostracizing that religion within the mainstream society? And so as a woman or as a Shia Muslim, but particularly as a woman, how do you push on the boundaries within religion or how do you talk about religious issues as a believer without ostracizing that religion within the bigger society?

David, postdoc (Israel), discussed how he shaped his philosophical work given that it is read by a mostly Christian audience:

> I've noticed that I, as a Jewish philosopher, working in this space, where most of my readers are either going to be Christians or naturalistic atheists, is that I end up almost subconsciously tailoring what I'm writing to a Christian audience. That is to say, I'm thinking, how might Jewish conceptions of atonement be interesting to Christians, who spend all this time thinking about atonement? And had I not been to loads of Christian conferences on the atonement, I might never have even thought about Jewish conceptions of atonement.... I'm not saying it as a negative thing, I'm very grateful to my Christian colleagues for what I've learned from them, but being a minority religious identity within this milieu, it just has as a consequence that you find yourself tailoring what you write and how you speak to the majority.

At the same time, David felt pressured to write in a distinctively Jewish voice, to fit expectations, as follows:

> A lot of my Jewish philosopher friends . . . they also worry, "Oh, but you're talking very distinctively Jewish!" If I have a response to the problem of evil, "but a Christian could have said it just as well, or a Muslim could just as well." So, on the one hand we're trying to tailor and cater ourselves to our mainly Christian audience, but on the other hand, we're also very eager to make sure that we must pepper our document with enough quotes from the Midrash otherwise . . . a Christian could have written it! I don't think my Christian colleagues have that kind of worry. Maybe they do, I don't know, does it sound Christian enough?

These concerns relate to testimonial silencing (Dotson 2011). Kristie Dotson (2011) starts from the observation that speakers cannot force their audience to receive their testimony, and so speakers depend to some extent on the goodwill and receptiveness of their audience. As a result of this, two forms of testimonial silencing occur: testimonial quieting and testimonial smothering. Testimonial quieting occurs when the audience does not recognize the speaker as a knower. Testimonial smothering comes from the speaker, who notices that the audience is unable or unwilling to receive her testimony and therefore modifies her testimony (as in David's case), for instance, by ensuring that "the testimony contains only content for which one's audience demonstrates testimonial competence" (Dotson 2011, 244). Both forms were discussed in both focus groups, albeit with more emphasis on testimonial quieting in the first group. For example, Zahra said that women who do not wear hijabs are not taken seriously as testifiers to Islam:

> When we get called to panels somehow there's some sense that this person [a female Muslim philosopher of religion] is probably more authoritative to speak for Islam because they are wearing a hijab or because they are dressed conservatively or dressed in a particular way . . . and not so much about how much knowledge they have or how much publications they might have on the topic or where they have studied. . . . [When] you are not wearing a hijab you have crossed a boundary, that you cannot now be considered an authority in Islam.

Given the prevalence of Christian philosophers in philosophy of religion, it is unsurprising that Christian philosophers did not feel compelled to modify their testimony in this way. The only Christian philosopher in either focus group who felt this pull was Jonathan, visiting assistant professor (US), who is part of orthodox Christianity, a minority tradition within philosophy of religion, although there are vocal proponents, such as Terence Cuneo (2016), who have discussed this tradition in detail in their work.

> I don't have exactly that worry, but being an orthodox Christian, which is a very small minority, I definitely do feel that pull personally. I feel like if I'm going to contribute something, I want to contribute something that is kind of distinctive to where I come from. So definitely I understand that feeling.

Key Finding 4: Gender and Intersectional Religious Identity

- Philosophers in both focus group studies had the perception that women were underrepresented in philosophy of religion, even relative to philosophy as a whole (which is male-dominated).
- People of all genders in both focus group studies noticed the underrepresentation of women, and tried to address it in their syllabi and work.
- They speculated that this might be because of traditional gender roles in particular religious traditions, such as Christianity, Islam, or Judaism, which do not recognize women as authorities to the same extent as men.

- As a result of such traditional gender patterns and expectations, gender intersects with epistemic authority in complex ways, and can give rise to intersectional invisibility for women, especially if they do not adhere to traditional gender norms and expectations.

People of all genders in both focus group interviews extensively discussed the underrepresentation of women in philosophy. It was not uncommon for women to be in a minority in conferences, for instance, as Sophia said:

> At one point I was in the room with pretty much everyone that was at the conference and there were 30 people, no, it was 31, and only three of them were women.

Some discussants expressed puzzlement at the lack of women in the discipline. For example, Simba said,

> I'm puzzled about why there are so few—even relative to the proportions in academia more broadly—so few female contributors in philosophy of religion. Just this semester I was looking—sometimes I use a reader, sometimes punchy books—for my philosophy of religion class and I was looking for short, punchy books by a female philosopher of religion. It's very hard to come across.

This gave rise to a discussion of possible hypotheses in the first focus group, initiated by Catherine. She asked whether "as a man in philosophy of religion, this topic of the male-dominatedness of philosophy of religion has been coming up more recently than in the past. I guess I wonder what your response is to that?" The men in the focus group did welcome the discussion and noticed that it had indeed become more commonplace. Raúl offered the following hypothesis:

> I'm familiar with more conservative Christian communities and in those communities it's pretty common for women to think that there's no available role for them to teach or to have a real voice about theological matters and I would think that that kind of community is less likely to yield women who are interested in philosophy of religion for similar reasons.

Participants in the second focus group also drew a connection between classical theism and masculinity, for example, Rose, assistant professor (Germany), said,

> I connected the whole objectivity versus standpoint objectivity and masculinity and metaphysics and a system of classical theism, and all of those things are distinct and should be kept separate and yet

somehow in my experience in philosophy of religion, they all end up running together.

According to Rose, masculinity is associated with purported lack of bias, and also with

> An attitude that does not take into account people's gender. Philosophical aptitude is tied up with masculinity, "we just take the best people," and contributors at conferences might explicitly mention that one is just there as the token woman.

She has now changed her views, as well as her research interests:

> I'm moving away from theism and doing more mysticism. I've changed my views. Neo-Platonism is another whole new world for me, but I found myself dissatisfied with the straightforward philosophy of religion and I think it's sort of correlated with the politics of philosophy of religion, but I'm not quite sure how.

In her analysis of epistemic injustice, Miranda Fricker (2007) draws attention to the relationship between credibility appraisals and epistemic injustice. She focuses on negative prejudices about particular groups, which undermine the epistemic authority of members of that group. As a result of negative stereotypes, members of particular groups are not regarded as reliable sources of information, and thus will not receive proper epistemic recognition. This gives rise to epistemic deficits. Given that women are often not regarded as proper religious authorities (in several religious traditions, e.g., Catholicism or orthodox Judaism they are also barred from holding positions of religious authority, such as priest or rabbi), they risk not to be seen as epistemic authorities about religion.

While Fricker's focus is on deficit, José Medina (2013) also looks at credibility excesses. In certain situations, a person is given more epistemic credit than they are due, which Medina deems harmful. For one thing, over time a person who has been granted too much epistemic authority can become arrogant, unmoved by dissent, etc. Thus, a thorough investigation of intersectionality in philosophy of religion would not only need to focus on the potential credibility deficit women suffer (as a result of negative stereotypes and lack of formal religious authority), but also potentially on credibility excesses men within certain religious communities enjoy.

Zahra, for instance, argues that men writing about Islam are benefiting from a credibility excess, whereas women suffer an epistemic deficit.

> I've often thought that because of the gendered norms within religion in general, there's a sort of moral authority that is awarded to

men within religious communities, that is completely unearned, that is disproportionate to the sort of knowledge they have, that is disproportionate to the character that they may possess, their religious character, the moral character they might have, at least in the communities that I am familiar with.

Key Finding 5: Harm and Philosophy of Religion

- In both focus group discussions, the topic of harm and patterns of exclusion came up.
- In the first focus group, discussion focused on how philosophers of religion can make sense of the topic of harm, particularly in the problem of evil. Participants felt the philosophical debate was often of poor quality, because it did not fully recognize the scope of this problem.
- In the second focus group, discussion focused on how particular religions (Mormonism, Christianity, and Judaism) excluded some people and had negative images, for instance about LGBTQ people, or about people outside of these religious traditions. Participants' work was in part driven by trying to pursue a theology or philosophy of religion within these traditions that moves beyond these negatives.

A topic of enduring interest in the philosophy of religion is the problem of evil: how can an omnipotent, omnibenevolent being allow so much evil to persist? Participants struggled with articulating philosophical answers that were coherent and that acknowledged the harm that people experience. In the first focus group, this was primarily about harm and the problem of evil. For example, Raúl noted:

> I find that many of my questions about God and evil straightforwardly arise from trying to live life with religious believers, and myself being one of those. You obviously confront people who are suffering and you run into pretty shallow answers that people throw out there and you naturally wonder, "Can we do better than that?", because that's not a very satisfying answer. I think we seek to find internal coherence for our big framework. We have questions about the internal coherence of it and many of the things that I find myself interested in, some of them, at least, fall into that kind of description.

Catherine agreed, noting what people said to her who have had bad experiences with religion:

> I think a lot of the research that I do now does spring from my own religious interests and experiences. One, just living in a community with people who have experienced religion in negative ways and

feeling like philosophy should have something to say to them, but being really dissatisfied with the traditional answers that are given to the problem of evil and feeling like if "I couldn't say this to my friend who is suffering, then should I be saying it at all?"

In the second focus group, discussion turned on traditional conceptions and patterns of exclusion. Sophia, who was raised Mormon said,

> That was part of what drove me into doing philosophy of religion, because I didn't like the dominant interpretation. It implied things that I didn't like, like the racism that's in Mormonism, the sexism that's in Mormonism, and the homophobia and transphobia. So all my work in philosophy of religion, not all of it, but a lot of it, is deeply personal, it's really an attempt to show that the tradition that I'm in did not have to be this way. There were lots of resources within the tradition that would have allowed Mormonism to go a different direction than it went. It was sort of a historical or arbitrary fact that it went in the direction that it did go.

David also sees his work in the philosophy of religion as a personal calling and response to harmful patterns of exclusion he perceives in Orthodox Judaism:

> My connection to Judaism is not doxastic primarily, it's kind of tribal and communal. It's this peoplehood that we're born into, or can join, of course. But as I became more and more committed to religious observance I was disturbed by some of the politics and the values that are most prominently expressed within observant orthodox Judaism, towards women, towards the LGBT community, towards non-Jews sometimes, on Israel-Palestine, on all sorts of things. So more and more I feel like for me philosophy of religion is something like a calling that I have some sort of responsibility to . . . I like what [Sophia] said, the resources are there. I'm trying to figure out: are there ways to articulate an authentically Jewish, recognizably in some sense orthodox, theology and philosophy that can move us beyond some of these negatives? So it is deeply personal, so personal that at times I didn't want to do it.

Allegra, associate professor (UK) working on Christian traditions, thinks having been part of a religious tradition does put her in a good position to criticize problematic features of religion without lacking empathy.

> I'm thinking particularly with respect to my work on religion and mental health, trying to enter into different mindsets, empathetically, but also not going with that kind of, "if something is someone's

religious beliefs, then you can't challenge it, because it's private, because it's religious." . . . It seems to me a very odd thing to say, "oh, it's their religious beliefs and therefore you can't step on people's toes or you can't challenge it." . . . So for example, some churches respond to people with depression by saying it's a symptom of sin, or of demonic possession, and they have self-help books about this. . . . And so it's worth calling people out on this kind of thing, where being critical and not thinking that you can't engage with people's beliefs. Those are quite extreme cases, but I think there are other cases as well where empathy and yet ability to criticize are wanted and that's because of my religious background.

Key Finding 6: Support and Encouragement in Specializing in Philosophy of Religion

- Participants were actively discouraged from specializing in philosophy of religion while in graduate school.
- Participants found their present department supportive, even if it consists mostly of atheists, agnostics, and people not interested in religion.
- Although participants shared the experience that they were discouraged from specializing in philosophy of religion, they found that this specialization conferred advantages too—it was sometimes easier to publish in, and one participant joked he came to philosophy of religion for the money (he got a postdoc position in this field, although his dissertation was not in the philosophy of religion).

Participants in both focus groups seemed to share an experience of being actively discouraged to graduate in philosophy of religion, while receiving support once they worked on the topic at the faculty level. For example, Anne had interests in both history of philosophy and philosophy of religion as a graduate student, and received the following advice:

> It's fine if I wanted to work on religion in history, but I should have a job-marketable AOS and history would be great—definitely don't just do AOS philosophy of religion, that was the explicit advice that I got from basically every person I talked to.

Chris' undergraduate mentor said it even more strongly:

> My close mentor, close undergraduate mentor at the time . . . was talking to me about my interests, and I mentioned that philosophy of religion was my area I wanted to go in, and he strongly, strongly discouraged me from going into it, for reasons much like the ones you said. You'll never get a job, it's a fringe area and I think that

even later, when despite his advice I started carving out an area of philosophy of religion that was of interest to me, just in talking to colleagues who were not in philosophy of religion, I did hear a lot of dismissive comments about the status of philosophy of religion in the professional arch.

Participants in both focus groups echoed this advice they received, one of them (Raúl) continues to give this advice to his own students, partly because he thinks it is important to get a good footing in a core discipline such as metaphysics or epistemology before one can meaningfully intervene in debates in the philosophy of religion. However, once participants reached the assistant professor or postdoc level, they felt supported in their work in philosophy of religion. For example, as Catherine says,

> My school is secular, but we have a large population of Christians here in [School], both among the student population and the faculty population. It's hard to say whether that contributes to the positive attitude, but I feel really supported by my colleagues and my chair, although I'm the only one doing philosophy of religion as such.

General Discussion and Conclusion

Several authors, such as Sandra Harding (1991), have argued that diversity among inquirers confers an epistemic advantage: people who are in underprivileged social positions are more likely to see patterns of social reality that elude more advantaged groups. This feminist standpoint epistemology has been criticized (see Rolin 2006, for discussion). For one thing, the claim that people who are socially disadvantaged would enjoy certain epistemic advantages seems to require that we are able to adjudicate which positions are less distorted than others, but standpoint epistemology denies that there is a privileged position from which we would be able to do this.

In response to this challenge, Helen Longino (1991) has argued that we have to think about knowledge not as something created by individuals applying a method, but by individuals who interact with each other in ways that facilitate revision in the face of criticism—this is why Longino ultimately favors a collective view of scientific objectivity, as something that is created by a community of interacting individuals, rather than the more individualist standpoint epistemology. Kristina Rolin (2006) argues that contextualism offers a way out of what she considers to be a false dilemma between a view from nowhere and radical framework relativism. Unlike the view from nowhere, contextualism does not put forward one position as the epistemically privileged one. Rather, contextualism holds that one is by default entitled to one's beliefs, but that these beliefs can be challenged by appropriate arguments and criticism. Unlike in radical framework relativism, no beliefs are beyond challenge.

Applying these considerations to philosophy of religion, what conclusions can we draw? This qualitative study looked at the social context in which academic philosophers of religion work, especially those who are underrepresented in the profession due to religious belief, gender, and race. I have used an intersectional framework where I explored, through two focus group discussions, how these identities intersect with each other and how they influence the practice of philosophy of religion. The use of focus groups with scholars from minorities was useful, because the assumptions under which philosophers of religion operate are likely to be less visible to scholars who belong to majorities in the philosophy of religion. Standpoint epistemology would predict that Christian, male, and white philosophers are less likely to see patterns of social exclusion that underlie their discipline. Given that these discussions rely on self-report it was therefore useful to focus on minorities in order to get a better insight into these patterns, and thereby challenge the notion that philosophy of religion is conducted from a view from nowhere.

My key findings support this notion: for participants in these focus groups doing philosophy of religion was deeply personal. They were motivated by personal experiences, often going back to early childhood, of engaging with religion and with religious communities, and their philosophical work interacted with their religious life experiences in complex ways (key finding 1). This pushes back against the view from nowhere, as these authors come from many different religious traditions and have a variety of experiences that inform their work, which enriches philosophy of religion. My participants were underrepresented in philosophy of religion, either by virtue of their religious beliefs, gender, ethnicity, or a combination of these factors. Standpoint epistemology would predict that people who are socially disadvantaged might be more clearly able to see how such non-epistemic factors influence their work. In a related paper (De Cruz 2018b), which used an open survey, I found that philosophers of religion who are part of the majority traditions (Christianity or naturalist atheism) also connected their work in philosophy of religion to personal faith and life experiences, so this finding further extends and supports my earlier results.

But given the focus on minorities, and the interactive nature of the focus group discussions, this study provides some unanticipated findings. In particular, the fact that minority philosophers themselves have difficulties diversifying their syllabus, due to student expectations and anthologies that emphasize a dichotomy between classical theism and naturalism, was unexpected (key finding 2). While one might expect that patterns of testimonial injustice and silencing could be at work in the philosophy of religion, it was nevertheless remarkable to observe how several participants felt compelled to keep within certain boundaries of their tradition, or to tailor their writing to fit expectations from the Christian majority (key finding 3). Another unexpected finding was that participants struggled with harm, not only in the abstract, as in the problem of evil and the engagement with this topic by philosophers, but also the harm that is done within particular religious communities (key finding 5). The topic of gender vividly raised discussion of intersectionality as participants discussed how certain patterns of gender expectations and religious authority negatively impacted the ability of women to be seen as epistemic authorities in their field (key finding 4). Finally, participants confirmed my expectation that philosophy of religion is actively discouraged as a subject of graduate study, but they felt supported by their department once they were at the postdoc or faculty level, and no longer saw philosophy of religion as a marginalized field (key finding 6).

While my main aim for this paper was diagnostic, identifying patterns of exclusion, credibility deficit, and testimonial smothering and quieting, rather than seeking to remedy such patterns, I will briefly conclude with some ways in which philosophy of religion can move forward (for a more extended treatment, see De Cruz forthcoming). One way to make philosophy of religion more inclusive would be to increase its diversity, both in terms of (religious) viewpoints and in terms of other relevant demographic characteristics, such as gender, class, sexuality, and race. Presently, philosophy of religion is dominated by male Christian theists, giving rise to a skewed epistemic landscape. Encouragement for religious and other minorities in philosophy to engage with philosophy of religion questions could come from graduate departments, focused conferences, and workshops on topics that are underrepresented in philosophy of religion and that might attract a more diverse public and more diverse contributions. A demographic change will not happen overnight. But through achievable changes in the broader social context of philosophy of religion as a practice, it may occur over the longer term. A second way to make philosophy of religion more inclusive is to offer resources for faculty members to teach beyond the (male-, white-, and Christian-) dominated canon. As focus group members expressed frustration at the difficulty they faced in making their syllabi inclusive particularly given lack of support and time, support could come from a variety of initiatives such as summer schools for faculty members, inclusive reading lists and syllabi distributed by philosophical societies, and also the commissioning of more minority perspectives in handbooks and anthologies (where editors tend to have a lot of leeway in who they invite and what topics they seek to address, even in an introductory handbook on philosophy of religion). A third course of action to effect change is to shape individual ways in which philosophers respond to others in the discipline, which sometimes expresses itself as boundary policing (how is this philosophy?) and in not according sufficient credibility to fellow voices in the discipline based on characteristics such as gender, religious background, and race.

Already, there are cultural changes along these lines afoot, but given implicit bias, it may be helpful for philosophers to try more actively to habituate themselves into inclusive attitudes.

In summary, this focus group study was a first exploration of how philosophers' social identity could impact their work, showing that philosophy of religion is not conducted in a social vacuum, but is intimately connected with issues relating to religious belief, gender, and ethnicity of flesh-and-blood philosophers.[3]

Appendix: Discussion Schedule

1. Tell me something about how you got interested in philosophy of religion.
2. Did you feel supported in your decision to specialize in philosophy of religion?
3. Philosophy of religion is a male-dominated field. How do you think this affects the practice of philosophy of religion and is there anything you wish to share about personal experiences regarding this?
4. Philosophy of religion, at least as practiced at Western institutions, is a white-dominated field. How do you think this affects the practice of philosophy of religion and is there anything you wish to share about personal experiences regarding this?
5. Philosophy of religion is, at least in Western academic institutions, focused on (mostly Protestant) Christianity and on naturalist atheism. How do you think this shapes philosophy of religion and is there anything about your personal work that you would like to share about this?
6. How do your personal religious beliefs (or lack thereof) interact with your work in philosophy of religion?
7. Are there any other thoughts you'd wish to share about philosophy of religion and how you relate to it?

Notes

1. www.theupdirectory.com/, Directory of Philosophers from Underrepresented Groups in Philosophy, self-identifications include black, Asian, Latino/a or Hispanic, multi-racial, person with a disability, LGBTQ, and woman.
2. The coding is done by hand, through careful reading of the text by the researcher. There are some limited options for machine coding using key words, but this was not utilized in this study due to the complexity and context-sensitivity of what was said). As there is no statistical analysis involved, coding of such studies tends to be done by the researcher rather than third-party coders, and this was the case for the present study.
3. Many thanks to Alicia Finch, Kevin Timpe, Blake Hereth, Michelle Panchuk, Katherine Dormandy, Johan De Smedt, and participants to the 2018 Logos Conference (Notre Dame) for very helpful feedback to an earlier draft, and to all discussants in the focus groups for their input to this study.

References

Alexander, Joshua. *Experimental Philosophy. An Introduction.* Cambridge: Polity Press, 2012.
Anderson, Pamela Sue. "Sacrificed Lives: Mimetic Desire, Sexual Difference and Murder." *Journal for Cultural Research* 4.2 (2000): 216–227.
Andow, James. "Qualitative Tools and Experimental Philosophy." *Philosophical Psychology* 29.8 (2016): 1128–1141.
Botts, Tina F., Liam Kofi Bright, Myisha Cherry, Guntur Mallarangeng, and Spencer Quayshawn. "What Is the State of Blacks in Philosophy?" *Critical Philosophy of Race* 2.2 (2014): 224–242.
Bourget, David and David J. Chalmers. "What Do Philosophers Believe?" *Philosophical Studies* 170 (2014): 465–500.
Bowleg, Lisa. "Intersectionality: An Underutilized but Essential Theoretical Framework for Social Psychology." In *The Palgrave Handbook of Critical Social Psychology*, edited by Brendan Gough, 507–529. London: Palgrave Macmillan, 2017.
Coakley, Sarah. "Dark Contemplation and Epistemic Transformation: The Analytic Theologian Re-Meets Teresa of Ávila." In *Analytic Theology: New Essays in the Philosophy of Theology*, edited by Oliver D. Crisp and Michael C. Rea, 280–312. Oxford: Oxford University Press, 2009.
Cova, Florian, Brent Strickland, Angela Abatista, Aurélien Allard, James Andow, Mario Attie, James Beebe, et al. "Estimating the Reproducibility of Experimental Philosophy." *Review of Philosophy and Psychology* (2018, online first): 1–36.
Crenshaw, Kimberlé. "Demarginalizing the Intersection of Race and Sex: A Black Feminist Critique of Antidiscrimination Doctrine, Feminist Theory and Antiracist Politics." *University of Chicago Legal Forum* 8 (1989): 139–167.
———. "Mapping the Margins: Intersectionality, Identity Politics, and Violence Against Women of Color." *Stanford Law Review* 43.6 (1991): 1241–1299.
Cuneo, Terence. *Ritualized Faith: Essays on the Philosophy of Liturgy.* Oxford: Oxford University Press, 2016.
De Cruz, Helen. "Prestige Bias: An Obstacle to a Just Academic Philosophy." *Ergo: An Open Access Journal of Philosophy* 5.10 (2018a): 259–287.
———. "Religious Beliefs and Philosophical Views: A Qualitative Study." *Res Philosophica* 95.3 (2018b): 477–504.
———. "Seeking Out Epistemic Friction in the Philosophy of Religion." In *Marginalized Identities, Peripheral Theologies: Expanding Conversations in Analytic Theology*, edited by Michelle Panchuk and Michael Rea. Oxford: Oxford University Press, forthcoming.
Descartes, René. "The Discourse on Method." In *René Descartes: Philosophical Essays and Correspondence*, edited by Roger Ariew, 46–82. Indianapolis: Hackett, 2000.
Dotson, Kristie. "Tracking Epistemic Violence, Tracking Practices of Silencing." *Hypatia* 26.2 (2011): 236–257.
———. "How Is This Paper Philosophy?" *Comparative Philosophy* 3.1 (2013): 3–29.
Draper, Paul and Ryan Nichols. "Diagnosing Cognitive Biases in Philosophy of Religion." *The Monist* 96 (2013): 420–444.

Fricker, Miranda. *Epistemic Injustice: Power and the Ethics of Knowing*. Oxford: Oxford University Press, 2007.

Hadewijch. *Visioenen*. Translated by I. Dros. Amsterdam: Prometheus, 13th century, 1996.

Harding, Sandra. *Whose Science? Whose Knowledge? Thinking from Women's Lives*. Ithaca: Cornell University Press, 1991.

Hens, Kristien, Herman Nys, J.-J. Cassiman, and Kris Dierickx. "The Storage and Use of Biological Tissue Samples from Minors for Research: A Focus Group Study." *Public Health Genomics* 14.2 (2011): 68–76.

Kelly, Thomas. "Disagreement, Dogmatism, and Belief Polarization." *Journal of Philosophy* 105 (2008): 611–633.

Leslie, Sarah-Jane, Andrei Cimpian, Meredith Meyer, and Edward Freeland. "Expectations of Brilliance Underlie Gender Distributions Across Academic Disciplines." *Science* 347.6219 (2015): 262–265.

Longino, Helen E. "Multiplying Subjects and the Diffusion of Power." *Journal of Philosophy* 88 (1991): 666–674.

Medina, José. *The Epistemology of Resistance: Gender and Racial Oppression, Epistemic Injustice, and the Social Imagination*. Oxford: Oxford University Press, 2013.

Purdie-Vaughns, Valerie and Richard P. Eibach. "Intersectional Invisibility: The Distinctive Advantages and Disadvantages of Multiple Subordinate-Group Identities." *Sex Roles* 59.5–6 (2008): 377–391.

Rolin, Kristina. "The Bias Paradox in Feminist Standpoint Epistemology." *Episteme* 3.1–2 (2006): 125–136.

Schilbrack, Kevin. *Philosophy and the Study of Religions: A Manifesto*. Malden, MA: Wiley-Blackwell, 2014.

Schwitzgebel, Eric and Fiery Cushman. "Philosophers' Biased Judgments Persist Despite Training, Expertise and Reflection." *Cognition* 141 (2015): 127–137.

Schwitzgebel, Eric and Carolyn Dicey Jennings. "Women in Philosophy: Quantitative Analyses of Specialization, Prevalence, Visibility, and Generational Change." *Public Affairs Quarterly* 31.2 (2017): 83–106.

Teresa of Ávila. *The Interior Castle or the Mansions*. Edited by B. Zimmerman. London: Thomas Baker, 1577 [1921].

Van Dyke, Christina. "Don't Get Your Panties in a Bunch: The Dilemma of Addressing the Absence of Women in the Philosophy of Religion." 2015. http://whimsyandwisdom.ghost.io/2015/09/20/dont-get-your-panties-in-a-bunch-the-dilemma-of-addressing-the-absence-of-women-in-the-philosophy-of-religion/.

Wilhelm, Isaac, Sherri Lynn Conklin, and Nicole Hassoun. "New Data on the Representation of Women in Philosophy Journals: 2004–2015." *Philosophical Studies* 175.6 (2018): 1441–1464.

Wilkinson, Sue. "Focus Groups." *Psychology of Women Quarterly* 23.2 (1999): 221–244.

2 That We May Be Whole
Doing Philosophy of Religion With the Whole Self

Michelle Panchuk

The first time I workshopped a paper on trauma, the emotional preparation seemed almost as strenuous as my frenzied writing. This was a new experience for someone accustomed to arguing about the status of abstract property-universals. My apprehension arose not from fear of public speaking or philosophical criticism, but from the prospect of having to maintain the appearance of dispassionate distance from a topic in which I was deeply emotionally invested. The prospect of discussing the sadistic abuse of a friend as if it had been inflicted on the abstract entities that populate philosophical thought experiments, rather than a flesh-and-blood child, made me feel sick—even morally suspect. I had exposed the wounds and souls of my friends and myself to being poked by those for whom analysis was merely an academic exercise, for whom nothing if import hung on the conclusion of the argument. These weren't *bad* people. *They* weren't even the source of my trepidation per se—disciplinary norms were. My project was philosophical. As such there was a tacit expectation that we would treat it as if it were neither personal nor political (Kittay 2009a).

Since then I have encountered a number of analytic thinkers whose work transgresses the boundaries between the personal, the political, and the philosophical. Many of them describe similar experiences of trepidation in bringing their whole person to bear on their philosophical endeavors. Elizabeth Barnes recalls thinking that she could not do philosophical work on disability because she herself is disabled (2016, viii ff.). Eva Kittay reflects on the emotional burden of defending her disabled daughter from professional philosophers who would deny her a place in the moral community (2009a, 607–608). Susan Brison and Melissa Burchard reflect on the philosophical insights that we gain by taking their first-person experiences of personal and secondary trauma seriously (Brison 2002; Burchard 2019). All argue persuasively that their personal investment in the subject matter, far from rendering them disadvantaged and problematically biased, gives them unique and valuable insight. Our philosophical conversations would not be complete without their contributions.[1] Within feminist philosophy and critical race theory the value of marginalized standpoints has come to be accepted almost as a given (as the abundance of work on standpoint epistemology shows), and theologians (our disciplinary cousins) have been working on theologies of gender, race, sexuality, ability, and postcolonial thought for decades. Yet, both their insights and the philosophical foundations that underlie them have been slow to gain traction within analytic philosophy of religion.[2] Here, the myth of the disembodied, dispassionate view from nowhere—which bears a striking resemblance to the view from cisgender, heterosexual, middle-class, white, able-bodied Christian males—reigns. In this chapter I set aside the question of whether or not the 'God's eye point of view' has any place as a regulative ideal in our theorizing. Instead, I draw on feminist theories of epistemic injustice and oppression to argue that we cannot afford to continue to pretend that we *actually* occupy that view or that those of us who remain uninvested and disinterested in the answers to particular philosophical puzzles manage to draw closer to it than others.[3] In the first two sections I sketch the dangers of attempting to do analytic philosophy of religion from this fictional perspective. In particular, I argue that it creates gaps in our collective knowledge—or what we might call, following Kristie Dotson, 'reliable ignorance.' Although not necessarily (initially) culpable, when embraced, reinforced, and then encoded in the structures and practices of the discipline, this ignorance becomes pernicious (2011).[4] It is pernicious in at least two respects. First, it distorts the results of our philosophical inquiry. Our theories end up incomplete at best, and false or positively harmful at worst. Second, though related, it does epistemic violence to members and would-be members of our philosophical community. Failing to see certain people as knowers, we quiet their testimony or encourage them to smother it themselves. In the third section I gesture towards some attitudes and practices that would help move analytic philosophy of religion toward greater epistemic justice, allowing more of us to practice philosophy with our whole selves.

The Epistemic Limits of the View From Nowhere

Bertrand Russell describes the view from nowhere (as the position occupied by the ideal philosopher) quite vividly:

> The free intellect will see as God might see, without a here and now, without *hopes* and *fears*, without the trammels of customary beliefs and traditional prejudices, calmly, *dispassionately*, in the sole and exclusive desire of knowledge—knowledge as *impersonal*, as purely contemplative, as it is possible for man to attain. Hence also the free intellect will value more the *abstract* and *universal* knowledge into which the *accidents of private history do not enter*, than the knowledge brought by the senses, and dependent, as such knowledge must

be, upon an exclusive and *personal point of view* and *a body* whose sense-organs distort as much as they reveal.

(Russell 1957, 160, emphasis mine)

Although rarely made this explicit, I suspect that similar assumptions about the 'proper' mode of doing philosophy linger within analytic philosophy of religion (as elsewhere). I will not, however, argue for the claim that these assumptions are widespread in the present chapter. Not only is it a supposition that I believe many of my readers will find plausible, it is also one for which it is difficult to obtain sufficient and reliable evidence. Doing so would require extensive empirical data about the attitudes, beliefs, and implicit biases of the members of the sub-discipline, the latter of which would be especially difficult to obtain. My goals are more modest. I argue that this perspective *would* have negative effects *if* it were indeed (implicitly or explicitly) endorsed by some critical mass of analytic philosophers of religion. In particular, I argue that this perspective artificially limits the range of topics to which philosophers of religion can and should apply themselves; it wrongly circumscribes the range of evidence available to us; and it unjustly limits the range of personal and social identities welcome within the subfield because it inflicts epistemic injustice upon those who cannot pretend to occupy the view from nowhere. Along the way, I offer anecdotes that, in addition to illustrating specific points, may support the plausibility, but not prove, the truth of my assumptions about the character of the field.

Among other things, Russell's description rejects emotion and particular, first-person, lived experience as playing legitimate roles in the project of analytic philosophy. Although he qualifies these claims with the phrase "as it is possible for man to attain," acknowledging the practical impossibility of perfect attainment of the ideal, it is clear that he believes that one should strive to limit these influences as much as is humanly possible. If this is the correct way to engage in analytic philosophy of religion, then it seems that analytic philosophers of religion should focus on topics that are universal and abstract, rather than particular, embodied, and concrete.[5] Questions about the existence of a divine being, the evidential significance of suffering, and the rationality of religious belief (in general) would be welcome areas of inquiry, while the existential problem of evil, racism as a manifestation of American Christianity, the performance of gender in religious communities, or the role of atonement theory in religious abuse would be precluded, or at least discouraged. In other words, on Russell's view, a whole range of social and political questions that philosophers of religion might be in a position to address, and which might benefit from the rigors of philosophical analysis, are completely inappropriate or at least philosophically suspect. Given that humans are inherently social and political beings, and given that most major world religions endorse things like obligations to members of one's family, love of neighbor, and care for the poor and socially disadvantaged, all of which are particular, embodied, and concrete, it would be both surprising and unfortunate if philosophers of religion had absolutely nothing to offer to our understanding of such projects.

One way to respond to this observation is to appeal to the intellectual division of labor. There are inevitably many valuable things that philosophers could do with their time that they do not do because they are busy with the demands of their chosen profession. In fact, most philosophers could probably make a greater practical impact on the world by choosing some other career path. But insofar as we think there is value in intellectual pursuits for their own sake, it would be odd to argue that we have a religious obligation to abandon our philosophical careers in order to pursue the common good in some more practical way. Similarly, there are many other valuable philosophical projects in which any given philosopher *could* engage, but doesn't. Insofar as we are *analytic* philosophers *of religion*, we have every reason to engage in those intellectual inquiries appropriate to *analytic* philosophy *of religion*—the abstract, universal, disembodied inquiries with which we are already engaged. And, of course, it would be uncharitable to ignore the various ways in which these abstract, universal, apolitical inquiries have actually contributed to the common good. If one thinks that religious faith is valuable, as I do, then removing barriers to it posed by the problem of evil or accusations of irrationality is a great good—one to which many analytic philosophers of religion have *in fact* contributed for the common good.

I have no wish to deny that this is true. I think philosophers of religion have done philosophical and practical good through their work. Nonetheless, when I look at the example of rigorous analytic philosophical work in feminist philosophy, philosophy of race, philosophy of disability, and applied ethics I cannot help but think that Russell's perspective artificially limits the range of topics to which analytic thought may be applied. Sally Haslanger's social ontology of gender is no less rigorous or analytic for taking on a topic that is particular, embodied, and inherently political (2000). So too for the work of Kristie Dotson, Elizabeth Barnes, Kate Manne, Charles Mills, Melissa Burchard, and a myriad of others (e.g., Dotson 2011; Dotson 2014; Barnes 2016; Manne 2017; Mills 1998, 2007; Burchard 2019). This demonstrates that seeing Russell's disciplinary norms as *essential* to the project of analytic philosophy is misguided. And I see no plausible reason to think that there is something about religion, as such, that requires exclusively abstract, universal, disembodied engagement with it. If I am right, then there is a whole range of issues that analytic philosophers of religion *could* be addressing, from which religious communities and society more generally might greatly benefit. Although I lack that data to say with any confidence what factors contributes to the paucity of engagement with these topics within analytic philosophy of religion, it seems plausible that assumptions about the appropriate mode of doing philosophy illustrated in the quote from Russell play a role to some degree. It may well be that philosophers of religion have systematically ignored these topics because of personal prejudice and the structural forces that such prejudice creates against the particular and the political.

Not only is it not the case that analytic philosophy of religion *must* be practiced in a dispassionate, ahistorical mode, but there may also be a whole range of valuable evidence, reasons, perspectives, and topics that we lose when we exclude emotion and lived experience from our theorizing. Consider first the value of lived experience. Recent work on transformative experience, pioneered by Laurie Paul, underlines the extent to which, at least for beings like us, what we are in a position to know and reason about is limited by our life experience (Paul 2015). Before leaving the black and white room, Mary does not and cannot know what seeing red is like, even though she possesses all the propositional knowledge there is to be had about the nature of color vision (Jackson 1986). Indeed, our knowledge isn't just limited by our experience as a matter of contingent fact. Given our finite human nature, our knowledge is necessarily limited.[6] A being like God may be able to occupy the view from nowhere *and* have access to the phenomenal knowledge of particular experiences (e.g., Zagzebski 2008), but beings like us only have access to the phenomenal knowledge of things we have experienced and those that are sufficiently similar for us to make accurate inferences about them.

Laurie Paul's primary point is that we cannot use the resources of standard decision theory to decide whether or not to undergo a transformative experience because we cannot know what the experience will be like and because we cannot access the values and preferences we will have after we undergo that transformation. We simply cannot occupy the proper frame of reference from which to assign values to possible outcomes. But the importance of lived experience and the phenomenal knowledge that it provides isn't limited to decision theory. It relates to a number of issues within analytic philosophy of religion. Of course, there has been a great deal of work done on the significance, reliability, and evidential value of experience both within and without philosophy of religion: is it rational to believe on the basis of religious experience?, what sorts of experiences count as religious experiences?, etc. . . . But the quote from Russell would help explain why there is greater hesitance to philosophize *with* or *through* that very same lived experience. Phenomenal knowledge may provide knowledge, evidence, and reasons that one would not otherwise have. Knowing what certain kinds of suffering *are like*—in the same way that Mary comes to know what seeing red is like—and having experienced the changes that they effect on one's value structures and preferences may be relevant for assessing the adequacy of a theory, for seeing the importance of a topic, for prudently navigating delicate philosophical issues. For example, knowing what it is like to experience religious trauma may better place one to evaluate the success of various theodicies and responses to the problem of divine hiddenness (Panchuk 2018). Not only does one come to know, phenomenologically, the kind of experience that a successful theory must account for, it also gives one access to the changes in values and preferences that impact whether a sufferer will be in a position to accept a particular theodicy. That is, the lived experience is important when responding to, and assessing responses to, the problem of evil both as a philosophical puzzle and as an existential problem. But no human trying to operate from the view from nowhere knows what that kind of trauma is like. Excluding the "accidents of private history" entails that, by definition, analytic philosophy of religion would lack this relevant range of insight. This is true across a number of issues that analytic philosophy of religion might otherwise address: male philosophers of religion do not know what it is like to experience religiously motivated misogyny; white philosophers do not know the pain of racial discrimination by those who claim to be brothers and sisters in the faith; some of us have never had a canonical religious experience, lost our faith, or converted to a new religion. All of these topics are ripe for analytic treatment, if only analytic philosophers of religion would abandon the view from nowhere and embrace the view from particular somewheres.

Not only does the exclusion of lived experience deprive us of epistemic resources relevant to the truth or falsity of our theories, it also makes it difficult, and perhaps even impossible, to see the negative practical impact that our theories may have. Black liberation, feminist, and womanist theologians often critique mainstream theology, not only for ignoring the experience of women and people of color in their theologizing, but for ignoring the ways in which theories that overlook the experiences of marginalized groups do positive, concrete harm to those already vulnerable communities (e.g., Williams 2013; Cone 2013; Brock and Parker 2001). For example, in *Proverbs of Ashes: Violence, Redemptive Suffering, and the Search for What Saves Us*, Rebecca Parker recounts her journey in realizing that the most prominent theories of the atonement valorize suffering in ways that have minimized and glorified the suffering of abused women and children. She recounts asking her congregation,

> Do we really believe that God is appeased by cruelty and wants nothing more than our obedience? It becomes imperative that we ask this question when we examine how theology sanctions human cruelty. If God is imagined as a fatherly torturer, earthly parents are also justified, perhaps even required to teach through violence. Children are instructed to understand their submission to pain as a form of love. Behind closed doors, in our own community, spouses and children are battered by abusers who justify their actions as necessary and loving discipline. . . . A God who [must punish] disobedience will

teach us to obey and endure when it would be holy to protest. . . . Atonement theology takes an act of state violence and redefines it as intimate violence, a private spiritual transaction between God the Father and God the Son. Atonement theology then says that intimate violence saves lives . . . mak[ing] intimate violence holy and salvific. Intimate violence ends sin.

(2001, 30–31; 49)

One need not agree with Parker's claims about the connection between atonement theory and abuse to appreciate that the claim itself, and any appropriate response to it, would have to draw on knowledge of the lived experience of vulnerable individuals. It is only as Parker engages with abuse survivors within her parish, outside of the 'ivory tower' of the academy that she becomes increasingly uneasy with mainstream approaches to the atonement, because only in that role does she confront the practical impact of those theories. While the task of discerning whether a particular point of theology is being misapplied or whether the appropriateness of a particular practical applications follows *logically* or *necessarily* from the doctrine is a fraught and challenging task, we are unlikely even to ask these questions if we strive to engage in analytic philosophy of religion only from the view from nowhere.

Similarly, James Cone describes his experience interacting with members of the black church:

The poison of White supremacy is so widespread and deeply internalized by its victims that many are unaware of their illness and others often do not have the cultural and intellectual resources to heal their wounded spirits. In my travels around the world, I am amazed at how much people of color want to be White. They want to look like Whites, talk like Whites, and even pray like Whites. Many are still worshipping a White God and a blond-haired, blue-eyed Jesus—still singing, 'Wash me and I will be Whiter than snow.'

(2004, 141)

No respectable theologian would claim that God or Jesus is white. And yet, because whiteness is so often invisible as an assumed default, white Christians have remained oblivious to how artistic and theological representations implicitly assume as much. God in Michelangelo's "The Creation of Adam" is an old white man who creates the first human to reflect that race. Blond-haired, blue-eyed Jesus hangs on the wall in many 'color-blind' churches. Few of us have ever considered how metaphorically associating darkness with evil and whiteness with good might serve to reinforce systems of oppression—how singing "black is the color of my sin, the wrong that will keep my heart from Him," in Sunday school might hurt a black child. We are confronted with the significance of the language we use to communicate abstract philosophical and theological ideas through the lived experience that Cone offers us in his testimony.

Finally, consider the relationship between emotion and knowledge. Although much of the philosophical tradition has been skeptical of the value of emotion, many feminist philosophers and virtue theorists affirm the importance of emotion in both epistemology and ethics. In her groundbreaking work "Love and Emotion," Alison Jaggar points out that the myth of the dispassionate investigator, far from protecting us from the ills of invested reasoning, actually intensifies this risk because it renders emotional investment, which we all inevitably experience, opaque and taboo, rather than transparent (1989). Furthermore, if one rejects the 'unintelligent view' of emotion according to which they are mere bodily perturbations (as I believe one should) in favor of a view on which emotions are intentional and involve concepts, then there is reason to think that emotions can give us insight that might otherwise be difficult or even impossible to obtain. For example, Eva Kittay points out that it isn't just that her love for her disabled daughter makes listening to Singer and McMahan's arguments about her daughter's exclusion from the moral community painful, but that both the experience and the existence of her love for her daughter reveals *facts* about the world that Kittay might not otherwise access (2009a, 623). Love, it is true, can distort one's perspective, making one insensitive to faults, unjustifiably hopeful, or encouraging one to unjustly favor the beloved over others; but it can also give one insight into the value of the other that one who does not love the other is likely to lack. The loving gaze is often a more insightful gaze because it enables the lover to see the beloved *as morally valuable*. Indeed, Kittay argues that the existence of her love for her daughter reveals that her obligations arise *not* from her own preferences, but from the nature of her daughter and the social relation in which she stands to her. Certainly one might accept on testimony that someone else is a member of the moral community. One might judge that another falls within the moral community based on facts about that other that one reads off of their medical chart. But another way to come to know the moral value of another is *to experience them as a moral subject*, an experience that may be facilitated by loving attention to that other. If this line of reasoning is right, then perhaps rather than vilifying the fetus-loving pro-lifer, the 'biased' parent of the gay child, or the angry atheist for their emotions, we can recognize that their emotions may enable insight that we ourselves do not have insofar as we do not share the emotional disposition that facilitates the insight. In other cases there may be little reason to think that an emotion is epistemically valuable, but where the emotion is still morally appropriate. Here the danger is not that the exclusion of emotion as such will be epistemically detrimental to our philosophizing, but that we may exclude members of the philosophical community from the philosophical conversation on the basis of morally appropriate responses to the content of the philosophical subject matter. This might make us philosophically worse off by excluding those who have valuable contributions to make. In fact, those whose lived experience gives them the philosophically valuable insight I mentioned above may be disproportionately among those excluded on the basis of their emotional engagement with the subject matter. Even if we don't think that Kittay, Haslanger, or Barnes had any special epistemic status with respect to disability or adoption, if we exclude them because they are emotionally invested in those topics, then we lose important voices.

If both lived experience and emotion can provide insight that we might not otherwise have, then a tacit commitment to dispassionate, disinteresting reasoning necessarily leaves gaps in our collective knowledge. In what follows I argue that these gaps are not morally benign because they constitute a kind of reliable ignorance that inflicts epistemic violence on members of our community.

The Silencing Effect of the View From Nowhere

It might initially seem that since all of us have and lack some lived experiences, and all of us experience emotions, a tacit exclusion of those things from philosophical discourse would limit us all equally in our philosophical endeavors. At worst it is a misfortune that we all share, not an *injustice*. Things are actually more complex. As I mentioned above, the view from nowhere often looks suspiciously like the view from the dominant group, so that the experiences and emotions most typical of cisgender, straight, able-bodied, white, Christian men aren't even recognized as particular experiences and emotions into which the accidents of personal history enter and which impact their philosophizing.[7] I remember a conversation I had a few years ago about the compatibility of the Christian faith with affirming the goodness of LBGTQIA+ (lesbian, bisexual, gay, transgender, queer, intersex, asexual, etc.) gender identities, orientations, and romantic relationships. My interlocutor suggested that the fact that I have a sibling and several close friends from this community makes me biased in my assessment, while they, lacking such relational attachments, are able to view the issue more objectively. They weren't wrong about me. I am deeply, personally invested in the question of LBGTQIA+ inclusion in religious spaces. My interlocutor's mistake (which they now acknowledge) was in thinking that their view, as a cisgender heterosexual man with no close LBGTQIA+ friends, was *less invested* or *less biased* than mine. We were merely *differently invested*. The difference was that my interlocutor's investment was opaque, while mine was transparent—their investment was mistaken for the God's eye point of view, while mine was quite obviously impacted by the "accidents of personal history."

The goal of this project is not to suggest that there is something inherently immoral about occupying that dominant perspective. I have no desire to expel the majority of analytic philosophers of religion from the discipline. Rather, it is to make their perspective—one that I, as a cisgender, white woman, largely share with them—transparent as a historically situated, invested, engaged position, with all of the limitations, biases, and insights that come along with it.[8] If we fail to do so, the gaps in our collective knowledge will remain and continue to have pernicious effects on those who do not occupy the dominant perspective. Because traditionally underrepresented members of the profession tend to be seen as the ones who are *especially* invested, *particularly* biased, and *inappropriately* emotional, those who do not occupy the dominant perspective are more likely to be unjustly assessed in their capacities as philosophers—and as knowers more generally. In this section I argue that when we remain ignorant of the fact that we ourselves fail to occupy the fictional view from nowhere, it is especially easy to inflict what feminist philosophers call *epistemic injustice* and even *epistemic violence* on our fellow philosophers.[9]

According to Kristie Dotson, epistemic violence in testimony "is a refusal, intentional or unintentional, of an audience to communicatively reciprocate a linguistic exchange owing to pernicious ignorance," where "pernicious ignorance" is a kind of ignorance that reliably arises from the gaps in the cognitive and hermeneutical resource available within a community and that has a tendency to harm others (2011, 242ff.). Here the "cognitive and hermeneutical resource" refers to the concepts, interpretations, images, and cultural scripts that are present within a particular community. Miranda Fricker notes that there are usually aspects of the life and experience of marginalized people and groups that members of the dominate group have little interest in trying to understand (Fricker 2007, 152). As a result, the community may fail to develop the vocabulary, theories, or scientific knowledge necessary for making sense of that category of experience. Fricker calls this kind of epistemic injustice *hermeneutical injustice*. Classic examples are the concepts of 'sexual harassment' and 'postpostpartum depression' prior to the women's movement, but we might also include things like 'white fragility' and 'religious trauma.' The absence of these conceptual resources makes it difficult for individuals who experience the relevant phenomena to successfully communicate about them to others, especially when those others haven't experienced them personally. All of us rely both on our interlocutors and on broader social factors for the success of our linguistic exchanges. The social imaginary (the range of 'live' possibilities or models that are socially imaginable), available hermeneutical resources, personal biases, and controlling images can all work against the speaker to make it impossible to get the desired uptake of their linguistic acts (Langton 1993, 22; Kukla 2014; Fricker 2007). In the case of epistemic violence, communication breaks down because interlocutors are reliably and perniciously ignorant. I contend that expectations within analytic philosophy of religion about philosophizing from the view from nowhere help to create an environment where reliable ignorance exists. The ignorance that concerns me in this paper is ignorance of the insight that individuals and groups may have in virtue of their particular, invested, historically situated identities—that is, the knowledge arising from their lived experience and their affective engagement with it.

Following Dotson, I suggest that this pernicious ignorance may inflict two kinds of epistemic violence on some members of the sub-discipline: testimonial quieting and testimonial smothering (2011, 242ff.). Testimonial quieting occurs when the audience fails to identify a speaker as a knower with respect to a body of knowledge. The audience need not discredit the speaker as a knower *tout court* or ascribe to them any form of irrationality or cognitive deficiency; rather, they simply fail to see the person as someone who might be in possession of the kind of knowledge in question in a particular linguistic exchange or domain. As a result, the testimony is goes completely unheard—because it is never solicited or attended to—or is not appropriately heeded. Nancy Eiesland describes this form of epistemic violence in her assessment of the American Lutheran Church's (ALC) failure to develop institutional policies that adequately reflect its ostensive theology of access. Eiesland diagnoses this failure as a refusal to place disabled people at the "speaking center" in the development of their theology:

> In the ALC theology of access, the able-bodied church is at the speaking center. Persons with disabilities are the topic. The document addresses itself to the able-bodied church urging it to promote the needs of persons with disability, rather than speaking directly to persons with disabilities within the denomination, empowering them to claim their voice and to assert their demands for justice. The comment features what the able-bodied church thinks it knows about persons with disabilities and how that differs from what it actually practices. Even on the level of semantics, persons with disabilities become third-person objects and the able-bodied church becomes the first-person subject.
>
> (1994, 82)

Individuals with disabilities were not invited to contribute to the development of the theology of access, and the history of the disability rights movement was largely ignored. Their testimony was quieted, either because it wasn't deemed important or because it was judged to be biased. As a result, only a few years later the very church that had resolved to work toward a theology of access barred people with "significant" physical or cognitive disabilities from ordination.

Although this example is drawn from a Christian denomination, it isn't hard to call to mind instances of similar quieting within analytic philosophy of religion. Take, for example, the controversy that arose within the Society of Christian Philosophers following a keynote address by Richard Swinburne at the Midwest meeting in 2016. In the course of the Q/A, Swinburne suggested that gay individuals should seek to be cured of their sexual orientation "just as" people with "any disability" should seek to be cured. Members of the audience cited disability-positive testimony as one reason to find this claim problematic, but Swinburne dismissed it out of hand. Later, when the president of the SCP made a public statement that included "regret regarding the hurt caused by the recent Midwest meeting of the Society for Christian Philosophers," one philosopher responded on social media by saying, "The only appropriate response is 'get over it.' This is why conservatives decry Millennials as precious snowflakes." Those who suggested that the 'hurt' involved was more than mere offense but the deep pain associated with the history of horrendous abuses that have been inflicted on LBGTQIA+ and disabled people in the name of curing them were dismissed for being 'emotional,' were laughed at and called names—silenced, not by physical coercion, but by suggestions that people 'like them' are incapable of the rigors of rational argumentation. Suggesting that emotional pain and personal vulnerability were worth taking seriously in a philosophical debate was enough to get them dismissed as reliable sources of knowledge or contributors to the pursuit of knowledge. While many of the individuals targeted by those attempts at silencing were privileged members of the profession (at least along some dimensions), and so were not greatly harmed by the attempts to silence them, interactions like this contribute to a culture where expression of emotion is grounds for downgrading the credence in or attention to an individual's argument. People who already lack privilege in the discipline are likely to be especially sensitive to even 'minor' challenges like this. If enough members of the profession engage in such quieting, those subjected to it, especially those who are vulnerable along a number of social dimensions, may be greatly harmed over the course of their careers. Their work might be unfairly rejected from conferences. They might not be invited to give talks or to participate in other professional events. Such exclusion from the venues in which our work is assessed, criticized, and improved through engagement with our peers is likely to have a negative net effect on the quality and quantity of work that the philosopher produces, which in turn would likely have a negative impact on their prospects in a difficult job market. In short, the harm could be quite great.[10]

Awareness of the frequency of such quieting and the harm it can do is one of many reasons that some knowers 'voluntarily' choose to remain silent, limit their contributions to what they expect will be well received by others, or hide significant aspects of their lives, experiences, and social identities that might otherwise contribute positively to philosophical discourse. Dotson calls this behavior testimonial smothering. Three conditions are characteristic of the phenomenon. First, the content of the testimony is unsafe or risky. Second, the audience demonstrates testimonial incompetence with respect to the content of the potential testimony. This incompetence may have already arisen in the context of the token conversation, or, as is more likely, it is a well-documented aspect of the cultural context. Third, "testimonial incompetence . . . follow[s] from, or appears to follow from, pernicious ignorance," as defined above (Dotson 2011, 244).

If analytic philosophy of religion privileges the view from nowhere in the spirit of Russell's description (as I suspect it does), then it is not difficult to imagine which speakers would be most likely to smother their own testimony. Even if emotion and lived experience can expand our knowledge as I argued above, they may also be used as grounds for dismissing or attacking another's argument, strong-mindedness, and philosophical rigor. In such an environment, it would be reasonable for a philosopher to worry that expressing their emotions or offering their lived experience as evidence is too risky. And given an implicit or explicit commitment to the view from nowhere, it wouldn't be unreasonable to assume that the risk arises from testimonial incompetence that follows from pernicious ignorance created by commitment to the view from nowhere. That is, the characteristic environmental features that contribute to testimonial smothering may well be present within analytic philosophy of religion. Furthermore, if those who are not cisgender, straight, able-bodied, white, Christian men are more likely to be seen as not occupying that view, as especially emotional and especially biased, then it follows that members of underrepresented groups in the profession are most likely to be in a position where they feel the need to smother their own testimony.

As I mentioned in the first section, many of the areas of inquiry where lived experience can give us important insight—religious trauma, horrendous suffering, racism—are the very kinds of experience that are likely to elicit strong emotional responses. In fact, those emotions may often be the morally appropriate responses to certain kinds of lived experience. Anger is an appropriate response to racism; sorrow and grief the right response to abuse; despair a sometimes unavoidable response to horrendous suffering. Some philosophers will not be able to engage with the issue into which they have unique insight without expressing (currently unwelcome) emotion. Others may be capable of stifling emotions, but believe that treating certain topics in a dispassionate manner is morally inappropriate or insensitive to the nature and content of the experience. This means that as long as expressions of emotion are assumed to have a skewing effect, those whose lived experience gives them insight, as well as those who have morally appropriate responses to it, are among those most likely to fall prey to testimonial silencing and smothering.

Let's return to Eiesland's example cited above. I have already suggested that the ALC's failure to place disabled people at the speaking center is a kind of testimonial quieting, but as Eiesland herself suggests, the quieting both results from and contributes to the phenomenon of testimonial smothering. She suggests that because people with disabilities are so rarely placed at the speaking center, and because it is so difficult to obtain uptake of their testimony about their experiences as disabled persons, they often remain silent or else craft their testimony in ways specifically designed to satisfy the expectations and abilities—the reliable ignorance—of their non-disabled interlocutors. They smother the testimony they would like to give, because that testimony is risky, and non-disabled people consistently demonstrate testimonial incompetence with respect to it. This is largely due to a social imaginary that can only cast disability as both negative (something that necessarily makes one worse off) and individual (not caused by socially structured lack of accessibility). Consider bell hooks's assessment of such situations:

> If the identified audience, those spoken to, is determined solely by ruling groups who control production and distribution, then it is easy for the marginal voice striving for a hearing to allow what is said to be overdetermined by the needs of that majority group who appear to be listening, to be tuned in. It becomes easy to speak about what that group wants to hear, to describe and define experience in a language compatible with existing images and ways of knowing, constructed within the social frameworks that reinforce domination.
>
> (1989, 15)

Of course, such testimonial smothering makes it less likely that disabled people will be placed at the speaking center in the development of theological resources. Their absence from that conversation perpetuates an environment in which they feel pressured to smother their testimony. And the vicious cycle continues.

Although I am sure that this phenomenon is most intense for individuals who live and work at the intersection of a larger number of marginalized groups than I myself do (after all, I am a white, cisgender, middle-class woman), I have felt this pressure myself. In my work on religious trauma, it is easy to allow the existing narratives and debates in philosophy of religion to determine the way that I frame the problem. It is easy to use detached, intellectualized, tidy narratives, rather than offering the invested, emotional, and messy reality of the phenomenon. It is easy to pretend that I count others, and not myself, among those who live in the wake of religious trauma, lest I be dismissed as angry, bitter, or biased (or at least angrier, more bitter, and more biased than merely working on the topic suggests). I have insight from lived experience that I usually do not share in conference presentations and published articles for fear of giving myself away—for fear of being stereotyped, dismissed, and misunderstood. This is perhaps most palpable in philosophical discussions of atonement theory. Rebeca Parker's critique of atonement theory cited above resonates with me because it aligns with my own experience of abuse in a Christian community. The fear and inner conflict of a child witnessing and subject to violence, who wants nothing more than to protect those she loves, but who believes that God blesses submission to abuse rather than resistance—that was my fear. Mine were the vain attempts to find joy in submitting to abuse inflicted in the name of God, the name of the cross, the name of the atoning Christ. When the cross is what you deserve, anything short of that is 'grace.' So I listen to defenses of penal substitution and vicarious punishment with shaking hands, racing heart, and tears welling in my eyes (Murphy 2009; Craig 2018). I stifle the desire to say, "Do any of you have the slightest idea what it feels like to watch helplessly while someone you are supposed to trust hurts someone you love? If you did, you would know that *this* could never be a just punishment for any sin, no matter how horrendous. You would know that *this* is not *grace*—that is not *mercy*," or "Do you know what it is like to try to love and trust someone who doesn't care *who* they get to hurt, as long as they get to hurt someone?" or "How can you all talk about this as if it is an abstract puzzle? Don't you know vulnerable people have lived and died, suffered or thrived, on the outcomes of your theory? Don't you know that some people's faith depends entirely on whether or not your theory of the atonement makes God out to be just like their abusers?" But I don't. I smother my testimony, my questions, my horror, and my grief. I don't trust the majority of my fellow philosophers to look on them, or me, with respect. I don't trust them to even consider the possibility that my revulsion arises from moral sensitivity, from moral insight, from knowledge. And I do not often trust myself or have the confidence to accept the value of my lived experience in the face of a profession that devalues it. The lines between self-confidence, intellectual honesty, epistemic humility, internalized self-doubt, and testimonial smothering are all too thin. And so, I write this wondering if I am brave enough to leave this paragraph in the final draft—if I am willing to take the very risk that I have argued there is epistemic value in taking.

I do not want to suggest that my or anyone else's lived experience renders our perspectives and critiques unassailable. No one claims that the testimony of those with lived experience is epistemically indefeasible. Like anyone, my own beliefs on these matters may be mistaken. Like any evidence, lived experience can be misleading. But none of this changes the fact that lived experience can be, and often is, epistemically valuable and that testimonial smothering and quieting in general are both bad for the philosophers subjected to it.

At this point, one might object not so much to the thesis of this chapter, but to my specific framing of the problem. One might claim that in the contemporary academy, and even in analytic philosophy of religion, it is not the perspective of women, people of color, abuse survivors, or LBGTQIA+ individuals that is underrepresented, silenced, and smothered; rather one might think that it is the perspective of conservatives, especially conservative white Christians, that is undervalued. It is true that there has been a shift in the views that dominate the academy in recent years, and those with more conservative views often feel less confident expressing them than they used to. It is undoubtable that in some cases and contexts traditional and conservative views are silenced. I do not want to claim that it is a necessary truth about the view from nowhere that it disadvantages women, people of color, LBGTQIA+ individuals, and liberal perspectives. This is one reason in the first section I included the Christian pro-life perspective as one that is often caricatured. However, when assessing this objection, it is important not to ignore the facts of the past and their lingering impact on our sub-discipline. While the winds of change have been blowing in the academy for some time, and they are beginning to blow in analytic philosophy of religion, for most of the history of contemporary philosophy of religion (and even its medieval manifestations), it has been dominated by cisgender, straight, white, able-bodied, conservative Christian men. The average analytic philosopher who doesn't work on philosophy of religion can name a host of prominent white male philosophers of religion with little thought (Alvin Plantinga, Peter Van Inwagen, William Alston, Richard Swinburne, William Hasker, John Hick, William Rowe, Robert Adams, etc.), possibly three women, and probably no philosophers of religion of color or from the LBGTQIA+ community.[11] This suggests that when we are assessing actual or potential epistemic violence, which is a phenomenon inherently tied to social forces and power dynamics, we must keep in mind that it is women, people of color, LBGTQ+ individuals, and other social identities who have been underrepresented. While it is possible for a conservative male philosopher to find his testimony silenced, or even smother it himself because of assumed testimonial incompetence, the silencing is likely to do him less harm as a knower and have fewer negative epistemic repercussions for the sub-discipline as a whole in the current, contingent conditions of the discipline than when members of other, less represented groups are silenced. Furthermore, it is unlikely that in any given instance a marginalized member of the profession would react badly to a conservative's perspective because of reliable ignorance. As a general rule, those who are marginalized within a community are more likely to have a working understanding of the traditional and more dominant perspectives—even, or especially, the ones they reject—than the privileged are to have an equal knowledge of non-dominant perspectives. This phenomenon is often called "double vision" (Medina 2013; Narayan 2007). The marginalized must understand the dominant perspective to 'make it,' while the privileged can completely ignore perspectives they do not share. This is why epistemic injustices are usually defined such that they only apply to marginalized groups (Fricker 2007).[12] Furthermore, the position I advocate for in this chapter is that we include more people, perspectives, testimony, and evidence, not less. Insofar as a view favors exclusion, harsh moral judgments of other identities, or a refusal to make the profession more welcoming and accessible to those others, it is *prima facie* more plausible that it will be epistemically violent than a view that promotes inclusion.[13]

In this section I have argued that our mode of philosophical theorizing has created a form of pernicious ignorance that is both epistemically violent and philosophically distorting. What is less clear is what we are to do about this as a sub-discipline. In the next section I suggest an attitude and a practice that would serve to ameliorate our ignorance so that it is less likely to be pernicious, though additional attitudes and practices are surely needed as well.

Ameliorative Attitudes: Making Room for the Whole Self

The alternative to the pernicious ignorance that arises from taking oneself to occupy (something close to) the view from nowhere requires both the attitude of epistemic humility and the practice of emotional labor. The first of these is one of the maxims suggested by Eva Kittay in her work on ethical practices in philosophical theorizing (2009b, 136). She argues that in order to theorize ethically, one must know what one does not know. In the context of this chapter, I suggest that the needed epistemic modesty will require (at least) two things: (1) recognizing the ways in which all of us are historically positioned, invested, and limited by our experiential knowledge and our social relatedness, (2) recognizing that others who are differently situated are also historically positioned and invested in ways that may give them insight that we lack. Both of these are involved in Fricker's description of the virtue of epistemic justice (2007, 86–108). Epistemic justice involves compensating for our tendency to downgrade the testimony of those who are socially marginalized by giving them a higher credence than we would otherwise tend to give them. I take this compensation for our learned credibility deficit to be a sort of epistemic humility—a willingness to lower our credence that our own perspective is superior and raise our credence in the perspective of marginalized others. On a practical level, this might involve actively pausing when we are swift to reject a critique or comment because of the social identity of our interlocutor or because of the emotions that they express. It might involve stopping to consider the possibility that they are right and we are wrong, perhaps especially when they espouse a view that conflicts with our assumptions and religious traditions.

What epistemic humility does not require is adopting a radical form of metaphysical or epistemic relativism, according to which there are not objective facts of the matter or it is impossible for us to gain objective knowledge. From the claim that it is practically and epistemically harmful for knowers *like us* to philosophize as if we can occupy a God's eye point of view, it does not follow that *God* does not or should not occupy such a view. In fact, part of my critique rests on the very assumption that there *are* objective truths that we are likely to miss when we engage in philosophy as Russell suggests.[14] Relatedly, epistemic humility does not require acquiescing or endorsing every position held by a traditionally marginalized philosopher of religion or every idea expressed with emotion. Underrepresented philosophers are no more a monolith than white men. We endorse a wide range of, often mutually exclusive, views. My proposal only requires that we not be excluded for failing to engage in philosophy free from passion and the "accidents of personal history."[15]

But merely acknowledging that others may have access to knowledge that we lack and adjusting our credences accordingly will be insufficient to prevent pernicious ignorance if our conceptual resources and assumptions prevent us from grasping the content of another's testimony to begin with. In the second section I mention the notion of hermeneutical injustice, which occurs when the hermeneutical resources available within a community are inadequate to express the experience of marginalized groups. Fricker suggests that to overcome the obstacles that this lack of resources creates we must develop the virtue of hermeneutical justice (2007). To this end, she argues that when a member of a marginalized group describes an experience in a way that initially sounds non-sensical to us, we should assume that they are trying to communicate something important. We should consider the possibility that either they or we lack the vocabulary or the conceptual framework to make this important reality mutually comprehensible. This forces us to listen charitably and respectfully and to work for mutual understanding *before* we attempt to evaluate the testimony. Something similar is required to overcome the barriers created by entrenched assumptions in our discipline. When a marginalized other speaks from lived experience, with emotion, from an obviously 'invested' position, I argue that we must do the emotional labor of seeking to *empathetically understand* what they are communicating and how it is relevant for our theorizing. This requires that we engage in the practice of empathy, which requires emotional labor.

We can learn something about the experience of those who occupy different positions from our own through quantitative data. Male philosophers of religion might read statistics about sexual harassment in the discipline, in the church, or in the mosque. Able-bodied philosophers can learn the history of abuse of the disabled community, including (and perhaps especially) abuse by religious communities. But this alone may be insufficient to understand what it is like to experience those things. If Laurie Paul is right, it is simply impossible to know what some experiences are like unless we have them for ourselves. Nonetheless, I believe empathetic listening can do much to overcome some of this inevitable cognitive gap. By empathy, I mean something like cognitively modeling the emotions and lived experience of another while maintaining the distinction between the self and the other. As Barrett Emerick points out, it involves not trying to figure out how you would feel in another person's shoes, but what it is like for them to occupy their own shoes (2016, 176). He suggests that it involves apprenticing oneself to the other and treating them as a knower of their own lived experience and emotional engagement with the world. This labor is not easy, and it is not without costs. It is painful to listen empathetically to the stories of gay religious individuals, of those traumatized by their faith communities, and of disabled people belittled and dismissed in the name of God. It requires listening to the arguments of those who express anger, grief, offense, emotional pain, and love without dismissing them, and accepting that these very emotional responses may provide insight into the topic they address. Yet, to abandon this labor of love is not only to abandon those who suffer; it is also to act irresponsibly, ignoring a range of epistemic resources in favor of our own privilege and comfort.

When we philosophize with our whole self and allow others to do so as well, we recognize and embrace the ways in which we are *all* personally invested. Only then can we work to correct our tendency to unjustly discount the arguments of others. We might grasp that when someone explains that in order to discuss a particular theodicy, they must first overcome the panic induced by hearing that their rape was an opportunity to foster intimacy with the divine, they are not confessing to a cognitive distortion. We might see the trans person who expresses outrage at claims of trans deviance as offering an important corrective, because we understand that cisgender philosophers are no less invested in being cis than transgender philosophers are in being trans. Such realizations can also force us to acknowledge the great responsibility we bear in our religious philosophical endeavors. Our theories and our arguments impact real people with real religious and non-religious lives. Finally, doing philosophy with the whole self allows us to subvert religious discourses that have been distorted by the fragmented modes of the past. With hard work and a bit of grace, philosophy of religion can become not just more inclusive, but more wholly truthful.

Notes

1. Barnes makes this point with regard to the perspective of adoptive mothers, such as Sally Haslanger, in the ethics of adoption (Barnes 2016, x).
2. Although, there has been a notable surge in interest in these topics over the past few years, as evidenced by this volume, the volume of *Res Philosophica* on "New Frontiers in Philosophy of Religion," and the volume that Michael Rea and I are editing (Panchuk and Rea, 2019).
3. Although standpoint epistemology also offers a helpful starting point for this discussion, I do not draw it to a significant degree in this chapter, both because I am not as competent in the literature as I would like to be and because I think it raises a number of issues regarding the nature of truth and knowledge that would need to be addressed for analytic philosophers of religion, but which I feel would take me too far afield.

4. My thanks to Kevin Timpe for suggesting this last step.
5. Admittedly, analytic philosophy of religion has concerned itself with a number of questions that are, in some sense or another, particular, embodied, and concrete, such as the incarnation, the doctrine of transubstantiation, and religious experience. However, much of this work has focused on abstract ontological or epistemic questions on these topics. What ontology of natures does one need to have to understand Christ's human nature? How is it possible for a substance to go out of existence while its accidents remain?
6. I take finitude to be an essential human property, and I take being a member of the substance kind one is to be an essential fact about that particular, so I take the finitude of our knowledge to be something essential about us. Even if that is wrong and our knowledge is only contingently limited, however, it is still a valuable direction for philosophical inquiry. I thank the editors, Kevin Timpe and Blake Hereth, for encouraging me to clarify this point.
7. Social epistemologists have theorized and documented this kind of opaque, but still predictable, ignorance that arises from being a member of a privileged group. See, for example, Medina 2013; Mills 2007.
8. There is an argument to be made that it is inherently more limited than other perspectives because subordinate groups are forced, in virtue of their subordination to develop what W.E.B. Du Bois calls "double consciousness." But I will leave these considerations to the side for the sake of brevity.
9. Gayatri Spivak first coined the term 'epistemic violence' in "Can the Subaltern Speak" (1988). Both Dotson and Miranda Fricker have identified various forms of epistemic harms and wrongs that are broadly related to this phenomenon. In addition to the two kinds of epistemic violence addressed here, they identify three kinds of epistemic injustices: testimonial injustice, hermeneutical injustice, and retributive injustice.
10. I do not intend to make any claims about whether or how many members of our profession are actually so treated. I hope that it is small, but I fear that it is not.
11. This is not an argument that representation should remain this way, only that as a matter of contingent and lamentable fact, it is currently this way. My hope is that these structural issues can be corrected and that we will achieve greater visibility of a wider range of analytic philosophers of religion in the coming years.
12. Although I have argued elsewhere that such definitions often make it more difficult for us to see certain kinds of harms, it is still important to recognize the differences (Panchuk unpublished).
13. I thank Michael Rea and the members of the audience at my presentation at the 40th Anniversary meeting of the Society of Christian Philosophers for pressing me to clarify this point.
14. Although we are working within different traditions and with different assumptions, Simmons's (2012) work has influenced my thinking on this point.
15. I thank several members of the audience at my presentation at the 40th Anniversary meeting of the Society of Christian Philosophers for pressing me to clarify this point.

References

Barnes, Elizabeth. *The Minority Body*. New York: Oxford University Press, 2016.
Brison, Susan. *Aftermath: Violence and the Remaking of a Self*. Princeton: Princeton University Press, 2002.

Brock, Rita Nakashima and Rebecca Parker. *Proverbs of Ashes: Violence, Redemptive Suffering, and the Search for What Saves Us*. Boston: Beacon Press, 2001.

Burchard, Melissa. *Philosophical Reflections on Mothering in Trauma*. London: Routledge, 2019.

Cone, James. "Theology's Great Sin: Silence in the Face of White Supremacy." *Black Theology* 2.2 (2004): 139–152.

———. *The Cross and the Lynching Tree*. Maryknoll, NY: Orbis Books, 2013.

Craig, William Lane. "Is Penal Substitution Unjust?" *International Journal for Philosophy of Religion* 83.3 (2018): 231–244.

Dotson, Kristie. "Tracking Epistemic Violence: Tracking Practices of Silencing." *Hypatia* 26 (2011): 236–257.

———. "Conceptualizing Epistemic Oppression." *Social Epistemology: A Journal of Knowledge, Culture and Policy* 28.2 (2014): 115–138.

Eiesland, Nancy. *The Disabled God: Toward a Liberatory Theology of Disability*. Nashville: Abingdon Press, 1994.

Emerick, Barret. "Empathy and the Life of Moral Endeavor." *Hypatia* 31 (2016): 171–186.

Fricker, Miranda. *Epistemic Injustice: Power and the Ethics of Knowing*. Oxford: Oxford University Press, 2007.

Haslanger, Sally. "Gender and Race: (What) Are They? (What) Do We Want Them to Be?" *Nous* 34.1 (2000): 31–55.

hooks, bell. *Talking Back*. Boston: South End Press, 1989.

Jackson, Frank. "What Mary Didn't Know." *The Journal of Philosophy* 83 (1986): 291–295.

Jagger, Allison. "Love and Knowledge: Emotion in Feminist Epistemology." *Inquiry* 32 (1989): 151–176.

Kittay, Eva. "The Personal Is Philosophical Is Political: A Philosopher and Mother of a Cognitively Disabled Person Sends Notes from the Battlefield." *Metaphilosophy* 40 (2009a): 606–627.

———. 2009b. "The Ethics of Philosophizing: Ideal Theory and the Exclusion of People with Severe Cognitive Disabilities." In *Feminist Ethics and Social and Political Philosophy: Theorizing the Non-Ideal*, edited by Lisa Tessman, 121–146. New York: Springer, 2009b.

Kukla, Rebeca. "Performative Force, Convention, and Discursive Injustice." *Hypatia* 29 (2014): 440–457.

Langton, Rea. "Speech Acts and Unspeakable Acts." *Philosophy & Public Affairs* 22 (1993): 293–330.

Manne, Kate (2017). *Down Girl: The Logic of Misogyny*. New York: Oxford University Press.

Medina, Jose. *The Epistemology of Resistance: Gender and Racial Oppression, Epistemic Injustice, and Resistant Imaginations*. Oxford: Oxford University Press, 2013.

Mills, Charles W. (1998). *Blackness Visible: Essays in Philosophy and Race*. Ithaca, NY: Cornell University Press.

Mills, Charles. "White Ignorance." In *Race and Epistemologies of Ignorance*, edited by Shannon Sullivan and Nancy Tuana, 11–38. Albany: State University of New York Press, 2007.

Murphy, Mark. "Not Penal Substitution but Vicarious Punishment." *Faith and Philosophy* 26.3 (2009): 253–273.

Narayan, Uma. "The Project of Feminist Epistemology: Perspectives from a Nonwestern Feminist." In *The Feminist Philosophy Reader*, edited by Alison Bailey and Chris Cuomo, 756–765. New York: McGraw Hill, 2007.

Panchuk, Michelle. "The Shattered Spiritual Self: A Philosophical Exploration of Religious Trauma." *Res Philosophica* 95 (2018): 505–530.

———. "Distorting Concepts, Obscured Experiences: Hermeneutical Injustice in Religious Trauma and Spiritual Violence." Unpublished.

Panchuk, Michelle and Michael Rea. *Marginalized Identities, Peripheral Theologies: Expanding Conversations in Analytic Theology*. Oxford: Oxford University Press, 2019.

Paul, L. A. *Transformative Experience*. New York: Oxford University Press, 2015.

Russell, Bertrand. *The Problems of Philosophy*. New York: Oxford University Press, 1957.

Simmons, J. Aaron. "Postmodern Kataphaticism: A Constructive Proposal." *Analecta Hermeneutica* 4 (2012): 1–19.

Spivak, Gayatri. "Can the Subaltern Speak?" *Die Philosophin* 14.27 (1988): 42–58.

Williams, Delores. *Sisters in the Wilderness: The Challenge of Womanist God-Talk*. Maryknoll, NY: Orbis Books, 2013.

Zagzebski, Linda. "Omnisubjectivity." In *Oxford Studies in Philosophy of Religion*, edited by Jon Kvanvig, 231–248. Oxford: Oxford University Press, 2008.

Section II
Religious Epistemology and Experience

3 Epistemic Injustice and Religious Experience

Kirk Lougheed

Introduction

This project/chapter connects work in feminist epistemology and the transformative experience literature to the philosophy of religion. Specifically, I apply the concept of epistemic injustice to religious experience. In her work on epistemic injustice Miranda Fricker (2007) explains that there are two kinds of epistemic injustice. First, testimonial injustice occurs when a speaker's credibility is unfairly lowered. For instance, the speaker is disbelieved because of her race. Second, hermeneutical injustice occurs when an agent lacks the interpretative resources she needs accurately to explain and understand her social experiences and this is puts her at a disadvantage (Fricker 2007, 1). For example, a woman is unable to understand her experience in the workplace as a victim of sexual harassment because her society lacks the concept of sexual harassment. She lacks the concept because her group lacks social power.

Epistemic injustice has interesting, and currently underexplored, implications for our assessments of the veracity of transformative experiences. I offer three relatively modest arguments in this chapter. First, I will argue that both speakers and hearers of transformative experiences are sometimes subject to epistemic injustice. Since at least some religious experiences are transformative experiences, it's possible that individuals who have religious experiences are subject to testimonial injustice on the basis of those experiences. Second, I will argue that those who report and hence testify about their religious experiences are in fact sometimes subject to testimonial injustice. Their testimony (and here I have in mind particularly those in the contemporary global West)[1] is unfairly downgraded because of prejudices about the speaker's epistemic reliability as a testifier. This isn't, strictly speaking, a project in social science and as such I make no claims about how often this type of injustice occurs. I only make the claim that it does in fact occur. Third, I suggest that as the West increasingly understands itself in naturalistic terms it's also possible that hermeneutical injustice sometimes occurs with respect to religious experience. For instance, someone who understands the world in (mostly) naturalistic terms may lack the conceptual resources fully to understand and explain her own religious experience (if indeed she has one). Again, I make no claims about the frequency with which this type of injustice occurs.

What Is Epistemic Injustice?

Before exploring the connection I want to make between epistemic injustice and religious experience it's important to be clear about what constitutes epistemic injustice. In this section I explain testimonial injustice and hermeneutical injustice. I will make no attempt at a complete survey of the epistemic injustice literature here.[2] I'll only highlight some the main themes in the literature, with particular reliance on Fricker's canonical work, which will be sufficient for my purposes.

Testimonial Injustice

Testimonial injustice occurs when a testifier is given less credibility in her report about proposition P than is (epistemically) deserved, simply because she is part of a certain social group. Fricker believes that part of the intrinsic value of humans is their rational capacity, and thus harming someone as a knower ultimately constitutes an intrinsic harm. She rightly observes that epistemic injustice also hurts the perpetrator since she might fail to gain new knowledge.

Fricker explains that "social power is a capacity we have as social agents to influence how things go in the social world" (2007, 9). Likewise, "whenever there is an operation of power that depends in some significant degree upon such shared imaginative conceptions of social identity, then *identity power* is at work" (2007, 14). The two types of identity power Fricker most often refers to are gender and racial power. She contends that the identity power is involved with how knowledge is passed from speaker to hearer (2007, 16). With respect to this testimonial exchange between speaker and hearer, Fricker suggests that hearers need to use social stereotypes to assess quickly the speaker's credibility. Stereotypes "are widely held associations between a given social group and one or more attributes" (Fricker 2007, 30).[3] Of course, it depends on the specific stereotype in question as to whether it is accurate or misleading with respect to the type of assessment of the speaker that it elicits. Fricker contends that when the stereotype is prejudice *against* the credibility of the speaker there are two harms. First, there is what she calls an 'epistemic dysfunction' between the speaker and hearer. By wrongly assessing the speaker's credibility the hearer loses out on knowledge. Second, the hearer has done something immoral since she undermines the rational capacity of the speaker as a knower (Fricker 2007, 16–17). The ideal hearer, then, needs to "match the level of credibility she attributes to her interlocutor to the evidence that she is offering the truth" (Fricker 2007, 19). She continues:

> We are picturing hearers as confronted with the immediate task of gauging how likely it is that what a speaker has said is true. Barring a wealth of personal knowledge of the speaker as an individual, such a judgement of credibility must reflect some kind of social generalization about the epistemic trustworthiness—the competence and sincerity—or people of the speaker's social type, so that it is inevitable (and desirable) that the hearer should spontaneously avail himself of the relevant generalization in the shorthand form of (reliable) stereotypes. Without such a heuristic aid he will not be able to achieve the normal spontaneity of credibility judgement that is characteristic of everyday testimonial exchange.
>
> (Fricker 2007, 32)

Of course identity prejudice can inform stereotypes and this can lead to what Fricker refers to as a *negative* identity-prejudicial stereotype. She defines this as "[a] widely held disparaging association between a social group and one or more attributes, where this association embodies a generalization that displays some (typically, epistemically culpable) resistance to counter-evidence owing to an ethically bad affective investment" (Fricker 2007, 35). When this consistently happens it is what Fricker refers to as a *systematic testimonial injustice*. Fricker's favorite example of a systematic testimonial injustice is from the all-white jury in the novel *To Kill a Mockingbird*, the members of which refuse to believe the testimony of a black defendant (2007, 23–27).[4] In sum, Fricker explains that:

> There is of course a purely epistemic harm done when prejudicial stereotypes distort credibility judgements: knowledge that would be passed on to a hearer is not received. This is an epistemic disadvantage to the individual hearer, and a moment of dysfunction in the overall epistemic practice or system. That testimonial injustice damages the epistemic system is directly relevant to social epistemologies such as Goldman's veritism, for prejudice presents an obstacle to truth, either directly by causing the hearer to miss out on a particular truth, or indirectly by creating blockages in the circulation of critical ideas. Further, the fact that prejudice can prevent speakers from successfully putting knowledge into the public domain reveals testimonial injustice as a serious form of unfreedom in our collective speech situation—and on Kantian conception, the freedom of our speech

situation is fundamental to the authority of the polity, even to the authority of reason itself.

(2007, 43)

I think it's safe to conclude that testimonial injustice does indeed occur and that it is epistemically significant. While Fricker is right to focus much of her book on the ethical harm of testimonial injustice, I will focus on the epistemic harms associated with wrongly assessing the credibility of the speaker who reports religious experience. In particular I'm going to be interested in assessments which give an unfairly low assessment of the speaker's credibility.

Hermeneutical Injustice

The second kind of epistemic injustice that Fricker examines is what she terms *hermeneutical injustice*. This occurs when someone lacks the conceptual resources to fully understand her experiences because of the social group to which she belongs. For instance, a woman may be unable to understand her experience of sexual harassment in the workplace in such terms because her society lacks the concept of sexual harassment. But it lacks the concept of sexual harassment because the group in question (i.e., women in the workforce) lack the requisite social power.[5] Thus, hermeneutical injustice is "the injustice of having some significant area of one's social experience obscured from collective understanding owing to a structural identity prejudice in the collective hermeneutical resource" (Fricker 2007, 155). Fricker explains that:

> One way of taking the epistemological suggestion that social power has an unfair impact on collective forms of social understandings is to think of our shared understandings as reflecting the perspectives of different social groups, and to entertain the idea that relations of unequal power can skew shared hermeneutical resources so that the powerful tend to have appropriate understandings of their experiences ready to draw on as they make sense of their social experiences, whereas the powerless are more likely to find themselves having some social experiences through a glass darkly, with at best ill-fitting meanings to draw on in the effort to render them intelligible.
>
> (2007, 148)

Throughout her book Fricker explores how both testimonial and hermeneutical injustice can be avoided by appealing to virtue theory. But my focus will not be on how to avoid epistemic injustice. Likewise, it's worth observing that the concept of hermeneutical injustice has received decidedly less attention in the literature than testimonial injustice. However,

I will argue that it has an important role to play when examining epistemic injustice with respect to religious experience.

What Is Religious Experience?

Introduction to Religious Experience

As stated in the introduction my main goals for this chapter involve applying epistemic injustice to religious experience. I believe that epistemic injustice has had a negative impact on the epistemic assessments of religious experiences both for those who have such experiences, and those who hear testimony about them. But before making these arguments, it's important to get clear on one more concept: religious experience. The difficulty in getting a grasp on religious experience—either in terms of necessary and sufficient conditions or something weaker like Wittgenstein's family resemblance—is that it is a wide-ranging and highly problematized subject. By this I mean it is (and has been) an object of (partial) study by numerous disciplines including, but not limited to, anthropology, cognitive science, philosophy, psychology, religious studies, sociology, theology, and even the medical sciences. For the sake of clarity and simplicity (and indeed feasibility) I will focus on just one type of religious experience, namely *intuitive knowing*. I'll also limit my examples of intuitive knowing to an analysis conducted by the philosopher Phillip H. Wiebe. Wiebe works from a database of *reported* religious experiences which will make the application to epistemic injustice all the more obvious.[6] Of course, this will generalize to other types of religious experiences which I will not discuss in this chapter.

Intuitive Knowing

Wiebe explains that intuitive knowledge represents the

> [t]he power of the intellect to grasp concepts and truths intuitively that are neither derivable from sense perception, such as the concept of infinity, nor justifiable by empirical evidence, such as inviolable principles of ethics, has been widely considered a characteristic that sets humans apart from all other earthly creatures.
>
> (Wiebe 2015, 1)

Plato and Aristotle both held that intuitive knowing was knowledge pertaining to matters that are eternal. In other words, "[t]he intellect came to be seen as capable not only of intuiting the reality of natural laws, a moral order, and an ontological order that includes God, but also of proving our immortality" (Wiebe 2015, 2–3). Augustine thought that intuitive knowing existed in intellectual visions; these are the visions that Wiebe examines in his study (2015, 3–5). These are distinct from corporeal visions (apparitions or ghost sightings). Part of my reason for limiting my discussion of religious experience to intellectual visions is because, at least historically, it is believed that they are superior to other types of religious experience (Wiebe 2015, 5). Finally, the fact that they are not repeatable and hence are directly inaccessible for people who haven't experienced them means knowledge of them can be gained *only via testimony*. To get a firmer grasp on what constitutes intuitive knowing let's look at two examples of it that Wiebe takes from the Alister Hardy Religious Experience Research Center:

Example 1

AMELIA: "It all began one spring morning when, as a little girl, I ran out of the house before breakfast and to the end of the garden which led to the orchard. In the night a miracle had been wrought, and the grass was carpeted with golden celandines. I stood still and looked, and clasped my hands and in wonder at the beauty I said 'God.' I knew from that moment that everything that existed was just part of 'that sustaining life which burns bright or dim as each are mirrors of the fire for which all things thirst.' Of course, I didn't put it in those words, but I did know that I and everything were one in the life. When I grew older and read philosophy I thought of all creation as the Shadow of Beauty unbeheld, and felt that Beauty was God." Amelia remarks that even in the inevitable changes that life brings, she has felt certain that "God is there, and in it all, and part of it all. So I could rest in Him." (Wiebe 2015, 66)[7]

Example 2

CAROL: "I looked up at the snows, but immediately lost all normal consciousness and became engulfed as it were in a great cloud of light and ecstasy of knowing and understanding all the secrets of the universe, and sense of goodness of the Being in whom it seemed all were finally enclosed, and yet in that enclosure utterly liberated. I 'saw' nothing in the physical sense . . . it was as if I were blinded by an internal light. And yet I was 'looking outward.' It was *not* a 'dream,' but utterly different, in that the content was of the utmost significance to me and in universal terms. Gradually this sense of ecstasy faded and slowly I came to my ordinary sense and perceived I was sitting as usual and the mountains were as usual in daily beauty." Carol says that the aftermath of the experience was in the form of a wonderful mental and spiritual glow, and then adds: "I became convinced later that a spiritual Reality underlay all earthy reality, and the ultimate ground of the universe was benevolent in a positive way, surpassing our temporal understanding. This conviction has remained with me, but in an intellectual form; it has not, however, prevented me from feeling acute personal depression and disappointment time and again, throughout my life." She also relates that later in life in she developed a strong interest in Buddhism, but after that felt that it was founded on a negative premise, whereas the universe seemed to her to be positive. (Wiebe 2015, 71)[8]

Before being in a position to formulate my arguments, I need to explain why experiences of intuitive knowing are transformative experiences. I also need to show that intuitive knowing ought to sometimes constitute evidence for particular propositions. After that I will be in a position to argue that there are cases where reports of intuitive knowing (among other types of religious experiences) are subject to epistemic injustice.[9]

Intuitive Knowing as Evidence

These two cases of intuitive knowing are meant, in part, to have evidential value similar to the way Fricker's examples are meant to have evidential value. The black defendant's testimony is *evidence* about the truth of whether he committed the crime. It's evidence for or against a particular proposition. The cases of intuitive knowing are analogous to this in that they're also evidence. Recall that Amelia says that she became aware of that "sustaining life which burns bright or dim as each are mirrors of the fire for which all things thirst." She subsequently identifies this feeling with God. Her experience led her to be convinced that God exists. It constituted evidence for the truth of the proposition 'God exists.' Likewise, Carol says that as a result of her experience she "became convinced later that a spiritual Reality underlay all earthy reality, and the ultimate ground of the universe was benevolent in a positive way, surpassing our temporal understanding." While at one time she identified this as support for a Buddhist understanding of universe, she seems to have concluded that some sort of positive divine reality exists. Carol's account is probably too vague to conclude that she believes in a theistic God because of her experience. But it seems this experience did constitute evidence for non-naturalism in some important sense.

We can't accurately assess the credibility of Amelia or Carol as testifiers since their accounts are anonymous reports without detailed background information. However, the type of case I have in mind is one from testifiers who are generally reliable testifiers in other domains. They are trustworthy people. Thus, while I can't evaluate Amelia's or Carol's credibility I assume that experiences of intuitive knowing have been reported by trustworthy people in the past. Thus, for my purposes I'm going to assume that Amelia and Carol are examples of reliable testifiers.

Epistemic Injustice and Religious Experience

In this section I argue that those who have religious experiences are sometimes subject to epistemic injustice. Thus, part of establishing my claims rests on establishing a particular understanding of the social status of religion in the West. Inasmuch as the social status of religion is marginalized, the reports of religious experience sometimes will be rejected because of negative stereotypes. Here are some examples from public figures which represent the type of sentiment about religion that I have in mind:

> Violent, irrational, intolerant, allied to racism and tribalism and bigotry, invested in ignorance and hostile to free inquiry, contemptuous of women and coercive toward children: organized religion ought to have a great deal on its conscience.
> (Hitchens 2007, 56)

> You don't get to advertise all the good that your religion does without first scrupulously subtracting all the harm it does and considering seriously the question of whether some other religion, or no religion at all, does better.
> (Dennett 2006, 56)

> The God of the Old Testament is arguably the most unpleasant character in all fiction: jealous and proud of it; a petty, unjust, unforgiving control-freak; a vindictive, bloodthirsty ethnic cleanser; a misogynistic, homophobic, racist, infanticidal, genocidal, filicidal, pestilential, megalomaniacal, sadomasochistic, capriciously malevolent bully.
> (Dawkins 2006, 51)

The New Atheists and their kin represent an attitude toward religion and religious believers that is growing in the West. Within the academy, sincere religious belief is often met with condescension and scorn. There is a very real sentiment that that religious believers are dumb, naïve, behind the times, and fundamentally irrational. Thus, my motivation in presenting these quotes isn't to evaluate their truth value. I simply intend them to be representative of how an increasing number of people in the West view religion.

Testimonial Injustice and Religious Experience

I'm now in a position to offer my first argument about religious experience and epistemic injustice. Here's an argument for the conclusion that those who report religious experiences are sometimes subject to testimonial injustice. Of course, this implies that those who receive such reports potentially lose out on knowledge:

1. T is a generally reliable and trustworthy testifier about their experiences.
2. If hearer H rejects testifier T's testimony about a religious experience R because of testimonial injustice, then both H and T are harmed.
3. Hearer H rejects T's testimony about religious experience R because of testimonial injustice.

Therefore,

4. H and T are harmed. (T isn't believed and H loses out on the truth about R.)

Notice that the harms in question here are *epistemic*. We could also add another conclusion which is that T is harmed in her rational capacity as a knower. But again, this isn't going to be my focus. Let's examine this argument in more detail. Premise (1) is simply the assumption that T is generally reliable with respect to R. Premise (2) represents the conditional statement that rejecting testimony because of epistemic injustice is a harm. (3) is the interesting premise and the one in need of an explanation. I'm not making any specific claims about how often (3) obtains. My suspicion is that it occurs quite frequently, but it only needs to happen once in order for this argument to apply to real-world cases. Though admittedly, this project becomes much less interesting if something like (3) rarely, if ever, obtains. A key to understanding (3) is to understand *why* when someone rejects a report of religious experience it could constitute a form of testimonial injustice.

If a testifier's report of religious experience is rejected on grounds akin to the ones in the above-mentioned quotes (which could very well be partly unconscious on the hearer's part) then it has been rejected unfairly. It has been rejected because of negative *prejudicial stereotypes* about the social group(s) to which the testifier (i.e. the religious believer) belongs.[10] Part of what I'm assuming here is that the New Atheist's attitude toward religion is epistemically irrational. If one takes them to have proven naturalism to be true, then their bias against religious belief is not necessarily unjust.[11] But if T is generally unreliable then it seems unfair to dismiss her testimony as having positive evidential value, even if one is a committed naturalist. Thus, in the argument testimonial injustice occurs and the hearer is epistemically harmed. Conclusion (4) logically follows from (1) through (3).

None of this is to say that reports of religious experience must always be believed if testimonial injustice is to be avoided. If the testifier in question is known to be unreliable on such matters then the hearer is within her epistemic rights to ignore or reject the testifier's report. Maybe the testifier is known to use psychedelic drugs, or prone to exaggeration, or often inappropriately posits supernatural explanations for events that have much simpler (and more obvious) naturalistic explanations. Nothing in my argument rules out rejecting testimony about religious experience based on these and other relevant considerations. In other words, it's possible for there to be (partial) defeaters to T's testimony about R. But if T is generally reliable, and in the case in question isn't experiencing cognitive dysfunction, etc., non-question-begging defeaters don't seem easily forthcoming. When reports of a religious experience are rejected merely for the reason that they happen to be religious, and not because of doubts about the testifier's reliability, it becomes an open question whether testimonial injustice has occurred. This concludes my first argument about religious experience and epistemic injustice.

Preemptive Testimonial Injustice and Religious Experience

The above argument leads to a different argument about what I believe is a kind of preemptive testimonial injustice.[12] This type of argument isn't found directly in the epistemic injustice literature, but it is closely related. There is social scientific evidence that *many* people fail to report their religious experience in the first place (or only report it to family members and close friends) because of the fear of prejudice. They fear that already existing (negative) prejudices about religion implies that their report won't be taken seriously by others. This is a kind of preemptive epistemic injustice since the negative biases of would-be hearers prevents the testimony from even occurring. This constitutes a kind of epistemic injustice because it is the bias of would-be hearers which causes the problem, along with the fact that the would-be hearer potentially loses out on the knowledge that would have been provided by the report.

5. If hearer would H reject testifier T's testimony about a religious experience R because of testimonial injustice, then both H and T are harmed.
6. If T reasonably believes that H would reject T's testimony about a religious experience R because of testimonial injustice then T doesn't report R to H at all.
7. T reasonably believes that H would reject T's testimony about religious experience R.

Therefore,

8. H never hears about R as a result of (preemptive) epistemic injustice.

Therefore,

9. Both T and H are harmed. (T doesn't testify and H loses out on the truth about R)

I'm not claiming that some kind of preemptive testimonial injustice necessarily occurs if T fails to report her religious experience. But there is social scientific data suggesting that (7) obtains frequently enough to create a legitimate worry. If this is right, then it follows that knowledge is lost as a result of a kind of preemptive testimonial injustice.[13]

Hermeneutical Injustice and Religious Experience

The other argument I want to put forward is about hermeneutical injustice. Consider the following argument for the conclusion that those who have religious experiences are sometimes subject to hermeneutical injustice:

10. If Agent S has religious experience R but rejects it (including to failing to understand it) because of hermeneutical injustice then S is harmed.
11. Agent S has religious experience R but rejects it because of hermeneutical injustice.

Therefore,

12. S is harmed. (S loses out on the truth about R.)

Premise (10) represents the conditional of a person rejecting a religious experience because of hermeneutical injustice. With respect to (11) it's worth observing that a growing number of people are raised in non-religious environments, particularly in the contemporary West. They do not have a specific shared religious faith within their family unit or her broader community. Likewise, their government does not take religious education to be one of its responsibilities. An increasing number of people in the West understand the world, from childhood even, in purely naturalistic terms. Not only that, but they tend to view religion in hostile terms. I make no normative claims about this situation in and of itself. Indeed, lessons from history may well suggest it's a good idea for governments to enforce religious freedom, while not embracing the truth of any one particular religion. This feature of liberal democratic societies is often viewed as a kind of moral progress. But all of this means that it's quite probable that there are people in the contemporary West who, if they had a genuine religious experience, would lack the conceptual resources to understand that experience as such. This isn't to assume that genuine religious experiences indeed occur. I'm merely making the observation that if they did occur there are people who couldn't make sense of them.

If (11) obtains it has the interesting result of possibly reinforcing naturalism even though the experience in question could actually be evidence *against* naturalism. This is because the person who has a religious experience and lacks the conceptual resources to count it as such won't count it as evidence against naturalism.

Objections

Religious Believers Don't Lack Social Power

One might object to my arguments by noting that a lack of social power is essential in Fricker's account of epistemic injustice. Testimonial injustice occurs because of the social group to which the testifier belongs. Hermeneutical injustice occurs because someone's social standing is so low that they don't have the conceptual resources to conceptualize appropriately the injustice. The objector might protest that those within who belong to the major world religious traditions are not downtrodden socially. Their social status precludes them from experiencing the type of epistemic injustice that I've been drawing upon from Fricker.

Reply

In cases where believer's social status precludes them from experiencing epistemic injustice (with respect to reporting or recognizing religious experience) then it's true that my arguments don't apply to such cases. But notice that I've been careful to limit the scope of my arguments. I have claimed that in the West, cases of epistemic injustice occur with respect to religious experience. But I haven't made any claims about how often they occur. In fact, the groups I've had in mind are the relatively educated middle and upper classes in liberal democratic societies. Of course in theocratic states, or secular states with more deference for religion, my arguments won't apply. And I never claim as much.[14]

Testimonial Injustice Is Incidental, Not Systematic

In explaining the difference between incidental and systematic injustice Fricker asks us to:

> Imagine, for instance . . . a panel of referees on a science journal have a dogmatic prejudice against a certain research method. It might reasonably be complained by a would-be contributor that authors who present hypotheses on the basis of the disfavoured method receive a prejudicially reduced level of credibility from the panel. Thus the prejudice is such as to generate a genuine testimonial injustice. . . . Although such a testimonial injustice may be grievous for the careers of the would-be contributors, and perhaps even for the progress of science, none the less its impact on the subject's life is, let us assume, highly localized. That is to say, the prejudice in question (against a

certain scientific method) does not render the subject vulnerable to any other kinds of injustice (legal, economic, political). Let us say that the testimonial injustice produce here is *incidental*.

(2007, 27)

Fricker concludes that while this is clearly a form of legitimate testimonial injustice, it isn't systematic. This is because "systematic testimonial injustices . . . are produced not by prejudice *simpliciter*, but specifically by those prejudices that track the subject through different dimensions of social activity—economic, educational, professional, sexual, legal, political, religious, and so on" (Fricker 2007, 27). The objection here is that epistemic injustice about religious experience is, at best, incidental and not systematic. This objection isn't so much a denial of the claim that those who report religious experiences are ever subject to testimonial injustice, it's an objection to the severity of the injustice I've discussed.

Reply

Even if this is objection is right, it ultimately doesn't detract from my main claims. As it stands, it's probably fair to characterize testimonial injustice about religious experience as somewhere between Fricker's example in *To Kill a Mockingbird* and the scientist example just mentioned in the objection. For my purposes, it does not matter whether this type of injustice turns out to be incidental or systematic. Even if it's only incidental, it still constitutes an epistemic harm in the particular cases in which it occurs. It still has the potential to limit a hearer's ability to gain new knowledge, or in this particular case evidence in favor of religious belief (or more broadly, against naturalism).

Likewise, while it's true that Fricker is primarily concerned with examining systematic epistemic injustice, she still acknowledges that incidental injustices are indeed injustices. For instance, she writes that "[t]o categorize a testimonial injustice as incidental is not to belittle it ethically. Localized prejudices and the injustices they produce may be utterly disastrous for the subject, especially if they are repeated frequently so that the injustice is *persistent*" (Fricker 2007, 29). This objection is about the scope and strength of the type of epistemic injustice I'm suggesting occurs with respect to religious experience. It does not hurt the main claims I've made here, even if it's right.[15]

There Are Conceptual Frameworks for Understanding Religious Experience

A similar objection can be raised regarding the strength of the hermeneutical injustice that occurs with respect to religious experience. Part of the idea behind hermeneutical injustice is that an agent lacks the conceptual resources to understand her experiences. The objector could point out that this hardly applies to religious experience. The major world religions come with a rich history and tradition, including conceptual frameworks for understanding religious experiences. Thus, someone who has a religious experience cannot experience hermeneutical injustice.

Reply

Fricker's argument for hermeneutical injustice is backwards looking in that up to the point of time at which an experience occurs there is no conceptual framework by which to understand said experience. My claim about religious experience is different in that it's forward looking in the sense that while in the past there may have been the conceptual resources required to understand the experience, such conceptual resources are no longer available for many people. It doesn't seem to matter which direction one looks. The main point is that one lacks the conceptual resources to understand the experience in question. This is true for the individuals in the West to which I refer, even if such conceptual frameworks exist for some.

Religious Experience Doesn't Provide Knowledge

The last objection I address suggests that reports of religious experience, even when not subject to epistemic injustice, do not provide evidence for religious belief. Religious experiences do not support the truth of propositions whose content describes a feature or doctrine of a particular religion.

Reply

It's simply not true that all cases of religious experience fail to support a specific proposition about religion. But I don't need to defend this claim in order to answer this objection. Fricker often uses the term 'knowledge' to refer to what the hearer may lose out on if she commits epistemic injustice. However, this understanding is consistent with a variety of epistemic ends such as true belief, rational belief, justified true belief, understanding, etc. One way to avoid positing specific religious propositions, the knowledge of which is lost out on when epistemic injustice occurs, is to claim simply that religious experiences like intuitive knowing are *evidence*. It's an open question what type and how much of evidence they constitute. It's an open question just what they support as evidence. But that naturalism has a difficult time explaining and understanding religious experience needs to be considered. Thus, religious experience may constitute evidence against naturalism, or evidence in favor of non-naturalism. I don't claim that my arguments say anything more than this about the epistemic significance of religious experience.[16]

Conclusion

In conclusion, it's worth observing that some may simply reject religious experience on the grounds that they're more sure that naturalism is true than that non-naturalism or supernaturalism is true. This is similar to the response that G.E. Moore offers in reply to the skeptic. I'm doubtful that this is a legitimate argumentative strategy, as it seems to do little more than beg the question against one's opponent. But even if this is an appropriate strategy the naturalist needs to acknowledge that when reports of religious experience occur, that they can't be legitimately ignored and that they might constitute evidence against naturalism. This is true even if she is rational to continue to believe that naturalism is true.

To date contemporary analytic philosophy of religion has had little to do with feminist epistemology in particular, and social epistemology more broadly. In this project I've offered one example of how to connect these two fields, though religious experience itself is hardly at the forefront of current research in the philosophy of religion either. I won't attempt to diagnose the reason(s) for this current state of affairs, but given the highly social nature of religious belief and practice there is surely much to be gained from making connections between those beliefs and practices with the ideas in social epistemology.[17] Both fields can enrich one another and I look forward to that taking place.[18]

Notes

1. By contemporary I mean no later than post WWII.
2. Since Fricker's 2007 book the literature on epistemic injustice has exploded. Likewise, in the last decade the literature on social epistemology has exploded more generally.
3. Fricker points to psychological literature to support her understanding of biases and heuristics. See Shelly E. Taylor 1982; Daniel Kahneman and Amos Tversky 1973, 1974. She believes this understanding is consistent with the current psychological literature which I won't explore here.
4. The setting of the novel is 1935 Maycomb County, Alabama, where racial tension between the black and white populations is high. In this fictional, though highly realistic story, the black defendant's testimony is unfairly downgraded and disbelieved because of racial prejudice. The white woman he is accused of assaulting is given a higher degree of credibility than she deserves, again because of racial prejudice.
5. Of course, the workplace is hardly the only place that such harassment can occur.
6. Wiebe's entire career has been devoted to the study of religious experience, including corporeal visions. For more see Wiebe 2015, 2014, 2004, 1997.
7. Here's an example of intersubjective sensory experience examined by Emma Heathcote-James (2002), and hence *not* an example of intuitive knowing:

   > Suddenly there was a man in white standing in front of the [baptismal] font about eighteen inches away. He was a man but he was totally, utterly different from the rest of us. He was wearing something long,

like a robe, but it was so white it was almost transparent. . . . He was just looking at us. It was the most wondering feeling. Not a word was spoken; various people began to touch their arms because it felt like having warm oiled poured over you. The children came forward with their mouths wide open. Then all of a sudden—I suppose it was a few seconds, but time seemed to stop—the angel was gone. Everyone who was there was quite convinced that an angel came to encourage us.

(Wiebe 2015, 47)

For more on other types of religious experiences not of intuitive knowing see Heathcote-James 2012; Maxwell and Tschudin 1990; Wiebe 1997.

8. There are underexplored connections between intuitive knowing and reformed epistemology. Indeed, it could be argued that reports of intuitive knowing somehow confirm the truth of reformed epistemology. This is a connection worth exploring, but it is well beyond the scope of this chapter. See Plantinga 2000 for more.
9. There might be important connections between religious experience and L.A. Paul's recent work on transformative experience. However, much of Paul's work focuses on the *choice* of whether to engage in a (potentially) transformative experience. While the experiences I am examining here are indeed transformative the individuals did not choose to experience them. For more see Paul 2014.
10. It's true that someone who reports having a religious experience might not be a religious believer. Indeed, sometimes these experiences are influential in one's conversion. But it's true, strictly speaking, that the reports of an experience does not necessarily entail that she is a religious believer. However, as long as there is a negative prejudice about religious belief, testimonial injustice about such experiences can still occur regardless of whether a religious believer is the one reporting it.
11. Though it might not be unjust in such a case, it's probably still unjust since it's rooted in biased reasoning.
12. My idea for this argument (and indeed, this entire section) comes from Travis Dumsday.
13. If one objects that the concept of preemptive epistemic injustice is inconsistent with Fricker's work, then simply replace the term with whatever concept one prefers. One can simply understand my argument as inspired by epistemic injustice. The key point is that knowledge appears to be potentially lost because of prejudice about religious belief.
14. While I haven't claimed as much for the kinds of cases I have in mind here, it is possible that certain religious minorities in the West (e.g., Jewish or Muslim groups) do lack the kind of social power Fricker mentions.
15. It's worth noting that as I write this paper in Canada in 2018 I believe that there's a strong argument to be made that this type of epistemic injustice about religious experience is leaning toward systematic injustice if it's not already there. It's true that I write this from my own anecdotal experience and perspective. And I'm not sure how one could definitively demonstrate this to be the case. Perhaps a social scientist could survey responses of certain groups in the West in an attempt to establish this claim. Still one should reflect on the recent challenges to the charity tax exempt status of religious organizations, accreditation challenges to religious schools, and other legal and political challenges religious believers have recently faced within Canada. I won't press these points further, as doing so is well beyond the scope of my project.

16. Of course, it's true that naturalistic explanations of religious experience could undermine them without epistemic injustice occurring. But I'm not evaluating those explanations here.
17. The epistemology of disagreement is perhaps starting to be an exception. For example, see Dormandy 2018; Holley 2013; Kraft 2007; Lackey 2014; Pittard 2014; Reining 2016; Thune 2010. But epistemic injustice, the testimony literature more broadly, epistemic paternalism, etc. are topics which remain largely unexplored by philosophers of religion.
18. I would like to thank Kevin Timpe and Blake Hereth for the opportunity to contribute to this volume. I'm also grateful to Nathan Ballantyne, Chris Dragos, Travis Dumsday, Jon Matheson, and Paul O'Hagan for taking the time to offer extremely helpful comments on earlier drafts of this chapter. This chapter was made possible, in part, by funding from the Social Sciences and Humanities Research Council of Canada.

References

Dawkins, Richard. *The God Delusion*. New York: Houghton Mifflin Company, 2006.
Dennett, Daniel. *Breaking the Spell: Religion as a Natural Phenomenon*. New York: Viking, 2006.
Dormandy, Katherine. "Resolving Religious Disagreements: Evidence and Bias." *Faith and Philosophy* 35.1 (2018): 56–83.
Fricker, Miranda. *Epistemic Injustice: Power & the Ethics of Knowing*. Oxford: Oxford University Press, 2007.
Heathcote-James, Emma. *Seeing Angels: True Contemporary Accounts of Hundreds of Angelic Experiences*. London: John Blake, 2002.
———. *They Walk Among Us: An Investigation into the Phenomenon of After-Death Materialisation*. London: John Blake, 2012.
Hitchens, Christopher. *God Is Not Great: How Religion Poisons Everything*. New York: Hachette Book Group, 2007.
Holley, David M. "Religious Disagreements and Epistemic Rationality." *International Journal for Philosophy of Religion* 74.1 (2013): 33–48.
Kahneman, Daniel and Amos Tversky. "On the Psychology of Predication." *Psychological Review* 80 (1973): 237–251.
Kraft, James. "Religious Disagreement, Externalism, and the Epistemology of Disagreement: Listening to Our Grandmothers." *Religious Studies* 43 (2007): 417–432.
Lackey, Jennifer. "Taking Religious Disagreement Seriously." In *Religious Faith and Intellectual Virtue*, edited by Laura Frances Callahan and Timothy O'Connor, 299–316. Oxford: Oxford University Press, 2014.
Maxwell, Meg and Tschudin, Verena (eds.). *Seeing the Invisible: Modern Religious and Other Transcendent Experiences*. London: Penguin, 1990.
Paul, L. A. *Transformative Experience*. Oxford: Oxford University Press, 2014.
Pittard, John. "Conciliationism and Religious Disagreement." In *Challenges and Moral and Religious Belief: Disagreement and Evolution*, edited by Michael Bergmann and Patrick Kain, 80–99. Oxford: Oxford University Press, 2014.
Plantinga, Alvin. *Warranted Christian Belief*. New York: Oxford University Press, 2000.

Reining, Stefan. "Peerhood in Deep Religious Disagreements." *Religious Studies* 52.3 (2016): 403–419.
Taylor, Shelley E. "The Availability Bias in Social Perception and Interaction." In *Judgement Under Uncertainty: Heuristics and Biases*, edited by Daniel Kahneman, Paul Slovic, and Amos Tversky, 190–200. Cambridge: Cambridge University Press, 1982.
Thune, Michael. "Religious Belief and Epistemology of Disagreement." *Philosophy Compass* 5.8 (2010): 712–724.
Tversky, Amos and Daniel Kahneman. "Judgment Under Uncertainty: Heuristic and Biases." *Sciences* 185 (1974): 1124–1131.
Wiebe, Phillip H. *Visions of Jesus*. New York: Oxford University Press, 1997.
———. *God and Other Spirits*. New York: Oxford University Press, 2004.
———. *Visions and Appearances of Jesus*. Abilene, TX: Leafwood Publishers, 2014.
———. *Intuitive Knowing as Spiritual Experience*. New York: Palgrave Macmillan, 2015.

4 Smelling God
Olfaction as Religious Experience
Joshua Cockayne

Introduction

Although it is commonplace within many religious traditions to talk of 'hearing God's voice' or 'seeing God at work,' or even 'being touched by God,' the fact that a chapter entitled "Smelling God" likely brought a smile to your face demonstrates the disconnect many of us will feel in speaking of olfactory experiences and religious experiences in the same breath. We are not used to people using olfactory language, even metaphorically, to describe their encounters with the divine, even though, if God is immaterial, it is surely true that God no more has a specific scent than he does an appearance or a sound.

But yet, as I will explore in this chapter, there is a rich history of using olfactory language in both symbolic and literal ways to explain religious experiences. In the Scriptures of the Hebrew Bible, language relating to smell is often used in describing the sacrificial and anointing rituals of the Jewish tradition, and God is often said to be pleased or displeased at the smell of the Israelites' worship. Moreover, as the Apostle Paul describes, Christians are to carry the *fragrance* of Christ into the world (2 Corinthians 2). In exploring recent work by Yael Avrahami (2012) and Susan Ashbrook Harvey (2006), I show how olfactory experience played an important role in the religious traditions described in Scripture and the early Christian church. As Harvey illustrates, by means of certain liturgical practices, early Christians described olfactory experiences as providing a kind of knowledge of God. And thus, she argues we should not interpret their claims in merely metaphorical terms (as modern readers may be tempted to do).

I will begin by considering why the olfactory sense lends itself well to the discussion of religious experience by showing how it differs from other sense modalities. Following this, I discuss the historical place of olfaction in theology. Note that the purpose of this chapter is not to explore all of the philosophical implications of the theological role of smell in Hebrew Scripture or in early Christian practice. But rather the chapter asks if we took seriously this emphasis on olfaction in the Christian theological tradition, how could we make sense of experiences of smell as examples of religious experiences today? For as we have already acknowledged, if God is immaterial, then it makes little sense to talk of smelling God in a literal way. The claim defended in this chapter is that whilst these experiences should not be thought of literally, neither should they be thought of in merely metaphorical terms.

How, then, can we make sense of the claim that olfactory experiences are encounters of God in a way that is non-metaphorical? This is the philosophical question which the latter half of this chapter focuses on providing an answer to. To give a response to this question, I begin by giving an overview of the categories of religious experience which are commonly used in contemporary philosophy of religion, before raising some issues with the narrowness of these categories. In particular, I argue that the typical way of thinking about religious experience, as a direct perception of God, is too narrow to accommodate the kinds of religious experience outlined in this chapter. Instead, by drawing on recent work by Adam Green (2009) on sharing attention with God, I argue that ordinary sense perception (seeing, hearing, touching, tasting, and, indeed, smelling) should be thought of as providing opportunities for indirect, but non-metaphorical experiences of God.

Finally, to fill this account out, I develop recent work on cognitive penetration of perception and its application to cases of religious perception, I explore what N. Russell Hanson (2002) and Michael Rea (2018) call experiences of 'seeing as.' Just as an ultrasound technician sees black blobs *as* the limbs of a fetus, I argue that we might experience the smell of sweet-smelling incense, or even freshly brewed coffee, *as* an encounter of the divine presence. And thus, since such experiences are indirect experiences of God mediated through the physical world, we can make sense of God's immateriality and yet still retain the idea that olfactory language is used in a non-metaphorical sense in reference to religious experience.

Why Smell?

Let me begin by highlighting some reasons why the olfactory sense is of importance for thinking about religious experience. There are some features of the olfactory sense which distinguish it from other sense modalities, and which provide us with good reasons for focusing on smell when thinking about encountering God.

First, as we will see stressed throughout the discussion in this chapter, olfactory experiences have an ephemeral, mysterious quality in which the location and character of the object of perception is mysterious. This feature of olfactory experience lends it well to thinking about experiencing the divine. We often cannot locate the specific character or location of a smell, even if we are undoubtedly experiencing it. As Gregory of Nyssa writes in a homily on the Song of Songs, smell seems particularly apt for experiencing God as transcendent. He writes that,

> the divine power is inaccessible and incapable of being contaminated by human thought processes, for to me it seems that by this statement there is conveyed something like the following: that the Nature that has no boundaries cannot be accurately comprehended by means of the connotations of words. . . . It is as if by certain traces and hints that our reason guesses at the Invisible; by way of some analogy based on things it has comprehended, it forms a conjecture about the Incomprehensible. For whatever name we may think up, she says, to make the scent of the Godhead known, the meaning of the things we say does not refer to the perfume itself. Rather does our theological vocabulary refer to a slight remnant of the vapor of divine fragrance. In the case of vessels from which perfumed ointment is emptied out, the ointment itself that has been emptied out is not known for what it is in its own nature. . . . Here, then, is what we learn from the words: the perfumed ointment of the Godhead, whatever it may be in its own essence, is beyond every name, and every thought, but the marvels discerned in each name and thought provide matter for our theological naming. By their help we name God wise, powerful, good, holy, blessed and eternal, and judge and saviour and the like. And all these refer to some slight trace of the divine perfume that the whole creation imitates within itself, after the manner of a jar unguents, by the wonders that are seen in it.
>
> (2013, 39–41)

Secondly, experiences of smell involve the object of experience as internal to the subject. Louise Richardson (2013a), in discussing whether olfaction is an exteroceptive (i.e., informative about the external world) or interoceptive (i.e., only informative about our own experiences) sense, expands more specifically on the unique nature of smell. She writes,

> In order to smell or taste something, we must take it into our bodies. In smell, or at least, in what we usually think of as smell, this happens when we breathe in through the nose, which is to say, when we sniff. For brevity I will use 'sniffing,' here, to include breathing through the nose, except if otherwise indicated. When we sniff, odiferous molecules are drawn up through the nostrils to the nasal cavity, and the receptive cells of the nasal epithelium. Sniffing harder increases the rate of flow through the nasal cavity—up to hurricane speeds with vigorous sniffing—and directs it upwards to the olfactorily receptive cells. As a result, more odiferous molecules reach the olfactory receptors. . . . Olfactory experience does not just involve awareness of certain qualities, such as vanillaryness or mustiness or whatever. It

also involves odours that have these qualities seeming to be brought into the nose when we sniff. To see this, consider how things seem to you when either breathing normally, or sniffing vigorously, never mind for now whether in so doing you're aware of anything odiferous. The experience you have is one of air being brought into the nostrils, from without, though the air is not represented as being at any distance or direction from you. Your experience of the air you breathe then is exteroceptive, even though the visual model of exteroceptivity is not appropriate to it. The point I want to make is that this is part of normal olfactory experience, too. In olfaction, odours seem to be brought into the nostrils, from without. In this way, olfactory experience, despite differing in its spatial character from vision, is nevertheless also exteroceptive: odours seem to be brought into the nose from without, and thus seem to be extra-bodily.
(Richardson 2013a, 9–10)[1]

Richardson's emphasis on the act of sniffing in experiences of smell highlights an important way of seeing why olfactory experiences of God have a religious significance that other sensory experiences might not. For in smelling, one takes an odor into one's body by the act of sniffing in order to experience the scent. There is no clear analog to this in seeing, hearing, or touching. The relationship between smell and taste is arguably more complex—there are clearly important connections between smell and taste (try tasting something fragrant whilst holding your nose, to experience this yourself), and there are surely important points to be made about taste and religious experience too, but I limit myself to discussing the olfactory sense here.[2] Smelling requires that the act of breathing (which is itself a life-giving act) takes in certain objects of perception into one's body. It is through this act of bringing an object of perception into the body, that one experiences smell.[3] This provides a helpful way for thinking about the way in which Christian theology emphasizes God's presence as distinct from us, but somehow within us—this is the foundations of a theology of being in union with God.[4] Like the odorous particles which we experience each day in our engagement with the world, the Holy Spirit is brought into the individual's body and is experienced both from within, but yet as distinct from oneself.

Thirdly, smell plays an important role in memory recollection and emotional attachment. As recent psychological work has shown, olfactory evoked memories are "associated with a higher emotional arousal that could not be accounted for by the perceptual stimulation alone" (Willander and Larsson 2007, 1659). By testing the role of smell in evoking memories of childhood in older individuals, John Willander and Maria Lasson show that such memories are more deeply rooted (i.e., they can attach to older memories) than memories evoked by verbal queues. They write that "odor-evoked memories were experienced as more emotional and pleasant, and associated with stronger feelings of being brought back in time as compared to events evoked by verbal cues" (2007, 1662). Again, this has theological implications for thinking about why smell is important for religious experience—for in using incense in liturgical practice, for instance, one is building memories of worship and engagement with God which are potentially more deeply rooted and emotionally attached than many other sensory or verbal engagements. If the spiritual life is thought of as the development of certain spiritual habits, then the use of smell in spiritual practice can play an important role in forming spiritual memories.

Finally, there are important connections to be made between smell and disability, which can provide us with motivation for giving an account of olfactory religious experience. A moving example of this can be found in Barbara Newman's description of her friend with autism who does not recognize people by sight, but rather by smell. Newman recalls her friend saying that, "I know all of you are looking forward to seeing Jesus in heaven, but I can't wait to smell him" (Timpe, "Disability in Heaven," n.d., 7.29). An over emphasis on the audio and visual senses in thinking about religious experience can exclude many for whom olfactory experience plays a central role in their experience of the world.

While it is clear that olfactory experience might have important religious significance, what is less clear is how best to interpret such experiences. We begin by considering the ways in which the olfactory sense has been used in the history of Christian and Jewish thought.

A Theological Sense of Smell

While the concept of smell as an experience of God might seem odd to the modern ear, it is important to see that our modern ways of thinking and experiencing the world are dominated by an emphasis on sight and sound. Even within my own prose, the eagle-eyed reader will notice, both vision and hearing metaphors have already been used to refer to our understanding of certain terms or concepts. Such use of metaphor is not uncommon. We talk of '*seeing* the point,' of some argument '*sounding* right' and of people 'coming to the light.' If points are less clearly communicated, we talk of claims 'falling on deaf ears.'[5] It is interesting to note that most of the metaphorical uses of smell that are used commonly in the English language in this way are negative. 'This smells fishy to me' or 'This smells off' are most often used to denote an argument's flaws or failures.[6]

This way of thinking has permeated our theological thinking too. We talk of spiritual enlightenment, and of experiencing visions and voices of the divine. In many contemporary contexts, worship is an almost entirely visual and auditory experience, involving listening to sermons and prayers and singing hymns from hymn sheets and projector screens. Apart from the practice of the Eucharist, in which participants engage their gustatory senses in worship, sight and sound are the dominant sense modalities of contemporary worship services. The olfactory sense is rarely, if ever, engaged in such a context. Moreover, as Harvey observes, "Modern scholars . . . have tended to privilege the visual in their treatment of ancient Christianity . . . and have utilized the imagery of sight and hearing as dominant themes for analysing the history of Western Christianity" (2006, 3). In contrast to this modern emphasis on sight and sound, as Harvey put it, "Christianity emerged in a world where smells mattered. They mattered for what they did. They mattered for what they meant" (2006, 1). Let us explore some of these historical emphases on olfactory experience.

In Jewish and Christian Scriptures, the olfactory sense plays an important role in various rituals and practices and experiences of smell are imbued with important meaning which speaks of how human beings and God are related. For instance, "sweet-smelling cinnamon" was an important component of the anointing oil used in the anointing of the tent of the meeting, the ark of the covenant, as well as in the consecration and anointing of priests (Exodus 30:22–33). In the ordination of priests, the writer of Exodus describes the Lord commanding that Aaron and his sons lay their hands on a ram to be slaughtered, preparing it for sacrifice by washing and cutting, and then smoking it on the altar to provide a "pleasing odor, an offering by fire to the Lord" (Exodus 29:15–18). In making atonement for sin offering, Leviticus describes the priest as taking "a censer full of coals of fire . . . and two handfuls of crushed sweet incense" to "incense of the fire before the Lord, that the cloud of the incense may cover the mercy seat that is upon the covenant" (Leviticus 16: 11–14). We are told in many places that God finds the odors of certain burnt offerings pleasing or displeasing (Genesis 8:20–21, Leviticus 26:30–31, Isaiah 3:24, Isaiah 34:3).

In the New Testament, the Apostle Paul talks of Christian believers as carrying 'the aroma of Christ' (2 Corinthians 2:15), which comes from knowing Christ and of the fragrance of 'death' that such aroma brings to those who are perishing. As Gregory of Nyssa describes, Paul's use of olfactory imagery highlights important theological points. He writes that Paul "said that he was the 'aroma of Christ' (2 Cor 2:15), capturing within himself the scent of that transcendent and unapproachable Grace and providing himself for others to have a part in according to their ability, as though he were an incense: others to whom, in accordance with the present disposition of each, the sweet smell became either life-giving or death-dealing" (2013, 101).

As Yael Avrahami explores in some detail in her work *The Senses of Scripture*, the writers of the Hebrew Bible did not think in modern terms about human senses.[7] More specifically, Avrahami argues, the biblical authors rejected the idea that the senses were mere "physical tools" (2012, 185) employed by the mind to further understanding. But rather, for the writers of the Hebrew Bible, the senses themselves play an important role in a person's understanding. The senses provide "a physical way of functioning that includes thought and action, obedience and disobedience, enjoyment and suffering" (2012, 185). The writers of Scripture describe our senses as playing an important role in our capacity for emotional experience, in perceiving help and harm, in understanding and knowing the world, in forming moral judgments, and in our capacity for autonomy. Surprisingly to our modern perspective, smell plays an important role in all of these capacities, and the writers of Scripture use olfactory language in describing these ways of relating to the world. It is not the case that such experiences furnish the mind with concepts to be understood and ordered, so that we might use sense data instrumentally to approach the world, but that our senses are an intrinsic part of our epistemological and moral judgments.

This emphasis on olfaction in relating to God and to the world was also present in early Christian thinking. As with its use in Scripture, olfactory language is used in a more than metaphorical sense in early Christian thinking and writing. As Harvey puts this point, antiquated use of olfactory language is "not based on symbolism as a disembodied language, but on the concrete view that smells participated in effecting the processes they represented. Odors could purify, ward off, or heal; they could contaminate, pollute, endanger" (Harvey 2006, 2). Olfactory senses were also thought to play an important role in relating to God and providing knowledge of God.[8] Through the use of various ritual practices, early Christians thought of the senses, including smell, to allow us encounter and experience God, thereby allowing for a kind of knowledge of God.[9]

There are many reasons why olfactory experiences were thought of in these terms; smell has an ephemeral and mysterious character to it, which lends such experiences well to religious contexts. Expanding on this thought in explaining Paul's use of olfactory language in 2 Corinthians 2, Harvey writes that in experiencing an odor, "one knows that it has a source: but the source need not be visible or even near.... Indelibly expressive of its source, a scent yet operated apart from it. An odor thus revealed something even as it concealed it" (2006, 115). Analogously, in the case of experiencing God through encountering those who carry the fragrance of Christ, we are able to acquire "distinct knowledge, of an indistinct source . . . such was the Christian witness to a God who defied the limits of human comprehension" (Harvey 2006, 115).

As with the use of olfactory language in the Hebrew Bible, the emphasis on God's revelation through smell has a particularly important role in ritual or liturgical practices. It is in the engagement with certain kinds of liturgies which early Christians were often most exposed to olfaction as a kind of religious experience. Writing on the sensory experience of God in liturgy, Dionysius the Areopagite (circa 500 AD) states that,

> it is quite impossible that we humans should, in any immaterial way, rise up to imitate and to contemplate the heavenly hierarchies without

> the aid of those material means capable of guiding us as our nature requires. Hence, any thinking person realizes that the appearance of beauty are signs of an invisible loveliness. The beautiful odors which strike the senses are representations of a conceptual diffusion. Material lights are images of the outpouring of an immaterial gift of life.
>
> (*Celestial Hierarchy*, 1:3, 146)

Dionysius is not claiming a relationship of analogy between the physical and the heavenly here.[10] But rather, the liturgy can act as a 'guide' to train the senses,

> so that they lead the believer to experience realities beyond the immediacy of the concrete situation. The immediate setting opens the senses, allowing them to blind the mundane, sensory experience of the worshipper to the celestial domain in which it must ultimately take place.
>
> (Harvey 2006, 136)

What is most notable here is the way in which olfactory experiences are thought of in literal terms to reveal something of the divine reality. The point is not, for Dionysius, that we extrapolate or infer from our experience to knowledge of God, but rather, our senses furnish us with an experience of God, thereby giving us knowledge of God. Indeed, as Harvey is keen to stress, the use of olfactory language in early Christian theology and practice was not merely symbolic. She argues:

> That such usage was never simply metaphor or analogy was clear from discussions about the incarnation. The notion of God become human lifted the role of sense perception in knowing God to intense significance: the senses perceived God through his handiwork in the natural world, yes. But in the incarnate Christ, the senses had perceived God himself; God has chosen to reveal himself according to the human capacity for knowledge gained sensorily as well as through the mind's understanding. . . . From the nativity to the resurrection, God had become known to humankind in and through the senses.
>
> (Harvey 2006, 127–128)

To summarize this brief foray into the history of the theology of smell, what we find in discussions of olfactory sense experience in the Hebrew Bible and the early Christian tradition is as follows:

1. Olfactory experience was more significant and more prominent in both of these sources than it is in a modern context.
2. Olfactory language was used in more than a merely metaphorical way.

3. Olfactory experience played an important role in understanding and relating to the world, but not as merely furnishing the mind with sense data.
4. Olfactory experiences were to sometimes be experiences of God and experiences which provided knowledge of God.

Let us now turn to consider the application of these insights to a contemporary religious context, before exploring what philosophical implications follow from this.

Olfactory Experience in Contemporary Religious Practice

While it is clear that experiences of smell do not play the same role in modern, Western religious contexts as they did at other times in the history of the Judeo-Christian tradition, contemporary religious thought is not entirely devoid of its olfactory sense. A quick web search of 'smell and religious experience' will rapidly expose one to the weird and wonderful world of pseudo-scientific spiritual writing on smell. One can also come across many descriptions of the olfactory sense in religious contexts which share many of presuppositions found in ancient Christian sources too. For instance, Kelly Isola, a Unitarian minister and blogger on issues pertaining to spirituality and mysticism writes,

> The activity of prayer effuses a trail of the most luxurious perfume, which I know as the presence of the holy. Smell is one of our external senses, that quickly attracts us to something or repels us. The spiritual sense of smell comes alive as our inner attraction for prayer and the Silence, to be still and wait to be drawn into oneness with loving attention. It's not that we are going to physically smell an aroma of Spirit, but rather it's as if the divine perfume is an irresistible and inescapable attraction to our encounter with our Source. We long to know and belong with God, real, attentive, and authentic. We experience the sweetness of this attraction as though Spirit were that delicious fragrance, like morning coffee, fresh flowers, or an ocean breeze, arising from within us and around us.
>
> (Isola n.d.)

Isola's use of perfume to describe the presence of the holy seems to resemble many of the ways in which Harvey describes ancient sources as thinking about olfactory experience. But yet, it is clear that Isola is keen to distinguish what she calls a 'spiritual sense of smell' and 'physical sense of smell.' As we have seen, olfactory language is used metaphorically in the Christian and Jewish traditions, but it is not the only use of such language. And there is nothing all that philosophically puzzling about how this metaphorical use of smell might be made sense of.

There are some instances of contemporary olfactory experience which are more philosophically puzzling. Let us briefly consider the way in which smell plays a role in certain liturgies to see that this is the case. Those who are familiar with certain Catholic, Eastern Orthodox, and High Anglican liturgical traditions will be familiar with the use of incense in worship. Those reflecting on these traditions often invoke the importance of smell to explain the significance of these practices. For instance, St. Michael and All Angels Church in London, explains on its website that

> in the Anglo Catholic liturgy we engage all our senses in the worship of God. Symbols and signs help us point our minds to the invisible in ways that are richer than words alone. . . . Incense symbolises three aspects of our worship. It signifies the presence of God; it is a symbol of prayer and it is a sign of offering. The rising of the smoke signifies our prayers rising up to God and its perfumed smell evokes a sense of God's presence—as the psalmist says in Psalm 141 'Let my prayer rise before you like incense.'
>
> (St Michael and All Angels, n.d.)

Similarly, as Andrew Gould describes the use of incense in Eastern Orthodox liturgies in the *Orthodox Arts Journal*,

> Incense truly sanctifies the seductive power of perfume! With it, the church forges in us a permanent emotional bond to the liturgy. Its positive influence is probably much greater than anyone suspects, as it works upon us so subconsciously—so different from liturgical texts and painted icons, whose meaning must be cognitively understood to be of much benefit. Rather incense is akin to the sound of bells—we never know what it means, but it pierces instantly to our hearts, and awakens in us an unexpected joy.
>
> (Gould 2014)

Finally, as St. Therese the Little Flower Catholic Church in Memphis, Tennessee explains on their website,

> As Catholics, we express our worship of Almighty God in words and gestures. The burning of incense is a prayer in itself; a prayer in action. Furthermore, for Catholics prayer is action, and that action becomes ever more present through the visual and sensory experience of incense. . . . Not only does the smoke symbolize the prayers of the faithful drifting up to heaven, incense actually creates the ambiance of heaven. . . . Incense connects us to God's altar in heaven and allows us to utilize all of our senses in our prayer. . . . Incense helps to support an atmosphere of solemnity and beauty that is fitting to

the greatest gift given by Christ to His Church, and the highest prayer the Church has to offer to God: the True Worship of God the Father as offered by Christ on His Cross. It helps us to understand that at Mass we enter into and are united with the worship offered God in Heaven by His Angels and Saints. If we are told, after all, that the angels stand amid clouds of incense singing God's praise in heaven, why shouldn't they do the same gathered around the altar, as they are, singing God's praise during the Holy Sacrifice of the Mass?

(St Therese the Little Flower n.d.)[11]

We can see, in these three accounts of the use and value of incense from three different Christian traditions, that many regard olfactory experience to be an important part of the Christian experience today. Some of the language used demonstrates thinking of olfactory experiences as pointing us towards an experience of divine presence (e.g., incense "*signifies* the presence of God"), but we can also see that a more literal understanding of olfactory experience as a religious experience is found in contemporary traditions (e.g., "Not only does the smoke symbolize the prayers of the faithful drifting up to heaven, *incense actually creates* the ambiance of heaven").

Thus, whilst an emphasis on smell in contemporary religious traditions may be uncommon, it is not entirely unprecedented. Moreover, the way in which olfactory language is used points to the significance of our embodied experiences as being imbued with religious significance, much in the same way that the early Church thought about sensory experience. The purpose of this chapter, however, is not to consider the philosophical implications of the practice of incense in Catholic and Orthodox liturgy (as interesting a task as this may be), but to think more generally about how our embodied experiences of smell might be thought of as religious experiences. Thus, whilst incense clearly has a rich religious tradition, this might not be the only olfactory experience which could be considered to have an important spiritual role for an individual. Could the smell of freshly brewed coffee count as a religious experience? Or might the smell of freshly cut roses somehow be thought of as an experience of divine presence? If we are happy to think that experiencing a beautiful sunset (see Plantinga 2000, 174–175) or a piece of sacred music (see Perlmutter 2016) can be an experience of the divine, then there is no reason to exclude olfactory experiences from having such significance too.[12]

It is this general question, of how olfactory experiences might be thought of as religious experiences in a non-metaphorical way, that I now consider. To provide such an account, I first outline the categories which contemporary philosophy of religion has typically used to think about religious experience, before considering how and where olfactory experience might fit in this analysis.

The Philosophy of Religious Experience

As William Lycan notes, "the philosophy of perception has been warped and skewed by its persistent focus on vision" (2000, 273), ignoring the important philosophical questions which emerge by thinking about our other senses, including the sense of smell. If this is the case for philosophical literature on perception more generally, it is even more the case for the philosophical discussion of religious experience. The philosophical literature on religious experience focuses almost entirely on accounts of visual, auditory, or mystical experiences of God.

Yet, despite this narrowness in the kinds of experiences considered, there has been a keen interest in the nature of religious experience in philosophy of religion over the past few decades. This discussion has largely focused on giving an account of mystical experiences and explaining how these can epistemically support, justify, or give warrant to, religious beliefs. William J. Wainwright (1981) in his philosophical work on mystical experiences specifies that the term 'mystical experience' should be restricted to:

1. 'unitary' states which are
2. noetic [i.e. connected to the intellect], but
3. lack *specific* empirical content.

In such experiences, he explains,

> [t]he distinctions which are ordinarily drawn between subject and object, between one object and another, and between different places and times are radically transcended. Although they are noetic, or perception-like, they are not experiences of specific items within the phenomenal world but intuitive apprehensions of the (character of) the space-time world as a whole or something which transcends it.
> (Wainwright 1981, 1)

Wainwright includes the *unitary* specification to emphasize that mystical experiences involve some sense of overcoming the distance between the object and subject of experience; in such experiences "distances are annihilated, and distinctions are overcome. If the experience has an object, the mystic experiences identity or union with that object" (1981, 5).

In writing on the noetic features of mystical experiences, Wainwright stresses the "perception-like" (1981, 1) quality of such experience. This is a point elaborated in detail in William Alston's influential work *Perceiving God*. According to Alston, in a typical mystical experience "it seems to the subject that something (identified by the subject as God) is directly presenting itself to his/her awareness as so-and-so" (1991, 67). Such experiences should count as perceptual since, he argues, it is both necessary and sufficient for a state of consciousness to be a state of perceptual consciousness that it (seem to the subject to) involve something's presenting itself to the subject, S, as so-and-so, as purple, zigzagged, acrid, loud, or whatever. A case of perceptual consciousness is a case of something's looking, smelling . . . so-and-so to S.

(1991, 38)

This "phenomenon of apparent presentation of an object" (Alston 1991, 37) distinguishes perceptual experiences from other modes of consciousness, and thus, mystical experiences should be regarded as perceptual. According to Alston, since God is "purely immaterial" (1991, 19) it makes little sense to say that he could look, sound, or, indeed, smell a certain way. Instead, Alston thinks, perceiving God should best be understood as a kind of non-sensory perception which involves mystical phenomenal qualia (although, it might also be accompanied by experiences of ordinary sensory qualia).

Along with mystical experiences, Wainwright states that there are a number of other kinds of religious experience, which he lists as:

1. "ordinary religious feelings and sentiments,"
2. "numinous experience," and
3. "visions, voices and such occult phenomena as telepathy, clairvoyance, and precognition."

(Wainwright 1981, 1)

On Wainwright's taxonomy, the other three categories of religious experience can be contrasted with mystical experiences in some way. For instance, *ordinary religious feelings and sentiments*, such as feelings of "love, awe, trust, fear, devotion, gratitude and other religious affections and sentiments" are all important instances of religious experience; however, such experiences lack the perceptual character that he suggests is essential for mystical experience; whilst such affections and sentiments have "a cognitive dimension" (Wainwright 1981, 3), they are not perceptual in the way that mystical experiences are. Furthermore, whilst *numinous experiences* share with mystical experiences "a sense of perception," which makes such experiences noetic, they are not unitary experiences (Wainwright 1981, 4). As Wainwright puts it, whilst mystical experiences invoke a sense of unity with the object of perception, numinous experiences involve "a sense of absolute otherness, or distance, or difference" (Wainwright 1981, 5). Like both mystical and numinous experiences, Wainwright thinks that *visions* and *voices* are perceptual, noetic experiences. Yet, unlike mystical experiences, such experiences lack specific empirical content and thus are "empirically falsifiable; in a way that mystical experiences are not" (Wainwright 1981, 7).

Where should we fit olfactory experiences within this taxonomy? Whilst olfactory experience might be the cause or stimulus of mystical and numinous perceptual experiences, it would seem strange to describe the smelling experience itself in these terms. Similarly, the descriptions Wainwright provides of religious feelings, sentiments, visions, and voices do not straightforwardly capture instances of olfactory experience such as those considered above. And so we ought to consider how religious experience might be thought of more broadly.

Broadening the Discussion of Religious Experience

Philosophers of religion have recently argued for a broadening of the categories of religious experience (Wynn 2009; Green 2009; Rea 2018). In particular, as Rea argues, the categories of religious experience considered by Wainwright, Alston, and others appear to ignore instances of "*garden-variety divine encounters*" (Rea 2018, 115; emphasis in the original), that is, "divine encounters that are not aptly described as visions, voices, or occult phenomena, are more than mere religious affections or sentiments, but do not rise to the level of being numinous or mystical experiences" (Rea 2018, 115–116). Such examples might include experiences of God's presence in liturgy, in nature, or through our engagement with friends (Rea 2018, 116).

As Mark Wynn notes, unlike many of the paradigm examples of religious experience discussed by philosophers of religion, there appear to be many cases which "may involve not so much a direct encounter with God, or some non-dualistic experience of God, as the recognition of the religious meaning of some material context" (Wynn 2009, 163). These experiences are "not fundamentally" those which involve seeing God as

> the efficient cause of certain events characterized in neutral or meaning-independent terms—rather, the sense of God is realized in some recognition of the existential meaning which attaches to a material context.
>
> (Wynn 2009, 149–150)

As Wynn highlights, there appear to be many examples of experiencing so called 'sacred spaces' which appear to be cases of religious experience, even if they are not perceptual experiences of God in the way that mystical experiences are. Our engagement with places, and particularly sacred or religious places, is often imbued with meaning and emotion, such that our experience of environments provides a kind of encounter with God. As Wynn puts it, in such cases, "it is not that God is encountered directly, or recognized as the cause of various neutrally characterized or 'objective' events, but rather that God is made known in apprehending the meaning which is borne by a particular place" (Wynn 2009, 157).

Similarly, Adam Green (2009), in his critique of Alston's model of mystical experience, contrasts the phenomenology of perception with that of interpersonal presence. As Green notes, we do not ordinarily experience a person's actions or emotions in a direct way, analogously to, say, perceiving a ripe apple on the table, but rather, our perception of a person's lowered brow and red eyes provides us with the experience that the person is sad. Similarly, even in many cases of paradigm mystical experience, individuals do not primarily report God as an object of perception, but rather, they describe God as 'strengthening,' 'forgiving,' 'sympathizing,' and 'speaking' (examples all taken from Alston 1991, 44). Green suggests that instead of thinking of religious experience in perceptual terms, we should think instead of such experiences as interpersonal engagements with God, which involve what psychologists have called 'shared attention' experiences. As Naomi Eilan defines it, shared attention occurs when

> each subject is aware, in some sense, of the object *as* an object that is present to both subjects. There is, in this respect a 'meeting of minds' between both subjects, such that the fact that both are attending to the same object is open or mutually manifest.
>
> (Eilan 2005, 5)

This basic kind of sharing attention with another person (sometimes called dyadic shared attention) can then give rise to a mutual object attention, whereby both participants are aware of one another's perception of other objects in their perceptual field (sometimes called triadic shared attention). According to Green, we can think of experiencing God in these terms too. In mystical experiences, Green thinks, individuals become aware (or come to believe) that God is sharing attention with them through ordinary acts of perception. As Green explains,

> using the shared-attention account, we can claim that sound, light, and affect are all mediums that can be manipulated by God in such a way as to reveal the mind of God toward the subject of the experience. The subject hears the sound of a voice reading a psalm that responds to his situation, a manipulation of auditory stimulation that evidences an awareness and concern for the subject by some theistically affiliated entity. He or she then experiences an unnatural light which seems patterned to reinforce the extra-natural nature of the reassuring voice. Then, the subject has the experience as of being loved and then one of peace. . . . The preceding pattern of light and audition does not seem epistemically incidental to the experience of being loved. The shared-attention model allows the preceding pattern of sensory imagery to enter into how one experiences whatever qualia were present in the experience such that it is experienced as being loved by God.
>
> (Green 2009, 463–464)

Thus, for Green, as on Wynn's account, our ordinary experiences of the physical world can be opportunities to experience God through the mediums of sense perception. What neither discusses directly is the role in which olfactory experiences might fit in such an account. In the next section, I turn to consider recent literature on what is often called 'cognitive penetration of perception,' and then to Rea's application of this literature to religious experience. I argue that this way of understanding perceptual religious experiences can accommodate many of the instances of smell we have been considering and provide a non-metaphorical account of smelling God.

Cognitive Penetration of Perception and Religious Experience

The philosophical literature on cognitive penetration of perception surrounds the question of whether perceptual states such as seeing, hearing, and smelling stand in a causal relation to cognitive states like believing or desiring. As Dustin Stokes defines it,

> A perceptual experience E is cognitively penetrated if and only if (1) E is causally dependent upon some cognitive state C and (2) the causal link between E and C is internal and mental.
>
> (Stokes 2013, 650)

Note that perception is cognitively penetrable only if it is possible for two perceivers to have experiences of distinct character or content whilst attending to the same object in the same conditions (i.e., the conditions of the two perceivers' sensory organs and environments are constant; Macpherson 2012). Moreover, as Susanna Siegel has shown, cognitive penetration can have both positive and negative epistemological value. For instance, it seems beneficial that the X-ray technician's perception of X-ray scans is cognitively penetrated by her beliefs (Siegal 2012, 201). Yet, if Jack interprets his spouse's facial expressions wrongly because he is angry at them, then this might weaken or defeat his justification for believing on the basis of his perception (Siegal 2012, 202).

Take the following example which is often cited in this discussion. Bruner and Goodman (1947) have shown in a series of experiments in which children were given carboard discs and coins of identical sizes that children consistently overestimate the size of the coins compared to the discs, despite their identical dimensions. What examples like this demonstrate, some philosophers have argued, is that the desire for wealth, or one's background beliefs about coins, alters one's perception of the objects. And thus, it is feasible that two subjects might have perceptual experiences of the same object with a different character or content because of the differences in how their cognitive states are related to their experiences.

Yet, as Dustin Stokes notes, many philosophers in the analytic tradition take "perception to be *cognitively impenetrable*," that is, they think that "cognitive states do not directly affect the way we see, hear, taste, and otherwise perceive the world" (Stokes 2013, 647). What is going on in cases like the coin perception, according to the defender of this view, is that the differences between subjects are entirely cognitive, and that their experiences are uniform. Thus, the fault comes in forming the wrong kinds of beliefs about one's veridical experiences of the coins, rather than one's beliefs altering one's experience in some way. It seems clear that no amount of empirical testing will fully determine the fact of the matter concerning cognitive penetration of perception, and we will have to make do with philosophical theories which provide the best explanations of the empirical data.

Yet, we need not delve too deeply into this contentious debate to see its application in the case of religious experience. For as Rea notes, regardless of our stance on whether perception is cognitively penetrable, we can see that there are many cases which we *describe* as perceptual, but which depend on certain cognitive states. For instance, an anxious person will see and hear a creaky house at night differently to a sober-headed individual (Rea 2018, 104). An ultrasound technician, in virtue of her training, sees a blob on a screen as the leg of an unborn child (Rea 2018, 102). These examples are all cases of what N. Russell Hanson (2002) calls 'seeing-as.' As Rea argues, it is possible to stay neutral on the cognitive penetration of perception debate, whilst using its insights to help make sense of cases of *seeing as*. As he puts it, by using the language of

> cognitive *contribution* to experience, or of *cognitively impacted* experiences, with the understanding that this way of talking is meant to be neutral on the question of whether cognition affects the character or content of the experience of itself or instead only affects our spontaneous responses to experience.
>
> (Rea 2018, 105)

In other words, the phenomenon of *seeing as* appears to occur, regardless of whether this phenomenon is best explained as an instance of cognitive response to experience or cognitive penetration of experience. And it is the phenomenon, not the causal explanation, which is useful for explaining examples of religious experience.

Rea argues that *seeing as* experiences (regardless of how we interpret the cognitive/perceptual causal connection) can help us to think about certain kinds of religious experiences. On Rea's view, religious experiences

> are cognitively impacted experiences whose stimuli (whether internal or external) are purely natural phenomena. The ability to experience natural phenomena in this way is, furthermore, a kind of skill—one

> that may not have been consciously or intentionally developed by the subject, but is, nonetheless, partly the product of socialization, training, and various other learned ways of experiencing and engaging with the world around her. . . . It is important to recognize that this characterization of divine encounters is fully consistent with the view that at least some of them are experiences *of* God, and even (e.g.) of *God's voice*; and so there is no reason to think that, in general, it casts doubt on experiencers' own characterizations of their experiences. . . . So long as the natural events stimulating these experiences were at least partly explained by God's intention that the subjects experience them in the ways that they did, it is appropriate to say that God communicated with them. . . . So long as God is intentionally causally involved in these encounters, it seems appropriate to speak of these experiences as veridical.
>
> (Rea 2018, 106–107)

Just as the training of the ultrasound technician means that her various background beliefs and other cognitive states incline her to have certain experiences *as* perceptions of arms and legs of fetuses, a person with the relevant cognitive states might perceive an internal sense, an audible voice, or a beautiful sunset as an experience *as* perceptions of God. As Rea argues, such experiences clearly do not fit within the schema offered by Wainwright or Alston, but yet, appear to be common experiences described by many ordinary religious believers. Indeed, Rea goes further, noting that it is plausible to think that

> all divine encounters—including apparent perceptions of external voices or visions, communications from God occurring wholly within the subject's own mind, and general senses (vague or vivid) of divine love, forgiveness, comfort, presence, and the like—involve entirely natural stimuli and require no special causal contact with God, and that cognition enters in as part of the explanation for why the stimuli are *experienced as* divine encounters.
>
> (Rea 2018, 121)

As I argue in the next section, this model provides a helpful framework for thinking about how ordinary experiences of smell can have religious significance in a non-metaphorical way.

Smelling God: Olfaction as Religious Experience

Let us turn to consider the application of Rea's account to olfactory examples. Rea writes that while his primary examples are cases of visions or voices, his account "obviously applies equally to encounters that have olfactory, tactile or gustatory character as well" (Rea 2018, 113). It is not difficult to see how the examples of encountering the sweet-smelling incense in the ritual of anointing the ark of the covenant, or the experience of smell in the Catholic scenting of the altar, might be interpreted as encounters with God by some individuals. For as Rea has highlighted, certain kinds of cognitive states can influence how one perceives or responds to one's perception of the world. And so, if one experiences an instance of inhaling the liturgical incense *as* an experience of smelling the presence of God, so long as God intended for such experiences to be understood in this way, then one encounters God through smell. The close connection between memory and smell noted previously seems particularly pertinent here; for these are often rituals which are embedded into a community, in which the experience of God is something which provides important connections to the past.

Thus, as we have seen, thinking about olfaction as a religious experience can be theologically helpful and such comparisons are ripe with symbolism. But we can also go further than metaphor, I think. It is important to see that interpreting olfactory experiences as non-metaphorical does not amount to saying that one is directly or literally smelling God. God does not have a scent any more than he has a sound or a specific appearance. Rea's model of 'seeing as' provides a way of providing a non-literal but yet non-metaphorical account of smelling God. *Smell as* experiences are those in which an experience of the material world is interpreted as having a particular religious content or significance. On this account, the very same smell, whether that be of freshly brewed coffee, or sweet-smelling incense, can be experienced differently (or can cause different spontaneous responses to experience) in different individuals. Given that we each have different background beliefs, and each have developed different associations with various smells in our memories, these religious experiences should be seen as interconnected, not competitive or exclusive.[13] And thus, it is possible that the experience of the religious believer who has olfactory experiences can be experiences of smelling the pleasing odor of God's presence. To my knowledge, such experience has been given little attention in the philosophical literature. But yet, I have attempted to show that philosophical reflection on such experiences can provide to be rich and, I hope, spiritually illuminating.

One benefit of this account is that it leaves room for the kind of subjectivity (or subject dependency) of religious experience. This can be seen by taking an overly literal reading of Paul's use of olfactory language in 2 Corinthians. A very good reason why the aroma of Christ is a sweet-smelling fragrance to some and a smell of death to others can be explained by thinking about the background cognitive states of each and how these background states influence one's experience or response to experience.[14] Those saved by Christ have the requisite desires and beliefs about Christ which make the experience of Christ's presence amidst his Church a pleasing experience, whereas those who are 'perishing' (to borrow Paul's language) lack these background cognitive states. And thus, to over-literalize Paul's point (but in a way which I think is instructive for many other cases), a religious believer might experience certain smells as having significance or meaning that a non-believer would not. The literature on cognitive contributions to perception can explain how experiences can differ from subject to subject, even if the object of experience is perceived in relevantly similar conditions.

Finally, what is helpful about the literature on cognitive penetration of (or contribution to) perception is that it emphasizes the way in which the Hebrew writers and the early Christian church thought about cognition and perception. For as both Harvey and Avrahami note, the modern distinctions between cognition and perception were less pronounced in such cultures and worldviews. Perception played an important role in thinking about human understanding and knowledge of the world in a way that many philosophers have since rejected. One way of making sense of these sources and ways of thinking in modern terminology is to see that such thinkers were committed to the cognitive penetration of perception (or something similar). This can help us to make sense of how olfactory language is non-metaphorical, but yet still retain the intuition that God does not have a scent or odor of any kind.

Conclusion

Is it possible to smell God? According to many in the Christian tradition, our olfactory experiences provide us with a way of encountering God. While it is tempting for us to think that all such language is metaphorical, or even non-sensical, I have shown that there are ways of making sense of such claims. It is possible, I have argued, in smelling some material object to encounter God.[15] While the philosophical discussion has been insufficiently narrow to accommodate such experiences as religious or encounters of God, more recent work in this area has shown how even the most mundane experiences might have religious significance and count as encounters of God.[16]

Notes

1. It is worth remarking how similar this account of smell is to that described by Avrahami in the Hebrew Scriptures—the connection between breath and smell is noted by both. Avrahami notes that, in the way it is described in Hebrew Scripture,

    > the nose does more than just smell. In many biblical verses, it explicitly refers to the breathing organ, with its connotation of life itself. When man was created, God "breathed into his nostrils . . . the breath of life" (Gen 2:7). Elsewhere the breath in the nostrils, or nose, is used to express life . . . (Job 27:3). The nose recurs as an organ containing the

spirit (i.e. breath) in descriptions of God... (Ps 18:16[15]).... The dual function of the nose as the smelling and breathing organ, together with the physiological basis of smelling as the intake of air, is strongly reflected in the interchange of meetings of the root [word] and its derivatives.... To sum, the nose in the Hebrew Bible is both the organ of smelling and of breathing, and the borders between both experiences are not easily discerned.

(2012, 125)

2. Richardson 2013b discusses the relationship between smell and taste in depth elsewhere.
3. It might be suggested that these differences are fairly superficial—in seeing and hearing we bring something external into the body (i.e., photons or sound waves). Yet, it is really the phenomenology of bringing a smell (or, indeed, a taste) into the body that interests me here, and this does seem to be importantly distinct from how we think about our experience of sight and sound. We experience an object as 'out there,' whereas, smells often have the phenomena of being brought from without to within, particularly, as Richardson argues, through the act of sniffing.
4. See Stump 2010 for a detailed philosophical account of being in union with God. As suggested by Kevin Timpe, an expansion of this discussion to the theology of taste would provide a rich analysis of the role of the Eucharist in engaging our senses.
5. As Kevin Timpe helpfully points out, the disability community has lots of thoughts about how these metaphors function. For instance, the move, in academic contexts, from 'blind review' to 'anonymous review' is an attempt to eliminate some of the bias against disability built into so much of our language.
6. Others include: 'I smell a rat,' or, 'Your argument stinks.' The only positive use I have so far come across is 'on the scent.'
7. Another helpful discussion of this can be found in Aviya Kushner's discussion of the role of the nose in *The Grammar of God*.
8. "Christians used olfactory experience to formulate religious knowledge: to posit knowledge of the divine, and, consequently, knowledge about the human" (Harvey 2006, 3).
9. Harvey writes that

Both through ritual practice and through related instruction . . . Christians granted value to the senses as channels through which believers could approach and encounter the divine. . . . A consensus was apparent that the sense body of the Christian in its received experiences and enacted responses yielded distinct knowledge of God.

(2006, 99–100)

10. Harvey 2006, 136.
11. Another use of smell in contemporary religious practice I have come across in discussing this chapter with colleagues and students can be found in the informal charismatic traditions of the Christian church. It is common in some charismatic traditions to talk of God providing 'words and pictures' to the mind, which one is encouraged to share with fellow believers. But in some traditions (which I have not experienced), believers are also encouraged to share prophetic smells or scents when praying for others.
12. As Blake Hereth suggests to me, it might be thought that olfactory experiences are relevantly different to these examples since it is often difficult to

trace the source of smells. On the account I develop, this does not rule out the possibility of smelling God, but it does give olfactory religious experience a distinct phenomenology.
13. Thanks to Kevin Timpe for raising this clarification.
14. As Blake Hereth helpfully points out, it is important to note that whilst my view can *accommodate* a very plausible explanation here, it is not the *only* thing that might explain these disparate experiences.
15. As Kevin Timpe helpfully points out to me, the medievals thought there was always a trace of the Creator in the creation. If this is correct, then the connections argued for in this chapter should not be surprising.
16. I would like to thank David Efird, David Worsley, Kevin Timpe, and Blake Hereth for their helpful feedback and comments on earlier drafts of this chapter. I would also like to thank members of the Logos Institute staff/student work in progress for their feedback and to the Templeton Religion Trust for their generous funding during the writing of this paper.

References

Alston, William. *Perceiving God*. Ithaca: Cornell University Press, 1991.
Avrahami, Yael. *The Senses of Scripture: Sensory Perception in the Hebrew Bible*. Library of Hebrew Bible/Old Testament Studies. New York: T&T Clark, 2012.
Bruner, J. S. and C. C. Goodman. "Value and Need as Organizing Factors in Perception." *Journal of Abnormal and Social Psychology* 42 (1947): 33–44.
Eilan, Naomi. "Joint Attention, Communication, and Mind." In *Joint Attention: Communication and Other Minds*, edited by Naomi Eilan, Christpoh Hoerl, Teresa McCormack, and Johannes Roessler, 1–33. Oxford: Oxford University Press, 2005.
Gould, Andrew. "An Icon of the Kingdom of God: The Integrated Expression of all the Liturgical Arts—Part 12: Incense—Heavenly Fragrance and Transfigured Light." *Orthodox Arts Journal* (2014). Accessed October 30, 2018. www.orthodoxartsjournal.org/icon-kingdom-god-integrated-expression-liturgical-arts-part-12-incense-heavenly-fragrance-transfigured-light/.
Gregory of Nyssa. *Homilies on the Song of Songs*. Translated with an Introduction and Notes by Richard A. Norris Jr. Atlanta: Society of Biblical Literature, 2013.
Green, Adam. "Reading the Mind of God (Without Hebrew Lessons): Alston, Shared Attention, and Mystical Experience." *Religious Studies* 45 (2009): 455–470.
Hanson, N. Russell. "Seeing and Seeing As." In *Philosophy of Science, Contemporary Readings*, edited by Yuri Balashov and Alex Rosenberg, 331–339. London and New York: Routledge, 2002.
Harvey, Susan Ashbrook. *Scenting Salvation*. Berkley: University of California Press, 2006.
Isola, Kelly. "Our Spiritual Sense, Part 1—Smell." No date. Accessed October 30, 2018. www.unity.org/resources/articles/our-spiritual-senses-smell.
Lycan, William. "The Slighting of Smell." In *Of Minds and Molecules: New Philosophical Perspectives on Chemistry*, edited by Nalini Bushan and Stuart Rosenfeld, 273–289. Oxford: Oxford University Press, 2000.
Macpherson, Fiona. "Cognitive Penetration of Colour Experience: Rethinking the Issue in Light of an Indirect Mechanism." *Philosophy and Phenomenological Research* 84 (2012): 24–62.

Perlmutter, Julian. "Desiring the Hidden God: Knowledge Without Belief." *European Journal for Philosophy of Religion* 8.4 (2016): 51–64.
Plantinga, Alvin. *Warranted Christian Belief.* Oxford: Oxford University Press, 2000.
Rea, Michael. *The Hiddenness of God.* Oxford: Oxford University Press, 2018.
Richardson, Louise. "Sniffing and Smelling." *Philosophical Studies* 162.2 (2013a): 401–419.
———. "Flavour, Taste and Smell." *Mind & Language* 28.3 (2013b): 322–341.
Siegal, Susanna. "Cognitive Penetrability and Perceptual Justification." *Nous* 46.2 (2012): 201–222.
Stokes, Dustin. "Cognitive Penetrability of Perception." *Philosophy Compass* 8.7 (2013): 646–664.
St. Michael and All Angels. "Incense." No date. Accessed October 30, 2018. www.smaaa.org.uk/worship/Incense.html.
St. Therese the Little Flower. "Why Do We Use Incense?" No date. Accessed October 30, 2018. https://littleflowermemphis.org/newcomers/why-do-we-use-incense/.
Stump, Eleonore. *Wandering in Darkness.* Oxford: Oxford University Press, 2010.
Timpe, Kevin. "Disability in Heaven." No date. Accessed February 7, 2019. www.youtube.com/embed/eIE1kYqfKhE.
Wainwright, William J. *Mysticism: A Study of Its Nature, Cognitive Value and Moral Implications.* Madison: The University of Wisconsin Press, 1981.
Willander, Johan and Maria Larsson. "Olfaction and Emotion: The Case of Autobiographical Memory." *Memory and Cognition* 35.7 (2007): 1659–1663.
Wynn, Mark. "Towards a Broadening of the Concept of Religious Experience: Some Phenomenological Considerations." *Religious Studies* 45.2 (2009): 147–166.

5 'Not My People'
Jewish-Christian Ethics and Divine Reversals in Response to Injustice

Joshua Blanchard

Introduction

In the Hebrew Scriptures, there are many familiar consequences for disobedience to God—destruction of holy sites, slavery, exile from the land, and death. But there is a particular consequence that is less familiar to casual readers and of special interest in this paper. Disobedience to God sometimes results in stark, devastating reversals in God's very relationship and experiential availability to the people whom God otherwise purportedly favors. For example, God's explicitly chosen people may, through particular forms of wrongdoing, remove God's very presence. In one of the most vivid instances, the prophet Amos proclaims,

> A time is coming—declares my Lord God—when I will send a famine upon the land: not a hunger for bread or a thirst for water, but for hearing the words of the LORD. Men shall wander from sea to sea and from north to east to seek the word of the LORD, but they shall not find it.
>
> (Amos 8:11–12)[1]

This is a curious form of punishment that not only threatens the very spiritual identity of the victims of the reversal, but—especially when combined with God's "loathing" and "spurning" of religious festivals, assemblies, and offerings (Amos 5:21–22)—seems to cut off their usual route to experience of and reconciliation with God.

This paper examines a phenomenon that I will call "divine reversal." In the second section, I explore different concepts of divine reversal and argue that each are present in both the Hebrew Scriptures and the New Testament.[2] After identifying the kind of divine reversal of most interest to me, in the "Two Examples" section I suggest some applications for understanding the contemporary relationship between social and religious groups and God, in particular as these relationships involve moral problems. I apply my analysis to two main examples: first, the relationship between the Jewish people and *Eretz Yisrael* (Land of Israel); and second, the relationship between the Church, gender, and sexuality. These are highly contentious topics, but that is why I have selected them. For purposes of illustration and argument, I will simply assume that the 'conservative' wings of the Synagogue and the Church, respectively, are correct in their positions on these topics rather than argue for that conclusion. This assumption is crucial, because one main aim of my reflection is to show that *even if* such positions are theologically or morally correct in the abstract, this does not settle the question of how God will relate to the issues and groups in question. It must be emphasized (both here and below) that this discussion is a kind of speculation. I regard my own concerns in this section as just that—concerns, albeit with substantial philosophical motivation. In the next section, I discuss more general implications of divine reversals for doing applied ethics from a Jewish or Christian point of view. In "Objections and Concerns" I address some worries about the general picture, and in the final section I offer some brief concluding reflections.

To spoil the main point, insofar as the self-identified people of God commit positive injustices against others, and even insofar as they are culpable for failing to prevent such injustices from occurring, devotees of the Hebrew Scriptures—so, devout Jews and Christians alike—ought to take seriously the possibility that God will, in ways that might seem shocking and offensive, side with those who suffer the injustices and even, in a sense, sanctify their life, practices, and identity. Such divine reversals pose a special problem for Jewish and Christian ethics, which must grapple with the possibility that God will seem, from the point of view of the Synagogue or Church, to adopt inconsistent moral positions across time—or at least inconsistent moral postures. The phenomenon of divine reversal generally complicates our understanding of the relationship between the will of God and Jewish/Christian ethics.

Three Kinds of Divine Reversal

It is worth briefly exploring two kinds of reversal that merely overlap but are not identical to the kind of interest to me in this paper.

One kind of reversal is the violation of human expectations. In both the Hebrew Scriptures and the New Testament, there is a prominent theme of tension between divine and human values. For example, Moses is surprised that God chooses him as the divine representative before Pharaoh.

> Moses said to the LORD, "Please, O Lord, I have never been a man of words, either in times past or now that You have spoken to Your servant; I am slow of speech and of tongue.... Please, O Lord, make someone else Your agent."
>
> (Exodus 4:10–11)

Additional examples abound, from God's surprising selection of leaders in the book of Judges to explicit prophetic speech that declares how God "did wonders we dared not hope for," which had "never [before] been heard or noted" (Isaiah 64:2–3).

This is a recognizable kind of reversal of expectation—human beings expect that p, but God asserts or makes it the case that $\sim p$. But this is not ultimately what I have in mind in this paper. That being said, it will become clear that the kind of reversal I do have in mind *can provide* instances of reversal of expectation.

Second, consider the reversal characteristic of a *change of mind*. Perhaps the most famous (for some, notorious) instance of an apparent divine change of mind in the Hebrew Scriptures is in the beginning of the flood narrative in the book of Genesis.

> The LORD saw how great was man's wickedness on earth, and how every plan devised by his mind was nothing but evil all the time. And the LORD regretted that He had made man on earth, and His heart was saddened. The LORD said, "I will blot out from the earth the men whom I created—men together with beasts, creeping things, and birds of the sky; for I regret that I made them."
>
> (Genesis 6:5–7)

This regret is indeed a kind of divine reversal. It involves God coming to think that something God did ought to be undone. In this instance, what is God's regret a reversal *of*, specifically? Based on the phrasing of the text, it seems to be a reversal of God's having "seen" exactly the opposite during creation, when "God saw all that He had made, and found it very good" (Genesis 1:31). Of course, God's change of mind is explicable in terms of humans having become wicked. But even more striking is God's further reversal after the flood, which occurs despite the fact that human beings have not changed.

> The LORD smelled the pleasing odor [of Noah's burnt offerings], and the LORD said to Himself, "Never again will I doom the earth because of man, since the devisings of man's mind are evil from his youth; nor will I ever again destroy every living being, as I have done."
>
> (Genesis 8:21)

As Shai Held comments,

> The text wants us to know that human nature has not changed after the flood—nor, seemingly, will it in any eon we could recognize. What has changed after the flood is not human nature but God's attitude toward it. The very same shortcomings that had called forth doom and denunciation now elicit forbearance and generosity instead.
>
> (Held 2017, 13)

This kind of reversal involves a chiefly internal change within God, albeit one that has (to put it mildly) dramatic externalities.

Although an internal change of mind is a kind of reversal—especially when the change is not based on a further external change 'on the ground'—it is not quite what I have in mind here. In an internal change of mind, there is a change of belief or attitude, a decision to do something different, but this is largely internal to the one whose mind has changed. As will become clear, the kind of reversal that interests me most can involve a divine change of mind, but a change of mind is not the essence of such reversals.

So, both of these kinds of reversal—violation of human expectation and divine change of mind—overlap but are not identical to divine reversal in the sense at issue in this paper. The sort of reversal I *do* have in mind is a non-regretful reversal of God's own commitments and pronouncements, but especially as they pertain to God's relationship with God's ostensibly chosen people. A few salient passages from the Hebrew Scriptures can illustrate what I have in mind when I talk about God's relational reversals. On the one hand, a Psalmist writes, "For the LORD will not forsake his people; He will not abandon His very own" (Psalm 94:14). Yet, God declares in the prophet Amos that, due to their transgressions, the same people "shall wander from sea to sea and from north to east to seek the word of the LORD, but they shall not find it" (Amos 8:12). Such reversals sometimes go in the other direction, extending to groups that are otherwise enemies of God's chosen people. Rather than the people of God becoming alienated from God, people who are *not* of God may be identified with him in some sense. Babylon, for example, is sometimes favored for divine purposes, so much so that its own actions are literally identified with divine action. "I will strengthen the arms of the king of Babylon and put My sword in his hand," God declares in Ezekiel 30:24. In Jeremiah 21:3–5, *in response to a plea from Jerusalem for divine help*, God promises the following:

> Thus says the LORD, the God of Israel: I am going to turn around the weapons in your hands with which you are battling outside the wall against those who are besieging you—the king of Babyon and the Chaldeans—and I will take them into the midst of this city; and I Myself will battle gainst you with an outstretched mighty arm, with anger and rage and great wrath.

Jeremiah implicitly identifies God's arm with the forces of Babylon, which would lay siege to the city.

Now, there are any number of hermeneutical approaches by which one might avoid taking these passages literally (see, e.g., Gellman 2016; for a Christian perspective, see, e.g., Boyd 2017). But to understand the potential offense of this kind of reversal, even as metaphor, for those who self-identify as belonging to God, we must contemplate what it would be like for synagogues or churches to be told that they are—at least for a time—not God's people; that even were they to seek out God's presence in earnest, God would not respond to them; and that the successes, oftentimes violent, of the groups that they perceive to be enemies are best interpreted (again, even if metaphorically) as actions of their God.

Part of what is interesting about divine relational reversals is that they seem to involve God acting or speaking in ways that are contrary to what would *prima facie* make sense, *given* other things that God has said or done. Given God's promises to never forsake Israel, for example, it would *prima facie* make sense that, even when Israel commits injustices, God would patiently remain with Israel—and, certainly, would still respond to those who "seek the word of the LORD," contrary to what Amos proclaims. Given that Israel and not Babylon is God's chosen nation, it would *prima facie* make sense for God to defend Israel from Babylon—and, all the more so, to do so when Israel cries for God's help.

Relational reversals are not the same as reversals of human expectations, mainly because they are not *merely* reversals of human expectations. Passages such as the ones I have quoted lead us to think about the possibility that God's relationship to those who are and who are not God's people has *really reversed* (again, even if this relationship is itself understood in some non-literal sense).

The concept in question is also, I argue, evident in the New Testament. Sometimes, the justification for divine reversals in the New Testament is precisely the relational effects that injustices can have on the victim groups' own actual and potential relationship to God. More specifically, whether and how the victims of the self-identified people of God will themselves experience God can be imperiled by the injustices that they endure. As the Apostle Paul adapts the Hebrew Scriptures in his letter to the congregation in Rome, "The name of God is blasphemed among the Gentiles because of you" (Romans 2:24; cf. Isaiah 52:5).[3] Moreover, some of Jesus's own harshest words are reserved for anyone who is responsible for what otherwise would be considered the failings of others: "It would be better for you if a millstone were hung around your neck and you were thrown into the sea than for you to cause one of these little ones to stumble" (Luke 17:2). Indeed, the parables and apocalyptic pronouncements of Jesus are something of a masterclass in divine reversals. In one of the more epistemologically upsetting statements of Jesus, he says,

> Not everyone who says to me, "Lord, Lord," will enter the kingdom of heaven, but only the one who does the will of my Father in heaven. On that day many to say to me, "Lord, Lord, did we not prophesy in your name, and cast our demons in your name, and do many deeds of power in your name?" Then I will declare to them, "I never knew you; go away from me, you evildoers."
>
> (Matthew 8:21–23)

In Jesus's famous story of the beggar Lazarus at a rich man's gate, he seems to suggest that starvation in the context of extreme wealth inequality alone is sufficient for a reversal of fate in the world to come, with seemingly very little attention to the religious identities or even deeds of the two figures.

> In Hades, where [the rich man] was being tormented, he looked up and saw Abraham far away with Lazarus by his side. He called out, "Father Abraham, have mercy on me, and send Lazarus to dip the tip of his finger in water and cool my tongue; for I am in agony in these flames." But Abraham said, "Child, remember that during your lifetime you received your good things, and Lazarus in like manner evil things; but now he is comforted here, and you are in agony."
> (Luke 17:23–25)

These examples suggest a picture in which not only what we take to be God's relationship to different people, but what really is God's relationship to different people, can be radically reversed or altered, in ways that are quite shocking.

The general concept of divine reversal in the relational sense, then, is that God's relationship to God's people can be—temporarily, at least—revoked. But not only that: in addition to revoking relational status, God can establish it elsewhere.

Two Examples

The Jewish People and Eretz Yisrael

The term 'Zionism' is a matter of considerable controversy in contemporary political life (not to mention in the Jewish community more narrowly), and so it is necessary to spend a moment clarifying how I will be using the term. 'Zionism' is probably most commonly used to refer to a distinctly nationalistic and even secular ideology, whose core tenants involve the establishment and maintenance of a recognizably Jewish state on largely political and humanistic grounds (for a classic statement of a version of this view, see Herzl 1917; see also Ha'am 1912). However, I will be using 'Zionism' in the sense of the distinctly *religious* Zionism that involves the combination of Orthodox Judaism with the basic commitments of a more secular Zionism. Religious Zionism says, in essence, that the land that currently constitutes the nation-state of Israel is part of what was promised to the Jewish people by God (*Eretz Yisrael*), and, crucially, that it is rightfully theirs on this basis. Even if the other political and moral arguments for Zionism were not cogent, God's promises would still, on this view, be sufficient grounds for the Zionist project. One of the main differences between secular and religious Zionism, then, has to do with the justifications given for the core view. But there are significant differences in practical upshot as well. For instance, a religious Zionist may, for obvious reasons, be considerably more likely to advocate for explicitly expansionist national ambitions, on the grounds of the biblical texts foundational to the view (see, e.g., Exodus 23:31).

I take no stand in this paper regarding which, if any, version of Zionism is true. Rather, the point here is to pose a particular kind of worry for those who think religious Zionism is true *and* that it settles certain salient questions.

Whatever one thinks about the plausibility of religious Zionism, it is natural to think that the central question about it is or would be over the factual question: *does God really promise Eretz Yisrael to the Jewish people?* Moreover, from the religious perspective, it is natural to think that settling the question of who the land belongs to will chiefly involve settling this question about what God has promised.

Although it is natural to think that this is the central question for anyone wondering about religious Zionism, it is worth asking why this is so. It seems to me that the naturalness of the question stems from the fact that *if* God really does promise *Eretz Yisrael* to the Jewish people, then this is morally significant for us here and now. The moral significance can be easily seen by reflecting on God's nature. If God is both omniscient and necessarily good, then if God approvingly promises that x *shall belong to* S, it would seem to follow that it would be good for S to possess x. More vividly, suppose you are arguing with someone over whether some bit of property is yours or theirs, and they demonstrably show that an omniscient and necessarily good God has declared that it is theirs (perhaps by successfully beckoning God's voice, or by producing a compelling passage from a text that you both recognize as authoritative). Putting it mildly, your opponent has produced good evidence for their proprietary claim.[4]

Here is where the sort of divine reversal prominent in the Hebrew Scriptures complicates matters. The fact that God has in some sense delivered *Eretz Yisrael* to the Jewish people is in fact not a sufficient condition for their rightful possession of it.[5] Those living in fidelity to the Jewish tradition must regard it as possible that God may (temporarily, at least) reverse fulfillment even of God's own most central promises, and this certainly includes the promise of land. In the Hebrew Scriptures, when God's people do not meet certain conditions of justice, God allows the very thing promised (the land) to be taken away, and worse. Interestingly, this is never taken to mean that God's promises are broken; it suggests, rather, that God's promises are reliable yet conditional. So, it can simultaneously be the case that *God promises* x *to* S and *God takes* x *away from* S. It can even be the case that *God gives* x *to* S*, where S and S* are different groups of people and even enemies (e.g., Israel and Babylon).

This possibility potentially has dramatic consequences for distinctly religious debates over the contemporary Israel-Palestine conflict.

Suppose two interlocutors are debating the question whether Israel has a right to this or that part of the land, or whether Israel is behaving justly. A religious Zionist may be inclined to offer religious arguments in favor of God's having promised the land to the Jewish people, and these arguments will seem especially cogent if the religious Zionist's interlocutor is at least committed to an overlapping, if not identical, theological framework. However, the possibility of divine reversal should worry the religious Zionist, because the possibility of reversal places a wedge between God's purported promises and questions of rights and justice. The religious Zionist's interlocutor may cogently say, "Perhaps God has indeed promised *Eretz Yisrael* to the Jewish people, but that in no ways guarantees even so much as rightful possession or justice here and now."

Now, as I said, I take no stand in this paper as to whether religious Zionism, political Zionism, some form of anti-Zionism, etc., is correct with respect to the Israel-Palestine conflict. That would be beyond the scope of this paper. The point here is simply to emphasize that a prominent theme in the Hebrew Scriptures—divine reversal in the sense specified in the previous section—should give pause to anyone offering typical arguments in favor of religious Zionism. Intuitively, we may think that "with God on our side" we have nothing to worry about, but the possibility of divine reversal makes conceptual room for God's being on our side yet against us for the time being, because of what we have done.

The Church, Gender, and Sexuality

Speculation over how God might relate to the relevant communities in the Israel-Palestine conflict is aided by the fact that possession of the very same land and attendant promises are an explicit issue in the Hebrew Scriptures, particularly as they relate to divine reversals. It is less clear how we might relate these themes to contemporary debates within the Christian church. In this section, I give an example of possible application.

Some of the intra-Christian debate about gender and sexuality structurally resembles the debate about religious Zionism. For instance, whatever one thinks about the plausibility of conservative Christian views on traditional gender norms and sexual life, it is natural to think that the central question about it for devout Christians is or would be over the factual question: *does God really command a traditional sexual ethic?* Moreover, from the religious perspective, it is natural to think that settling the question of which sexual ethic is correct will chiefly involve settling this question about what God has commanded.

Divine reversal in the New Testament is presented in a different mode than in the Hebrew Scriptures.[6] Whereas God's relationship to human beings is largely presented via sweeping narratives in the Hebrew

Scriptures, the New Testament relies much more heavily on explicit didactic teaching. Because we do not have, for instance, long prophetic judgments of this or that church, or of this or that period of the Church's life, it's less obvious how to draw lessons regarding divine relational reversal.

So, to illustrate the concept of divine reversal as it might apply to the New Testament and contemporary debates around Christian views of gender and sexuality, it is useful to draw on a somewhat fraught comparison between how conservative Christians view LGBTQ+ individuals and how the religious leaders of Jesus's day viewed tax collectors, prostitutes, and other 'sinners,' which is an issue that is given some narrative shaping. Now, even suggesting a comparison between LGBTQ+ individuals, on the one hand, and the New Testament's categories of sexual and other 'sinners,' on the other, risks immediate offense and thus undermining of the entire project of this paper. So, one must be careful to bear in mind the narrow purpose of the comparison. Remember that I am assuming *for the sake of argument* that the conservative position on contemporary issues of gender and sexuality is correct. My aim here is to develop a challenge that arises from *within* that perspective, just as my aim in the previous subsection was to develop a challenge that arises from *within* a religious Zionist perspective. The point here is not to say that LGBTQ+ individuals *really are* in the same category—morally, spiritually, or otherwise—as the New Testament's various 'sinners.' The point is that, *from the standpoint of the conservative Christian position on gender and sexual ethics*, the comparison would hold. What each side of this debate can agree on, I suspect, is that LGBTQ+ individuals and the New Testament's various sinners historically share something in their social standing relative to the religious leaders in their respective communities.

So, from an intra-Christian point of view, it is natural to think that the central question for anyone wondering about the conservative Christian gender and sexual ethic is whether God really wills it. As with religious Zionism, the naturalness of this thought stems from the fact that *if* God really does will a conservative ethic, then this is morally significant for us here and now. As before, the moral significance seems obvious from reflection on God's nature. If God is both omniscient and necessarily good, then if God approvingly wills that p, it would seem to follow that it would be good if p. Suppose you are arguing with someone over whether some gender self-identification or sexual choice is right for a person, and they demonstrate that God has declared that it is not (perhaps by successfully beckoning God's voice, or by producing a compelling passage from a text that you both recognize as authoritative). As before, it seems that your opponent has produced good evidence for their claim.

But God's favoring of a particular gender or sexual ethic does not settle the question of who is rightly related to God on this issue. With all of this in mind, consider the following pronouncement of Jesus, from the Gospel of Matthew:

> Truly I tell you, the tax collectors and the prostitutes are going into the kingdom of God ahead of you. For John came to you in the way of righteousness and you did not believe him, but the tax collectors and the prostitutes believed him; and even after you saw it, you did not change your minds and believe him.
>
> (21:31–32)

Jesus speaks these words to an audience that is presumed by the text to be on the *right side* of moral questions regarding tax collection and prostitution. In this case, it seems that what makes the difference is belief in the preaching of John the Baptist, not correctness on moral questions regarding tax collection and prostitution. But the general theme of surprising results with respect to who enters "the kingdom of heaven" is persistent in Jesus's teaching. Notice that Jesus even accuses the religious leaders of positively *blocking* entrance into the Kingdom of God, *despite* their being correct on matters of doctrine and morals. Indeed, in a passage from the Gospel of Matthew, these two statements are put virtually one after the other in the text:

> Jesus said to the crowds and to his disciples, "The scribes and the Pharisees sit on Moses' seat; therefore, do whatever they teach you and follow it; but do not do as they do, for they do not practice what they teach. They tie up heavy burdens, hard to bear, and lay them on the shoulders of others; but they themselves are unwilling to lift a finger to move them. . . .
>
> "But woe to you, scribes and Pharisees, hypocrites! For you lock people out of the kingdom of heaven. For you do not go in yourselves, and when others are going in, you stop them."
>
> (23:1–4, 13)

Much can be said about these passages, of course, and the point of this paper is not to engage in New Testament exegesis.[7] The point is to simply issue a kind of warning or challenge regarding the relationship between being right about some moral or other matter, on the one hand, and being in right relationship to God with respect to that issue, on the other. The New Testament continues and interprets the theme in the Hebrew Scriptures of divine reversal when it comes to who is favored *vis-à-vis* moral questions, including those of gender and sexual ethics. Not only is being in some sense correct insufficient for being in right relationship to God, but it is not clear that it is even necessary in many cases.

Applying this to the case at hand, devout Christians should acknowledge that it can simultaneously be the case that the conservative Christian gender and sexual ethic is formally correct, yet it still be the case that the piety of those who follow the ethic is regarded by God as worthless, and that those who do not follow the ethic "are going into the Kingdom of God" before those who do. Moreover, a devout Christian should worry that holding to and even teaching the correct ethic is compatible with "lock[ing] people out of the kingdom of heaven." Whereas it might be tempting to simultaneously feel secure in one's own standing next to God as well as one's judgment that those who think or live wrongly are far from God, precisely the opposite may be the case on account of one's own very words and actions. This latter, haunting concept suggests that a person's distance from God and God's will may be attributable to someone other than themselves; indeed, it may be attributable to oppressions and burdens that they face precisely from those who are correct about God and God's will!

This has dramatic consequences for religious debates over gender and sexual ethics. Suppose two interlocutors are debating the question whether non-conforming gender identities are compatible with God's will, or whether the Church oppresses people with non-heterosexual sexual orientations. A conservative Christian may be inclined to offer religious arguments in favor of God's willing a conservative ethic, and these arguments will seem especially cogent if the conservative Christian's interlocutor is at least committed to an overlapping, if not identical, theological framework. However, the possibility of divine reversal should worry the conservative Christian, because the possibility of reversal places a wedge between God's purported will and questions of gender and sexual obligations. The conservative Christian's interlocutor may cogently say, "Perhaps God has indeed willed a conservative ethic, but that in no ways guarantees that those living and speaking according to the ethic are closer to God than those who are not."

The crucial point is not merely the banal observation that even people with the right moral beliefs can go wrong in their behavior. It is, rather, that God may positively refuse to relate to those who are right *and* positively welcome those who are wrong, and in the course of doing so deny or temporarily suspend the very relationship with God's putatively favored people that made their beliefs seem so important.[8]

As with Zionism, I take no stand in this paper as to whether a conservative, liberal, or some other position is correct with respect to Christian approaches to gender and sexuality. My purpose here is simply to emphasize that a prominent theme in both the Hebrew Scriptures and New Testament should give pause to anyone who connects the conservative gender and sexual ethic to being in right relationship to God. Intuitively, God's will is an ethical trump card and those living according to it are in the best place they could be. But the possibility of divine reversal makes conceptual room for somehow holding many of the right beliefs and even behaviors—yet, in the end, being on the losing end of God's favor.

Lessons for Applied Ethics From a Jewish-Christian Point of View

It is natural for devout Jewish and Christian theists to think that debates in applied ethics are or would be settled by successful appeals to timeless divine commands. This thought is also natural for other theists (e.g., Hindus) and even atheists who think God's commands *would* play this role if God existed. Although the traditional framework of divine command theory can justify this thought via God's commands constituting what is good or right, one need not be a divine command theorist to have it. Even if God is not the origin or ground of moral truths, God's goodness and knowledge plausibly guarantee that God's commands and moral assertions are consistent with moral truth. If God wills some morally evaluable p, then it must be good that p.[9]

But the possibility of divine reversal means that someone may both be right that God wills that p yet wrong that those who are living and speaking in accordance with the truth that p are in right relation to God—even in that respect. Israel's injustices sometimes made God reject their sacrifices—even though such sacrifices were offered in accordance with the Torah, and those sacrifices per se were not instruments of injustice. The oftentimes impeccable piety of the religious leaders of Jesus's day did not yield the *prima facie* appropriate hierarchies in the eyes of God. The first lesson to learn, then, is that correctness about doctrine and morals can be pulled apart from not just divine favor but also real relationship and covenantal standing, even divine favor and standing *with respect to those very matters that one is correct about*.

A second lesson is that just as religious epistemology should be informed by a view of the *purposes* of knowledge, religious ethics should be informed by a view of the *purposes* of action.[10] As many authors have pointed out, for example, a conservative Christian gender and sexual ethic is plausibly motivated by many *underlying ends*—faithfulness, imaging God, protecting children, and so on—that may nevertheless be harmed in a conservative context and pursued in a non-conservative context. It may very well be that, even if the conservative position is correct on these matters, its correctness is nevertheless not more important in practical situations than the values that undergird it. Hence, although it may seem paradoxical from the conservative point of view, God may in some contexts bless, sanctify, or otherwise favor what the conservative opposes, provided that the relevant underlying values are present.[11]

Third, more work needs to be done on what it means that God might command or promise something at time t, and then seem to temporarily reverse matters at time $t+1$. As another example of divine reversal, consider this peculiar proclamation from the prophet Jeremiah:

> [W]hen I freed your fathers from the land of Egypt, I did not speak with them or command them concerning burnt offerings or sacrifice. But this is what I commanded them: Do My bidding, that I may be your God and you may be My people; walk only in the way that I enjoin upon you, that it may go well with you.
>
> (Jeremiah 7:22–23)

This passage is surprising, because God is said to have commanded burnt offerings and sacrifices at precisely the time in question.[12] Nevertheless, it appears in the context of a familiar theme from the Hebrew Scriptures, that there is a hierarchy of divine ethical concern, with justice, care for strangers, orphans, and widows, at the top, and concerns about sacrifices and cultic practices generally below those.[13]

Overall, there is a question for Jewish and Christian applied ethicists in thinking about the contingent aspects of seemingly universal or objective prescriptions. It is not just a matter of the familiar Kantian questions about not only doing the right thing, but doing it for the right reasons, or bringing about the right thing in the right way. It is also a matter of doing and thinking the right thing *in the right institutional, historical, cultural, and political context*. A Jewish or Christian ethicist must worry that God may have, as it were, a normative plan B in the event that the presumed people of God act unjustly.[14] From the point of view of the religious ethicist, this can sound absurd: how could wrongdoing by S somehow mean that acts that *were* wrong are (perhaps temporarily) no longer so? And how does the question of being in right relationship to God relate to obedience to God's various strictures?

Jewish and Christian ethicists cannot simply do ethics in the usual mode, taking intuitions, values, etc., and applying them to various contentious issues. Even if these intuitions and values are informed by religious tradition, there is still something missing—the consequences of thinking of human life as involving determinate relationships to God on both individual and group levels.

Objections and Concerns

It would be reasonable for a critic to wonder if I haven't really just identified two orthogonal issues: there's the truth about various doctrinal and moral matters, on the one hand, and the truth about who God favors on the other.

I don't think that this would be a full, fair characterization of the picture offered in this paper. We should, of course, care about the truth regarding doctrinal and moral matters, but we should also care about the fundamental values that undergird the importance of seeking the truth on any particular matter. For all I've said, at the end of the day, the conservative Jewish position on religious Zionism and the conservative Christian position on gender and sexual ethics could be objectively true. But this is not a problem for anything I've said in this paper, because my point has been that the possibility of divine reversal should worry even those who have things right by their own lights. Second, the questions of this paper to some extent *do* bear on the truth. For instance, even if, in some ultimate sense, God wills a particular, narrow model of human gender or sexual life, it may be that, *for the time being* and even for quite a while, God not only permits but sanctifies alternative models that serve the underlying values at issue.

More to the point, it seems from foundational religious texts that God at times simply ceases to care about this or that moral or ritual matter, or that God at times seeks to welcome people into the people of God regardless of their standing and behavior. As a provocative example from the New Testament, consider Jesus's parable involving guests to a wedding banquet. A man prepares a banquet, but all of his original guests are too busy to attend. The parable ends on a shocking note.

> [T]he master told his servant, "Go out to the roads and country lanes and compel them to come in, so that my house will be full. I tell you, not one of those who were invited will get a taste of my banquet."
> (Luke 14:16–23)

It seems that undeserving guests are invited to the banquet *merely on the grounds that the original invited guests wouldn't come*, not on the basis of anything else having to do with their beliefs or moral behavior.

Because of the two examples that I have chosen in the paper, someone might worry that the only kinds of "beliefs or moral behavior" at risk for divine reversal are conservative beliefs and behavior. But optics aside, this isn't the case. I see no reason why liberal Jews and Christians—provided that they are theistic realists—should not be equally concerned that being factually correct in their liberalism is insufficient for God's really being on their side. In fact, I think they should be. Religious Zionism and conservative Christian perspectives on gender and sexuality just happen to be presently contentious topics where the issues of this paper arise in a direct and straightforward manner. For any debate where someone thinks that God is on their side on account of favoring their belief or way of life, one lesson of this paper is that this does not settle the debate in their favor. If they are committing injustice, for example, in a way that directly implicates the debate, then devout Jews and Christians should see divine reversal as a real possibility.

All the talk in this paper of committing injustice highlights a conceptual worry about the very notion of divine reversals. Consider that divine reversals might really just amount to one outcome of conditional promises or commitments, typically in the context of covenant. When God promises the land to the Jewish people, for instance, the promise comes with conditions of behavior.

But even if translated into the languages of covenant and conditional promises, acknowledgment of the possibility of divine reversal would radically reshape debate on issues like the two discussed in the "Two Examples" section. In a debate about possession of *Eretz Yisrael*, for instance, "God has promised this to me" is far more decisive than "God has promised this to me provided that I practice justice, care for the stranger...." So, I am in fact somewhat amenable to the incorporation of the ideas of this paper into the standard language of covenant and promise rather than the somewhat more idiosyncratic notion of divine reversal.

However, I am still partial to the choice to conceptualize the phenomenon in terms of divine reversal. In a Jewish and Christian context, ethical debates have an upshot with respect to where and how one stands in relation to God and God's will, plus many people take God's view on moral issues (God's normative plan A) to be decisive in moral debate. The language of covenant and promise undersells the dramatic nature of one's failure totally reversing one's relationship to God.

Finally, there is a reasonably worry that divine reversals are in tension with a notion of God as perfect.[15] Divine reversals (especially when they involve a divine change of mind, as in the flood narrative) can appear as a kind of bait and switch that, in addition to directly contradicting God's immutability, undermines the sense in which God is reliable—and reliability (the reliability of, for example, commands and promises), indeed perfect reliability, seems like a plausible component of perfect goodness.

In response to this concern it is worth flagging a methodological difference when it comes to unpacking what it means to say that God is perfect, from within the perspective of a religious tradition like Judaism or Christianity. We can distinguish between a methodology that begins with *a priori* rational reflection on perfect goodness and then seeks to fit textual and experiential tradition into the resulting philosophical theory. This is the methodology most commonly associated with Western philosophical theology. Alternatively, we might begin with the textual and experiential tradition and then seek to mold our rational reflection on perfect goodness according to it. Especially because I have based my discussion on suggestive and provocative material from the Hebrew Scripture and New Testament, I suspect that the second approach is more congenial to the resulting picture of God than the first, *a priori* approach. In actual intellectual practice, however, I suspect that a theological application of the method of *reflective equilibrium* is more common. This third approach takes as *data* both tradition and rational intuition, and seeks to develop a systematic view that reasonably balances these two sources in a way that is constrained by theoretical virtues.[16] It may simply be that divine reversals are somewhat counter-intuitive but nevertheless best accommodate a combination of rational reflection, tradition, and experience.

Conclusion

In summary, Jews and Christians seeking to engage in applied ethical debate in which reference to God's will is fair game and, moreover, who wish to do so in fidelity to a conception of God founded in traditional sources, must take seriously the fact that the *prima facie* warrant provided by even a successful appeal to God's will may be defeated by one's own failing to live in ways that reflect the values that undergird the very idea that one is right about. This fact is, or should be, especially salient in cases where one stands in an oppressive relationship to those whose lives one is speaking about.

Notes

1. All quotations from the Hebrew Scriptures are from the Jewish Publication Society translation, as published in *The Jewish Study Bible* (2004).
2. I will use "Hebrew Scriptures" to neutrally refer to the *Tanakh*—that is, the Torah, Prophets, and Writings that comprise what Christians and many secular people refer to as the "Old Testament." But I will still use "New Testament" to refer to the distinctly Christian Scriptures, as calling them "Christian Scriptures" obscures the fact that, like the Hebrew Scriptures, they were also largely written by Jews.
3. All quotations from the New Testament are from the New Revised Standard Version, as published in *The Jewish Annotated New Testament* (2017).
4. Of course, within Jewish tradition, such evidence is in fact defeasible and, if the debated proposition is one of *halacha* (Jewish law), possibly even irrelevant. See one of the most famous and foundational texts from the Babylonian Talmud, *Bava Metzia* 59a–b.
5. Of course, it is also not a necessary condition, provided that there can be secular grounds for rightful possession of land. But this is less surprising than the sufficiency claim.
6. See Hazony 2012 for an approach to distinguishing the Hebrew Scriptures from the New Testament. While I disagree with Hazony's apparently Hellenized (and, hence, apparently de-Judaized) reading of the New Testament, I agree with his characterization of the Hebrew Scriptures as offering philosophical arguments in narrative form, and of the New Testament as offering something more in the genre of proclamation.
7. Generally speaking, the perspective here on offer is probably most congenial to the approach to the New Testament associated with N.T. Wright, in which questions of covenantal membership are prioritized over questions of salvific beliefs. See, e.g., Wright 1997.
8. Cf. Dietrich Bonhoeffer's provocative remark that "the church is the church only when it exists for others" (1971, 382).
9. Of course, on some views it may be permissible for God to lie, even about moral matters. For instance, Boyd 2017 argues that God allowed biblical Israel to partly experience God in ways that were in fact contrary to the divine

nature, as part of God's "incarnational" relationship to Israel as an ancient Near Eastern people.
10. On how the purposes of religious knowledge should shape religious epistemology, see especially Moser 2008.
11. For a similar approach in a Jewish context, see Tucker n.d.
12. There is scholarly debate about whether this passage represents a separate textual/intellectual tradition from that which produced the text that clearly does involve burnt offerings and sacrifices at the time of the Exodus (cf. Leviticus 7:37–38). However, this would not explain why the compilers and editors of the Hebrew Scriptures maintained this text as is.
13. Hence, when Jesus cites Hosea 6:6 ("I desire goodness, not sacrifice; obedience to God, rather than burn offerings") at Matthew 9:13 to the same end, he is speaking squarely within the Jewish prophetic tradition. Cf. Yohanan ben Zakkai's use of the passage in *The Fathers According to Rabbi Nathan* (1990, ch. 4).
14. A more or less explicit case of a normative plan B occurs in the biblical narrative telling of the origins of Israel's monarchy. The desire for a king is understood by God in the text as being more or less a form of idolatry born of jealousy: a desire to put a human being in the place where God should be, on account of wanting to resemble other nations. Moreover, it's deemed objectively bad for the people. Yet, God establishes a way for having what was understood to be objectively bad at an earlier time. See 1 Samuel 8.
15. See Nagasawa 2017 for an up-to-date discussion (and defense) of perfect being theology.
16. See Wood 2014, 191 for appeal to reflective equilibrium in this context.

References

Bonhoeffer, Dietrich. *Letters and Papers from Prison*. New York: Touchstone, 1971.
Boyd, Gregory. *The Crucifixion of the Warrior God*, 2 vols. Minneapolis: Fortress Press, 2017.
The Fathers According to Rabbi Nathan. Translated by Judah Goldin. New Haven: Yale University Press, 1990.
Gellman, Jerome Yehuda. *This Was from God: A Contemporary Theology of Torah and History*. Brookline, MA: Academic Studies Press, 2016.
Ha'am, Ahad. *Selected Essays*. Philadelphia: Jewish Publication Society, 1912.
Hazony, Yoram. *The Philosophy of Hebrew Scripture*. Cambridge: Cambridge University Press, 2012.
Held, Shai. *The Heart of Torah*, vol. 1. Lincoln: University of Nebraska, Jewish Publication Society, 2017.
Herzl, Theodor. *The Jewish State*. Dover, 1917.
The Jewish Annotated New Testament, 2nd ed. Oxford: Oxford University Press, 2017.
The Jewish Study Bible: Torah, Nevi'im, Kethuvim, 2nd ed. Oxford: Oxford University Press, 2004.
Moser, Paul. *The Elusive God: Reorienting Religious Epistemology*. Cambridge: Cambridge University Press, 2008.

Nagasawa, Yujin. *Maximal God: A New Defence of Perfect Being Theism*. Oxford: Oxford University Press, 2017.
Tucker, Ethan. "Category Shifts in Jewish Law and Practice." *Mechon Hadar*. No date. www.hadar.org/torah-resource/category-shifts-jewish-law-and-practice.
Wood, W. Jay. *God*. New York: Routledge, 2014.
Wright, N. T. 1997. *What St. Paul Really Said*. Grand Rapids, MI: Wm. B. Eerdmans, 1997.

Section III
Non-Human Animals

6 Eschatology for Creeping Things (and Other Animals)

Dustin Crummett

Introduction

Analytic philosophy of religion, like many things, has traditionally been pretty anthropocentric. This has changed somewhat in recent years. More attention has been paid to theological issues surrounding non-human animals, such as their post-mortem fate and the implications of their suffering on the problem of evil (e.g., Murray 2008; Pawl 2014; Graves, Hereth, and John 2017). The importance of these issues arises partly because of the importance of non-human animals themselves,[1] but also partly because of differences between non-human animals and humans (or, in some cases, most adult humans) which raise significant theological questions, preventing us from simply applying answers developed for humans to the animal case. For instance: non-human animals apparently lack moral agency of the sort that could make them deserve to suffer, or be responsible for missing out on a good afterlife; they've existed longer than humans, so it is hard to see how their suffering could be the result of the biblical Fall; their comparatively limited reflective capacities may make it harder to see how they could benefit from suffering; Scriptures and traditions tend to say a lot less about them, so that matters concerning them involve more in the way of philosophical speculation; there is more dispute over whether it's metaphysically possible for them to survive death; etc. Less attention has been paid to the possibility that the many differences *between* non-human animals might also have important theological implications. Authors often *say* they are discussing all, or all sentient, non-human animals, but give arguments which could only apply to members of 'higher' animal species, such as mammals, and often only to some members of those species (cf. Crummett 2017, 73, esp. fns. 2–3).[2]

This is understandable, since the literature is comparatively small, and had to start somewhere. But I think it's important to move beyond treating non-humans as a mostly undifferentiated group. The best way to argue for this is probably just to do it, and show that interesting results follow. In any event, that's what I tried to do in an earlier work (Crummett 2017). There, I discussed the implications for the problem of evil of focusing on "creeping things," by which I meant, basically, insects and relevantly similar animals.[3] I argued that it was plausible that many creeping things could suffer, and that, if they did, certain facts about them—such as their numbers, their method of reproduction, and their level of psychological sophistication—might make their suffering harder for theists to address than the suffering of the 'higher' animals who get attention from theodicists.

Here, I will discuss animal universalism, which I define as the view that all non-human animals with interests will eventually receive eternal, infinitely good afterlives. When I say that an animal "has interests," I mean that things can be good or bad *for that animal*. I think that sentience is a necessary and sufficient condition for having interests, but some philosophers have thought that non-sentient creatures might also have interests, and even (implausibly) that some sentient animals don't have interests (Crummett 2017, 75–77). I mostly won't need to take a stand on those issues here. For purposes of this chapter, I assume that creeping things have interests, which I've argued elsewhere (74–77) is credible, though uncertain. I will also assume that theism is true. When I discuss what I call "arguments for animal universalism," what I really mean are arguments that, *conditional on theism (and sometimes certain other beliefs which theists often hold)*, animal universalism is true.

In this chapter, I have two primary aims. The first is just to evaluate the major arguments for animal universalism. I discuss six arguments: a *beneficence* argument, a *harm avoidance* argument, a *divine love* argument, a *relationship* argument, a *compensation* argument, and an *equality* argument. I claim that the beneficence and divine love arguments succeed, that the relationship argument fails in its original form but can be made powerful, and that the compensation argument fails but can provide support for a controversial premise shared by the previous arguments. I claim that, taken together, these four arguments provide a strong case for animal universalism, while the remaining arguments require further development if they are to work.

The secondary aim is to show how attending to the differences between animals can illuminate this discussion. Both the harm avoidance argument and the currently existing form of the relationship argument probably establish that *some* non-human animals will receive good afterlives, but fail to establish animal *universalism* because they invoke considerations which can probably only be applied to *some* non-human animals with interests. Recognizing this fact is important for developing better versions of these arguments in the future.

Before moving on, I note that there is at least one possible argument for animal universalism which, for reasons of space, I don't discuss at any length. Call it the *theodicy argument*. One might think that the best explanation for why God allows animal suffering has to do with some benefit which accrues to the animal, such as soul-making or a closer relationship with God (cf. Pawl 2014; Murray 2008, ch. 4). And it might be thought that such an explanation requires some form of animal afterlife, either because so many animals die in their suffering and apparently don't reap the relevant benefits, or because reaping these benefits would require that their cognitive faculties be enhanced in some way beyond what they enjoy in their earthly lives. A good animal afterlife might then be a kind of theoretical posit invoked to explain why God allows evil. This differs from the compensation argument, discussed later. The theodicy argument suggests that an afterlife is necessary to explain why God allows animal suffering in the first place. The compensation argument grants that God's reason for allowing suffering in the first place may be something with no particular connection to an animal afterlife or to animal well-being, but suggests that God should compensate animals for their suffering, and that such compensation requires an afterlife. All I will say about the theodicy argument is that I have argued elsewhere (Crummett 2017, 85–86) that theodicies of the relevant sort can be applied much more easily to some animals than others. So, attempts to mount a theodicy argument for animal universalism must also attend to the differences between non-human animals.

The Beneficence Argument

One good argument for animal universalism is extremely straightforward. The basic idea is that giving animals eternal, infinitely good afterlives would sure do them a lot of good, and wouldn't hurt anything, and so seems like something God ought to do. Specifically, I formulate the argument like this:

1. If an agent can benefit an individual with moral standing and there is no sufficiently good reason for the agent not to provide the benefit, the agent has a duty to so benefit the individual.
2. Non-human animals with interests are individuals with moral standing.
3. God is an agent who can benefit non-human animals with interests by giving them eternal, infinitely good afterlives.
4. There is no sufficiently good reason for God not to do so.
5. God has a duty to benefit non-human animals with interests by giving them eternal, infinitely good afterlives (from 1–4).
6. God acts in accordance with God's duties.
C. Animal universalism (i.e., the view that all non-human animals with interests will receive an eternal, infinitely good afterlife) is true (from 5 and 6).

As far as I know, this argument is original to me, though it's reminiscent of a beneficence-based argument for human universalism given by Eric

Reitan and John Kronen (2011, ch. 5). There are a number of differences between their argument and mine. Apart from the fact that I focus on non-humans where they focus on humans, the most notable one is that they treat beneficence as a kind of free-standing divine attribute, whereas I (for purposes of this argument) treat it as arising from God's moral goodness. In doing this, I assume that God has moral obligations, and that the fundamental moral principles governing divine action are more or less the same as those which apply to other agents. This is slightly controversial (e.g., Adams 2017; Murphy 2017), but I can't defend it here. Readers who deny that God has duties of the sort that I think, but who agree that God is beneficent, are welcome to reinterpret the argument accordingly.[4] (For an argument *against* treating beneficence as a freestanding attribute, at least if it is taken to be an *essential* divine attribute, see Murphy 2017, ch. 2.)

Premise (1) is a statement affirming what W.D. Ross (1930, ch. 2) would have called a "duty of beneficence"—a *prima facie* duty to benefit others. When I say that an all-things-considered duty to benefit exists when there is "no sufficiently good reason for the agent not to provide the benefit," I want to be pretty liberal about what *sort* of thing might count as a sufficiently good reason. Such reasons could include (either individually or jointly) that providing the benefit would conflict with another duty the agent has, that it would cost the agent more than morality can reasonably demand, that the beneficiary has waived their claim to the benefit, that the beneficiary is very bad and deserves to suffer, and so on.

With this broad understanding of "sufficiently good reason" in mind, I think Premise (1) is very plausible. If I could press a conveniently located button and thereby provide a huge benefit to a stranger in Kazakhstan, and I have no reason (other than the mild cost of reaching for the button) not to press it, I think it would be, not just nice, but *obligatory* for me to press it—the stranger could reasonably blame me for the fact that I literally refused to lift a finger in order to provide them a great benefit. There are some nihilists and some hard-nosed libertarians who will reject this. But I think most people will accept the premise, or something near enough the premise as to make no difference to the argument.[5]

Premise (2) states that non-humans have moral standing, which means, roughly, that they are directly owed some kind of moral consideration. You and I have moral standing, but rocks don't; how I treat a rock might be morally important, but only derivatively, because of some connection it has to a being with moral standing. (Maybe it's your pet rock.) Note that this doesn't entail any strong thesis about the moral *equality* of humans and non-human animals (though I think such a thesis is also plausible). All it requires is that non-human animals are sources of moral claims of *some* strength: nothing I do can wrong a rock, but many actions could wrong a cat. Again, some people will deny this. But denying it is absurd.

Premise (3) says that God can benefit non-humans by giving them eternal, infinitely good afterlives. There are two ways one might dissent. First, one might claim that animals couldn't benefit from an eternal afterlife. This seems implausible. All I need is the claim that there's *some possible* environment, or series of environments, which would make continued life good indefinitely for each non-human animal. Whether this would involve, say, the beatific vision, or else just cat toys and things to climb on, it seems clear to me that God could come up with *something* for each animal with interests which would indefinitely be better for it than non-existence.

Alternatively, one might claim that it's not possible for animals to have *any* afterlife. The ground would presumably be that animals don't have souls, or the right *kind* of soul (e.g., to use Thomistic terms, a rational, as opposed to a merely animal or vegetative soul), where a soul, or the right kind of soul, is necessary to survive death. But I think this is also very implausible. One would need to establish the relevant thesis about animal souls. But one would also need to defeat the various suggestions about how humans might survive death if some form of materialism is true (e.g., van Inwagen 1978). Even if dualism is true about humans, so that God doesn't need to resort to these measures, God could still use them on animals, if materialism is true for them. I'll also present another reason for rejecting this line of argument in "The Compensation Argument" section.

Premise (4) says that there is no sufficiently good reason for God not to benefit non-humans with interests by giving them eternal, infinitely good afterlives. Because we're talking about an *infinite* benefit, the *pro tanto* obligation to provide the benefit will have tremendous force, and any reason sufficient to defeat it would need to be correspondingly impressive. What could this reason be? Excluding humans from paradise is generally thought to be justified either on grounds of retributive justice or respect for autonomy, but neither of these considerations seems likely to provide a sufficient justification for excluding non-human animals from heaven.[6] There doesn't seem to be anything else which would benefit animals more, and which a good afterlife rules out. It's not as though God has finite resources, so benefiting non-humans in this way wouldn't detract from benefiting us. And it doesn't seem that God must exert effort, or otherwise bear any sort of unreasonable cost, to save animals from death.

Some skeptical theists might complain that this line of reasoning involves a so-called *noseeum* inference—an inference from the fact that we can't see a good reason for God to do something to the claim that God has no good reason to do it. They will say that our cognitive faculties are so puny that such inferences are unjustified. I agree that the argument I've given involves such an inference. There are two things to note. First, endorsing even very strong versions of skeptical theism as a response to the problem of evil does not require the claim that we can *never* employ noseeum inferences to determine what a good God would do. For instance, Michael Rea (2013, 483) defines skeptical theism as the thesis that "No human being is justified (or warranted, or reasonable) in thinking the following about any evil *e* that has ever occurred: there is (or is probably) no reason that could justify God in permitting *e*," noting that this "leaves open the possibility that an evil might someday occur about which we can justifiably think that it is gratuitous." So, for instance, this allows that we can safely conclude that God couldn't have a sufficiently good reason to condemn a group of innocent people to eternal torture, even while we're (supposedly) unable to conclude the same about actual evils. As I suggested above, God's *pro tanto* obligation to give animals a blissful afterlife is *extremely* weighty: any countervailing consideration would need to justify denying these animals an *infinite* benefit. It's consistent to say that we can judge it very unlikely that any such consideration exists while denying that the same is true of the evils we observe around us. So, a skeptical theist at least doesn't *need* to reject my argument.

The second point—which I'll state even though I know it's controversial, and I can't defend it here—is that I think philosophical reasoning about God's action in general requires us to make certain noseeum inferences, so that any *in principle* objection to these inferences would undermine our ability to reason about God's actions more broadly. In other words, *any* time we judge that God would or wouldn't do something, we are committed to the judgment that God doesn't have adequate reason for acting otherwise. Indeed, I agree with the claim, made by some authors (e.g., Wielenberg 2010; Hudson 2014), that even our ability to trust divine revelation depends on a noseeum inference, since it relies on the claim that God would not deceive us, which in turn requires the claim that God doesn't have sufficient reason to deceive us. So, if the problem with this premise is an in principle objection to noseeum inferences, I think the same reasoning will lead to untoward implications elsewhere.

The rest of the argument is easy. Premise (5) follows from Premises (1–4). Premise (6) says that God complies with God's duties. Everyone accepts that. (Even people who think that God has no duties will agree that, for all the duties God has, God complies with them.) From Premises (5) and (6), animal universalism follows.

The Harm Avoidance Argument

A subtly different argument for animal universalism comes from Shawn Graves, Blake Hereth, and Tyler John (2017, 181; Hereth 2017, 175–179). They claim that animals have a "right to avoid harm," and that this provides others with a duty not to deny animals the opportunity to avoid harm. For instance, they claim that "it would be a violation of an animal's right to avoid harm to deny that animal the opportunity to flee from attackers or seek shelter from a lightning storm" (Graves,

Hereth, and John 2017, 181). They suggest that ceasing to exist would be extremely bad for an animal, and this gives God a strong obligation to grant animals immortality.

This differs from my beneficence argument in that it appeals, not to the claim that continued existence would be *good* for animals and an attendant duty of beneficence, but instead to the claim that the cessation of existence would be *bad* for animals and an attendant duty to help others avoid harm. I see two ways in which this argument might seem to have an advantage over the beneficence argument. First, it might seem clearer that we have a duty to help others avoid harm than that we have a duty to benefit them; this would provide additional support for the analog of the beneficence argument's Premise (1). Second, it might seem plausible that the duty to help others avoid harm tends to be stronger, *ceteris paribus*, than the duty to help them. This would provide additional support for the analog of the beneficence argument's Premise (4). These are advantages, but I don't think they are big ones, since, given the reasons surveyed in the previous section, I think Premises (1) and (4) of the beneficence argument are already very well supported. Meanwhile, the harm avoidance argument faces a unique difficulty of its own.

My worry has to do with the sense in which the cessation of existence is taken to be a *harm* which others have a duty to help one avoid. Whether the cessation of existence is a harm at all has been a topic of debate among philosophers at least since Epicurus, and continues to be one now. If it's *not*, then, of course, the harm avoidance argument doesn't work. In laying out their case, Graves et al. seem tacitly to rely on the so-called preference-satisfaction theory of well-being, which identifies well-being with desire satisfaction and ill-being with desire frustration (cf. Crummett 2017, 75–77), writing that "animals are harmed when their basic creaturely desires are frustrated, setback, or defeated" (Graves, Hereth, and John 2017, 181). Within this framework, their explanation of how cessation of existence would harm animals has two elements.

The first element is that the cessation of existence "marks the end of any possible future desire satisfaction" (181). The idea is that it constitutes a harm because it deprives the animal of future flourishing. (Certain difficulties arise in the case of animals who would have had bad lives had they not died, but set that aside. See Hereth 2017, 176–177.) This proposal is in line with Ben Bradley's suggestion that death is bad for non-human animals if and only if it "makes that individual's lifetime wellbeing level lower than it would otherwise have been" (2015, 51). This view in turn meshes well with the so-called "comparative account of harm," according to which "a harmful event is an event that makes things go worse for someone, on the whole, than they would have gone if the event had not happened" (Bradley 2012, 396). But the comparative account of harm doesn't seem right, and if it's true, harm doesn't seem to have the special normative significance which would differentiate the beneficence and harm avoidance arguments. Suppose I request that Bill Gates hire a fulltime chef to prepare me tasty but reasonably nutritious vegan cookies. Suppose Gates refuses my request, and that in the nearest possible world where he doesn't refuse my request, I receive much more desire satisfaction, since he grants it. The comparative account of harm implies that Bill Gates's refusal harms me, since, in the closest possible world where it didn't occur, I was much better off (cf. 397). But this doesn't seem right. Further, even if Gates does harm me, his harming me in this way clearly can't be worse than his failing to provide me with a proportional benefit, since it just *is* his failing to provide me with a benefit.

I don't have my own account of harm, and providing one is extremely difficult (Bradley 2012). But my own sense is that God's failing to provide creatures with future desire satisfaction via an afterlife would be relevantly like Bill Gates's failing to provide me with future desire satisfaction via a pastry chef, insofar as both represent a failure to benefit but not a harm or a failure to help one avoid harm (or at least, not a harm in the sense that makes the act especially significant). As the beneficence argument indicates, failures to benefit can also be extremely morally weighty. But insofar as this is the concern, I think we would do better to just focus directly on the duty to benefit, while sidestepping questions about harm.

But Graves et al. also provide another explanation for why cessation of existence is supposed to be harmful. It's that it involves the "ultimate and final frustration of the animal's desires" (181). The preference-satisfaction theory views desire frustration as *positively bad* for you, and so might allow us to see how cessation of existence is harmful, in the relevant sense. (So, if I have only one desire and it's frustrated, I'm worse off than if I had no desires, even though I have no *fulfilled* desires in either case.) But it seems that the only desires which can be frustrated just by my ceasing to exist are ones which are about the *future*. Sitting here writing this, I want to do certain things in the future: to finish and publish this chapter; to go with my significant other, Xia, to Pittsburgh tomorrow; to ensure the continued well-being of my cats, Artemis and Apollo; and so on. If I were to die in the next second, all these desires would be frustrated. I also have certain desires about the present moment: I want the bed I am sitting on to be comfortable, not only in the future, but also right now. However, if I only ever have desires about the present, then ceasing existence will never frustrate any of my desires. After all, the moments at which I don't exist are ones at which I have no desires to frustrate.

Whether this argument works for non-human animals, then, depends on whether they have future-directed desires which can be frustrated if they cease existing. Is it the case that all non-human with interests—which, given the preference-satisfaction theory of well-being, means all non-humans with desires—have future-directed desires? Some don't think so. Peter Singer argues that having future-directed desires requires "the capacity to see oneself as an individual existing over time" (1993,

119). He thinks (ch. 4) that some non-human animals, like perhaps healthy adult members of some great ape species, have this capacity, but that most animals do not. For instance, a fish may "struggle to get free of the barbed hook in its mouth," but Singer thinks this is merely the result of a "preference for the cessation of a state of affairs that is perceived as painful or frightening," not the result of the fish "preferring their own future existence to non-existence" (95). Accordingly, given the preference-satisfaction view of well-being, a fish could not be harmed in the relevant way by a painless death. (The preference-satisfaction view, combined with Singer's utilitarianism, is also partly responsible for his notorious views on the permissibility of killing infants and other humans who arguably lack future-directed desires. The moral repugnance of these views suggests that we should be wary in general of thinking that the frustration of future-directed desires is what makes it wrong to let individuals die.) Other views about the capacity to have future-directed desires will be more inclusive. For instance, there are some insects who engage in what appears to be long-term planning, and certain theories of mind will treat this as good evidence of future-directed desires (Crummett 2017, 76). However, Graves, Hereth, and John (2017, 161) define animal universalism as the view that "all sentient animals will be brought into Heaven and remain there for eternity." Even if many more animals than we think possess future-directed desires, it would require much more in the way of argument to show that *all* sentient animals have future-directed desires, and thus fall within the scope of the harm avoidance argument.

We are now in a position to see how the harm avoidance argument, as given by Graves et al., falters. Perhaps it would succeed *if* all non-humans with interests had minds basically like those of, say, healthy adult great apes. But I claim that Graves et al. pay insufficient attention to the differences between non-human animals. Blake Hereth (2017, 176), in arguing that cessation of existence constitutes a harm for non-human animals, generalizes from one case: that of Sadie, a dog who dies just before she gets to play on a beach, a prospect which has excited her throughout a long car ride. It seems plausible that Sadie has a future-directed desire which would be frustrated if she ceased to exist. But what isn't obvious is whether we can generalize from this case. It turns out that the harm avoidance argument, as stated, most clearly applies only to a fairly narrow class of animals, so that it has not been shown that it can establish animal *universalism*.

The proponent of the argument now has a number of options. They might attempt to show that all non-humans with interests (or, as Graves et al. put it, all sentient non-humans) have future-directed desires after all. This would likely involve a great deal of empirical investigation, with careful attention to neurological and psychological differences between different species, and between individuals within species. Alternatively, one might argue that death is harmful for reasons besides the frustration of future-directed desires. For instance, Frances Kamm (1998, ch. 3) argues that (on the assumption that there is no afterlife) death is harmful because, in taking what an individual had, it constitutes a kind of *insult*, and because it represents the final extinction of a life, which is bad for one in and of itself. If these factors apply to humans, they plausibly would also apply to non-humans with interests. Or perhaps thinking about the ethics of letting die will ultimately convince us that allowing someone to cease to exist would be wrong for some reason *besides* being harmful or representing a failure to provide a benefit—say, for some deontological reason—which might provide a novel argument for animal universalism. I will not pursue any of these lines here. My aim has instead been to show where more work is needed.

The Divine Love Argument

Graves, Hereth, and John (2017, 166–172) present another argument for animal universalism which I will term the "divine love argument." The basic idea is that God, being perfect, would also be perfectly loving, and this perfect love would lead God to benevolently ensure the truth of animal universalism. (This is similar to an argument for human universalism from Reitan and Kronen 2011, 38–40.) Because I think this argument is sound as it stands, I won't have much to say about it here. I will instead note that it and the beneficence argument each add something to the other. For purposes of the beneficence argument, I assumed that God had moral obligations, and that these obligations were established by basically the same principles which establish our obligations. As I noted, this assumption, while popular, is controversial. Some authors, such as Marilyn McCord Adams (2017), have denied that God has any moral obligations to us, but have held that God's *love* would nonetheless lead God to act in certain benevolent ways towards us. On the other hand, Mark Murphy (2017, ch. 2) argues that divine freedom means that God would not *necessarily* be loving in any way which goes beyond what God is obligated to do. (Murphy happens to think that God isn't obligated to do anything for us, but that God, happily, does happen to love us more than God is obliged to. But both of these positions are separable from the argument in question.)

The beneficence and divine love arguments, then, may be able to gain traction against somewhat different audiences. For those who deny that God has moral obligations but who agree that God is loving in the relevant way, the divine love argument may have force which the beneficence argument lacks. On the other hand, for anyone who agrees with Murphy that divine freedom constrains the degree to which God will be necessarily loving, but who agrees with me that God has moral obligations which are basically similar to those which we have, the beneficence argument may have force which the divine love argument lacks. The arguments, then, can serve as complements. (Of course, it is also possible to think, like me, that *both* arguments are sound.)

The Relationship Argument

Another argument from Graves, Hereth, and John (2017, 172–174) appeals, not to the love of God for animals, but rather to the love of God for the *blessed humans* who *themselves* love animals. Thomas Talbott (1999, 136–140) argues for human universalism on the grounds that those humans who *are* saved could not be completely happy while knowing that some of their loved ones had not been saved. If, as seems plausible on independent theological grounds, heaven is to be a place of perfect happiness, then God must also save the loved ones of anyone who is saved, and Talbott argues that this ultimately implies that God must save *all* humans. (We will return shortly to the question of how Talbott reaches that conclusion.) Graves et al. extend an analogy of this argument to non-human animals. They suggest that "those who have relationships with particular animals care about the wellbeing of these animals, and would be adversely affected by the knowledge that they have permanently lost their lives," such that "those humans in heaven who had meaningful relationships with animals during their mortal lives could not flourish maximally while knowing that their animal companions had been lost forever" (2017, 174). If I arrived in heaven constituted as I currently am and learned that my cats had been annihilated, I think this would indeed prevent my being perfectly happy. Perhaps there are measures God could use to change this—erasing my memory of my cats, or altering me psychologically so that I no longer cared about them—but these changes seem problematic for other reasons. So, it seems plausible that if I am to be perfectly happy, my cats will need to be there, too. Perhaps this alone is enough to provide some additional support for the claim that animals can survive death, and so for Premise (3) in the beneficence argument and its analog in the divine love argument. If we have reason to think I really will be perfectly happy in heaven, and if this requires that my cats survive death, then we have reason to think it's possible for my cats to survive death. If they can, presumably other non-human animals can, too.

But treating this *directly* as an argument for animal universalism requires confronting the fact that many non-human animals are not involved in any "meaningful relationships" with human beings. It might seem that being good to the blessed humans wouldn't require God saving those animals. In response, Graves et al. appeal to a "profound web of interconnectivity" which allegedly links all non-human animals together. Not only would God need to save those animals with which human beings had relationships:

> Each of these animals, in turn, would flourish maximally only if they were able to live in heaven with their non-human families, and with those other animals that they had relationships with prior to their deaths. Humans in heaven would be better-off if all of their animal companions lived alongside them, flourishing maximally, and would therefore be better-off if all of their animal companions' non-human friends and families were ushered into heaven—along with *their* respective friends and families, and so on—for eternity as well.
>
> (Graves, Hereth, and John 2017, 174)

Maximizing my flourishing requires maximizing the flourishing of the animals I care about, which requires maximizing the flourishing of their animal pals, etc. Graves et al. also add that "each individual animal matters to God. God loves each individual animal, and the loss of these animals would be a great relational loss to God, who looks after each animal and desires their well-being and their companionship" (174). However, insofar as this consideration requires the claim that God would love non-human animals and therefore want to save them, it seems to be parasitic on the considerations driving the earlier divine love argument. If the claim about divine love is *essential* to the relationship argument, it seems to me that the relationship argument would not really constitute a "second argument" as Graves et al. (172) claim, so I will set this consideration aside for now.

Can appeal to this "web of interconnectivity" between animals help us establish animal *universalism*? It may be able to do quite a lot of work. I am not sure whether my cats love, or even remember, their relatives, and their relationships with the squirrels and birds they see through the window don't seem loving. But maybe *someone's* cats love their relatives, and some of these relatives love their relatives, and so on. Perhaps we could then construct a chain that included many or even all cats, along with at least some of our cats' evolutionary ancestors, along with at least some of the evolutionary descendants of those ancestors, along with various members of other species who cats have established relationships with (the other day I saw a video of cats who were friends with a duck), along with the relatives of *those* animals, etc. But I doubt this can justify including *all* animals with interests, especially if it turns out that creeping things have interests. It seems plausible to think that many insects, say, do not have the ability to love each other. Some of them may be loved by members of other species: perhaps someone loves the ants on their ant farm. But because those ants don't love and aren't loved by other ants, it will not be possible to establish a chain. So, some ants living in an isolated part of the wilderness, even if they are sentient, may be out of luck, so far as this argument is concerned. We again see that attention to the diversity among animals threatens the ability of an argument to establish animal *universalism*.

Eschatology for Creeping Things 153

However, I suspect we can rehabilitate the relationship argument by drawing further on Talbott's work. Talbott himself recognizes that, even to establish *human* universalism, he must address the question of "those who are not our loved ones": if there are humans who are not loved by any of the blessed, and are not loved by anyone loved by any of the blessed, etc., could God leave them out to dry? Talbott's response (which Graves et al. don't discuss) is that if there are any other humans who we currently do not love in the relevant way, this is because "our capacity for love is not yet perfected" (139). However, in heaven, our capacity for love will be perfected. (He suggests that such perfection is necessary for our achieving "supreme happiness," but of course there are various other reasons why one might expect such perfection in heaven.) Even if we do not love everyone *as much as* those closest to us, we will nonetheless love everyone enough that we would be precluded from supreme happiness if we knew they weren't in heaven. Accordingly, if God is to make any of us supremely happy *in our perfected state*, God really will need to save *everyone* (or else prevent from us knowing the truth about the lost, or do some other problematic thing).

We can see the potential application. It may be that none of us *currently* experience the relevant kind of universal love for animals. As my research agenda attests, I think I care far more about insects than most people do: on the assumption that they have interests, I would be willing to make sacrifices to protect their sufficiently great interests. But this is largely the result of a detached judgment. I don't think I currently *love* any insects, much less *all* insects, in the way needed for their well-being and mine to be bound up in the relevant way.[7] Were I to arrive in heaven as I am currently constituted and learn that insects didn't make it, I would think that was too bad, but I don't think it would pose a serious threat to my happiness. Honestly, it might not make me more unhappy than, say, the treatment of Luke Skywalker's character in the new *Star Wars* movies. If it prevented my being perfectly happy, I might nonetheless be trivially close to perfectly happy. This is probably partly due to general facts about human self-centeredness. (Unless you have some sort of personal connection, the current war in Yemen, for instance, probably doesn't have much of an impact on your day-to-day happiness, even if you recognize how terrible it is.) And it's probably partly due to the specific fact, which presumably has some sort of evolutionary explanation, that we don't feel much sympathy for bugs.[8]

However, it might seem that my detachment is a kind of defect, or at least limitation, in me, a failure on my part to appreciate the value of other creatures and which would have to change for me to reach a perfect state in heaven.[9] St. Isaac of Ninevah (1923, 341) wrote that a merciful heart is characterized by:

> The burning of the heart unto the whole creation, man, fowls and beasts, demons . . . so that by the recollection and the sight of them

the eyes shed tears on account of the force of mercy which moves the heart by great compassion . . . it is not able to bear hearing or examining injury or any insignificant suffering of anything in the creation. And therefore even in behalf of the irrational beings . . . at all times [the person with a merciful heart] offers prayers with tears that they may be guarded and strengthened; even in behalf of the kinds of reptiles, on account of his great compassion which is poured out in his heart without measure, after the example of God.

If I possessed the kind of heart St. Isaac describes, I'm not sure how I would feel about Luke Skywalker, but I'm sure I couldn't forget the creeping things. So, it may be that maximal goodness to me will wind up requiring that God save all the animals with interests after all.

Note that the relationship argument has at least one potential advantage over the ordinary divine love argument. Some authors have expressed a great deal of skepticism over our ability to know what divine love would involve (e.g., Rea 2018). This might serve as the basis for an objection to the divine love argument: perhaps we aren't in a position to know whether divine love would lead God to promote the flourishing of non-humans in the relevant way or not. Such skeptical arguments might appeal to various considerations about divine transcendence, and so forth, and so not rule out our ability to know what perfect *human* love would be like. So, if we know (from revelation, or whatever) that God will be maximally good to the blessed, and if we can know through reflection on human love that this will require saving the animals, we have a love-based argument for animal universalism which allows us to avoid the kind of philosophical speculation about divine love to which the imagined skeptic objects.

The Compensation Argument

Some have suggested that God has a duty to give creatures who suffer an afterlife as a way of making their suffering up to them (Murray 2008, 125; Hereth 2017, 179–183). The moral judgment underlying this claim may seem reminiscent of W.D. Ross's (1930, ch. 2) "duty of reparation," the duty to compensate those one has wronged. Of course, God won't do anything *wrong*. But it also seems plausible to think that agents take on a duty to compensate others when they *transgress their rights*, even if they do so permissibly. So, if during a snowstorm, my breaking into your unoccupied cabin and burning the furniture for warmth is the only way to save my life, I transgress your property rights but do so permissibly, since your rights are overridden by the importance of my life (Feinberg 1978). But while I did not *wrong* you, I nevertheless owe you compensation. Contrast this with a case where I break into the cabin looking for the map of the bombs you placed around the city. Here, it seems plausible that your property right against me actually has no moral force: it is not merely overridden but has been *forfeited* by you, so that I do not transgress your right. And here you are not owed compensation.

Non-human animals clearly experience severe harms as a result of God's creative choices, with many having earthly lives containing far more suffering than flourishing. God could prevent these harms, but does not. God presumably has some good reason for all this, and so doesn't act wrongly, but it does seem plausible that God infringes the rights of the animals—perhaps the right against being harmed, or the right to help in avoiding harm mentioned by Graves et al. So, it seems plausible that God has a *pro tanto* obligation to compensate them. And God is capable of providing compensation, and indeed, is often the only agent capable of doing so. So, there's some reason to expect that God will compensate them. Since such compensation could apparently only occur in the afterlife, there's then some reason to believe in an animal afterlife.

Unfortunately, the compensation argument cannot establish animal universalism as I have defined it. It shows only that God has an obligation to grant post-mortem compensation to non-humans who have been harmed during their lives, and it is not clear that this is true of every animal with interests. Further, it could not establish that even animals who are owed compensation are owed *eternal, infinitely good* afterlives, rather than just enough to make up for their suffering. (One might claim that some earthly suffering is so bad that no finite amount of good can outweigh it, but this is implausible. The arguments from Crummett 2017, 80–83, can be adapted to show this.) Accordingly, all the argument can show is that some amount of post-mortem compensation, for some humans and animals, is necessary.

Blake Hereth (2017, 175, 179–183) responds to these worries, making two main points. In response to the claim that the argument can show only that animals are owed a finite amount of compensation, Hereth writes that "because [the animals] would be unjustly harmed again if they were brought to a good afterlife and then sent to a harmful afterlife or perpetual nonexistence, the good afterlife must be a perpetual one" (175). And in response to the suggestion that only animals who suffered need to be compensated, Hereth writes that "it would be unfair to restrict an escape from death . . . to animals who have been unjustly harmed" (ibid.), so that others must be included, too.

But I doubt these moves work. Consider the first point. Note that it presupposes that going out of existence would be harmful, which I argued earlier required further defense. But grant that it would be harmful. If the claim is that God wouldn't allow this harm because God wouldn't deprive an animal of an opportunity to escape this harm, then the argument becomes parasitic on the harm avoidance argument. On the other hand, if the worry is just that animals would be owed compensation for this harm, then unless we presuppose something like the comparative account of harm, it isn't clear to me why God couldn't compensate animals *in advance* for the harm of going out of existence, while they yet exist.[10] So, suppose my earthly suffering will be outweighed by X years of heavenly life, and the harm of ceasing existence by Y years of heavenly life; it's not clear why God couldn't appropriately compensate me by providing me with X+Y years of heavenly life, and then letting me cease existing. (Perhaps there's something odd about compensating someone for a *wrongful* act in advance, but there's nothing similarly odd about compensating them for a justified rights transgression. For instance, before breaking into your cabin, I might Venmo you an appropriate amount of money.)

Now consider the second point. Hereth's reason for endorsing the claim that it would be unjust to grant immortal bliss to animals who are harmed but not those who aren't is that if an "animal has not suffered unjust harm, then that animal should not be permitted to be worse off on grounds of having not suffered unjust harm, and should therefore share the same fate as other animals (i.e., immortality)" (183). This is an expression of a moral principle which I will question in my discussion of the equality argument. But grant it for now. This principle still requires giving unharmed animals immortal bliss only if harmed animals also get immortal bliss. So, it requires the success of the previous point, which I argued doesn't succeed. So, I think the compensation argument fails.

Of course, if God saves *some* non-humans and sustains them post-mortem for *some* length of time, one might wonder why God wouldn't just go ahead and save them all and sustain them forever. After all, it doesn't seem like it would hurt anything, and it would certainly help the animals. This brings us back around to the beneficence argument, and in fact, I want to suggest that the best use for the compensation argument is probably as support for Premise (3) ("God can benefit non-human animals with interests by giving them eternal, infinitely good afterlives") of the beneficence argument, and for the analogous premises in the divine love and relationship arguments.[11] If the moral claim underlying the compensation argument is correct, then, conditional on letting non-humans suffer, God has a strong *pro tanto* obligation to grant them post-mortem compensation. If God will be unable to make good on this obligation, then that would be a reason not to let them suffer to begin with. But God does let them suffer to begin with; that God would have strong reason not to do this if God could not compensate them therefore provides good evidence that God is able to compensate them. And if non-humans who suffer are able to survive death, presumably others are, too. The reason God sustains *all* non-humans with interests *forever* has to do with beneficence or love or relationships rather than compensation, but a more restricted duty to compensate provides evidence that this is possible.

Of course, I don't claim that this argument is decisive. Clearly something overrode God's reasons not to let animals suffer to begin with. Maybe something could also override God's reasons not to let them suffer without compensation. But my point here is just that the duty to compensate provides additional evidence for a premise which, for reasons discussed previously, I think already has much to be said for it.

The Equality Argument

A final way of arguing for animal universalism is suggested by Graves, Hereth, and John (2017, 174–180). Their equality argument attempts to show that there is no morally relevant difference which would favor allowing humans, but not sentient non-human animals, into heaven; from this, it concludes that, assuming humans get into heaven, excluding sentient non-human animals would be an unjust form of speciesist discrimination. They summarize the argument as follows:

> There is no morally relevant property that distinguishes animals from human beings with respect to whether it is good to have an opportunity to enter and remain within heaven. But if there is no morally relevant property that distinguishes animals from human beings with respect to whether it is good to have an opportunity to enter and remain within heaven, then if human beings are offered an opportunity to enter and remain within heaven, then it is a requirement of justice that animals be given an opportunity to enter and remain within heaven. Human beings are offered an opportunity to enter and remain within heaven. Therefore, it is a requirement of justice that animals be given an opportunity to enter and remain within heaven.
>
> (2017, 180)

Note here a major difference between the equality argument and, say, the beneficence argument. The beneficence argument says that non-humans animals have a claim to immortality which, so to speak, stands on its own two feet (or four or six or eight). From that perspective, divine justice would require animal universalism even if there were no humans. By contrast, the equality argument claims that, because God gives humans the opportunity to obtain a blessed afterlife, God must also give such an opportunity to non-human animals. It is compatible with accepting the equality argument to say that, if God had denied humans a chance at immortality, it would be permissible to do the same to non-humans. What is bad (so far as this argument is concerned) is not allowing animals to perish *itself*, but rather allowing them to perish *while* giving humans the opportunity to escape death.

The moral principle here is essentially a 'luck egalitarian' one. Luck egalitarianism—a position borne out of the literature on distributive justice—asserts, roughly, that it is unjust for one individual to be worse off than another due to factors for which they are not responsible (cf. Anderson 2010). And indeed, Hereth elsewhere (2017, 175) approvingly quotes a statement of luck egalitarianism from Larry Temkin: "It is bad—unjust and unfair—for some to be worse off than others through no fault of their own." However, there are trenchant criticisms of luck egalitarianism, including from other egalitarians. And I think the reliance on something like luck egalitarianism proves the undoing of the argument in its current state.

Suppose we start out with a distributively just situation, one where no one is worse off than another due to bad luck. As part of this situation, suppose I have some tasty and reasonably nutritious vegan cookies, ones which I am permitted to keep and eat. But I'm nice, and decide to offer a cookie to the next neighbor who passes my house. Graves et al. write that "perfect justice compels God to offer non-arbitrarily distributed opportunities" (175, fn. 36). And I have arbitrarily distributed the opportunity to get a cookie: my neighbor is no more *deserving* than anyone else because they happened to be passing by at that time, nor can anyone really be considered responsible for missing out on the opportunity, given its unforeseeable nature. (We could even make it so that my neighbor exercises *no agency at all* in being given the opportunity—maybe I pick someone I know at random from the phonebook.) So, others may now be worse off than my neighbor, through no fault of their own. Have I done something even a little unjust? Do I now have even a *pro tanto* obligation to offer a cookie to everyone who passes my house? To everyone in the phonebook? To everyone in the world?

I don't think so. Of course, if I *didn't* get offered a cookie, and I really wanted one, I might feel some resentment. But this reaction would be driven by envy, not justice. The morally correct reaction would be for me to be glad that you graciously offered one of your cookies to someone else, and happy for whoever had the opportunity to get one (cf. Anderson 2010). Of course, if, for some independent reason, you had an *obligation* to offer me one of your cookies, I might justifiably feel resentment that you didn't. But then the fact that you offered someone else a cookie wouldn't really be doing the work, and, as mentioned, the equality argument can't assume that God has an independent obligation to offer non-human animals a place in heaven, on pain of begging the question.

But isn't equality important? Of course. I believe so-called *social egalitarianism* provides a superior picture of its significance. Social egalitarians see equality as fundamentally being about, not the strictly equal distribution of well-being, but rather the existence of equal *relationships* between individuals. What they oppose is not some being luckier than others, but rather the existence of oppressive hierarchies in which some individuals are dominated, disrespected, disregarded, or exploited (Anderson 2010; Crummett forthcoming b). I think this is a more philosophically attractive view, as well as one which better accords with the aims of actual egalitarian liberation movements.

Social egalitarianism will require equal treatment *of certain sorts in certain contexts*. For instance, where people with certain characteristics are already unjustly disadvantaged, discriminating on the basis of those characteristics can exacerbate existing oppression (cf. Anderson 2013); this is at least part of why the law treats discrimination on the basis of "protected characteristics" differently. At other times, unequal treatment will constitute an insult, thereby creating, constituting, or reinforcing a degrading status hierarchy. For instance, I think a society could be just without having an institution of legal marriage. However, I think it's unjust for a state to offer marriages to heterosexual couples but only "civil unions" to gay couples, even if the same legal rights and benefits attach to both. This is at least partly because, once the government gets into the business of giving special honorific designations to straight relationships, refusing them to gay relationships signals that the government thinks those relationships aren't worthy of the designation, even if it wouldn't have signaled that had the government stayed out of the honorific designation business altogether (cf. Crummett forthcoming a, forthcoming b). At yet other times, a group of people have engaged in some sort of cooperative endeavor, and each has a *prima facie* claim to an equal portion of the fruits of that endeavor, however large that portion winds up being. In these cases, allowing some to claim a bigger piece of the pie can constitute a form of exploitation. Avoiding this is major reason for favoring economic equality (Crummett forthcoming b). I suspect that the intuitive appeal of the luck egalitarian premise which appears in the equality argument results from our inaccurately generalizing from the many cases where unequal treatment really is wrong.

However, this may also suggest a way forward for the equality argument. I think that plausible forms of social egalitarianism will also require that we avoid subjecting non-human animals to speciesist oppression. (For instance, factory farming, in which animals are kept in degrading and torturous conditions so that they may be more cheaply exploited for food and other products of their bodies, will clearly be ruled out, in addition to being wrong for other reasons.) Given that social egalitarianism condemns *some* forms of unequal treatment, and given that any plausible social egalitarianism includes non-human animals, it may be that attention to the *particular* reasons why unequal treatment can be wrong will reveal that some of these reasons would also tell against God's distributing opportunities for a good afterlife on the basis of species. Of course, I would welcome this result.

Notes

1. An example of what I mean: consider *star universalism*, which states that every star which has ever existed will exist forever in the New Heaven. There is a lot say about this position philosophically—it implicates various questions about mereology, gappy existence, etc.—but no one has said it, because

whether star universalism is true doesn't, comparatively speaking, matter very much. On the other hand, whether animal universalism is true matters a lot. And this is because animals matter a lot.
2. A major exception is Pawl 2014, which represents the sort of thing I think we need.
3. My grouping all these very different creatures under one heading may well turn out to be an instance of the phenomenon I am criticizing. But, again, we have to start somewhere.
4. The argument might go something like:
   1. If a perfectly beneficent agent can benefit an individual with moral standing and there is no sufficiently good reason for the agent not to provide the benefit, the agent will so benefit the individual.
   2. Non-human animals with interests are individuals with moral standing.
   3. God can benefit non-human animals with interests by giving them eternal, infinitely good afterlives.
   4. There is no sufficiently good reason for God not to do so.
   5. If God is a perfectly beneficent agent, God will benefit non-human animals with interests by giving them eternal, infinitely good afterlives (from 1–4).
   6. God is a perfectly beneficent agent.
   C. Animal universalism (i.e., the view that all non-human animals with interests will receive an eternal, infinitely good afterlife) is true (from 5 and 6).
5. For instance, Blake Hereth reported that if "the benefit to the Kazakhstani, who is already exceptionally happy, is to increase his happiness in the slightest possible way," then "it isn't obvious to me that doing so is *obligatory*, although certainly a maximally beneficent person (such as God) would do it." If we wanted to accommodate this, we might replace Premise (1) with a weaker premise stating, for instance, that an agent has a duty to benefit another when they can provide them with a *tremendous* benefit, and there is no sufficiently good reason not to do so. This would give us a kind of circumscribed version of the Rossian duty of beneficence. Since what's at issue is whether God should give an *infinitely great* benefit to non-human animals, the circumscribed principle will still let us get the conclusion I want. (I don't myself think we need to circumscribe the principle in this way. Of course, the *prima facie* duty of beneficence will be weightier when the benefit is larger, but why would there only be a *prima facie* duty *at all* when the benefit is sufficiently large [or the one benefited sufficiently poorly off]? But the point is that the option of circumscribing the principle is there.)
6. I don't mean to deny that non-human animals can act autonomously. Perhaps some are even moral agents, though it's less clear to me that even they would be appropriate targets of retributive justice. The point is just that I don't think these factors, insofar as they apply to non-human animals, could justify their exclusion from paradise. We all recognize that, for respect for autonomy to justify our allowing an individual to make bad choices, certain conditions regarding their understanding of the situation, their capacity to weigh and act on the relevant reasons, etc. must be met, with the conditions being more stringent the worse the decision. For instance, human children have some autonomy, and this can justify allowing them to make decisions which are *somewhat* bad for them. But adults are nonetheless justified in all sorts of paternalistic interference in their actions, even where the stakes are comparatively low. Do any non-human animals meet the conditions

necessary to justify God's respecting choices which would cause them to miss out on an *infinite* good? I doubt it. It's hard enough defending the claim that any humans do.
7. Although Blake Hereth tells me that ze suspects that ze would be devastated by the news that some sentient animals hadn't made it to heaven. This might make the move I suggest in the next paragraph unnecessary.
8. Don't I *desire* the flourishing of insects? Of course. Does this mean the preference-satisfaction view will count their flourishing as bound up with mine? No. Plausible forms of the view need to somehow restrict detached, purely altruistic desires from counting towards my well-being. Cf. Parfit 1986, 494–495.
9. It doesn't follow that a lack of strong emotion would represent such a failure on the part of everyone. Most obviously, it might mean something very different when experienced by people who are neurodivergent in certain ways. Cf. Bommarito 2018, ch. 4.
10. If we presuppose the comparative account of harm, then an instance of God's failing to provide us with a benefit would constitute an instance of God's harming us. Then God's failing to provide animals with an infinitely good afterlife would constitute an infinitely severe harm to them, and perhaps might call for infinite compensation—in the form of an infinitely good afterlife! But I expressed my worries about the comparative account earlier. If the harm is instead something like the frustration of a finitely strong future-directed desire to continue living, then a finite amount of compensation seems sufficient.
11. Modifying the compensation argument to support the claim that God is able to give non-humans immortality is also briefly suggested by Graves, Hereth, and John 2017, 182, fn. 53.

References

Adams, Marilyn McCord. "A Modest Proposal? Caveat Emptor! Moral Theory and Problems of Evil." In *Ethics and the Problem of Evil*, edited by James Sterba, 9–26. Bloomington, IN: Indiana University Press, 2017.

Anderson, Elizabeth. "The Fundamental Disagreement Between Luck and Relational Egalitarians." *Canadian Journal of Philosophy* 40.1 (2010): 1–23.

———. *The Imperative of Integration*. Princeton, NJ: Princeton University Press, 2013.

Bommarito, Nicolas. *Inner Virtue*. Oxford: Oxford University Press, 2018.

Bradley, Ben. "Doing Away with Harm." *Philosophy and Phenomenological Research* 85.2 (2012): 390–412.

———. "Is Death Bad for a Cow?" In *The Ethics of Killing Animals*, edited by Tatjana Visak and Robert Garner, 52–64. Oxford: Oxford University Press, 2015.

Crummett, Dustin. "The Problem of Evil and the Suffering of Creeping Things." *International Journal for Philosophy of Religion* 82.1 (2017): 72–88.

———. "Expression and Indication in Ethics and Political Philosophy." *Res Publica*, forthcoming-a.

———. "Introduction to the Left." In *Ethics, Left and Right: The Moral Issues That Divide Us*, edited by Bob Fischer. Oxford: Oxford University Press, forthcoming-b.

Feinberg, Joel. "Voluntary Euthanasia and the Inviolable Right to Life." *Philosophy & Public Affairs* 7 (1978): 93–123.

Graves, Shawn, Blake Hereth, and Tyler M. John. "In Defense of Animal Universalism." In *Paradise Understood: New Philosophical Essays About Heaven*, edited by T. Ryan Byerly and Eric J. Silverman, 161–192. Oxford: Oxford University Press, 2017.
Hereth, Blake. "Two Arguments for Animal Immortality." In *Heaven and Philosophy*, edited by Simon Cushing, 171–200. London: Lexington Books, 2017.
Hudson, Hud. "Father of Lies?" *Oxford Studies in Philosophy of Religion* 5 (2014): 147–165.
Isaac of Nineveh. *Mystic Treatises*. Translated by A. J. Wensinck. Amsterdam: Uitg. der Koninklijke Akad. van Wetenschappen, 1923.
Kamm, Frances. *Morality, Mortality Vol. I: Death and Whom to Save from It*. Oxford: Oxford University Press, 1998.
Murphy, Mark. *God's Own Ethics*. Oxford: Oxford University Press, 2017.
Murray, Michael. *Nature Red in Tooth and Claw: Theism and the Problem of Animal Suffering*. Oxford: Oxford University Press, 2008.
Parfit, Derek. *Reasons and Persons*. Oxford: Oxford University Press, 1986.
Pawl, Faith. "The Problem of Evil and Animal Suffering: A Case Study." Doctoral dissertation. St. Louis, MO: Saint Louis University, 2014.
Rea, Michael C. "Skeptical Theism and the 'Too-Much-Skepticism' Objection." In *The Blackwell Companion to the Problem of Evil*, edited by Justin McBrayer and Daniel Howard-Snyder, 482–505. Malden, MA: Wiley-Blackwell, 2013.
———. *The Hiddenness of God*. Oxford: Oxford University Press, 2018.
Reitan, Eric and John Kronen. *God's Final Victory: A Comparative Philosophical Case for Universalism*. New York: Continuum, 2011.
Ross, W. D. *The Right and the Good*. Oxford: Oxford University Press, 1930.
Singer, Peter. *Practical Ethics*. Cambridge: Cambridge University Press, 1993.
Talbott, Thomas. *The Inescapable Love of God*. Eugene, OR: Universal Publishers, 1999.
van Inwagen, Peter. "The Possibility of Resurrection." *International Journal for Philosophy of Religion* 9.2 (1978): 114–121.
Wielenberg, Erik. "Skeptical Theism and Divine Lies." *Religious Studies* 46.4 (2010): 509–523.

7 Exploring Theological Zoology
Might Non-Human Animals Be Spiritual (but Not Religious)?

Faith Glavey Pawl

Introduction

The aim of this chapter is to explore the possibility that some non-human animals (henceforward 'animals') might have conscious awareness of divine presence or action in the world, much like humans are thought to have according to various theological traditions. Mystics, authors of sacred texts, and ordinary religious believers alike use the language of seeing, tasting, touching, smelling,[1] and feeling when they speak of experiencing God—either directly, or through experience of God's goodness as suffused in the world. In a similar vein, William Alston hypothesizes that humans have certain kinds of religious experiences by way of a unique mode of perception epistemically on par with our ordinary powers of sense perception of everyday objects. The language of perception pervades the discourse of theological anthropology. In what follows, I will focus on this discourse as situated in the Christian theological tradition in order to fill out in more detail about what spiritual perception might consist in, but my hope is that what I argue can generalize to other religious traditions as well.

However powerful human cognitive machinery might be, the claim that humans can have anything like perceptual awareness of an invisible, immaterial God is truly remarkable. As understood in the Christian tradition, this is only possible because God's acts of self-revelation accommodate human epistemic limitations. God bends down to our limited condition in order to be known and loved—a radical act of divine humility. But does God bend down only so low as *our* species? We are not the only creatures capable of perceptual awareness of the world around us. If awareness of God can be mediated by something *like* or *dependent on* human perceptual faculties, perhaps other creatures endowed with perceptual faculties can be aware of God too.

Christian theism claims that God is personal, and that spiritual perception is possible for humans because God chooses to make Godself known. Thinkers like Thomas Aquinas extend this further to say that God's self-revelation is always communicated in the way best suited to the condition of the knower. This is, in fact, one of Aquinas's most repeated refrains—that whatever is received is always is received according to the mode of the receiver (eg. Aquinas 1920, Ia. Q 75 a. 5). The idea is that humans can have knowledge of God because God makes Godself accessible to the human intellect in ways best suited to human cognitive machinery. So how might God make Godself known to animals, given what we know about animal cognition?

To explore this admittedly speculative question, I begin by briefly considering two helpful models for thinking about human awareness of God. Then I offer reasons we might think it unlikely that animals might be capable of something similar. After arguing that those reasons are not decisive, I give a positive theological argument for thinking that a personal, loving God would want to be known by all creatures God has made, to whatever extent those creatures are capable of knowing. I look to research on primate social intelligence in order to make the case that given what is supposed about God's nature and human spiritual perception and given what we know about the nature of many socially intelligent animals, we should not be surprised if some animals have spiritual perception too. I conclude with some brief suggestions for how the development of a theological zoology that takes seriously the possibility of animal spiritual perception might be applied in ethics and philosophy of religion.

Two Models for Thinking About Human Awareness of God

In the last few decades of analytic philosophy of religion, the most influential model for thinking about human awareness of divine presence or action has come from William Alston's landmark work, *Perceiving God*. Alston argues there that certain kinds of beliefs about God can be justified in the very same way that ordinary perceptual beliefs are. He focuses on what he calls M-beliefs, beliefs about purported manifestations of divine presence or action. M-beliefs are "beliefs to the effect that God is doing something currently vis-a-vis the subject—comforting, strengthening, guiding, communicating a message, sustaining the subject in being—or to the effect that God has some (allegedly) perceptive property—goodness, power, lovingness" (Alston 1993, i). We can be justified in holding M-beliefs, Alston argues, because we (purportedly) acquire them through a mode of perception that is distinct from but epistemically akin to sense perception. He says, "If we think of perception in the most general way, in which it is paradigmatically exemplified by but not confined to sense perception, putative awareness of God examples this character" (1993, 9). By attending to firsthand reports of religious experiences of various kinds, Alston argues that spiritual perception shares its essential features with sensory perception, insofar as both involve, direct, presentational experience of something.

Alston contrasts the direct, presentational character of many kinds of reported religious experiences—whether deeply mystical or decidedly more mundane—with other kinds of mental states, like thinking abstractly about God, calling up mental images, or remembering. In perceiving God, he says, people experience God being "presented or given to their consciousness, in generically the same way as that in which objects in the environment are (apparently) presented to one's consciousness in sense perception" (1993, 14). The presentational character of these God-perceptions sometimes carries sensory phenomenal content, and sometimes does not. But what all such experiences have in common is that they convey presence, as opposed to absence.

Alston is careful to note that when he talks about awareness of or perception of God, he does not mean to use either "awareness" or "perception" as success terms. That is, he does not mean to suggest that whenever someone takes themselves to be aware of God through spiritual perception, they are in fact in some kind of causal contact with God. His goal is not to offer a proof for God's existence by way of religious experience, but rather to explore the conditions under which a person may be epistemically justified in holding an M-belief. I follow his convention of canceling any implication of success in using the terms in question in what follows. Someone can certainly be mistaken as to whether they are perceiving God. And since the basic claim I wish to argue for here is conditional—that if humans are capable of spiritual perception, some animals are likely capable of spiritual perception too—one can accept my conclusion without actually affirming that God exists.

Since Alston's purpose is to explore the implications of perceptual awareness of God for the epistemology of religious belief, the overarching goal of his book is not relevant for my inquiry. Though awareness of God is an important ingredient in the kind of complex, culturally conditioned attitudes humans can take toward God, we shouldn't look to animal awareness of God to play some kind of similar role for animals, since those epistemic norms may not apply to them. That is, M-beliefs need not play the same kind of role in an animal's psychology as they do in a human's psychology. What is relevant in Alston's account, however, is the direct, presentational character of the experiences whereby humans acquire M-beliefs. Might animals have simple experiences of the same kind?

The second model for human awareness of God I want to consider does not claim that experiential awareness of God comes by way of some species of perception, but rather by means of something that is highly perception-like. In the defense against the problem of evil that she mounts in *Wandering in Darkness*, Eleonore Stump gives an account of what she calls 'Franciscan knowledge,' or knowledge of persons. Knowledge of persons is a kind of knowledge by acquaintance, as opposed to propositional knowledge (or knowledge *that* such and such is the case).

Knowledge of persons, she contends, cannot be reduced to propositional knowledge.

Stump argues for the distinctness of knowledge of persons by adapting Frank Jackson's famous Mary thought experiment in order to show that knowledge of persons requires second-person contact (Stump 2010, 51; Jackson 1982). If poor Mary had been locked in a prison with only third-person descriptions of other people for her whole life, but had never had a face-to-face contact with anyone, she would not know anyone *as a person*. No amount of propositional knowledge gained from biographical sources could suffice for Mary to know her own mother in the way she would know her if she were to encounter her face to face.

In recent work attempting to draw out the epistemic implications of knowledge of persons for the philosophy of religion, Matthew Benton argues that "treating someone second-personally involves an 'I-you,' subject to subject interaction, wherein some of what one learns about others is learned from, because it is given to one by, the person themselves" (Benton 2018, 424). Benton goes on to claim that gaining this kind of interpersonal knowledge requires an encounter where both parties treat each other as persons. Benton's characterization resembles what Stump says about what she calls 'second-person experience.' She explains,

One person Paula has a second-person experience of Jerome just in case

1. Paula is aware of Jerome as a person,
2. Paula's personal interaction with Jerome is of a direct and immediate sort, and
3. Jerome is conscious.

(Stump 2010, 112)

The underlying ability in question for both Benton and Stump roughly maps onto what psychologists call 'mind-reading.' Mind-reading offers a person a direct sort of insight into the mind of the other, and this is at the root of the social cognition many scientists believe is sub-served by the mirror neuron system.

The building blocks of mind-reading begin very early in life for humans. Before human infants even begin to develop abilities for language, they are able to relate to their caregivers in a second-personal kind of way. As Stump explains, citing the work of developmental psychologist Peter Hobson, a typically developing infant can "know her primary care-giver as a person, and even, as it were—read the mind of her care-giver to a certain extent" (2010, 66). As infants bond with and attach to their caregivers, they establish the emotional connections that form the initial basis of their relationships with them. Stump quotes Hobson, who says,

> To be emotionally connected with someone is to experience the someone else as a person. Such connectedness is what enables a baby . . . to

differentiate people from things.... It is through emotional connectedness that a baby discovers the kind of thing a person is. A person is the kind of thing with which one can feel and share things, and the kind of thing with which one can communicate.

(Hobson 2005, 59)

This basic ability to distinguish between persons and non-persons, agents from non-agents, is at the heart of an infant's cognitive development.

Second-person experiences can vary widely, from the rudimentary, primarily affective kinds of experiences infants can share with their caregivers to the rich and complex meeting of minds between two old friends engaging in deep conversation. And germane to the inquiry at hand, figures throughout the history of the Christian tradition think that it is possible to know God, at least to some extent, by way of knowledge of persons.[2] In fact, for Stump, that kind of knowledge is precisely what we are after when we try to characterize what it is to have experiential awareness of divine presence or action in the world.[3] So we should also ask, is it possible for any animals to have similar knowledge of persons of God?

Reasons for Skepticism

Since the goal here is to find something analogous to human spiritual perception in the animal world, the theologian might begin to worry that humans are supposed to be the sole bearers of the image of God. The scientist might begin to worry that only humans have the kind of rational capacities one might need to even think about a transcendent being. Before I go on to show how the two models described above might be extended to cases involving animals, I want to consider two formidable objections that reflect these worries about human uniqueness. I hope to show that those worries might not have as much force as we would initially think. The first objection says that the limits of animal cognition preclude the possibility of animal awareness of God. The second says that there is paltry evidence from observation of animal behavior that suggests animals are in any sense religious.

To begin with the first objection, you might think that in order to be able to be aware of God, an individual would have to be able to employ abstract concepts about God. And since it seems unlikely that animals could have such concepts, they can have no such awareness. The objection is a sensible one. How could a creature have mental content about an immaterial, invisible being if it has no concepts of divinity, power, goodness, etc.? Surely no animal (expect for maybe Balaam's ass) has ever thought about a being as possessing all the Anselmian perfections.

There are two ways to respond to this first objection. The first way is simply to deny that abstract concepts are required for *humans* to have awareness of God as described on either of the models above, so we should not expect that concepts are required for animal spiritual perception. Recall that for Alston, one the defining characteristics of M-beliefs is that they come from experiences that are direct and presentational. For him, the kind of experience one has in spiritual perception is in explicit contrast to the kind of experience one has when engaging in abstract thought (Alston 1993, 17). When considering God-perceptions that lack sensory phenomenal content, he admits there is something peculiar about the notion of non-sensory experiences that are presentational in character. He asks though,

> Many people find it incredible, unintelligible, or incoherent to suppose that there could be something that counts as presentation, that *contrasts with abstract thought* in the way that sense perception does but is devoid of sensory content. So far as I can see, this simply evinces a lack of speculative imagination. Why suppose that the possibilities of experiential givenness, for human beings or *otherwise*, are exhausted by the powers of *our* five senses?
>
> (Alston 1993, 17)[4]

Alston's point here is that some quality need not be sensory in order for it to be present to us with immediacy. I think his point can be extended further. If God-perceptions are essentially presentational in nature, why not think it possible that a creature who lacks abstract concepts might nevertheless have awareness of God as present? Perhaps in such a case a creature has no abstract concept featuring as the content of its awareness, but it can still sense something—something very different from any other thing—which is present and relating to it. In other words, why think that the possibilities of experiential givenness are exhausted by our powers for abstract representation?[5]

If we think about human awareness of the divine along Stump's model, then the worry that awareness of God requires capacities for abstract thought recedes even further into the background. If experiential awareness of God comes primarily through second-personal encounter, we need not ask if animals must possess abstract concepts, but only if they are capable of having second-person experience. Stump herself say that the details of her account may very well have application outside of the human sphere, but whether they do depends on "whether the animals in question have the cognitive and conative abilities that allow for relationship" (Stump 2010, 379). I address the possibility of animals having second-person experience in more detail below in section "Animal Awareness of God". But here recall that for Stump, even human infants are capable of having second-person experiences, and of knowing their caregivers as persons, even though infants lack concepts like 'person,' 'parent,' or 'love.' If an infant can experience what it is like to be related to another person, or to be loved, why couldn't an animal? In fact, I take it to be a point in favor of this first line of response to the first objection that it leaves open the possibility that *humans* lacking conceptual capacities, or humans who have rather limited capacities for abstraction, can still be aware of God's presence or God's love.

A further point in favor of denying the necessity of conceptual sophistication for spiritual perception is that many people who have mystical experiences report that they are unable to express the content of their experiences in ordinary language. While some people may be able to communicate what they learn through their perceptions of God, many others struggle to find the words to communicate something so familiar and yet foreign at the same time. The ineffability of these kinds of mystical experiences might suggest that some kinds of experiential awareness of God do not depend on the deployment of abstract concepts, as abstract concepts themselves might be inadequate for the task of comprehending the object of perception. Exploring connections between Franciscan knowledge and the ineffability of certain kinds of religious experiences, Lorraine Keller says, "Knowledge of God is ultimately personal in a way that is irreducible to propositional knowledge, and this is why such knowledge is, in some sense, incommunicable" (Keller 2018, 349).

The second way to respond to the first objection is to argue that some animals in fact have conceptual capacities—or something close enough—that could be useful for perception of God. Whether or not this is the case is widely debated in philosophical and psychological literature, and much depends on how we define 'concept.' One team of proponents of the view that some primates have rudimentary conceptual capacities, Dorothy Cheney and Robert Seyfarth, argue that some primates are able to employ higher-order cognitive rules. These rules allow monkeys to streamline the way they process very complex information about their social surroundings. In their studies of baboons who live in very large groups organized in very complicated dominance hierarchies, Cheney and Seyfarth found that baboons are remarkably skilled at keeping track of where they and all of their conspecifics fall in the social order. This is remarkable as there can be up to 150 monkeys in a baboon troop, and there are not any obvious physical attributes off of which a baboon could read any individual's spot in the various hierarchies within one troop.

How can we explain how baboons are able to keep track of where everyone falls in the hierarchy and who is related to or mating with whom? How are baboons able to sort out these facts about each other's social attributes as quickly as they do? Given that there are "thousands of dyadic relations (and tens of thousands of triadic relations)" they must track, baboons need to have either incredible memories or else some way to schematize relations between animals in order to be able to successfully predict one another's behavior (Cheney and Seyfarth 2015, 61). Seyfarth and Cheney suggest that the latter offers the more parsimonious explanation of baboon behavior, and that baboons are able to employ higher-order cognitive rules that make the relevant classifications easier. These higher-order rules for schematizing relations between baboons function like concepts—presumably concepts like 'parent,' 'rank,' 'kin,' 'pair,' and so on. Seyfarth and Cheney's suggestion is not that baboons possess explicit, linguistic concepts about social relations, but rather that they have something concept-like, and that they implicitly associate one another with their familial and social roles (Cheney and Seyfarth 2015, 61).

Cheney and Seyfarth's suggestion, that our best guess at what kind of concepts monkeys might employ suggests they are social ones, fits well with the Social Intelligence Hypothesis. The Social Intelligence Hypothesis says that animals have evolved to have the complex and flexible cognitive skills they do primarily because of the social pressures they have encountered (2008, 121ff.). Many species of primates have adapted to group living because there are benefits that come from living in large groups, but there are many costs as well. Though the evolution of the primate brain has no doubt been shaped by the ecological challenges primates have had to overcome (where to find food, how to navigate their home range, how to judge distances between trees, etc.), the Social Intelligence Hypothesis claims that social pressures have been the main driver of primate cognitive evolution. As ethologist Frans de Waal and neuroscientist Pier Francesco Ferrari explain, "Primates are intensely social, hence continuously challenged to compete with, work with, to understand each other. Their brains have been designed for social connection" (de Waal and Ferrari 2012, ix).

Might there be some kind of implicit social concept a monkey could apply to God, then? Might a monkey conceive of God as 'parent' or 'friendly affiliate'? Either of those concepts might fill in the content of what is predicated in an M-belief or token of knowledge of persons about God. As we come to learn more about animal social cognition, this second line of response to the first objection stands to gain more evidence for its support.

These responses to the first objection are admittedly very quick, and there is much more that can and should be said to address them. In section "Animal Awareness of God" below, I discuss additional findings in research on primate social intelligence that will help fill out the speculative picture I have in mind in more detail. But the second objection given above, that there is little evidence in animal behavior that animals are at all religious, cuts to the heart of the difficulty we face in trying to make comparative claims about human and animal psychology and behavior. How can we look for the animal analog to something that seems to be so distinctively human, since the human experience of religion is so intimately wrapped up with language and culture?

Pioneering animal behavior scientist Hans Kummer writes that the ancient Egyptians thought hamadryas baboons raised their arms in prayer to the gods every morning. He titled his account of his years in the field with the hamadryas *In Quest of the Sacred Baboon* but reports that he never witnessed the animals in the legendary pose of reverence firsthand. However, other field researches share anecdotes about behaviors they couldn't help but classify as religious. Jane Goodall tells of chimpanzees in the Gombe Reserve who sit calmly gazing at a waterfall, repeatedly throwing in rocks in a ritualistic fashion. Goodall hypothesizes that the chimps are engaging in some kind of rite that expresses a sense of awe and wonder (King 2016).

Perhaps there is something special about Gombe, as baboon researcher Barbara Smuts tells a strange tale of witnessing something peculiar there that she had never seen before in a troop of baboons.

> The Gombe baboons were traveling to their sleeping trees in the day, moving slowly down a stream with many small, still pools, a route they often traversed. Without any signal perceptible to me, each baboon sat at the edge of a pool on one of the many smooth rocks that lined the edges of the stream. They sat alone or in small clusters, completely quiet, gazing at the water. Even the perpetually noisy juveniles fell into silent contemplation. I joined them. Half an hour later, again with no perceptible signal, they resumed their journey in what felt like an almost sacramental procession. I was stunned by this mysterious expression of what I have come to think of as baboon sangha. Although I've spent years with baboons, I have witnessed this only twice, both times at Gombe. I have never heard another primatologist recount such an experience. I sometimes wonder if, on those two occasions, I was granted a glimpse of baboon life they do not normally expose to people. These moments reminded me how little we really know about the 'more-than-human-world.'
>
> (Smuts 2001, 300–301)

I am not sure how to weigh the evidence from these kinds of anecdotes. Perhaps these researchers really did get a glimpse of something like religious behavior in the primate world. It would be difficult to confirm *or* deny. My own suspicion is that Goodall and Smuts's interpretations veer too far into anthropomorphism, and in any case (as admitted by Smuts in the quotation above) such reports are very rare.

If animals are capable of having awareness of divine presence or action in the world, why don't we see more behavioral evidence to confirm that? But then what exactly *should* we be looking for as evidence that an animal has had such an experience? My tentative response is that to ask for evidence of religion is to ask too much.

Religion is a distinctly human phenomenon. Consider Emile Durkheim's classic definition:

> A religion is a unified system of beliefs and practices relative to sacred things, that is to say, things set apart and surrounded by prohibitions—beliefs and practices that unite its adherents in a single moral community called a church.
>
> (Durkheim 2001, 46)

In order to be able to systematize beliefs and to construct practices that express that system, you need language. You need to be able to take reflective, evaluative attitudes toward your beliefs. In order to have a moral community, you must have morally free agents who are able to communicate their values with one another. It would be a leap to attribute any of those capacities to animals.

Unlike animals, humans are meaning-makers. We make sense of our lives and the world around us by constructing narratives that tie our experiences together, narratives saturated with the cultures we inhabit. When humans report having instances of awareness of God, we weave those experiences into our narrative histories. Religion, even in its simplest forms, is a highly complicated thing. But awareness of God itself needn't be. It makes some sense to say that awareness of God, at least in many paradigm cases, is what precedes religion. While I concede that animals are probably not capable of being religious, that does not preclude the possibility that they might be, in some sense, spiritual.[6] There is no reason to expect that whatever role spiritual experiences play in the formation of the complex forms of religious experience human report, animal's awareness of God would need to play the same role in their mental lives.

An Argument From Analogy

To make a positive case for animal awareness of God now, I wish to begin by considering what the Christian tradition takes to be the final end or purpose of human nature. Why is it good for humans that we have consciousness and intersubjectivity? Why didn't God make a world full of beings that lack consciousness—a world teeming with life, beauty, and reflections of divine creativity, but with no conscious awareness on the part of any creatures? Why not have a world of distinct individuals with no awareness of the content of other minds? From a purely naturalistic standpoint, consciousness and intersubjectivity confer all sorts of fitness advantages on humans, and great goods like knowledge, friendship, and aesthetic appreciation depend on our having these endowments. You might even think they are necessary for our very humanity. But in the Christian tradition, the human capacities for consciousness and

Exploring Theological Zoology   173

intersubjectivity find their fulfillment and highest expression in relation to God. Why would God make other creatures, then, who have analogous capacities for consciousness and intersubjectivity, and yet not make possible some kind of experience of Godself?

The basic point of this question can be expanded in an argument from analogy.

1. The God of Christian theism is personal and desires to be known and loved by God's creatures.
2. Loving and knowing God both require some awareness of God.
3. Humans are able to know and love God because God has endowed them with capacities that allow them to be aware of God (or God's activity in the world), and because God communicates Godself to them in ways suited to their capacities.
4. There are animal analogs of those human capacities which are tied to awareness of God.

(C) Thus, we should expect that animals endowed with such capacities can have awareness of God.

The first conjunct of Premise (1) states a foundational belief of traditional Christian theism. The second conjunct of Premise (1) is either just entailed by the first, or else highly plausible on most interpretations of God's being personal, combined with the biblical narrative of God's involvement in history. We need not look further than the opening words of our catechisms to see the very existence of humans explained by their final end of knowing and loving God (e.g. Shorter Westminster Catechism: Q. 1; Catechism of the Catholic Church 1994, Prolog).

The key notion of knowledge at play in Premise (2) is knowledge of persons, detailed in Section "Two Models for Thinking about Humane Awareness of God". The conception of love I have in mind comes from Aquinas, where love is a feature of the will, and consists in having desires both for union with the beloved and for the good of the beloved for the beloved's sake (Aquinas 1920, I–II q. 27 a. 1). Premise (2) is admittedly vague, in order to leave room for disagreement over the extent to which someone must be aware of someone else in order to know or love that person. The aptness of a person's awareness of the identity of the other can come in degrees, and for the moment I will leave to one side what degree of apt awareness is sufficient for love or knowledge. What seems plausible enough is that at least *some* awareness is required.

Premise (3) underscores another point important in Christian theology, that humans are able to relate to God primarily because of God's initiative. This is the case both for how God has made humans, and for how God relates to them. Though God is personal, God is also transcendent. There is an ontological gulf between God and humans—what philosopher Marilyn Adams calls a size-gap (Adams 2000, 49)—and God is not an object of awareness at all like any other kind of object. God is immaterial and invisible.

For the kind of comparative purposes of this argument, it is important to remember that even though Christianity takes humans to be made in the image of God, the size-gap between God and humans is far larger than any between humans and animals.[7] So while it may seem outrageous to claim that animals can have awareness of God, we should remember that the claim that humans have such awareness is itself bold. And nonetheless, figures throughout the history of the Christian tradition have reported that they have sensed God, or sensed God's goodness, or been aware of being loved by God, or have other such experientially rich instances of awareness of the divine.

That brings us to Premise (4), which I take to be the most difficult to defend. First, how do we know with any specificity which human capacities are actually involved in awareness of God? We may speak in general terms about consciousness and intersubjectivity as necessary components of such awareness, but the actual capacities that underlie spiritual experiences are likely a complex combination of psychological functions. On Alston's model, there is no one psychological system, no module hypothesized as the seat of spiritual perception. And even though on Stump's model we have some sense of where to look in human psychology, we would still have to be able to locate the relevant parallels in animal cognition. Such tasks of translation are notoriously difficult. Any attempt to justify Premise (4) will be very speculative.

Animal Awareness of God

Now I wish to consider whether, given the models of human awareness of God outlined above, it makes sense to say any animals can have similar experiences. One figure in the Christian tradition who answers in the affirmative is St. Francis of Assisi, the namesake for Stump's characterization of knowledge of persons. When we think of Francis and animals, we likely think of how his love for them is sentimentally depicted in garden statuary. There is more to the way Francis related to animals than just syrupy affection, however. He thought not only that animals could relate to God, but also thought they could direct praise toward their creator.[8] Francis, often portrayed as preaching to wild animals such as birds, seems to have taken a fairly literal interpretation of some biblical passages about the way creation relates to creator. The psalmist exhorts everything that has breath to praise the Lord (Psalm 150:6). In another psalm, the monsters from the depths of the sea and all the beasts, cattle, creeping things, and flying birds are exhorted to praise the Lord (Psalm 148:7–10).

The chronicler Thomas of Celano (2004) reports that after his first sermon to the birds, Francis was embarrassed that it had never occurred to him before that animals needed to hear the message that they, too, have the duty and privilege to praise God. In this sentiment we see both that Francis thought animals could direct their attention to relating to God with an attitude of praise, and that he was calling at least some of them out for not actually practicing the task of which they were capable. The point here is not that animals were morally culpable for failing to praise God, but that there was something pitiable in such a condition, and Francis responded to this deficit out of compassion for the animals.

Of course, there is an alternate way of interpreting those same Psalms that inspired Francis. This interpretation says all of creation gives glory to God just by reflecting God's goodness as a creator, much in the way that a masterpiece gives glory to the sculptor who created it. On that reading, the bird offers praise merely by actualizing its avian nature—by excelling at being a bird—and not necessarily by directing its song toward its creator.

To consider how the fulfillment of avian nature might allow a bird to direct praise toward God, though, we would have to take a closer look at what it is that makes a bird the kind of creature it is. If we consider one genus of birds—corvids—it is clear that what makes them distinct is not merely the ability to sing, but their remarkable social intelligence. There is some evidence that European magpies can recognize themselves in a mirror—a capacity theorized to be a building block of perspective-taking (Prior, Schwarz, and Güntürkün 2008). Scrub Jays are able to tell where their conspecifics are directing their gaze and alter their behavior according to whether they think other birds are able to see them or not (Emery and Clayton 2004). Crows have a prodigious ability for recognizing and remembering individual faces (ibid.). This research suggests that, like primates, birds in this genus seem to have minds built for processing social information. Why *not* think that sentient creatures, especially ones with rich capacities for social cognition, can relate to God in a way that involves their capacities for social connection? Relating to other beings, after all, is part of what it takes for many creatures to excel at being the sorts of things that they are.

This brings us to consider what it is that animals know about other minds. Much of the literature on primate social intelligence focuses on the question of whether any apes or monkeys have a Theory of Mind: the ability to detect or attribute distinct mental states to other agents. Experiments about Theory of Mind very often focus on what animals and humans know about what other agents *believe or know*. For example, much speculation about Theory of Mind in animals focuses on whether animals try to deceive one another, since the ability to try to manipulate another agent's beliefs presupposes a sense that the other agent's beliefs are distinct from one's own.

The results are mixed concerning which species of animals, if any, are able to have this sophisticated kind of Theory of Mind.[9] De Waal surmises, though, that focusing too closely on beliefs and knowledge as the only targets of Theory of Mind makes for "a rather narrow angle for inter-subjectivity" (de Waal 2012, 138). For one animal to know what is going on 'inside' another animal, they need to have insight into much more than just beliefs and knowledge, but also emotions, perceptions, goals, motivations, and desires. Cheney and Seyfarth contend that while most primates lack the kind of Theory of Mind that allows them to know what other animals know or believe, many primates (and animals across other taxa as well) do in fact have rudimentary Theory of Mind when it comes to the intentions, motives, and emotions of their fellow creatures (Cheney and Seyfarth 2008, 2015).

The ability to have insight into the mind of others and sensitivity to their affective states is crucial for both the models of awareness of God described above. M-beliefs present God as "doing something currently vis-a-vis the subject." Taking God to be doing something to or for you might just be equivalent to attributing intentions, motives, and emotions[10] to God. Likewise, attributing intentions, motives, and emotions is central to what is shared in second-person experience.

Recall that Stump says of second-person experience that,

> One person Paula has a second-person experience of Jerome just in case
>
> 1. Paula is aware of Jerome as a person,
> 2. Paula's personal interaction with Jerome is of a direct and immediate sort, and
> 3. Jerome is conscious.
>
> (Stump 2010, 112)

Immediately we face a terminological problem on Stump's model, as the term 'second person' seems to imply that both parties in a second-person experience need to be persons. I do not wish to argue here that any animals are persons (though I am certainly open to the possibility that we might learn some are). I think it would be more fruitful to ask whether there is some other term to substitute for 'person' that would still allow us to capture what Stump thinks is important in second-person experience. Perhaps the best substitute for 'person' is 'individual agent.'

Animals would have to be able to think of others as individual agents, then, in order for them to have second-person experience. Cheney and Seyfarth explain that "individual recognition is widespread in animals" (Cheney and Seyfarth 2015, 58). Animals are able to integrate information about faces, vocalizations, and smells in order to distinguish various individuals from one another. Baboons, for example, are able to recognize each other by their distinctive calls, and can pick out when they are the intended target of another baboon's vocalization even when they cannot see the other animal (Engh 2006). Furthermore, they are able to associate each individual baboon with its social attributes (like its rank and kin), and personality traits (like friendliness or aggression) (Seyfarth, Silk, and Cheney 2012). On the basis of those associations, they have strong preferences for spending time and grooming with particular baboons over others (Cheney and Seyfarth 2012; Smuts 2007). And given their ability to attribute motives and intentions to each other, it does not seem like stretch to say they think of each other as individual agents. Thus, we can say of baboons that they have second-person experiences with each other.

If animals like baboons can have second-person experience with each other, then that capacity might also be directed toward God. It is difficult to imagine how that works, since baboon-to-baboon second-person experiences are mediated through the integration of sensory cues. But then again, human-to-human second-person experiences are mediated through the integration of sensory cues. If we take it that humans can have knowledge of persons of God, our inability to imagine how animals might too is likely just another failure of our speculative imagination.

I would wager that most people who live with companion animals or work with service animals simply take it for granted that they have some sort of relationship with them that involves at least some reciprocity (even if it is easy to exaggerate the degree to which those relationships are reciprocal). If it is meaningful to say that someone's dog or horse can relate to and be emotionally connected to their human—to someone who is ontologically very different than they are—it should not be such a stretch to think they might be able to relate and emotionally connect to God.

The picture I have in mind, then, is one where an animal that has even a limited Theory of Mind and the ability to detect other agents as individuals might have some encounter with God where it senses God's presence or action. Maybe the animal senses God as a loving parent—an experience marked primarily by positive affect in the animal. That positive affect helps it bond and attach to God and constitutes a great good for that animal.

I use the language of bonding and attachment here because the basic neurobiology of bonding and attachment is widely shared across species with long periods of maternal care (namely, in mammals and some birds). An animal (or human) infant bonds with and attaches to her caregiver when their caregiver nurtures her in close causal contact, and the effect is reciprocal. In mammals with smaller brains, this is primarily achieved by way of olfaction, and is limited to the mother-child relation. In animals with larger brains, bonding and attachment can be achieved via cognitive means, and can extend to other caregivers besides just the mother (Keverne 2006, 101ff.).

I offer this image of bonding and attachment as a kind of metaphor to help us imagine how it could be that an animal might orient itself toward God in a way that constitutes a great good for that animal. When

I imagine what that looks like, I think of the work of Jaak Panksepp, a pioneer in the field of affective neuroscience. Panksepp garnered the nickname "the Rat Tickler" because of his research on positive affect in rats. He suspected that most other mammals were capable of experiencing emotions like joy, as the brain systems most likely responsible for joy do not depend on the pre-frontal cortex, but on sub-cortical systems shared across many species (Panksepp and Biven 2012).

Pankseep and his team discovered that when rats are engaged in joyful play, such as when they are tickled, they emit high pitched squeals. The squeals are imperceptible to the human ear without the help of ultrasonic equipment. But sure enough, when experimenters would tickle the rats, they would 'laugh' (Panksepp and Burgdorf 2003). Better yet, when the experimenters tasked with the tickling would simply walk into the room, the rats would 'laugh' in anticipation. (They emitted no such sounds when non-tickling experiments would come in). Perhaps animals might take similar joy in the presence of God and emit expressions of that affective attachment in sounds imperceptible to the human ear.

Applications and Conclusion

What might be the practical upshot of this possibility, that some animals might be able to have conscious awareness of divine presence or action? Should we join St. Francis in his mission to preach to wild creatures? Should we baptize our pets and include them in the liturgical life of our religious communities? I think the answer is no. If God had intended that animals' experience of communion with God be so dependent on human intervention, I think God might have made that clearer in revelation. As much as I would like to model my life after Francis, I think there are probably better ways for most of us to respect whatever special dignity animals might have.

For if the story I have suggested is true, an animal's ability to commune with God depends on its ability to develop its natural tendencies—to live the kind of life specific to the sort of creature it is. Here our practical choices can have serious impact. Many of the ways we interact with animals today seriously imperil their ability to live out the kinds of life that are most fitting to their natures. As I have argued in particular elsewhere, many of our practices undermine the kind of natural social flourishing many animals are capable of (Pawl 2016). We might not be able to evangelize animals, but we may be capable of being a stumbling block to them by standing in the way of their development as relational beings. We have good reason to avoid such harm on the story I am telling here.

One philosophical implication of the possibility of animal awareness of God is that there may be a broader range of responses available to the theist for developing theodicies or defenses for animal suffering than is typically assumed. The existence of animal suffering poses a unique challenge to the rationality of theism, because the kinds of stories theists typically tell about why God might allow humans to suffer don't really seem to be very promising as justification for why God allows animals to suffer. Some offer stories about God's permission of animal suffering that have nothing to do with the well-being of the animals themselves (van Inwagen 2009, 113–135). Others have suggested that animals would have to undergo a radical change in the afterlife in order for their suffering to be defeated (Dougherty 2014). But if I am right that some animals are capable of experiencing communion with God in *this* life, it might be the case that we can come up with better stories. As the next generation of philosophers of religion take up the problem of animal suffering—a problem the surface of which has only been scratched—we may need to indulge possibilities as speculative as the one I have sketched here.[11]

Notes

1. See Joshua Cockayne's entry in this volume on olfaction and religious experience.
2. In connection with this claim, it could be fruitful to explore work in biblical studies about various understandings of the Hebrew verb to know, 'yada.' I am grateful to Meghan Fisher for this suggestion.
3. We might ask then what relation Alston's conception of spiritual perception bears to Stump's conception of knowledge of persons of God. At first glance, the two accounts seem to be describing different phenomena. After all, Alston focusses on the kinds of experiences that yield M-beliefs, and M-beliefs are propositions—*that* God is doing something for me, *that* God is comforting me, or *that* God is loving, good, etc. For present purposes, I only wish to ask whether either model can be extended to animal cognition, and I think there are elements to both that might have such application. My own suspicion is that second-person experience of God is what is more fundamental, and M-beliefs are what are formed on the basis of second-person experience. For a fascinating comparison between Alston's account and second-personal approaches, see Green 2009.
4. The first two sets of italics are mine, the third is Alston's.
5. The key to filling out what this consists in would have to trade on the idea that M-belief-generating experience is basically awareness of some kind of personal presence. But caution is in order here. Euan Grant raises a helpful objection, that if animals entertain thoughts (or something equivalent) about God under the aspect of predicates not apt of God, animals might be something like natural idolaters. That is, they likely would be mistaking the Creator for some created thing. This objection is worth taking very seriously. When humans mistake created things for the Creator, their understanding falls short of the kind of picture of God they ought to have, given their intellectual capacities and whatever revelation they have been given. To whom much has been given, much is expected. But there might not be anything epistemically or religiously wrong with animals failing to understand God as we can. My suspicion is that animals aren't subject to the same kinds of norms that make idolatry problematic for humans.

6. This playful take on the now-common designation "spiritual but not religious," does not quite map onto the meaning it's usually interpreted to have. For a helpful discussion, see Carey 2018.
7. The point here is that the difference between creator and created thing is so sharp a contrast that even if humans are the most godlike material beings that exist, they are still fundamentally other than God. God is not a being among other beings, at least not in the theological tradition from which I'm drawing. Humans and animals can be said to be in the same genus of beings, but no such claim can be made of humans and God. Which all just gets terribly messy when we consider Christology.
8. By regarding animals as his brothers and sisters, Francis seemed to recognize in them an ability to commune with God, an ability that he shared in common with these beasts. He also saw in them something he knew well from his own experiences and those of the humans to whom he ministered, the need to be called back into relationship with God.
9. One worry about Theory of Mind research is that it is very difficult to design experiments where the results aren't subject to underdetermination. The philosopher Robert Lurz (2011) charges that current research on primate mind-reading is at an impasse. To illustrate the problem, Lurz draws attention to experiments designed to test whether chimps have a sense that others 'see,' where 'seeing' is a particular sort of mental state that stands in contrast with merely having something within one's line of gaze, or having one's eyes oriented toward an object. A chimp might act strategically to pursue food outside its rival's line of sight because it knows its rival cannot see the food, or because it knows to pursue food whenever its rival's eyes are not oriented toward the food. On the former hypothesis the chimp reads his rival's mind by reading his behavior. On the second, the chimp just reads behavior. The question of whether the chimp attributes the mental state 'seeing' to the rival is simply underdetermined.
10. The Classical Theist who takes God to be impassible might object to the attribution of emotions to God. This worry can be avoided either with a characterization of divine emotions that is compatible with the Theory of Impassibility, or else by focusing on the emotions of Christ's human nature in the Incarnation.
11. I am grateful to Blake Hereth and Kevin Timpe for insightful comments on an earlier draft of this chapter. I am also indebted to the students and faculty of the Logos Institute for Analytical and Exegetical Theology at the University of St. Andrews for helpful comments on a seminar presentation of this same topic.

References

Adams, Marilyn McCord. *Horrendous Evils and the Goodness of God*. Ithaca, NY: Cornell University Press, 2000.

Alston, William P. *Perceiving God: The Epistemology of Religious Experience*. Ithaca, NY: Cornell University Press, 1993.

Aquinas, Thomas. *The Summa Theologica of St. Thomas Aquinas*. Translated by Fathers of the English Dominican Province. Online Edition. Newadvent.org, 1920.

Benton, Matthew A. "God and Interpersonal Knowledge." *Res Philosophica* 95.3 (2018): 421–447.

Carey, Jeremiah. "Spiritual, but Not Religious? On the Nature of Spirituality and Its Relation to Religion." *International Journal for Philosophy of Religion* 83.3 (2018): 261–269.

Catholic Church. *Catechism of the Catholic Church*. Vatican City: Libreria Editrice Vaticana, 1994.
Cheney, Dorothy L., and Robert M. Seyfarth. *Baboon Metaphysics: The Evolution of a Social Mind*, 1st ed. Chicago, IL: University of Chicago Press, 2008.
———. "The Evolutionary Origins of Friendship." *Annual Review of Psychology* 63.1 (2012): 153–177.
———. "The Evolution of Concepts About Agents." In *The Conceptual Mind: New Directions in the Study of Concepts*, edited by Eric Margolis and Stephen Laurence, 57–76. Boston, MA: MIT Press, 2015.
de Waal, Frans B. M. "A Bottom Up View of Empathy." In *The Primate Mind: Built to Connect with Other Minds*. Cambridge, MA: Harvard University Press, 2012.
de Waal, Frans B. M., and Pier Francesco Ferrari, eds. *The Primate Mind: Built to Connect with Other Minds*. Cambridge, MA: Harvard University Press, 2012.
Dougherty, Trent. *The Problem of Animal Pain: A Theodicy for All Creatures Great and Small*. New York: Palgrave Macmillan, 2014.
Durkheim, Émile. *The Elementary Forms of Religious Life*. Translated by Carol Cosman. New York: Oxford University Press, 2001.
Emery, Nathan J. and Nicola S. Clayton. "The Mentality of Crows: Convergent Evolution of Intelligence in Corvids and Apes." *Science* 306.5703 (2004): 1903–1907.
Engh, Anne L., Rebekah R. Hoffmeier, Dorothy L. Cheney, and Robert M. Seyfarth. "Who, Me? Can Baboons Infer the Target of Vocalizations?" *Animal Behaviour* 71.2 (2006): 381–387.
Green, Adam. "Reading the Mind of God (without Hebrew Lessons): Alston, Shared Attention, and Mystical Experience." *Religious Studies* 45.4 (2009): 455–470.
Hobson, Peter. "What Puts the Jointness into Joint Attention?" In *Joint Attention: Communications with Other Minds*, edited by Naomi Eilan, Christoph Hoerl, Teresa McCormack, and Johannes Roessler, 185–204. New York: Oxford University Press, 2005.
Jackson, Frank. "Epiphenomenal Qualia." *The Philosophical Quarterly* 32.127 (1982): 127–136.
Keller, Lorraine Juliano. "Divine Ineffability and Franciscan Knowledge." *Res Philosophica* 95.3 (2018): 347–370.
Keverne, E. B. 2006. "Neurobiological and Molecular Approaches to Attachment and Bonding." In *Attachment and Bonding: A New Synthesis*, edited by Carter, C. Sue, et al., 101–117. Boston, MA: MIT Press, 2006.
King, Barbara J. "Chimpanzees: Spiritual but Not Religious?" *The Atlantic*, March 29, 2016.
Kummer, Hans. *In Quest of the Sacred Baboon*. Translated by M. Ann Biederman-Thorson. Princeton, NJ: Princeton University Press, 1997.
Lurz, Robert W. *Mindreading Animals: The Debate over What Animals Know About Other Minds*. Cambridge, MA: A Bradford Book, 2011.
Panksepp, Jaak and Lucy Biven. *The Archaeology of Mind: Neuroevolutionary Origins of Human Emotions*, 1st ed. New York: W. W. Norton & Company, 2012.
Panksepp, Jaak and Jeff Burgdorf. "'Laughing' Rats and the Evolutionary Antecedents of Human Joy?" *Physiology and Behavior* 79.3 (2003): 533–547.

Pawl, Faith G. 2016. "Flourishing and Suffering in Social Creatures." In *On Earth as It Is in Heaven: Cultivating a Contemporary Theology of Creation*, edited by David Meconi, SJ., 159–173. Grand Rapids, MI: Wm. B. Eerdmans.

Prior, Helmut, Ariane Schwarz, and Onur Güntürkün. "Mirror-Induced Behavior in the Magpie (Pica Pica): Evidence of Self-Recognition." *PLoS Biology* 6.8 (2008).

Seyfarth, Robert, Joan B. Silk, and Dorothy L. Cheney. "Variation in Personality and Fitness in Wild Female Baboons." *Proceedings of the National Academy of Sciences* 109.42 (2012): 16980–16985.

Smuts, Barbara B. "Encounters with Animal Minds." In *Between Ourselves: Second-Person Issues in the Study of Consciousness*, edited by Evan Thompson. Charlottesville, VA: Imprint Academic, 2001.

———. *Sex and Friendship in Baboons*, 2nd ed. New York: Aldine Transaction, 2007.

Stump, Eleonore. *Wandering in Darkness: Narrative and the Problem of Suffering*. New York: Oxford University Press, 2010.

Westminster Assembly, Douglas F. Kelley, Philip B. Rollinson, and Frederick T. Marsh. *The Westminster Shorter Catechism in Modern English*. Phillipsburg, NJ: Presbyterian and Reformed Pub. Co., 1986.

Thomas of Celano. *The Francis Trilogy of Thomas of Celano: The Life of Saint Francis, the Remembrance of the Desire of a Soul, the Treatise on the Miracles of Saint Francis*. Hyde Park, NY: New City Press, 2004.

Van Inwagen, Peter. *The Problem of Evil: The Gifford Lectures Delivered in the University of St. Andrews in 2003*. Oxford: Clarendon Press, 2009.

8 Animal Gods

Blake Hereth

Introduction

It's ridiculous that non-human animals have received so little attention within analytic philosophical theology.[1] Doubtless this reflects widespread speciesist assumptions about them. Aquinas, for example, believed animals lacked souls and thus couldn't survive death (Dougherty 2014, 159–161). And some philosophers believe animals lack moral status altogether (Dougherty 2014, 56–76). Fortunately, the tides are changing. Philosophical theology is beginning to address issues of animal ethics (Miller 2012; Clough 2018), eschatology (Graves, Hereth, and John 2017; Harpeth 2018), and the problem of evil (Murray 2008; Dougherty 2014; Crummett 2017). But any philosophical theology is incomplete without a consideration of whether, how, and why non-human animals take their place within theology proper—that is, within the doctrine of God. This chapter defends a particular view within philosophical theology proper: the view that some non-human animals are divine. Call this view *zootheism*. If zootheism is true, then a lack of attention to non-human animals within philosophical theology is not only a glaring omission but an *impious* one, for excluding *them* is excluding *God*.

Three 'High' Views of Animals

Let's first distinguish between three possible 'high' views we might take of animals in theology proper. The views are 'high' insofar as they elevate the status of animals. We might think that some god or gods *manifest* as animals. This appears to be the view of Ancient Egyptians, whose divinities include Khepre, who appears as a beetle, and Anubis, who appears as a hybrid human-jackal; Hindus, with Ganesha, who appears as an elephant, and Vishnu, whose ten incarnations include four as animals, including a fish, a turtle, a boar, and a hybrid human-lion (Haberman 2018); Ancient Greeks, who believed Zeus and other gods appeared as animals (Thumiger 2014); and Christians, who maintain that the Holy

Spirit descended on Jesus during his baptism embodied as a dove. Let's call this *zoomorphism*, and let it be the following view:

Zoomorphism: Some divine person appears as an animal.

As a view of the status of animals, zoomorphism can qualify as a 'high' view. Christian theologians and philosophers have long believed it an honor that God would take human form (Anselm 1998; Swinburne 1994). Of course, it's possible to appear as an animal without being one. Xenophanes, for example, once remarked that if horses and oxen had a conception of God, then God would look remarkably like horses and oxen (Diels and Kranz 1952, B15). Thus, zoomorphism doesn't entail the stronger view that animals are worthy of worship or that they're divine. We can thus further distinguish between two other positions, the first of which is:

Zoolatry: Some animal is worthy of human worship.

Examples of this might include certain pagan, neo-pagan, and indigenous North American traditions in which animals are revered or worshipped either as divine or quasi-divine individuals (Kemmerer 2012). Assuming that divinity necessarily possesses other properties such as omniscience and omnipotence, and that those properties are distinct from worship-worthiness, zoolatry doesn't entail the existence of any divine animals. We can therefore identify at least one further position:

Zootheism: Some divine person is an animal.

This view, unlike zoomorphism, maintains that divine persons don't *merely* appear to be animals. They *are* animals. As divine individuals, they are worthy of worship, but also omnipotent and omniscient. This was, historically, a popular view among Greeks in Antiquity (Aston 2014).

There are, I assume, *theistic* and *deistic* variants of zootheism. We might call these *zootheism* and *zoodeism*, respectively. On a zootheist view, divine animals exist and are involved with the affairs of the world. Perhaps they created the world or sustain it, are involved with schemes of earthly redemption, and the like. On a zoodeist view, divine animals exist but aren't involved in these ways. Perhaps they play other roles, such as explaining moral facts and principles or the rationality of belief in God. The paper ahead defends a variant of zootheism/zoodeism.

Anselmian Theism

When arguing that God has some property, many philosophical arguments appeal to a principle of divine perfection. For example, when arguing that God is omniscient, it is often argued that because God is perfect and because knowledge is a good-making property with an intrinsic maxima, ontological perfection entails omniscience and thus God is omniscient (Morris 1991, 83; Flint 1998, ch. 1). Saint Anselm of Canterbury is often identified with the view that God is *ontologically* or *metaphysically* perfect, possessing all the composible properties of perfection (Anselm 1998). Anselm's views have received extensive treatment and defense elsewhere (Morris 1989; Nagasawa 2017; Rogers 2000), so I shall forego a defense of them here. Here's Thomas Morris's explication of Anselmian theism:

> It is the strongest of intuitions for the traditional theist that God is a greatest possible, or maximally perfect, being. Informing this conception are value intuitions regarding what properties are, objectively, perfections. That goodness is one of those properties is about as strong a value intuition as there can be, whose content borders on analyticity.
>
> (Morris 1989, 50)

Let's distinguish between the *procedural* commitments of Anselmianism from its *substantive* commitments. The latter includes commitments to properties like simplicity, omniscience, and omnipresence, whereas the former is more basic. It includes only a commitment to the view that God is necessarily maximally perfect. Call this basic commitment Anselmianism.

Anselmianism: Necessarily, God is a maximally perfect being.

I shall assume Anselmianism in this chapter. All of my argumentation relies on the view that God is a perfect being, and I draw inferences from this perfection as other philosophers have done. While I am uninterested in defending Anselmianism from objections, I shall endeavor to defend the inferences I draw from it. If my arguments succeed, Anselmianism entails zootheism.

The Power Argument

Principles of Fair Power Distribution

The first argument for zootheism concerns a fair distribution of power. To get the argument started, I'll begin with a highly plausible claim:

Divine Asymmetry: If God is both omnipotent and a member of group G, and if S is neither a member of group G nor omnipotent (and if no one else outside of G is omnipotent), then G has a decisive power asymmetry over S.

Everyone should believe this claim. Omnipotence entails possessing, at the very least, all the powers it's logically possible to have. Some, like Cartesians, think it entails having even more powers than that. But even if you think omnipotence means having *less* than all the powers it's logically possible to have, it certainly entails having the *most* powers of everyone with powers. That is, we should all believe that if God is omnipotent, then no one is *more powerful* than God, and individuals who are less than omnipotent have *less power* than God. And, of course, we think that omnipotence entails more than a marginal power advantage; it entails a decisive advantage, even over those who are very powerful.

Let's move away from God for a moment and talk about political philosophy. As it so happens in the world, individuals have powers. They can vote, express their views, engage in rational reflection, move their limbs to lift, push, and pull, and coerce people to do what they want. These powers are distributed unevenly in our world, either by nature or design. Sometimes we think it's *unjust*, or at least *less than fully just*, when individuals have unequal power. This is true, for example, in cases where individuals have equal moral interests but unequal power over them. To give one such example, consider:

> *Maleficent Whites*: The white citizens of Terra make up 50% of Terra's population, but fully control the city's politics. The mayor is white, the city council is white, and all the eligible voters are white. White politicians and voters decide how and when elections are conducted, who is eligible for them, who can acquire a driver's license, and which neighborhoods are closer in proximity to the city's dangerous waste dumps and volatile gas lines. All of this, of course, has an intentionally, disproportionately negative impact on Terra's non-white population, none of whom consented to the current arrangement of power.

The actions of the white citizens of Terra are clearly impermissible. They culpably violate the rights of the non-white residents of Terra, which is unfair. Now consider a different example, which I'll call:

> *Beneficent Whites*: The power dynamics in the city of Stella are the same in Terra: White residents have decisive power and make up 50% of the city's population. But *unlike* Terra, the white rulers of Stella are beneficent: They make decisions that benefit white and non-white citizens alike, and benefit them equally. Thus, non-white residents are full citizens who can vote, speak their minds, and live where they please. But as in Terra, the non-white residents never consented to this arrangement of power.

As a city, Stella is a clear improvement on Terra. The rights of non-white residents aren't violated at all, much less routinely and systematically. In fact, their rights are *respected* and thoroughly defended by Stella's white rulers.

We might even say that there's nothing *unfair* about the arrangement of power in Stella. Suppose, for example, that Stella used to be solely white and that a provisional (and white) government was arranged at that time, voted upon unanimously by the residents of Stella. The rules in Stella are such that the existing government will remain in place unless 51% or more of voters elect a new government. Since each and every white citizen votes to elect the existing white government, and since they make up 50% of the citizenry, the white government never changes hands. Plausibly, a government that's elected in this manner isn't unfair.[2] Nor are the decisions made by the white government of Stella unfair: they respect and defend, and never violate, the rights of any citizen.

Still, there's something rotten in the city of Stella. Although non-white voters have their interests well-represented, fairness concerns not simply *what* is decided but *who* is deciding. And although the white government is democratically elected and followed a fair process, the exclusion of non-white citizens from power in Stella is less than maximally fair. Said another way, although it's not unfair that the government is white, it would be *fairer still* if the government wasn't all-white.[3] This is intrinsically fairer because self-representation is fairer than other-representation. Said another way: paternalism is presumptively less fair than non-paternalism between individuals sufficiently capable of caring for their own welfare, or whose welfare isn't threatened. But it's also fairer because of the possibility of abusing power. In the event that the white rulers of Stella became less beneficent—perhaps coming to resemble the white rulers of Terra—the non-white citizens of Stella would be at a decisive (and unfair) disadvantage. Whereas the actual misuse of a skewed power distribution is unfair, it's nevertheless better (because it's fairer) to have a less skewed and more equal distribution of power. So, although there's perhaps nothing unfair about the government of Stella, it's not ideal from the viewpoint of fairness. Generalizing this point, we should say that:

> **Equal Power Presumption:** If A and B have morally equal interests concerning X and their (pre-consensual) distribution of power over X is maximally fair, then A and B have *presumptive equal power* over X.[4]

The equal power is 'presumptive' because it can be forfeited.[5] For example, suppose an ideal society is constructed such that white and non-white citizens have equal power, but white citizens wield their power unjustly against non-whites. In that case, it seems less than maximally fair, and indeed unfair, that the perpetrating white citizens maintain their equal power. But where morally equal interests hold, the *presumption* of equal power is entailed by maximal fairness. I also note that the fairness of this power distribution is *pre-consensual* because if A and B consent to a different distribution of power, that may change which distribution is fairest.[6] Thus, the Equal Power Presumption is about which distributions are fair prior to consensual arrangements.[7]

Let's consider two additional claims about fairness. Both concern cases in which moral interests are not equally shared. The first concerns what maximal fairness entails in cases where there are unequal but comparable moral interests. In those cases, both parties have a moral interest over X but they have those interests to different degrees. To imagine such a case, consider the case of:

> *Bedroom Window*: Jacobi and Hargun live together. One day during the spring, the carbon monoxide levels reach dangerous levels in the house, prompting the need for either Jacobi's bedroom window to be opened or Hargun's bedroom window to be opened. Jacobi is mildly photosensitive and thus prefers his window to remain shut, but Hargun has severe allergies during the spring and will suffer more than Jacobi if his window is opened.

In this case, both Jacobi and Hargun have an interest in *their* bedroom window remaining closed and opening their roommate's bedroom window instead. But Hargun has the stronger interest between the two of them, since his allergic reaction is worse for him than Jacobi's (mild) photosensitivity is for him. Thus, when debating whose window to open, Hargun's preferences should take priority over Jacobi's. Because of this, maximal fairness entails that Hargun should be empowered to open Jacobi's window, but not vice versa. There are other, but more controversial examples of this. For example, many think that potential gestators have stronger bodily interests than non-gestators (other than, perhaps, fetuses), and thus that gestators should have proportionally greater say and influence over their reproductive options (Little 1999; Denis 2008). Call this underlying principle the

> **Unequal Power Presumption:** If either A has a moral interest concerning X and B doesn't, or if A has a sufficiently greater interest concerning X than B, and if their (pre-consensual) distribution of power over X is maximally fair, then A will have *proportionately greater power* than B over X.

I think both the Equal Power Presumption and the Unequal Power Presumption are true. But even if you reject them, you should accept one further principle, which I'll call the

Shared Power Presumption: If A and B both have moral interests concerning X and their (pre-consensual) distribution of power over X is *maximally fair*, then *neither A nor B has presumptive decisive power* over X.

If, for example, A has *decisive* power over X (and B doesn't), then B lacks meaningful power over X. But that's less than maximally fair because B's interests concerning X are meaningful. This is true even if we distinguish between *having* decisive power over X and *using* decisive power over X. Thus, even if the non-white citizens of Stella have *greater* interests than the white citizens, this at most entitles them to *greater* political representation on (for example) the city council. It wouldn't entitle them to total control of the city council or veto-proof majorities.

From Principles to Zootheism

Let's now return to the first claim I made in this section:

Divine Asymmetry: If God is both omnipotent and a member of group G, and if S is neither a member of group G nor omnipotent (and if no one else outside of G is omnipotent), then G has a decisive power asymmetry over S.

Suppose now that God became incarnate as a human (and thus is a member of the group Human) but *didn't* incarnate as a non-human animal (and thus isn't a member of the group Animal). Let's also suppose that no non-human animal is either divine, human, or omnipotent. Assuming that many, if not most, members of both Human and Animal have moral interests, it follows that the group Human has *decisive* power over Animal.[8] But this is less than maximally fair, according to the Shared Power Presumption. If you think even some members of Animal have even some proportionately strong or equally strong moral interests with members of Human, you'll also think this power distribution violates the Equal Power Presumption.

Such a distribution is incompatible with an essential divine property: *being maximally fair*. We should think not only that God avoids being *unfair*, which is the minimum standard of fairness, but that God is instead the exemplar of moral perfection. This property requires not only that God be fair with existing individuals and groups, but that representatives of those individuals and groups exist within the Godhead.[9] Moreover, it's not enough for those individuals to exist *contingently* within the Godhead, for contingent membership in the Godhead is contingent power in the Godhead and contingent power is contingent maximal fairness. Thus, animal members must enjoy *necessary* membership in the Godhead and share eternally in the Godhead's power. It's not enough for there to be animal divines who come into existence whenever non-divine animals exist, and then cease existing when animals disappear. There must be no divine individual who possesses decisive power over a divine animal. The Godhead, therefore, must at every time come 'pre-equipped' with a membership that covers all possible interest-possessing creatures, including animals. Where moral interests are equal or roughly equal, the power must be equally or roughly equally shared.

Which Animals Are in the Godhead?

What animals have a place in the Godhead? I'll make four speculative comments on this. I'll briefly support each of my comments.

The first is that such animals must be *sentient* and *possess some degree of intentionality*. The former is necessary for having moral interests whatsoever, and the latter is essential to *sharing* power (Cochrane 2018, ch. 2). Those incapable of exercising intentional power are also incapable of sharing it, and principles like the Shared Power Principle assume a capacity for some minimal exercise of power. It's worth noting that this is a very low cognitive bar: the ability to choose, whether explicitly or tacitly, one state of affairs over another. Call this *agency* or *executive power*. This doesn't require deliberative (or reflective) agency, but rather the kind of agency characterized by having preferences or desires (Donaldson and Kymlicka 2011, 112). These animals act on the basis of reasons, whether propositional or merely perceptual. As Jeff Sebo (2017, 6–8) argues, many non-human animals have the latter kind of agency.[10] Dogs, for example, exercise perceptual agency when they place their faces in piles of food because they view the food as *to-be-eaten*, or a lion experiencing "her cubs as *to-be-protected*" (Sebo 2017, 11).

Second, divine animals *don't* have to be moral agents in either the propositional or perceptual senses (Sebo 2017). Many animals have moral interests, including very strong ones, without possessing moral agency of any kind, and excluding them from sharing power in the Godhead on that basis would be less than maximally fair.[11]

Third, I take no stance on whether maximal fairness requires *maximal membership* in the Godhead (i.e., whether each and every animal is in the Godhead).[12] One natural reaction to the Shared Power Presumption is that it entails maximal membership because particular individuals have particular interests and distributing power to interest *types* over interest *tokens* thereby permits some individuals to have decisive power over other individuals with the same interest type, which is less than maximally fair. To see what I mean, consider citizenship theory: if A and B have morally significant interests, then the *starting place* for A and B is to be empowered and for neither A nor B to have decisive power over the other. If maximal fairness requires that each and every individual with interests be divine, then you and I are divine, as are our animal companions. On the other hand, if maximal fairness requires only that *interest kinds* be represented in the Godhead, then it's enough that there is a divine individual who shares our interest-kind (e.g., our interest against suffering or our interest against heteronormativity).

Fourth, there's reason to prefer either a social monotheist or polytheist variant of zootheism over a strict monotheist view. I'll first explain the models. The first is a *strict monotheist* view on which there's a single divine individual who's uniquely God and who instantiates the various metaphysical properties (e.g., kinds, interests, and perspectives) required by divine moral perfection. The second is a *social monotheist* view on which multiple divine individuals who jointly constitute God and who instantiate the relevant, perfect-making properties. The third is a *polytheist* view on which there are multiple divine individuals, each of whom is God, who individually instantiate divine perfection. I'll briefly defend my view that there's reason to prefer either a social monotheist or polytheist model over a strict monotheist one.

The first reason to prefer either a social monotheist or polytheist variant of zootheism is that a single divine individual can't instantiate supreme love. In "Trinity and Polytheism," Wierenga develops and defends a social model of the Christian Trinity. The central idea of social trinitarianism is that the oneness of God can be explained by appeal to social or relational properties that the members share. For Wierenga, this means showing that there can be three divine persons without there being three gods. He makes the following proposal:

> That is, something is *a* God just in case it *is* God. The *Quicunque Vult*, however, says, in effect, that something can be a divine Person without being identical with God. One might have uncritically been inclined to accept [that being divine entails being God], but the *Quicunque Vult* denies it. One thing I think reflection on the doctrine of the Trinity does is to call into question such uncritical acceptance. Perhaps, in fact, a thing is identical with God just in case it is a trinity of divine Persons.
>
> (Wierenga 2004, 291)

As motivation for this claim, Wierenga appeals to an argument by Richard of St. Victor that "divine goodness and love requires that there be more than one divine person" (Wierenga 2004, 291). The argument has also been defended by Richard Swinburne (1988). If a divine person loved only themselves, they would lack "fullness of charity" (Richard 1979, 375) that comes from loving others. Moreover, since "the existence of a third" divine person "is sufficient to permit divine persons to share in supreme love," there's no need for more than three divine persons (Wierenga 2004, 291). Reconstructed, the argument goes like this:

Richard of St. Victor's Love Argument for Trinitarianism

1. If God exists, then God is supremely loving.
2. If the God is supremely loving, then God shares in supreme love.
3. If God shares in supreme love, then God (a) loves themself, (b) individually loves another person equally worthy of love, and (c) jointly loves yet another person equally worthy of love.
4. Necessarily, if God is worthy of love and some distinct individual X is equally worthy of love, then X is a Divine Person.
5. Therefore, if God exists, then there are at least three Divine Persons.

The central premise is (3). As a premise, it doesn't require much to believe it. It's hard to see how supreme love is compatible with a lack of self-love. Those who don't love themselves could love *better* than they do. We often think, for example, that those who fail to engage in self-care are making a mistake, and it's a mistake of love. Similarly, we often think that those who love *only* themselves lack supreme love. That's true in cases where self-love becomes self-obsession, vanity, or selfishness, but even virtuous self-love is inadequate for supreme love where when there's no one else to love. In a universe emptied of all but one person, that person, no matter how much they love themself, lacks a kind of love that's crucial for supreme love. Finally, it's a great good of love that two individuals who love each other *share* their love with another. This establishes both cooperation between the two towards the third, and selflessness on the part of the second. What social monotheist and polytheist models have that strict monotheism lacks are multiple divine individuals who can instantiate this supreme love. The Love Argument strikes me as very strong, and thus there's very strong reason to prefer social monotheism or polytheism over strict monotheism.

The second reason to prefer either a social monotheist or polytheist model is because strict monotheism can't accommodate the various identities that the Power Argument supports. Because the Power Argument supports not only the inclusion of non-human animals within the Godhead, but also disabled individuals, people of color, queer individuals, women, etc., it supports invariably many identities within the Godhead. This raises the worry that no single individual can instantiate *all* of these identities, or at least not at once. For any divine individual G and time t, either G is disabled at t or G isn't disabled at t; and if G isn't disabled at t, then non-disabled individuals have decisive power over disabled individuals at t, which is less than perfectly just.

Limiting Power

Since the Power Argument supports the existence of multiple divine individuals, either within one Godhead or as separate gods, how is the power distributed between divine individuals? What's a maximally fair distribution of power between them? Let's begin with an example from William Rowe (1979, 337):

> *Suffering Fawn*: In some distant forest lightning strikes a dead tree, resulting in a forest fire. In the fire a fawn is trapped, terribly burned, and lies in terrible agony for several days before death relieves its suffering.

Imagine now that two divine individuals, a non-human animal (Fawn God) and a human (Human God), *foresee* Rowe's suffering fawn.[13] Let's also suppose that Fawn God and Human God have species-typical intelligence, and that (as a result) Fawn God is less intelligent than Human God. Suppose now that Human God dislikes fawns and is happy to see them suffer, and so is unwilling to rescue Rowe's fawn despite having the power to do so. Alternatively, suppose that Human God *is* compassionate and has the power to save Rowe's fawn, but Fawn God lacks this power because of their cognitive limitations.

Under either scenario, Human God has powers that Fawn God doesn't. In the first case, Human God is able to forego saving Rowe's fawn for speciesist reasons—a power Fawn God apparently lacks. If Human God refuses to save the fawn for this reason, this also goes against the moral interests of Fawn God who, being a fawn, has an interest in avoiding discrimination against fawns—a moral interest that Human God doesn't share, at least not to the same degree. This would violate the Unequal Power Presumption. In the second case where Human God is empowered to save Rowe's fawn but Fawn God isn't, there's no discrimination at play here. So, we might suppose that Fawn God has no special interest in the saving of Rowe's fawn, and thus that Human God and Fawn God have *equal interest* in the salvation of Rowe's fawn. But if that's true, then the Equal Power Presumption tells us that Human God and Fawn God should have *equal power* with respect to saving Rowe's fawn, which they don't. Thus, maximal or perfect fairness requires either that *both* Human God and Fawn God can save Rowe's fawn, or that *neither* can. Which view should we prefer?[14]

Generally speaking, there's reason to think that the powers of some divine individuals need to be limited. There's *also* reason to think that the powers of some divine animals need to be enhanced. As I pointed out in section Which Animals Are in the Godhead," those incapable of exercising intentional power are also incapable of sharing it, and thus the fair power principles I've defended concern those capable of sharing forms of intentional power. This simultaneously entails the inclusion of animals like fawns and dogs who possess executive power, and the exclusion of animals like wasps and plankton who lack executive power. Perhaps Fawn God has executive power and can, merely by wishing it, save

Rowe's fawn, which is also something Human God can do. If I'm right that *all* divine individuals have some form of executive power (or agency), however limited, then in cases where they all have equal moral interests with respect to X, one divine individual has power over X if and only if every other divine individual has equal power over X. Thus, if Human God can save Rowe's fawn, so can Fawn God.

I have assumed that God's power is metaphysically decisive: if God wills the salvation of Rowe's fawn, then it follows that Rowe's fawn is saved. But that's a case where God wills F and F occurs. What about cases where one can will F only by willing E, but willing E is cognitively complex? In that case, Fawn God might be unable to will F because it requires the cognitively complex willing of E, but Human God *can* will G (and thus can will F). I am inclined to think that there's no possible case like this: that there either are no precondition cases or that, if there are, then willing F entails willing E whether or not it's clear to the agent that ~E → ~F. On that view, Fawn God isn't at a power disadvantage with respect to F even if they can't (directly) will E. But suppose there can be cases like this. Or, at the very least, suppose that willing E itself is cognitively complex.[15] If either of these claims is true, then we need a new path to fair power. One tempting suggestion is to exclude cognitively complex individuals from the Godhead. But that would be less than maximally just, since some cognitively complex individuals share equally strong moral interests with cognitively less complex individuals. The same would be true if cognitively less complex individuals have their cognitive abilities enhanced (e.g., if willing E requires knowledge of particle physics and Fawn God knows particle physics), since then there wouldn't be cognitively less complex or even cognitively disabled members of the Godhead. Nor is it a solution to exclude cognitively *more complex* individuals from the Godhead. So, if we are to include them all while excluding greater power, then those members of the Godhead capable of forming cognitively complex aims are *unable to actualize those aims*. That is, they are able to intend those aims, but they can't bring them about.

The chief alternative to this position is that such members of the Godhead *can't even intend* those aims, but has the metaphysical power to bring them about. For example, a member of the Godhead could *accidentally* bring about things they can't intend. But I think we have at least two good reasons to reject this alternative view. First, this latter view makes less sense of common theistic beliefs about divine praiseworthiness and blameworthiness. If God can intend X but not actualize it, then God can be praiseworthy or blameworthy for intending (or failing to intend) X. But if God can't even intend X, then God is neither praiseworthy nor blameworthy for intending (or failing to intend) X. Second, this view needlessly limits God's power. The general principle here is that if A is unable to intend X (but could accidentally do X) while B is able to intend X (but can't actualize X), then A has weaker agency than B. If you can't even intend X, then you could at best do X accidentally, and accidents can't be attributed to an *agent's* strength. While it might seem that B's agency is weaker than A's because B's intentions can be frustrated whereas A's can't, which seems like a genuine difference in power, the fact is that A can neither intend nor actualize X whereas B can at least intend X. We want to preserve maximal agency within the Godhead, compatible with the (prioritized) moral perfection within the Godhead (Funkhouser 2006). That means preferring a view on which an agent's *actions* are limited but their *intentions* aren't.

The Incarnation Argument

Morally Proper Incarnations

The second argument for zootheism is about incarnations. More specifically, it's an argument grounded in traditional arguments *for* an incarnation (typically a Christian one). Here's how that argument generally goes:

> Because God truly loves us, and loves us perfectly, God is not content to leave us alone. God desires to share in our experiences, our joys and our sorrows, and to meet us where we are. Doing that as a distant but sympathetic bystander is insufficient for maximal love and sympathy, since there is a great chasm between God's interests and our interests. Thus, the best way to share our moral interests is to share in our nature and become one of us, to take on our flesh and to live among us—that is, to become incarnate.

Versions of this argument have been given by Saint Anselm of Canterbury (1998), Richard Swinburne (1994, 216–220, 2010, 40),[16] Alvin Plantinga (2004, 2013), Marilyn McCord Adams's *Christ and Horrors* (2008, 53–79), and others. I'll assume that this fundamental view of God is correct. That is, I'll assume that a morally supreme God would indeed become incarnate to share in the plight of the oppressed. It's not enough for God to become just *anyone*, therefore. As black liberation theologian James Cone argues, a morally supreme God would come to identify *particularly with the oppressed*:

> The blackness of Christ clarifies the definition of him as the *Incarnate One*. In him God becomes oppressed humanity and thus reveals that the achievement of full humanity is consistent with divine being. The human being was not created to be a slave, and the appearance of God in Christ gives us the possibility of freedom. By becoming a black person, God discloses that blackness is not what the world says it is. Blackness is a manifestation of the being of God in that it reveals

that neither divinity nor humanity resides in white definitions but in liberation from captivity.

(Cone 2018, 128)

Extending this line of thinking to non-human animals, who also suffer due both to natural harms and to human-caused harms, is only natural. As Nicola Hoggard Creegan observes, "God in Christ suffers with all that suffers, human and non-human alike" (2013, 60). She continues:

> Nevertheless, in the coming of the Christ, in incarnation and in Spirit, God has come very close to us and has born our suffering and taken this suffering into the very being of who God is. We do not suffer alone. There is a growing understanding that in taking on human flesh God was also drawing close to all flesh, for our bodies are studded with the signs of the animals out of which we have emerged. Read in this light it is significant that Jesus was born in a stable, with animals perhaps for company.
>
> (Creegan 2013, 79)

If God suffers with non-human animals without *becoming* one, is that problematic? Theologian David Clough motivates the view that there's something problematic about God incarnating *only* as a human:

> For in the scandalous particularity of God becoming incarnate in the man, Jesus of Nazareth, and defeating sin and death through the cross of Calvary and resurrection from the town, it seems that all laborers up to this point have been in vain. Here, it seems, is the final and decisive evidence that God is concerned with one species, rather than the multitude of creatures I have been seeking theologically to remember, and that Christianity will never be able to escape a blinkered preoccupation with only one kind of animal: God became human.
>
> (2013, 81)

Clough continues:

> One possible theological move immediately presents itself. If God became human for human beings, perhaps God became or will become dolphin for dolphins, gorilla for gorillas, ostrich for ostriches, herring for herrings, ant for ants and plankton for plankton. We know nothing of such incarnations—why should we?—but our ignorance is not a disproof of the thesis. Such a theory of multiple incarnations would allow us to keep Jesus Christ as God's human project, while remaining open to the idea that other animals may also have their Messiah.
>
> (2013, 82)

Although Clough ultimately rejects non-human animal incarnations, he argues for its status as a serious theological proposal and notes that the motivation for such a view is clear.[17] Were God to descend from heaven and incarnate as a 21st-century white, male, cisgender, heterosexual billionaire, it's doubtful God would be *fully* partaking in our joys and sorrows or making (all of) our interests God's interests. This is because these natures are *socially privileged* in the sense that to occupy them is to distance yourself from certain kinds of oppression. Insofar as God's aim is to join us in our oppression, God must incarnate as an oppressed person. To do otherwise is to identify with creaturely oppression only minimally. This is why, in the Christian tradition, Jesus didn't incarnate as a Roman ruler or a child of an influential family, but instead was born a person of color to a low-income Jewish family under imperial occupation. But the same is true of non-human animals. They are oppressed in ways most humans are not, and God displays a lack of solidarity with them unless God suffers *as* they suffer. This requires God to incarnate as a non-human animal. Just as the world needs not only a white savior but a *black* savior, so also the world needs not only a human savior but an *animal* savior.

Fitting Incarnations

> First, human nature is such a good thing that given that he has created it, it is a fitting nature for God to adopt. There is in humanity a unique mixture of the rational (humans see and pursue the good as such), the sensory (have sensations, and are influenced by nonrational desires), and the physical (operate through bodies situated in a beautiful law-governed universe). It would be appropriate for its creator to put on such a nature, as it is for a designer to wear a coat he has designed. Thereby he evinces solidarity with his creation.
> (Swinburne 1994, 218)

According to Swinburne, this is an explanation endorsed by both Augustine and Aquinas. It's a curious explanation for an incarnation, but not one I'm ready to reject. I'll simply note that if these are reasons for adopting human nature, they are also good reasons for adopting other animal natures, all of which God has also created (and all of which are therefore *good* on this view). All animals have bodies, most have sensations, and many possess substantive forms of rationality. Swinburne, like Augustine and Aquinas before him, maintain that humans *uniquely* possess this mixture, but that's problematic. If it's meant to exclude animals on the grounds that they lack a kind of propositional or moral agency and are thus 'inappropriate' or 'unfitting' vessels for God, the same should be said of cognitively disabled humans who also lack these capacities.[18] I also have my doubts that *all* non-human animals lack the requisite cognitive capacity Swinburne mentions: seeing and pursuing the good for its own sake. Instances of non-human animal empathy, for example, are good evidence for the conclusion that many animals have the kind of moral agency where recognition and pursuit of the good is actual (de Waal 2016, 132–133; Rowlands 2012, ch. 9). And, at any rate, the lack of these properties is not *essential* to non-human animalkind anymore than its presence is essential to humankind. Thus, even if it were 'inappropriate' or 'unfitting' for God to incarnate as a cognitively typical animal, this is no impediment whatsoever to incarnating as a cognitively *atypical* animal.

There's also reason to doubt that cognitive abilities like believing, intending, knowing, and the like are *comparative* cognitive perfections to their cognitive counterparts.[19] As one ancient and early critic of Christianity, Celsus, remarks,

> And if it is said that human beings are better than the irrational animals because we live in cities and occupy prominent offices and the like—I say this proves nothing: ants and bees do as much; or at any rate, the bees elect leaders and a stratified social system of leaders, attendants, servants; they have their weapons and wage their ways, slay the vanquished, build cities and even suburbs. They share in the work of their society and punish the idlers—that is to say, in driving out the drones to fend for themselves. And the ants are no less clever, for they pick out the unripened fruit for themselves to keep it throughout the year—and set a place apart as a graveyard for those of their number who have died. Indeed, the very ants meet in council to plan strategy; this is why they do not lose their way. They have a fully developed intelligence—and it seems they have as well a clear-cut notion of certain universal laws, and even a voice to make the experience of their learning known to others of their kind.
> (Celsus 1987, 83–84)

Arguably, the comparative perfection of any cognitive system depends upon how well it fulfills its cognitive design plan. Thus, if cognitive system C1 is tasked with *A*-ing and C2 is tasked with *B*-ing, and if C1's success rate is 60% and C2's is 90%, then C2 is a comparatively better design. Maybe this isn't the *only* measure of comparative cognitive perfection. For example, the *quality* of the thing sought by cognitive systems might make a difference to a system's perfection. But even if justified beliefs or the successful seeking of moral knowledge is more intrinsically worthwhile than designing a hive (as bees do) or knowing precisely how to make a long-distance flight without external instruments (as pigeons do), the cognitive *successes* of the latter abilities ought to be part of an *overall* calculation of comparative cognitive perfection. And it's not obvious to me that the typical human cognition will emerge victorious in the contest, and this challenge was of serious concern to early Christian philosophers and theologians, such as Augustine and Origen (Miller 2018, 43). Celsus concludes with the following remarks:

> But of course, the Christians postulate that everyone is a sinner, so that they are able to extend their appeal to the public at large. Now, it is perhaps the case that everyone is inclined to sin—though not everyone does sin. But if it is the case that everyone sins, why did their god not merely call mankind in general to salvation rather than the wicked? I mean, *why on earth this preference for sinners?*
> (Celsus 1987, 75, emphasis mine)

I don't think Celsus's argument succeeds, but a more successful variant of it helps make the case for a non-human animal incarnation. Within God's creation, there are sinners and non-sinners alike. The vast majority of non-human animals, for example, aren't sinners. A God who incarnated to show solidarity with the sinful while ignoring the non-sinful is problematic because the non-sinful struggle and also suffer. Non-human animals are a profoundly oppressed group, and to prioritize loving and showing solidarity with the sinful—including, in most instances, the *perpetrators* of unjust animal suffering—is to show greater solidarity with the oppressors than with the oppressed.[20]

Ways to Incarnate

There are three possible ways a divine person might incarnate as an animal and dwell among us on Earth: by merely *appearing* as an animal, by *becoming* an animal, and by *preexisting* as an animal. Call these possibilities the Appearance View, the Transformation View, and the Preexistence View, respectively. I'll evaluate each of these in turn and defend the Preexistence View.[21] Thus, my view is *not* simply a defense of the view that God might incarnate in multiple forms (Pawl 2016a, 2016b), though I think that view is true. Indeed, I think we should expect *each and every* divine individual to incarnate. Instead, it's a defense of the view that at least one divine person is *eternally* an animal.

Let's start with the Appearance View. As a view, it's analogous to the ancient Christian heresy Docetism according to which Jesus didn't become human but merely appeared as one. There are, as I see it, two problems with such a view. First, as the Christian tradition has emphasized, it's incompatible with divine perfection. If God merely appears as one of us, then God doesn't *share* in our struggles and sufferings, and is therefore less than maximally sympathetic. Second, if God merely appears as an animal without taking on their oppression, then God engages in a kind of 'animalface': a privileged individual deciding to pass as an oppressed individual. This is morally non-ideal, if not impermissible, and thus incompatible with the divine moral nature.[22]

The Transformation View lacks the deficiencies of the Appearance View. On this view, God wasn't an animal before but becomes one. The purpose of doing so is to share in animal life and animal suffering, to identify with animals as unjustly oppressed individuals. But the Transformation View has problems of its own, the first of which is appropriation. Prior to incarnating, God either *was* oppressed in morally similar ways to animals, or God *wasn't* oppressed in morally similar ways to animals.[23] If the latter is true, then by becoming an animal, God does something morally inappropriate by *appropriating* animal suffering. God, as a person of privilege, takes on animal nature—yet another kind of animalface.[24,25] If, on the other hand, God *was* oppressed in much the same way as animals prior to incarnating, then this problem disappears because God doesn't appropriate their oppression, but is already with them in the struggle. But animal oppression is itself unlike other kinds of oppression, such as ableism or racism, although these forms of oppression sometimes intersect (Monroe 2018; Mills 2015). So, although one may be oppressed in other ways, one doesn't experience the kind of oppression animals experience unless one *is* an animal. Thus, if God was oppressed in ways morally similar to animals prior to incarnating, then God *was* an animal prior to incarnating. The second objection to the Transformation View is this: if God became an animal but wasn't previously an animal, then God wasn't always sharing in animal life and struggles, and therefore wasn't always maximally an ally in their plight. It's better to sympathize with, fight for, and commiserate with the oppressed when they're first oppressed than to sympathize, fight, or commiserate with them later. And it's better not just in some generic sense, but with respect to *justice*. The longer God occupies a particular position of comparative privilege while the oppressed suffer under that privilege, the less just God is.

This brings us to the final view, the Preexistence View. On this view, God is, but never became, an animal. Thus, God was always an animal. Assuming the plausible premises that each and every divine individual is always at least a member of God and that God exists necessarily (Rogers 2000), it follows that there's a necessarily existing divine individual who is also an animal. That's zootheism. Moreover, since theism plausibly entails animal incarnation which plausibly entails zootheism, theism entails zootheism.

Final Remarks and a Religious Experience

This chapter defends the speculative view that some non-human animals may be divine. This is a thesis about divine membership. As one example, Christians have historically believed that exactly three persons are divine, and one of them (the Holy Spirit) is often represented as a dove. Perhaps the Holy Spirit *is* a dove—a particular dove who is also divine. I called this view zootheism and I distinguished it from other, related views, such as zoomorphism (the view that divine persons sometimes appear as non-human animals) and zoolatry (the view that non-human animals are proper objects of worship). Next, I offered two arguments for zootheism: the Power Argument and the Incarnation Argument. According to the first argument, God's perfect justice entails a presumption of shared power such that among two or more persons with interests, none of them has *decisive* power over the other. Since non-human animals have interests but would be decisively outpowered if God is omnipotent and there are no divine non-human animals, it follows that there are divine non-human animals. The Incarnation Argument says that a perfectly just and loving God would incarnate as an oppressed person to share in the suffering of the oppressed. Not only that, but God would *avoid* incarnating (exclusively) as someone possessing privilege over other groups. If God incarnated exclusively as a human in a speciesist world like ours, God would thereby incarnate as a privileged individual and fail to join (and identify closely with) non-human animals in their suffering. After considering several ways God might incarnate as a non-human animal—by merely *appearing*, or *becoming*, or *preexisting* as one—I concluded that only the third option, the Preexistence View, is satisfactory. Since the Preexistence View entails zootheism, zootheism is true.

As I conclude, I would like to reflect, briefly, on my own experiences with non-human animals. I suspect experiences such as these are widely held and could furnish further arguments for zootheism, though I won't develop those arguments here. The theologian C.S. Lewis once remarked that humans will be deified in such a way that, if we knew them in their deified state, we'd be tempted to worship them. He writes,

> It is a serious thing to live in a society of possible gods and goddesses, to remember that the dullest and most uninteresting person you talk to may one day be a creature which, if you saw it now, you would be strongly tempted to worship.
>
> (Lewis 2001, 45)

I confess that I've experienced a temptation like that, but rarely with humans. My deepest sources of moral inspiration—experiences of sharp shame, of caring, and of desiring to be better—have arisen from my interactions with the moral qualities of *animals*. I have approached many animals, such as my late, canine sister Margaret, with moral awe. I found in her, and sometimes in other animals, a moral purity unmatched elsewhere. And I am not alone in this reaction to animals, as other philosophers point out:

> People who have risked their lives to save others—running into a burning house, jumping into a freezing river, breaking cover to help a fallen comrade—often say they did not stop to reflect. They

responded directly to a situation of need in which they perceived they could act. We consider these people moral heroes. Moral action is not just about doing things out of commitments to abstract justifications; it is about moral character and action, and motivations such as love and compassion and fear and loyalty.

(Donaldson and Kymlicka 2011, 116)

In 2006 a beagle named Belle became the first nonhuman animal to receive the annual VITA Wireless Samaritan Award. This award recognizes individuals in the U.S. who use their "wireless phones to save lives, stop crime and help in other emergency situations." Belle had received special training to recognize when her diabetic owner's blood sugar dropped to dangerous levels and to respond. One morning when her owner slipped into a diabetic seizure, Belle retrieved his wireless phone and pushed the preprogrammed button to dial emergency medical services. "I am convinced that if Belle wasn't with me that morning, I wouldn't be alive today," her owner claimed. "Belle is more than just a life-saver; she's my best friend."

(Miller 2012, 1)

Like some other non-human animals, Margaret's kindness, her old soul, her compassionate cuddles, and her soft but eager yearn for affection betray a *godlike* nature. These religious experiences are not so easily discounted without begging the question against zootheism, at least not by theists who accept the possibility of religious experiences.[26] Perhaps my temptations to feel as though Margaret was as close to God as I have ever come and to worship her were not so misguided after all. Perhaps Margaret was simply one incarnation of the divine. Christians have for centuries offered a basic argument for the conclusion that Christ was divine: that Christ was profoundly good and did no wrong (Davis 2009). That sounds like Margaret to me.

Notes

1. Unless otherwise noted, "animals" refers to "non-human animals" throughout this chapter. I prefer the shorthand for purposes of clarity and concision only. Nothing of normative significance is being implied by my usage.
2. If you think *term limits* are a requirement for any just state, modify the example so that new elections are held but the white voters always elect a *new* white government. Term limits won't guarantee *who* acquires power, only that someone new does.
3. If you think it's *unfair* and not merely *less fair*, then an even stronger version of the Power Argument applies.
4. For those who think it's unfair (and not merely less fair) for A and B to have unequal power, you should still accept the Equal Power Presumption. If you think it's not only less fair, but *unfair* than A and B have unequal power over X where their moral interests concerning X are equal, then you'll certainly

think maximal fairness entails equal power since you'll think even minimal fairness entails it.
5. It can't be waived since the fairness is *pre*-consensual, and waiving rights is intrinsically consensual. Thus, the Equal Power Presumption is about the *initial* conditions of fairness.
6. Then again, this may change nothing. It seems to me at least conceptually possible that two or more individuals might consent to a less than maximally fair arrangement, since at least some facts about fairness (as we've seen) are agreement-independent. But I'll avoid making any firm commitments on this here.
7. The distinction between pre-consensual and post-consensual fairness won't make a direct difference to my argument for zootheism, but a pre-consensual variant of the Equal Power Presumption strikes me as the less presumptuous, and so more plausible, principle.
8. On my view, inclusion in the Godhead tracks *interest* kinds and not *natural* kinds, although I accept that kinds of interest might be correlated with natural kinds.
9. Edward Wierenga makes a similar argument for the conclusion that a property such as *being maximally loving*, which God is widely assumed to possess, entails not only that God loves each individual maximally, but also that there are *multiple* divine individuals. See Wierenga 2004.
10. My endorsement of Sebo's distinction isn't meant to endorse his more central claims about agency and moral status.
11. By contrast, it *wouldn't* be less than maximally fair to exclude individuals who can't exercise power, since there's literally no way of sharing power with them. A requirement for fair distribution of resources is that those resources *can* be distributed.
12. If this were true, it would plausibly support atheism. If it's true that the existence of God entails the equal power of everyone with interests, then the fact that there are power asymmetries in the actual world (e.g., between some humans and some dogs) entails that God does not exist. Cf. Moti Mizrahi's (2014) argument that natural evils of this kind are a special and unexplored variant of the problem of evil.
13. I'm not assuming that there *is* a divine fawn. Perhaps there is, but nothing I say here commits me to it.
14. As I'll argue below, this implication has significant implications for the problem of evil.
15. Presumably there are some propositions whose actualization requires complex cognitive machinery to understand. For example, willing it to be the case that a mathematician solves Fermat's Last Theorem due to its intrinsically interesting mathematical properties doesn't seem achievable for mere perceptual agents.
16. Swinburne (2010: 40) goes so far as to claim that because God has allowed creatures to suffer, God is morally obligated to share in their suffering.
17. Clough rejects animal incarnations for four reasons. First, because it's "odd and over-complex" to posit one God and argue for multiple redemptive actions. Second, because God's incarnate redemptive actions aren't species-specific, so there's no need for further redemptive incarnations. Third, because we would have to embrace agnosticism about God's redemptive purposes for non-human animals. Fourth, because (as evolutionary biology tells us) species aren't finely delineated, and thus a redemptive program that assumes otherwise is suspect. See Clough 2013, at 82. These reasons aren't persuasive. Since oppressions differ, it's neither odd nor over-complex to posit a God who shares our suffering under multiple oppressions. Moreover,

that animals suffer intensely from both natural and human causes clarifies at least some of God's central redemptive purposes, so embracing global agnosticism is unnecessary. While we might be left with some agnosticism, since God's redemptive purposes might extend beyond these aims, that's already true of *human* redemption, so this leaves us with no more agnosticism than we began. Nor does any of this depend on the view that non-human animals are a clearly delineated natural kind. It's enough that they are *perceived* and *treated as if* they are other natural kinds to motivate incarnating as a non-human animal, or at least with the *appearance* of one, so as to endure the same oppression and liberate from within.

18. This strikes me as not only ableist, but also undermines the primary purpose of an incarnation: to enjoin solidarity with *all* of creation, including the cognitively disabled, and to share in our predicaments. To think of cognitive disability as 'unfitting' or 'unworthy' of incarnation because it's an imperfection therefore misses the point entirely: *if* cognitive disability is an imperfection as suffering is (which I deny, but the objector assumes), then that's *all the more* reason to incarnate as disabled (i.e., it's a condition eminently *worthy* of incarnation).

19. My use of the term "cognitive perfections" over "epistemic perfections" is meant to designate a broader array of cognitive abilities, goals, and successes than are arguably covered under "epistemic perfections," which tend to be more doxastic in nature. For example, when bees are more efficient at construction than humans due to their less deliberative, more instinctual cognitive machinery, it's unclear this is an *epistemic* perfection, since it has little to do with what bees *believe* or *intend*. Rather, it has to do with how they *avoid* developing certain beliefs or intentions (e.g., the intention to build only if others agree), which seems like a cognitive perfection but not an epistemic one. But I don't mean to signal any difference beyond that.

20. Multiple incarnations can solve the problem of identifying too strongly with less oppressed groups. I am not advocating a kind of 'oppression Olympics' for incarnations, where God seeks to identify *exclusively* with members of a maximally oppressed group. For example, if God incarnated once as a human woman and again as a non-human animal, then God would identify with both groups effectively.

21. Some might express surprise at anything other than the Transformation View counting as a view about *incarnation*, since an incarnation without transformation isn't really an incarnation. Incarnation requires *becoming* something that one isn't. I'm agnostic about this conceptual dispute. But my view preserves a view on which an embodied God comes to be with their suffering people, which strikes me as the most important feature of any incarnation account.

22. There's a variant of the Appearance View wherein God *involuntarily* appears as an animal on Earth. But that makes a divine incarnation involuntary, which is problematic. Moreover, a perfect God wouldn't be such that they involuntarily appear as an animal without being one, since that's a kind of built-in appropriation.

23. Kevin Timpe has expressed skepticism about my view that appropriation can occur even if the transformation is complete. But my claim isn't that the *successful transformation* is appropriative, only that the *decision to transform* is appropriative.

24. This is also my standard for sufficient moral similarity in oppression: S1 is oppressed in a morally similar way to S2 such that, if S1 attempts to share in the oppression of S2, then S1 does nothing morally inappropriate (or appropriative).

25. It might be objected that God isn't appropriating animal oppression if God *becomes* an animal. But this is morally analogous to claiming that Rachel Dolezal wouldn't have appropriated black oppression if she had succeeded at becoming a black woman. At the very least, we should think there's something morally problematic about transforming our race or species as a means of identifying with the oppressed.
26. For a traditional theistic approach to the epistemology of religious experience, see William Alston 1993 and Alvin Plantinga 1967, 2000. For a general approach to which I'm more sympathetic, see Burns 2017. For a skeptical view, see Fales 2005.

References

Adams, Marilyn McCord. *Christ and Horrors: The Coherence of Christology*. New York: Cambridge University Press, 2008.

Alston, William P. *Perceiving God: The Epistemology of Religious Experience*. Ithaca, NY: Cornell University Press, 1993.

Anselm of Canterbury. "Why God Became Man." In *Anselm of Canterbury: The Major Works*, edited by Brian Davies and G. R. Evans, 260–356. New York: Oxford University Press, 1998.

Aston, Emma. "Part-Animal Gods." In *The Oxford Handbook of Animals in Classical Thought and Life*, edited by Gordon Lindsay Campbell, 366–383. New York: Oxford University Press, 2014.

Burns, Aaran. "A Phenomenal Conservative Perspective on Religious Experience." *International Journal for Philosophy of Religion* 81.3 (2017): 247–261.

Celsus. *On the True Doctrine: A Discourse Against the Christians*. Translated by R. Joseph Hoffmann. New York: Oxford University Press, 1987.

Clough, David L. *On Animals: Volume 1: Systematic Theology*. New York: Bloomsbury T&T Clark, 2013.

———. *On Animals: Volume 2: Theological Ethics*. New York: Bloomsbury T&T Clark, 2018.

Cochrane, Alasdair. *Sentientist Politics: A Theory of Global Inter-Species Justice*. New York: Oxford University Press, 2018.

Cone, James H. *A Black Theology of Liberation*. New York: Orbis Books, 2018.

Creegan, Nicola Hoggard. *Animal Suffering and the Problem of Evil*. New York: Oxford University Press, 2013.

Crummett, Dustin. "The Problem of Evil and the Suffering of Creeping Things." *International Journal for Philosophy of Religion* 82.1 (2017): 71–88.

Davis, Stephen T. "Was Jesus Mad, Bad, or God?" In *Oxford Readings in Philosophical Theology: Volume 1: Trinity, Incarnation, and Atonement*, edited by Michael C. Rea, 166–185. New York: Oxford University Press, 2009.

Denis, Lara. "Animality and Agency: A Kantian Approach to Abortion." *Philosophy and Phenomenological Research* 76.1 (2008): 117–137.

De Waal, Frans. *Are We Smart Enough to Know How Smart Animals Are?* New York: W.W. Norton & Company, 2016.

Diels, H. and W. Kranz. *Die Fragmente der Vorsokratiker*. Dublin and Zurich: Wiedmann, 1952.

Donaldson, Sue and Will Kymlicka. *Zoopolis: A Political Theory of Animal Rights*. New York: Oxford University Press, 2011.

Dougherty, Trent. *The Problem of Animal Pain: A Theodicy for All Creatures Great and Small*. New York: Palgrave Macmillan, 2014.
Fales, Evan. "The Road to Damascus." *Faith and Philosophy* 22.4 (2005): 442–459.
Flint, Thomas P. *Divine Providence: The Molinist Account*. Ithaca, NY: Cornell University Press, 1998.
Funkhouser, Eric. "On Privileging God's Moral Goodness." *Faith and Philosophy* 23.4 (2006): 409–422.
Graves, Shawn, Blake Hereth, and Tyler M. John. "In Defense of Animal Universalism." In *Paradise Understood: New Philosophical Essays About Heaven*, edited by T. Ryan Byerly and Eric J. Silverman, 161–192. New York: Oxford University Press, 2017.
Haberman, David L. "Hinduism: Devotional Love of the World." In *Routledge Handbook of Religion and Ecology*, edited by Willis Jenkins, Mary Evelyn Tucker, and John Grim, 35–42. New York: Routledge, 2018.
Hereth, Blake. "Two Arguments for Animal Immortality." In *Heaven and Philosophy*, edited by Simon Cushing, 171–200. Lanham, MD: Lexington, 2018.
Kemmerer, Lisa. *Animals and World Religions*. New York: Oxford University Press, 2012.
Lewis, C. S. *The Weight of Glory and Other Essays*. San Francisco: Harper, 2001.
Little, Margaret Olivia. "Abortion, Intimacy, and the Duty to Gestate." *Ethical Theory and Moral Practice* 2.3 (1999): 295–312.
Miller, Daniel. *Animal Ethics and Theology*. New York: Routledge, 2012.
Miller, Patricia Cox. *In the Eye of the Animal: Zoological Imagination in Early Christianity*. Philadelphia, PA: University of Pennsylvania Press, 2018.
Mills, Charles W. "Bestial Inferiority: Locating Simianization Within Racism." In *Simianization: Apes, Gender, Class, and Race*, edited by Charles W. Mills and Wulf D. Hund, 19–42. London: LIT Verlag, 2015.
Mizrahi, Moti. "The Problem of Natural Inequality: A New Problem of Evil." *Philosophia* 42.1 (2014): 127–136.
Monroe, Hannah. "Ableism, Speciesism, Animals, and Autism: The Devaluation of Interspecies Friendships." In *Animaladies: Gender, Animals, and Madness*, edited by Lori Gruen and Fiona Probyn-Rapsey, 89–99. New York: Bloomsbury, 2018.
Morris, Thomas V. *Anselmian Explorations: Essays in Philosophical Theology*. South Bend, IN: University of Notre Dame Press, 1989.
———. *Our Idea of God: An Introduction to Philosophical Theology*. Downers Grove, IL: InterVarsity Press, 1991.
Murray, Michael J. *Nature Red in Tooth and Claw: Theism and the Problem of Animal Suffering*. New York: Oxford University Press, 2008.
Nagasawa, Yujin. *Maximal God: A New Defense of Perfect Being Theism*. New York: Oxford University Press, 2017.
Pawl, Timothy. "Thomistic Multiple Incarnations." *The Heythrop Journal* 57.2 (2016a): 359–370.
———. "Brian Hebblethwaite's Arguments Against Multiple Incarnations." *Religious Studies* 52.1 (2016b): 117–130.
Plantinga, Alvin. *God and Other Minds: A Study of the Rational Justification for Belief in God*. Ithaca, NY: Cornell University Press, 1967.
———. *Warranted Christian Belief*. New York: Oxford University Press, 2000.

———. "Supralapsarianism, or 'O Felix Culpa.'" In *Christian Faith and the Problem of Evil*, edited by Peter van Inwagen, 1–25. Grand Rapids, MI: Wm. B. Eerdmans, 2004.

———. "Comments on 'Satanic Verses: Moral Chaos in Holy Writ.'" In *Divine Evil? The Moral Character of the God of Abraham*, edited by Michael Bergmann, Michael J. Murray, and Michael C. Rea, 109–114. New York: Oxford University Press, 2013.

Richard of St. Victor. *The Trinity*, Book 3, Chapter 2. In Richard of St. Victor, *Twelve Patriarchs, The Mystical Ark, Book Three of the Trinity*, translated by Grover A. Zinn. New York: Paulist Press, 1979.

Rogers, Katherin A. *Perfect Being Theology*. Edinburgh: Edinburgh University Press, 2000.

Rowe, William. "The Problem of Evil and Some Varieties of Atheism." *American Philosophical Quarterly* 16 (1979): 335–341.

Rowlands, Mark. *Can Animals Be Moral?* New York: Oxford University Press, 2012.

Sebo, Jeff. "Agency and Moral Status." *Journal of Moral Philosophy* 14.1 (2017): 1–22.

Swinburne, Richard. "Could There Be More Than One God?" *Faith and Philosophy* 5 (1988): 225–241.

———. *The Christian God*. New York: Oxford University Press, 1994.

———. *Was Jesus God?* New York: Oxford University Press, 2010.

Thumiger, Chiara. "Metamorphosis: Humans into Animals." In *The Oxford Handbook of Animals in Classical Thought and Life*, edited by Gordon Lindsay Campbell, 384–413. New York: Oxford University Press, 2014.

Wierenga, Edward. "Trinity and Polytheism." *Faith and Philosophy* 21.3 (2004): 281–294.

Section IV
Disability

9 The Resurrection of the Minority Body
Physical Disability in the Life of Heaven

David Efird

Introduction

On the day Stephen Hawking died, the artist Mitchell Toy 2018 published this illustration on his Twitter account:

Reactions to the illustration were polarized. Some thought that the cartoon expressed the freedom Hawking now has in the afterlife, having previously been bound to a wheelchair; others thought that the cartoon overlooked the fact that, during his natural life, Hawking's wheelchair was a source of freedom for him. Commenting on this illustration, Ellis Palmer, a disabled person, writes,

> For me, the most troubling moment in the reaction to Prof Hawking's death was when an image of him standing out of his wheelchair went viral on social media.
>
> What this image suggested was a rather damaging trope: the disabled person should always seek to not use a wheelchair, rather than the impairment being something positive to reflect and work with. Society still seeks to create an image of a disabled person's life as pitiable or a burden on society. This can be incredibly damaging to a disabled person's mental health and their perception of themselves.
>
> (Palmer 2018)

Another reaction came from Ace Ratcliff, who was diagnosed with Ehlers-Danos syndrome at the age of 27. Commenting on this illustration, as well as the language used in Hawking's obituaries, Ratcliff writes,

> Language influences and shapes our experience. When the media insists on discussing Hawking's disability as something he "overcame" or "conquered," it's playing into repetitive and inaccurate tropes that describe disability as something that stifles innovation, something that cannot exist beside great intellect, something that staunches creativity. That mindset encourages inaccessibility, the denial of access to medical treatment, the mockery of disability. Perpetually describing disability as negative by default instead of as a normal or neutral form of variation means it becomes something to be eradicated, fixed, removed.
>
> Hawking didn't discover what he did about the way the universe works "in spite of" his disability. He did so as a disabled human, fully informed by the reality of his existence, living it every single day – as those of us who are disabled do. Illustrating Hawking, an atheist, walking away from his wheelchair to his afterlife is as offensive an erasure as is the implication that disability and genius, success and satisfaction can't ever go hand in hand. Instead of playing into the same tired cliches, it's time to rewrite the narrative. Accepting disability as one of the myriad ways in which humans can and do exist is the first move toward building a more accepting and accessible world.
>
> (Ratcliff 2018)

In this paper, I aim to support Ratcliff's thought, at least with regard to the life of heaven. That is, I will argue that, in the life of heaven, having a physical disability is 'one of the myriad ways' in which resurrected bodies can exist.¹ To use Elizabeth Barnes's (2016a) phrase, there could be minority bodies in heaven.²

Taking Ratcliff's point that Hawking, being an atheist, wouldn't be the best example for my argument, I introduce one more, that of Cardinal Francis E. George, OMI, Archbishop Emeritus of Chicago.³ When he was 13 years old, he contracted polio. As a consequence of the disease, he had a pronounced limp and so wore a large, metal brace on his left leg. He was buried with this brace, at his request (Martin and Duriga 2015). While we don't know why Cardinal George made this request, let's assume, for the sake of argument, that Cardinal George expected, or even desired, to retain his physical disability in heaven. But such an expectation, or desire, seems confused when the weight of Christian tradition is brought to bear. For, on the traditional view, there couldn't be physical disabilities in heaven, since God unilaterally (that is, acting on his own) eliminates them before, or at the time of, a person's re-embodiment in heaven. For some, God does this because a person's physical disability is a punishment for their sins; for others, God does this because physical disabilities are effects of the Fall.⁴ In contrast, I argue that it's the tradition, rather than Cardinal George, that is confused. To do this, I'll begin by introducing what I take a physical disability to be and characterizing what the life in heaven might be like. I then argue that God has no reason either to eliminate or to retain physical disabilities in the life of heaven unilaterally. Next, I'll argue that God could give a saint, that is, a person in heaven, who had a physical disability in their earthly life the choice to retain that physical disability in their heavenly life, and they would be reasonable in choosing to do so. Finally, I'll conclude that there could be minority resurrected bodies.⁵

Physical Disability and the Life of Heaven

To begin, I take a resurrected body to be numerically identical with a body which has died (Merricks 2009, 476).⁶ This seems to be implied by Jesus being raised in the same body he had before he died (Luke 24:1–6), a body which retained the scars of his crucifixion (John 20:25, 27), and his resurrection being the model of our own (Philippians 3:20–21). Moreover, that our resurrected bodies will be numerically identical with our bodies that have died seems to run through Paul's most extensive discussion of the resurrection of the dead in 1 Corinthians 15. Now, some bodies which have died had physical disabilities; do the resurrected bodies, which are numerically identical with those bodies which have died, have physical disabilities? To answer this question, I should say something about what I take a physical disability to be. Having already given the examples of Professor Hawking and Cardinal George, I follow Barnes in defining the concept of physical disability by ostension: blindness, deafness, mobility impairments, and so on (2014, 89).⁷ So, our question then is: could there be blindness, deafness, mobility impairments, and so on, in the life of heaven?

To answer this question, we need to think about what our bodies are good for in the life of heaven, and that's going to depend on what the life of heaven is like. To begin, following Richard Swinburne (2017), the life of heaven is the life supremely worth living. The primary feature of such a life is the enjoyment of the beatific vision (cf. 1 Corinthians 13:12). This 'vision' is an intellectual vision, rather than a sensory one,[8] where a person comes to know God personally, and immediately, by experiencing him second-personally and sharing attention with him completely and uninterruptedly.[9] This is the intellectual aspect of the life supremely worth living. As to its corporeal aspect, there seem to be two ways we could live the beatific life: in a physically dynamic way, where our bodies change and we can do things with them, or in a physically static way, where our bodies don't change and we can't do things with them.[10]

On a physically dynamic life of heaven, our bodies are good for taking us places, such as through fields, down valleys, and up mountains, assuming heaven has that kind of geography,[11] and doing things in those places with our bodies, like maybe playing rugby.[12] On this conception of the life of heaven, our question then becomes: if the life of heaven is one where we do things like go places and play ball games, could there be blindness, deafness, mobility impairments, and so on?

Alternatively, on a physically static life, since we can't do anything with our bodies, they don't seem to be good for anything.[13] However, following Aquinas, there is something our bodies could be good for, even if they don't do anything, namely, they could provide another dimension, beyond the intellectual, for enjoying God. He writes,

> For the soul desires to enjoy God in such a way that the enjoyment also may overflow into the body, as far as possible. And therefore, as long as it enjoys God, without the fellowship of the body, its appetite is at rest in that which it has, in such a way, that it would still wish the body to attain to its share.
>
> (*ST* I.II. Q.4. A.5. ad.4)

On this conception of the life of heaven, our question then becomes: If the life of heaven is one where we enjoy God both intellectually and bodily, could there be blindness, deafness, mobility impairments, and so on?

For both ways of putting the question, there are three ways to answer it: (1) no, because God unilaterally (that is, without the request, or even consent, of the person who was physically disabled in their earthly life) eliminates physical disabilities in the life of heaven; (2) yes, because God, unilaterally (that is, without the request, or even consent, of the person who was physically disabled in their earthly life) retains physical disabilities in the life of heaven; and (3) yes, because God could give those who have physical disabilities in their earthly lives the option to retain them in their heavenly lives, and they could choose to do so. In the next section, I'll argue against the first of these answers, that God unilaterally eliminates physical disabilities in the life of heaven.

Against the Unilateral Elimination View

James Barton Gould defines 'the elimination view' as "people with disabilities will be healed in heaven when God restores all things to what they were meant to be" (2016, 317). He thinks that this view is implied by the biblical argument for healing. The story line of Scripture can be understood as a drama with three acts.

1. In the beginning God created all things good. We are meant to function without disease or impairment of body and mind.
2. Then sin entered creation—and now the world is not the way it should be. The fall results in illness and dysfunction, which are detrimental to human flourishing.
3. God acts to restore wholeness—including physical health and mental ability—to what is broken.

Holistic functioning is both the origin and destiny of human persons.
(2016, 318)

Now, this story line of Scripture, as recounted by Gould, presupposes that, all disabilities are themselves detrimental to human flourishing, presumably, in the life of heaven (cf. Gould 2017, 99). For physical disabilities being detrimental to a person's flourishing in their earthly life provides no reason for eliminating them in their heavenly life. It's only if they're detrimental to their heavenly life that God has a reason to eliminate them. So one way to argue against the elimination view is to argue that disabilities aren't so, which is what I aim to do so in this section.

To begin, I'm going to take it that a person's flourishing is constituted by their well-being: the more well-being a person has, the more they flourish, and vice versa. Now, following Ian Stoner (2016), I'm going to take 'well-being' in its pre-theoretic sense, where it concerns what makes for a good life: such as having enough food, water, and sleep; feeling safe and secure; having loving relationships and belonging to a community; respecting yourself and being respected by others; using your talents and abilities in pursuit of a goal; and being part of something bigger than yourself.[14] When you have more of these things, you're better off, and when you have less, you're worse off.[15]

Next, I'm going to introduce a distinction made by Barnes, that between a difference being a 'bad-difference' and a difference being a 'mere-difference.' A bad-difference is something about you that differs from other people and, in and of itself, makes you worse off. A mere-difference is something that something about you that differs from other people and, in and of itself, doesn't make you worse off. For instance, having brown hair is a mere-difference I have. I'm also gay. That's a mere-difference I have, but some think it's a bad-difference I have. That's for another paper. As applied to physical disabilities, we can think of the distinction between their being a bad-difference and a mere-difference this way: if justice were achieved for disabled people, would their disabilities still make a difference to their well-being? If physical disabilities were 'bad-differences,' then they would; if they're 'mere-differences,' then they wouldn't, as Barnes explains:

> According to bad-difference views of disability, not only is having a disability bad for you, having a disability would still be bad for you even if society was fully accommodating of disabled people. . . . According to mere-difference views of disability, having a disability makes you nonstandard or different, but it doesn't by itself make you worse off.
>
> (2014, 89)

According to Barnes (2014, 2016a), physical disabilities are mere-differences in this life. Are they so in the life to come? To answer this question, we need to think about the two ways the life of heaven might be with respect to the body: either physically dynamic or physically static. On both ways, I argue that they're mere-differences. I'll take the latter case first, as it's easiest to deal with.

If the life of heaven is physically static, the only thing the body is good for is to provide another dimension of enjoying God beyond the intellectual, at least as Aquinas argues. Now, as Christopher Brown (2009, 239) observes, for Aquinas, perfect human happiness comes in degrees. It might, then, be argued that a saint with a physical disability consisting in the loss of a limb can't enjoy God to the same bodily extent as a saint with all their limbs, and so the loss of a limb constitutes a bad-difference as opposed to a mere-difference in a physically static life of heaven. But such an argument would be absurd. For it would also imply that I have overwhelming prudential reason to gain as much weight as possible, so I would bodily enjoy God to the greatest possible extent in the life of heaven. That might make good news for the diet I'm trying to keep to, but I can't imagine it's true. Thus, the only physical disabilities that would be bad-differences, as opposed to mere-differences among resurrected bodies, would be physical disabilities that are so painful that they prevented the saint from experiencing God second-personally and sharing attention with him. So, apart from such bad-difference physical disabilities, physical disabilities in a physically static life of heaven are mere-differences.

Turning now to the case of heaven being physically dynamic, such a life might be very much like this one, where time passes and we engage in bodily activities. Now, if it's a life supremely worth living, then it can't be an entirely easy life. For it must be a life where achievement is at least possible. As Gwen Bradford writes,

> It is a commonly held view, among both philosophers and non-philosophers alike, that achievements of one kind or another are one of life's greatest sources of meaning, and that dedicating ourselves to a worthy pursuit is precisely what we should aim for if we want to have a worthwhile and meaningful life.
>
> (2015, 2)

While 'achievement' might be used to refer to anything we do, the sense of 'achievement' here is something we do that requires some effort, in other words, something we do that's difficult (Bradford 2015, ch. 2). So, if the life of heaven is both supremely worth living and is physically dynamic, then it has physical challenges. For such challenges afford greater scope for achievement, which then allows for a better life. Think about that game of rugby we might be playing in heaven. If we win, and it takes no effort, like the England team playing against the local secondary school, we would quickly quit playing. For it would be boring.[16] Without any difficulty, there's no challenge, and if there's no challenge, there's no interest. So, a physically dynamic life would be boring if it were always physically easy. And if it were boring, it wouldn't be a life supremely worth living.[17] Writing in another context, Eleonore Stump states, "There is something small and unworthy about a life lived totally at ease" (2018).[18]

Presumably, at least some of these achievements would have a physical aspect, such as winning a race, being first up a mountain, discovering something at the bottom of the ocean, or exploring a new planet, assuming heaven has that kind of geography. So, some of the things we do in our heavenly lives have to be physically difficult, requiring us to expend some effort. Now, the effort we expend can't be negligible. It can't be so because, otherwise, we would run into what Bradford terms 'the ridiculous conclusion':

> An extremely minimal amount of effort expended over a very, very long time comes out as *more* effort than an extremely intense effort expended for a shorter time. As a result, for any intensely effortful activity of finite duration, there is always an activity of extremely minimal intensity of effort that requires *more total effort*.
>
> (2015, 48; emphasis in the original)[19]

Avoiding this 'ridiculous conclusion' is particularly relevant for the life of heaven, as it lasts forever: expending a very small amount of effort over billions of years (assuming we can measure time that way in heaven) to raise your arm might come out to be more effort than to climb a mountain in a day, but the former shouldn't count as an achievement while the latter should. So, in the life of heaven, assuming it's physically dynamic, we'll be expending non-negligible effort to do things with our bodies, and thereby achieve things. This then means that our bodily powers in the life of heaven must be limited, since, other things being equal, a being with unlimited bodily powers experiences no difficulty, or at most negligible difficulty, in achieving things of a physical aspect.[20] So, if the life of heaven is physically dynamic, resurrected bodies will have limited bodily powers.[21]

Now, one of the ways that our bodily powers can be limited is through our bodies having physical disabilities.[22] I think we can safely assume that heaven, a place where justice, mercy, and peace are fully realized, and all people are allowed to flourish to the greatest extent possible, is accommodating to those with physical disabilities.[23] Ben Mattlin expresses a hope that this is the case, along with anticipating the issues of identity I'll discuss in the following section, in the following radio interview:

> A few years ago a friend of mine died unexpectedly at 39. We both used motorized wheelchairs and needed assistance with tasks such as washing, dressing and eating, but his disability came from a motorcycle accident 14 years earlier. Mine is from birth, the result of a congenital neuromuscular condition. So I'm used to being quadriplegic. He wasn't. He would sometimes ask, with startling frankness, "How do you do it? How do you manage?" I never knew how to answer.
>
> One morning my friend's attendant found him dead with a smile on his face, we were told, at the packed memorial service. A young minister explained that he'd been, quote, "a free spirit, trapped in an unresponsive body. Now that spirit is truly free." We were told he'd gone to a place where he could walk again. His dad added "Walk? He's probably playing basketball in the nude." The words stung. Mourners need to believe their loved one has gone to a better place. Yet what was the message here? Death sets you free and cures disability? Was he better off dead than disabled? I realize I'm biased. I have never ridden a motorcycle or done half the other physical things my friend used to love, but I do know one can live a pretty full life with a disability.
>
> Indeed, some people find life after disability more intense, more deeply appreciated than it was before. My lifelong experience, with disability, has made me a creative problem-solver, and, ironically, perhaps, a diehard optimist, if only because I've had to be. It's taught me a great deal about patience, tolerance and flexibility. My disability is part of who I am. Why couldn't my friend's family value the disabled man he'd become? How limited is this vision of life, and of the afterlife? Are there no wheelchairs in heaven? I'm not buying it. For

me, if there is a heaven, it's not a place where I'll be able to walk. It's a place where it doesn't matter if you can't.

(Mattlin 2005)

Thus, in a physically dynamic life of heaven, the only physical disabilities that would be bad-differences would be physical disabilities that prevent a person from achieving anything,[24] or achieving the properly tuned desires of the heart,[25] or experiencing God second-personally and sharing attention with him.[26] So, apart from such bad-difference physical disabilities, physical disabilities in a physically dynamic life of heaven are mere-differences.

Against this argument that, in a physically dynamic life of heaven physical disabilities are mere-differences, it might be objected:

> Rather than showing that physical disabilities are mere-differences in the life of heaven, the argument actually shows physical disabilities are positive differences, that is, differences that are better for you, in the life of heaven because they allow for a greater scope of achievement, which allows for a greater sense of fulfilment. Consequently, God should not only unilaterally retain the physical disabilities of those who have them in their earthly lives, but also cause unilaterally those who didn't have them in their earthly lives to have them in their heavenly lives. But this would be absurd. So, the argument for physical disabilities being mere-differences in the life of heaven must be unsound.[27]

For the sake of argument, I'm willing to grant that, on a physically dynamic conception of the life of heaven, physical disabilities are positive differences and that God knows this. That is, God knows that if he causes a person who had not been physically disabled in their earthly life to be physically disabled in their heavenly life, their heavenly life will go better for them than it would have gone had he not caused them to be physically disabled. Even if that's the case, it doesn't follow that God should cause them unilaterally to be physically disabled in their heavenly life because it would harm them unjustifiedly, or so I argue.

To begin, God would harm them because they would experience transition costs in becoming disabled, typically involving significant pain and difficulty in adapting to this new bodily state,[28] and also suffering, because it may well be opaque to them why they are experiencing this pain and difficulty.[29] This harm would be unjustified because the harm, short-term though it may be, is for the person's future benefit rather for than the prevention of a future cost worse than the harm itself, and they haven't consented to it.[30]

Let me explain. Say that I've collapsed and am unconscious. You take me to the hospital, and I need surgery to save my life. My consent isn't required for the surgeons to perform this life-saving operation, even though it's a harm that will cause me significant pain in recovery. This is relevantly different from the case where if I'm an actor, and you knew that I would get cast for this role that I really wanted if I got a nose job. We haven't discussed it, but you took it upon yourself to render me unconscious, and have a plastic surgeon give me a nose job. Afterwards, I do get the job, but it was wrong of you to do that, because I preferred to keep the nose I had and not have the role.

Similarly, God causing a person to have a physical disability wouldn't be for the prevention of a worse harm, but rather for something better for them in the future. So, God would need their consent for him to do this justifiedly. But he doesn't have that.[31] So, it would be wrong of God to unilaterally cause a person to have a physical disability even if it's a positive difference. So, even if physical disabilities are a positive difference in the life of heaven, God can't cause people who haven't had them in their earthly lives to have them in their heavenly lives. Consequently, the objection isn't successful.[32]

We can use this response to give a further reason for thinking that God can't eliminate physical disabilities in the life of heaven unilaterally on a physically dynamic conception of the life of heaven. For there can be transition costs to having a disability eliminated.[33] We can grant for the sake of argument that these costs are for a future benefit, that is, a life without this disability. Now, it may be opaque to the person the nature of this future benefit, to be discussed below, since they can't imagine what it would be like to live a sighted life, say, if they were blind from birth. Thus, these costs constitute suffering for them, which they haven't consented to. Consequently, it would be wrong of God to eliminate physical disabilities unilaterally in the life of heaven.[34]

Having argued that either on a physically static or a physically dynamic conception of the life of heaven, physical disabilities are mere-differences among resurrected bodies, God has no reason to eliminate them unilaterally in the life of heaven. I turn now to argue that God also has no reason to retain physical disabilities unilaterally in the life of heaven.

Against the Unilateral Retention View

The primary reason for thinking that God retains unilaterally physical disabilities in the life of heaven is that, if he were to eliminate them, he would eliminate the person who had them. In discussing a film produced by the American Association of Retarded Citizens entitled "Prevent Retardation," Stanley Hauerwas writes:

> [T]here seems to be something deeply wrong or disturbing about this film and its message, "Prevent Retardation." Perhaps part of the difficulty involves the disanalogy between preventing mental impairment

and preventing cancer, polio, or heart diseases, as these latter diseases exist independent of the subjects having the diseases. The disease can be eliminated without eliminating the subject of the disease. But the same is not true of the person mentally impaired. To eliminate the disability means to eliminate the subject.

(1984, 68–69)

Hauerwas's final sentence in this passage has come to be known as 'Hauerwas's dictum.'[35] But what is its scope? That is, for what disabilities, if any, does it hold? Well, Hauerwas seems to have had in mind cognitive disabilities, and, as mentioned, such disabilities are beyond the scope of this paper. Does it hold for physical disabilities? Well, not acquired ones, since a person isn't killed by acquiring a physical disability.[36] So if Hauerwas's dictum holds at all for physical disabilities it has to hold for congenital ones. But does it?

It seems from the testimony of those with physical disabilities that it does. Recall that as part of his account of how he hopes heaven to be a place where physical disabilities don't matter, Mattlin says, "My disability is part of who I am." But I'm not sure that Mattlin's claim should be interpreted as the claim that if his physical disability were eliminated, he would be eliminated. To see what I'm getting at, consider another account from a person with a physical disability, Emma:

> We all have an identity. It's what makes us who we are. Muscular Dystrophy and my wheelchair are part of who I am. So does my disability define me? Yes, it does. Is that a bad thing? Only if I make it one.
>
> For a very long time, I thought my disability didn't define me. Maybe I got caught up in the whole "my disability doesn't define me" mantra. Who knows? I certainly wasn't ashamed or resentful of my disability. I guess I wanted people to see me not just my disability, but like I said, my disability is part of me. It can't be hidden and it isn't going anywhere. I've come to realise that it's a big part of my life and I'm totally ok with that.
>
> Would I be the same person if I could walk or live independently on my own? I'd like to think I would be, but with my disability, it's brought its fair share of struggles as well as strengths and I have little quirks as a result of it. I'm proud of those quirks and you should be proud of yours. Without my disability, I wouldn't have those qualities that make up my identity.
>
> (2017)

So, Emma agrees with Mattlin that her physical disability is part of who she is, but she also says that she would "like to think" that she would be the same person if she didn't have it. It seems that, on Emma's view, her physical disability is part of her identity in one sense of 'identity' but not part of her identity in another sense of 'identity.' How could that be?

Following Christine Korsgaard, we can distinguish a person's *theoretical identity* from their *practical identity*.[37] Theoretical identity consists in a metaphysical description of who you are, whereas practical identity consists in a description under which you value yourself. Korsgarrd writes,

> The conception of one's identity in question here is not a theoretical one, a view about what as a matter of inescapable scientific fact you are. It is better understood as a description under which you value yourself, a description under which you find your life to be worth living and your actions to be worth undertaking. So I will call this a conception of your practical identity. Practical identity is a complex matter and for the average person there will be a jumble of such conceptions. You are a human being, a woman or a man, an adherent of a certain religion, a member of an ethnic group, a member of a certain profession, someone's lover or friend, and so on. And all of these identities give rise to reasons and obligations. Your reasons express your identity, your nature; your obligations spring from what that identity forbids.
>
> (Korsgaard 1996, 101)

As examples of a person's practical identity, Korsgaard gives a number of different descriptions under which a person might value themselves.[38] As examples of a person's theoretical identity, we might include, depending on your metaphysics of personal identity, one or more of the following:

- Being an immaterial soul or ego (Foster 1991).
- Being a bundle of mental states (Campbell 2006).
- Being a material body (Thomson 1997).
- Being a body-soul complex (Swinburne 1997).
- Being a material simple (Lowe 1996).
- Being an animal (Olson 1997).
- Being a person materially constituted by, but non-identical with, animals (Baker 2000).
- Being a part of a brain (McMahan 2002).

Now, a person's practical identity can come apart from their metaphysical identity. For instance, while being gay is part of my practical identity, something it took me a long time to achieve, but not part of my theoretical identity, or at least that's how it seems to me: if my sexual orientation were changed overnight, that wouldn't kill me. But what of physical disability?[39]

Some physical disabilities a person has from birth, and they come to know they have them. And so, it seems, they would be part of a person's practical identity, as that's the only way a person has ever known themselves. Nancy Eiesland seems to be saying something like this in the following account of her experience:

> As a person with a disability, I could not accept the traditional answers given to my own query of "What is disability?" Since I have a congenital disability, I have had opportunities to hear and experience many of these so-called answers through the years. They included "You are special in God's eyes, that's why you were given this painful disability." Imagine it didn't seem logical. Or "Don't worry about your pain and suffering now, in heaven you will be made whole." Again, having been disabled from birth, I came to believe that in heaven I would be absolutely unknown to myself and perhaps to God. My disability has taught me who I am and who God is. What would it mean to be without this knowledge? I was told that God gave me a disability to develop my character. But by age six or seven, I was convinced that I had enough character to last a lifetime. My family frequented faith healers with me in tow. I was never healed. People asked about my hidden sins, but they must have been so well hidden that even I misplaced them. The theology that I heard was inadequate to my experience.
>
> (Eiesland 2001/2002, 2)

But what of physical disabilities that a person acquires during their lifetime? These, too, can become part of a person's practical identity, as Susan Wendell seems to suggest in her own account of her experience. Diagnosed with myalgic encephalomyelitis/chronic fatigue syndrome, Wendell writes,

> Yet I cannot wish that I had never contracted myalgic encephalomyelitis, because it has made me a different person, a person I am glad to be, would not want to have missed being, and could not imagine relinquishing, even if I were "cured."
>
> (Wendell 1996, 84)

Robert Merrihew Adams also seems to suggest this in commenting on the following passage from Leibniz: "You will insist that you can complain, why didn't God give you more strength [to resist temptation]. I answer: if He had done that, you would not be you, for He would not have produced you but another creature" (1948, 327; cited in Adams 1979, 53). Adams rejects Leibniz's assertion when given Leibniz's view that criteria of identity are extremely strict: if I underwent but one change, I would fail to exist. But, Adams thinks, there is some truth in Leibniz's claim, when 'identity' is understood differently, and in the sense I have termed 'practical identity,' "that we would not be ourselves without many and great evils" (1979, 53). In particular,

> [t]here are evils that happen to people, without which they could, strictly speaking, have existed, but which shape their lives so profoundly that wishing the evils had not occurred would be morally very close to wishing that somebody else had existed instead of those particular people.
>
> (1979, 64)[40]

As an example, he cites Helen Keller who, at a young age, became deaf and blind, and, as a result suffered significantly, until she learned sign language by touch and became a great success. Now, it's unfortunate, at least in my view, that Adams equates disability with evil, but regardless of this, Adams's point remains, that, for people who acquire a physical disability during their lives, while this disability is part of their practical identity, it's not part of their theoretical identity.

Given that physical disability, whether had from birth or acquired during a person's earthly life, is part of a person's practical, but not theoretical identity, it seems that God wouldn't be killing them by eliminating their physical disability in the life of heaven. So, this removes the primary reason for thinking that God unilaterally retains physical disabilities in the life of heaven.

For the Optionality View

Having argued that God unilaterally neither eliminates nor retains physical disabilities in the life of heaven, I now argue that he gives those who had physical disabilities in their earthly lives the option of either having them eliminated or retained in their heavenly lives. To begin, I return to Gould's argument for the elimination view, which he summarizes as follows:

1. If God heals disease and disability in this life, then God will heal disease and disability in the next life.
2. God does heal disease and disability in this life.
3. [So,] God will heal disease and disability in the next life.

(2016, 323–324)

But God heals disease and physical disability in this life only following a request for healing from either the person themselves, or, if they are a child, their parent. For instance, consider this story of Jesus's healing ministry:

> Now in Jerusalem by the Sheep Gate there is a pool, called in Hebrew Beth-zatha, which has five porticoes. In these lay many

invalids—blind, lame, and paralysed. One man was there who had been ill for thirty-eight years. When Jesus saw him lying there and knew that he had been there a long time, he said to him, "Do you want to be made well?" The sick man answered him, "Sir, I have no one to put me into the pool when the water is stirred up; and while I am making my way, someone else steps down ahead of me." Jesus said to him, "Stand up, take your mat and walk." At once the man was made well, and he took up his mat and began to walk.

(John 5:2–9)

Note that there were many people with physical disabilities in the porticoes. Jesus didn't eliminate everyone's physical disabilities indiscriminately. Rather, he asked one man if he wanted "to be made well," and hearing what he took to be a positive response, Jesus eliminated his physical disability. This suggests that, in the next life, God doesn't eliminate physical disabilities unilaterally,[41] but rather offers a person having a physical disability in their earthly life the choice as to whether to retain it or having it eliminated and, if a person requests that God eliminate their physical disability, God will do so.[42] But for this to be possible, it first must be possible for God to give a person with physical disabilities in their earthly life the option to have them either eliminated or retained. This does seem to be possible for the following reason.

"What do you want me to do for you?", so asks Jesus of Bartimaeus, a blind man. "My teacher, let me see again," Bartimaeus responds, and immediately he regained his sight (Mark 10:51–52). If physical disabilities in the life of heaven are mere-differences, God has no reason to eliminate them unilaterally, that is, without our consent and regardless of our own desires, as he has no reason to eliminate other mere-differences among humans in the life of heaven, such as differences in height or gender (Aquinas, *ST* Suppl. Q.81.A.2, A.3). And if God has no reason to eliminate physical disabilities in the life of heaven, he could give a person with a physical disability in their earthly life the choice to retain the disability or have it eliminated.[43]

Now, even if God could give a person who has a physical disability in their earthly life this choice, for there to be physical disabilities in the life of heaven, it must be possible for a person to have their physical disability retained. Now, at the point this choice is made, the person will have all of the relevant information, and their cognitive capacities will be functioning optimally. And so, if it's possible for them to choose to have their physical disability retained, it must be possible for them to do so rationally. But is this possible? John Harris thinks it not. He writes, "[P]hysical or mental conditions that constitute a harm to the individual, which a rational person would wish to be without" (2000, 98). In contrast to Harris, I think it a person with a physical disability could reasonably choose to retain it on three counts.

First, there seem to be some physical disabilities, such as congenital blindness, such that it wouldn't be rational to request that they be eliminated. For their elimination would constitute 'transformative experiences,' which, according to L.A. Paul (2014, ch. 1) are both epistemically and personally transformative.

- An epistemically transformative experience is an experience such that the only way to know what it's like to have it is to have it yourself (such as seeing a color for the first time).
- A personally transformative experience is an experience such that it changes your point of view, including your preferences (such as encountering new cultures).
- An experience is a transformative experience just in case it's both epistemically and personally transformative (such as becoming a parent, undergoing a religious conversion, or becoming bereaved).

Let's go into these kinds of experience in a bit more detail. Consider Frank Jackson's famous thought experiment about Mary, the color scientist, which he uses an argument against physicalism, the view that everything true about the world can be learned from the physical, chemical, and biological sciences:

> Mary is a brilliant scientist who is, for whatever reason, forced to investigate the world from a black and white room via a black and white television monitor. She specialises in the neurophysiology of vision and acquires, let us suppose, all the physical information there is to obtain about what goes on when we see ripe tomatoes, or the sky, and use terms like 'red,' 'blue,' and so on. She discovers, for example, just which wave-length combinations from the sky stimulate the retina, and exactly how this produces *via* the central nervous system the contraction of the vocal chords and expulsion of air from the lungs that results in the uttering of the sentence "The sky is blue."(It can hardly be denied that it is in principle possible to obtain all this physical information from black and white television, otherwise the Open University would of *necessity* need to use color television.)
>
> What will happen when Mary is released from her black and white room or is given a color television monitor? Will she *learn* anything or not? It seems just obvious that she will learn something about the world and our visual experience of it. But then it is inescapable that her previous knowledge was incomplete. But she had *all* the physical information. *Ergo* there is more to have than that, and Physicalism is false.
>
> (Jackson 1982, 130; emphasis in the original)

Whether or not Jackson's thought experiment tells against physicalism,[44] it does suggest that Mary's epistemic position is, in some way, improved upon seeing color for the first time. Consequently, she can't project from her black-and-white experiences what it would be like to have a, say, red-experience. Thus, when she comes to see, say, red for the first time, she has an epistemically transformative experience. In the same way, it might be said that a blind person can't project from their non-sighted experiences what it would be like to have a sighted experience, and so coming to have sight for the first time would be an epistemically transformative experience for a blind person.

> It might also be argued that a congenitally blind person coming to have sight is a personally transformative experience as well. To see that, let's consider the following experience Jerry Falwell reports on how he came to renounce racism:
>
> In my adolescence and young adult years I don't remember hearing one person speak of the injustice of segregation. To the contrary, all my role models, including powerful church leaders, supported segregation.
>
> I have never once considered myself a racist. Yet, looking back, I have to admit that I was one. Unfortunately, I was not quick enough or Christian enough or insightful enough to realize my condition until those days of tumult in the 1960s.
>
> But believe me, it wasn't the Congress or the courts that changed my heart. [The] demonstrators, in spite of their courage, didn't move me to new compassion on behalf of my black brothers and sisters. The new laws and the loud protest marchers may have helped to enforce the change and to speed it up, but it was God's still small voice in my heart that was the real instrument of change and growth for me.
>
> One Saturday morning in 1963 I sat in the end chair of Lee Baca's shoe-shine business on Main Street in Lynchburg. It was my Saturday morning ritual to have Lewis, an elderly black man, shine my shoes at 10 A.M.
>
> "I heard your sermon on television last week, Reverend," Lewis said as he began dusting a week of dirt off my shoes. "I sure do like the way you preach."
>
> "Why thank you, Lewis," I replied, looking closely at the thin, muscular man in his middle sixties whose curly gray hair framed his shiny, smiling face.
>
> Every week Lewis shared his faith with me. And every week I left his chair feeling his ministry in my life. Then on that particular Saturday morning Lewis asked me a question that he had never asked before.
>
> "Say, Reverend," he began softly, so that no one else could hear, "when am I going to be able to join that church of yours over on Thomas Road?"

> I felt like a boxer who had been punched directly in the stomach. For the first time in years, I was speechless.
>
> I puzzled over the question that next week and in the months that followed. I had no good reason that Lewis could not join my church. He was kind enough not to ask me for an explanation, because he knew that there was none. I had excuses, but I had no reason.
>
> (Falwell 1987, 294–296)[45]

This experience, Falwell reports, changed his life. In a similar way, it might be argued that some physical disabilities, whether they are acquired or eliminated, change a person's life. As Stephen M. Campbell and Joseph A. Stramondo write, "disabilities tend to be what we call *high-impact traits*—that is, traits that have a substantial causal impact on how a person's life unfolds" (2017, 166; emphasis in the original). Presumably, then, for specifically high-impact physical disabilities, their causal impact would involve changing how a person understands themselves, the world, and their place in it, and the values by which they life their lives. Thus, a congenitally blind person coming to have sight would seem to be a personally transformative experience.

A congenitally blind person coming to have sight would be a transformative experience *simpliciter*, as it's both epistemically and personally transformative, in Paul's terms. Now, as Paul (2014, ch. 2) argues, such experiences pose a challenge for rational choice. Because you wouldn't know what such an experience is like, it's hard to see how choosing to have such an experience could be an informed choice, and because such experiences change your preferences, it's hard to see what preferences should guide your choosing. So, it may be that people with certain physical disabilities couldn't rationally choose not to have them.

Secondly, and more generally, a person may reasonably choose to retain their physical disability because it's part of the person's practical identity, as discussed above. Holly Woodward, who uses a wheelchair, says something along these lines:

> My disability isn't a negative, it's a part of me, it's helped form my view of the world, given me determination (or stubbornness), the ability to laugh at myself, and makes me more grateful for the great people in my life. I love my life and I can honestly say given the chance I wouldn't take my disability away. . . .
>
> I would love to get to a stage where people are just people and disability is seen as a difference in ability rather than a negative or a description of someone.
>
> (2016)

Because it's part of her practical identity, Woodward wouldn't want to be without her physical disability.

The Resurrection of the Minority Body 229

Finally, a person may choose to retain their physical disability as a sign of love for God. To see how this might be so, consider Augustine's account of the resurrection of the body. While he thinks that most physical 'defects' or 'deformities' will be eliminated in the life of heaven, he thinks that some will be retained, namely, the scars of bodily wounds of the martyrs (1998, 22.19). Rather than being defects or deformities, according to Augustine, the scars from these wounds would be marks of virtue, or glorious marks, showing the love the martyrs had for God. In a similar way, as Scott Williams (2018, 4) argues, a person with an earthly disability might choose to retain that disability in the life of heaven as a mark, or sign, of their love for God, that they persevered in this love despite their suffering in their earthly life. And these disabilities, just as the scars of the martyrs, would be marks of virtue, or glorious marks, showing God's defeat of the suffering they endured in their earthly lives.[46]

Thus, we have three reasons why a person who has a physical disability in their earthly life may choose to retain that disability in their heavenly life, namely, it wouldn't be rational for them to choose to have it eliminated, they think it part of their practical identity, and they think it a mark of their love for God. And saints might then make different choices: some might choose to have their physical disability retained; some might choose to have their physical disability eliminated, which, as Williams writes, "is consistent with God's desire for human diversity" (2018, 5).[47]

Conclusion

Having argued that God could offer a person who has a physical disability in their earthly life the choice to retain their physical disability in their heavenly life, and it would be reasonable for them to choose to retain it, we can now conclude that there could be physical disabilities in the life of heaven. Consequently, for all we know, Cardinal George will be wearing a leg brace in his heavenly life, climbing mountains, and maybe even playing a game of rugby.[48]

Notes

1. The modality used here and throughout this paper is epistemic. That is, I aim to argue that, for all we know, there are physically disabled resurrected bodies. The reason for formulating the argument and conclusion of this paper in this way is that I'm conscious of our, or at least my, limited outlook on the life of heaven. As C.S. Lewis puts the point,

    I think our present outlook might be like that of a small boy who, on being told that the sexual act was the highest bodily pleasure should immediately ask whether you ate chocolates at the same time. On receiving the answer 'No,' he might regard absence of chocolates as the chief characteristic of sexuality. In vain would you tell him that the reason why lovers in their carnal raptures don't bother about chocolates is that they have something better to think of. The boy knows chocolate: he does not know the positive thing that excludes it. We are in the same position. We know the sexual life; we do not know, except in glimpses, the other thing which, in Heaven, will leave no room for it.

(1960, 159–160)

2. While the question of whether resurrected bodies could have disabilities has been discussed previously (e.g., Ehrman 2015; Mullins 2011; Yong 2007, 2009, 2012), the discussion has typically not distinguished between physical and cognitive disabilities. I focus only on physical disabilities in this paper.
3. I'm grateful to Fr. Benjamin A. Roberts for bringing the example of Cardinal George to my attention.
4. For a range of reasons from Christian tradition for why God eliminates physical disability in the life of heaven, see Brock and Swinton 2012.
5. For further arguments for the possibility of minority resurrected bodies, see Timpe forthcoming; Williams 2018.
6. I should acknowledge that this seems impossible, at least for bodies which have long died and thoroughly decayed. Peter van Inwagen makes the point forcefully with the following analogy:

> Suppose a certain monastery claims to have in its possession a manuscript written in St. Augustine's own hand. And suppose the monks of this monastery further claim that this manuscript was burned by Arians in the year 457. It would immediately occur to me to ask how this manuscript, the one I can touch, could be the very manuscript that was burned in 457. Suppose their answer to this question is that God miraculously recreated Augustine's manuscript in 458. I should respond to this answer as follows: the deed it describes seems quite impossible, even as an accomplishment of omnipotence. God certainly might have created a perfect duplicate of the original manuscript, but it would not be that one; its earliest moment of existence would have been after Augustine's death; it would never have known the impress of his hand; it would not have been a part of the furniture of the world when he was alive; and so on.
>
> Now suppose our monks were to reply by simply asserting that the manuscript now in their possession did know the impress of Augustine's hand; that it was a part of the furniture of the world when the Saint was alive; that when God recreated or restored it, He (as an indispensable component of accomplishing this task) saw to it that the object He produced had all these properties.
>
> I confess I should not know what to make of this. I should have to tell the monks that I did not see how what they believed could possibly be true.
>
> (1978, 116–117)

For philosophical defenses of the possibility of a person's earthly body being numerically identical with their resurrected body, see van Inwagen 1978, which proposes a 'body-snatching' model of the resurrection of the body and Zimmerman 1999, which proposes a 'falling-elevator' model of the resurrection of the body.

7. More, of course, could be said about how this relates to more theoretical accounts of defining a disability, such as the medical or social model, but this will be sufficient for our purposes. For compelling critiques of such models,

see Barnes 2016a, ch. 1. It may be impossible to demarcate precisely physical from cognitive disabilities because, as Kevin Timpe observes, it seems that *all* disabilities involve bodily features or conditions in the disability itself. Be that as it may, there are some core cases of physical disabilities, as mentioned above, and it's these cases I'll focus on.

8. So, there's no contradiction in a blind person experiencing the beatific vision.
9. For an account of personal knowledge which involves second-personal experience and sharing attention, see Stump 2010, ch. 4.
10. I exclude the possibility that our bodies change but we can't do anything with them, that is, such changes are all involuntary. Such an eschatological version of locked-in syndrome doesn't seem to be characteristic of a life supremely worth living. Thanks to Blake Hereth for bringing this possibility to my attention.
11. Richard Swinburne seems to favor such a conception of the life of heaven when he writes, in agreement with Augustine, "The Fathers all agree that the Blessed (the inhabitants of heaven) will be free from pain and suffer no disability; the body will go [as Augustine writes,] 'wherever the spirit wills'" (Swinburne 2017, 356). It's important to note that Swinburne excludes (presumably) physical disabilities and pain from the life of heaven, something I will soon challenge.
12. There's a familiar joke about rugby in heaven: two 90-year-old men, Mike and Joe, have been friends all of their lives. When it's clear that Joe is dying, Mike visits him every day. One day Mike says, "Joe, we both loved rugby all our lives, and we played rugby on Saturdays together for so many years. Please do me one favor, when you get to Heaven, somehow you must let me know if there's rugby there." Joe looks up at Mike from his death bed and says, "Mike, you've been my best friend for many years. If it's at all possible, I'll do this favor for you." Shortly after that, Joe passes on. At midnight a couple of nights later, Mike is awakened from a sound sleep by a blinding flash of white light and a voice calling out to him, "Mike, Mike." "Who is it?" asks Mike sitting up suddenly. "Mike, it's me, Joe." "You're not Joe. Joe just died," says Mike. "I'm telling you, it's me, Joe," insists the voice. "Joe! Where are you?" asks Mike. "In heaven," replies Joe. "I have some really good news and a little bad news," Joe continues. "Tell me the good news first," says Mike. "The good news," Joe says, "is that there's rugby in heaven. Better yet, all of our old friends who died before us are here, too. Better than that, we're all young again. Better still, it's always spring time and it never rains or snows. And best of all, we can play rugby all we want, and we never get tired." "That's fantastic," says Mike. "It's beyond my wildest dreams! So, what's the bad news?" "You're in the team for this Saturday," replies Joe.
13. They would seem to be, in Christina Van Dyke's words, "nothing more than glorious hood ornaments" (2015, 291).
14. These do, of course, correspond to Maslow's (1943) hierarchy of needs, which I use for illustrative purposes only. It's important to note, though, that these things illustrate what it is to have a good *earthly* life and may not carry over to illustrating what it is to have a good heavenly life. For example, according to Aquinas (1948, ST Suppl, Q.81 A.4), we won't eat, drink, or sleep in heaven, and so having enough of those would be irrelevant to having a good heavenly life. What the important things to have for a good heavenly life depends on the nature of that life.
15. Up to a point, of course. Sleeping all the time, while it may appeal to teenagers, certainly wouldn't make for a good life.
16. I mean 'boring' in a physical sense. As Blake Hereth pointed out to me, if I could easily climb the highest of mountains, it might still be interesting,

for I could take in the spectacular views. But it would be physically boring, because it would have required no effort. So, overall, it would be more interesting if I were to climb the highest mountain and it took effort for me to do so, which, it seems, would then be a better fit for a life supremely worth living.
17. Bernard Williams (1973) famously argues that heaven would be boring because we would run out of things to do. On this argument, heaven would become boring much quicker than on Williams's, because, even if we still have things to do, we wouldn't want to do them as they would be too easy.
18. The life Stump is discussing is our earthly life, rather than our heavenly life. She thinks our heavenly life will be quite different from our earthly one. But on this conception of the life of heaven, where it's physically dynamic, there isn't such a great difference.
19. This conclusion is, of course, analogous to Derek Parfit's 'repugnant conclusion':

> For any possible population of at least ten billion people, all with a very high quality of life, there must be some much larger imaginable population whose existence, if other things are equal, would be better, even though its members have lives that are barely worth living.
>
> (1984, 388)

20. Consequently, Augustine's account of how resurrected bodies achieve things must be wrong:

> I do not venture to give any bold account of what the movements of such [resurrected] bodies will be in the world to come; indeed, I cannot even imagine it. But everything there will be seemly in its form, in motion and in rest, for anything that is not seemly will not be there. It is certain also that the body will go immediately to wherever the spirit wills; and the spirit will never will anything which is not seemly either to the spirit or to the body.
>
> (1998, 22.30, 1178; cited approvingly in Swinburne 2017, 356)

21. Thus, echoing Van Dyke's criticism of Aquinas's account of the intellect in the life of heaven, Augustine's account of the body in the life of heaven, as given in the previous footnote, "represents less a fulfilment of human nature than a transcendence of what it means to be human" (2015, 292).
22. But that's not the only way, since, more generally, it's in the nature of having a human body (whether resurrected or not) that our bodily powers are limited, and limited in different ways (cf. Creamer 2009, 93–94; Barnes 2016a, 132; Cross 2016). Thus, when God-the-Son became incarnate, he experienced the limitations inherent in having a human body. Such limitations are, of course, easier to accommodate in a kenotic model of the Incarnation, but such a model isn't required. For discussion, see Green 2017. Thanks to David Worsley for bringing the connection to the Incarnation to my attention.
23. Chong-Ming Lim argues that the thought that disability reduces a person's overall well-being "depends on our considerations about the costs and extent of change involved in accommodating individuals with a particular disability trait" (2017, 323). I assume that given the infinite resources of heaven, accommodating any particular disability trait is possible. But, as Lim notes, "when we shift our focus to accommodating multiple disability traits, we see that accommodating one trait may make things difficult for

another trait" raising the possibility that it's impossible to accommodate, at the same time, two or more disability traits (2017, 326–327). Again, given the infinite resources of heaven, I don't think that this purported possibility is really possible for heaven, but, to be sure, we would have to know a lot more about heaven than we do and about how accommodating different disabilities interact with each other, something well worth exploring on another occasion.

24. For the same reasons that resurrected bodies in a physically dynamic life of heaven have limited bodily powers, such bodies will experience pain, but not suffering, since it will be transparent to the person the benefits of the pain they are experiencing, whereas such benefits of suffering is typically opaque to the sufferer (Stump 2010, 14).

25. As Stump defines it, a person's 'heart's desire' is a "particular kind of commitment on her part to something—a person or a project—that has great value for her in virtue of her care for it but that need not be essential to her flourishing" and is "at or near the center of the web of desire for her" (2010, 7). Given the nature of heaven, which consists primarily in union with God, it's hard to see that physical disabilities could prevent a person from achieving their heart's desires in the life of heaven. I thank Kevin Timpe for this point.

26. For a discussion of how physical pain can prevent a person from sharing attention with another, see Stump's (2012) discussion of Christ's cry of dereliction from the cross.

27. This objection is, of course, a descendent of the argument that if physical disabilities are mere-differences, it's permissible to cause a person who doesn't have a physical disability to have one; but that's absurd, so physical disabilities aren't mere-differences. This argument is made by, among others, Harris 2001, Kahane 2009, McMahan 2005, and Singer 2001, which Barnes 2016a rebuts. For a rebuttal to Barnes's argument, see Kahane and Savelescu 2016; for Barnes's reply, see Barnes 2016b.

28. While God could perform painless surgery on a person to cause them to be disabled, they would still likely experience pain and suffering in adapting to this new state.

29. Even if God informed them that their becoming disabled is better for them, and they believed him, it's likely that they wouldn't understand the reasons for this, and so it would still be opaque to them why they're experiencing this pain and difficulty.

30. For further discussion of the role of consent in the justification of harm, see Stump 2010, ch. 13.

31. But if we're united with God in the beatific vision, we would want what God wants, which is always the best for us, and so, if God wants the good that a physical disability would make possible for us, we would want that, too; consequently, if God tells us that becoming physically disabled is best for us, we would trust him, and God would therefore have our consent. I thank Kevin Timpe for this objection.

   In reply, if, in the beatific vision, God did ask us and we did consent, call this 'actual consent,' then God does have our consent, and so it wouldn't be wrong of him to cause us to be physically disabled. But if, in the beatific vision, God didn't ask us but merely relied on knowing that we would consent if asked, call this 'hypothetical consent,' then I don't think he would have our consent, and so it would be wrong of him to cause us to be physically disabled. In essence, in the beatific vision, God needs our actual consent rather than our hypothetical consent in order to be justified in causing us to be physically disabled. The reason is that, in the beatific vision, we don't submit to God but rather surrender to him. And hypothetical consent is sufficient for justified harm only if we submit to God. So, God needs our actual consent in order to be justified in causing us to be physically disabled.

Of course the main driver in this response is the distinction between submission and surrender, a distinction I take from Stump:

> For Paula to submit to Jerome is for Paula to desire that something be done or that something be the case just because she believes that Jerome desires that she desire *this*, even when she herself would desire the opposite of *this* if it were not for her belief that Jerome desires that she desire it and her fear of what Jerome would do if she did not desire what he desires her to desire. It is certainly possible for Paula to submit to Jerome in this way while she helplessly hates Jerome. By contrast, in the sense of surrender at issue here, for Paula to surrender to Jerome is for Paula to come to desire *Jerome*. It is for her to desire him and union with him after a period of resistance to him. On this way of thinking about the difference between submission and surrender, one can submit to someone without surrendering to him, and one can surrender to someone without submitting to him. Paula could desire Jerome and union with Jerome without thereby desiring *that* something-or-other be the case or be done just because she knows that Jerome desires that she desire this. Paula might in fact desire what Jerome desires, but only because she herself desires it as good, and not for the reason that Jerome desires that she desire this. On the other hand, Paula might desire Jerome but actually not desire what Jerome desires; she might instead desire that Jerome change *his* desires to bring them into harmony with what *she* desires. So, surrender is not to be confused with submission.
>
> (2010, 169; emphasis in the original)

In the beatific vision, we surrender, rather than submit to God, because we desire union with him while retaining control of our wills. And being in control of our wills, means that God needs our actual, rather than hypothetical, consent, in order to be justified in causing us to be physically disabled, even if he knows what we will will.

32. As Blake Hereth pointed out to me, there is another reply to the objection that could be made: even if physical disabilities are value-positive in the life of heaven, they need not be the only value-positive differences in the life of heaven. It may well be that being non-disabled is also a value-positive difference in the life of heaven, and, if that is the case, there is no motivation for changing from a physically disabled body to a non-physically disabled one.
33. According to Jonathan Glover (2006, 19–23; cited in Barnes 2014, 96), after a man, who had been blind from infancy, had his vision restored by a surgical procedure, he fell into a deep depression and died less than two years afterwards.
34. Again, God would require our actual consent rather than our hypothetical consent as argued above.
35. It's cited approvingly in Yong 2007, 270, 2009, 61, and argued against in Mullins 2011 to which Yong 2012 responds. Timpe forthcoming also discusses it.
36. I thank Kevin Timpe for this point.
37. There's a close relationship between practical identity and narrative identity, where, according to Marya Schechtman, "a person creates his identity by forming an autobiographical narrative—a story of his life"' (1996, 93). Thanks to Joshua Cockayne for this observation.

38. Anthony Appiah (1990) gives an insightful discussion of race, ethnicity, and gender as what he terms 'ethical identities,' which seem relevantly similar to Korsgaard's practical identity.
39. In their introduction to their volume, *Disability and the Good Human Life*, Jerome E. Bickenbach, Franziska Felder, and Barbara Schmitz seem to elide this distinction, or take it to be a distinction without a difference, when they write,

    > [W]hen an impairment such as blindness or lower-body paralysis is so thoroughly internalized as to form part of one's identity, it seems insensitive and factually incorrect to continue to insist that impairment is both an objective harm and an essential detriment to that individual's good life.
    >
    > (2014, 5–6)

    For it seems that it's "factually incorrect to continue to insist that impairment is both an objective harm and an essential detriment to that individual's good life" only if a person's physical disability is part of their theoretical identity, but it's 'insensitive' to do the same only if a person's physical disability is part of their practical identity. In the same volume, Thomas Schramme seems to be aware of this distinction, and thinks it makes a difference, when he writes that "disability almost by its nature is, or can become, a part of a person's identity" (2014, 88) but makes clear that it's the practical concept of identity he means when he writes in the following page, "The person who had an accident or who was born blind *could* have had another life, or he *might* be cured in a conceivable world" (2014, 89; emphasis in the original).
40. Furthermore, as Hauerwas argues, making what happens to a person to become part of them can be an important part of their response to suffering:

    > We often find that essential in our response to suffering is the ability to make what happens to me mine. Cancer patients often testify to some sense of relief when they find out they have cancer. The very ability to name what they have seems to give them a sense of control or possession that replaces the undifferentiated fear they had been feeling. Pain and suffering alienates us from ourselves. They make us what we do not know. The task is to find the means to make that which is happening to me mine—to interpret its presence, even if such an interpretation is negative, as something I can claim as integral to my identity. No doubt our power to transform events into decisions can be the source of great self-deceptions, but it is also the source of our moral identity.
    >
    > (1984, 82–83)

41. I emphasize that this passage merely suggests that God won't unilaterally eliminate physical disabilities. I don't think we can conclude, merely on the basis of this passage, that he won't. It simply adds to the case that I've been presenting in this paper. Thanks for Kevin Timpe for prompting me to clarify this.
42. Here I assume that the person has the capacity for consent. The case of young children and those with severe brain injury raise interesting questions about those who cannot consent. For the case of children, it may be that they are allowed to mature in a kind of limbo until they achieve the capacity for consent (see Timpe 2015). For the case of those with severe brain injury, this would be a kind of cognitive disability, and I've no argument for how God would deal with such cases. This illustrates Timpe's point that it's hard

to draw an exclusive distinction between physical and cognitive disabilities. Thanks to Joshua Cockayne for drawing my attention to cases of severe brain injury.
43. Determining just what mere-differences God could offer a person the choice to retain or have changed is beyond the scope of this paper, but it would be interesting to think about what they might be: sex or gender? race or ethnicity? body shape or size? hair or eye color?
44. For a range of assessments of Jackson's thought experiment, see Ludlow, Nagasawa, and Stoljar 2004.
45. For a skeptical viewpoint on this incident, see Harding 2000, 26–28.
46. A precedent may be Paul's 'thorn in the flesh' (2 Corinthians 12:7–9), sometimes associated with the effects of his stoning in Lystra (Acts 14), which would have caused significant bodily injury. Yet Paul glories in this weakness, praising God for it. Thanks to David Worsley for this point.
47. Now, it might be objected that a person might be conflicted in their desires: a person with a physical disability in their earthly life might both desire to have that disability eliminated in their heavenly life, but desire not to have that desire; or a person with a physical disability in their earthly life might both desire to have that disability retained in their heavenly life, but desire not to have that desire. And so, it might be thought, it's unclear whether being physically disabled is part of their practical identity, which means that it's unclear what God would do, thereby making problems for the optionality view. (This is a version of the authority problem raised by Irving Thalberg 1978 and Gary Watson 1975 against Harry G. Frankfurt's early hierarchical account of freedom [1971], which Stump [unpublished manuscript]. discusses in connection with the possibility of disability in heaven.)

In response, I don't think that this putative possibility is a genuine possibility. For, when a person comes to have the choice as to whether their physical disability is retained, their desires will be integrated around a desire for the good, and, if it is indeed good for them, as I've argued to very well might be, to be physically disabled in their heavenly life, then that is what they will wholeheartedly desire; however, if it's not good for them, they will wholeheartedly desire not to be physically disabled in their heavenly life. If both states, of being physically disabled and not being physically disabled, are good for them, and neither is overall better for them, then I think there will be some arbitrariness concerning which desire will become wholehearted, but one of them will, because their desires will indeed be integrated, that is, without fragmentation. And so I don't think that there could be a conflict in a person's desires regarding retaining or eliminating their physical disability.
48. Many thanks to Joshua Cockayne and David Worsley for helpful comments on previous drafts of this paper, and also to the editors, Blake Hereth and Kevin Timpe for their helpful comments and work on this anthology.

References

Adams, Robert Merrihew. "Existence, Self-Interest, and the Problem of Evil." *Noûs* 13 (1979): 53–65.

Appiah, Anthony. " 'But Would That Still Be Me?' Notes on Gender, 'Race,' Ethnicity, as Sources of 'Identity.' " *The Journal of Philosophy* 87 (1990): 493–499.

Aquinas, Thomas. *Summa Theologicae*. Translated by Fathers of the English Dominica. Province, 5 vols. London: Christian Classics, 1948.

Augustine. *The City of God Against the Pagans*, edited and translated by R. W. Dyson. Cambridge: Cambridge University Press, 1998.
Baker, Lynne Rudder. *Persons and Bodies: A Constitution View*. Cambridge: Cambridge University Press, 2000.
Barnes, Elizabeth. "Valuing Disability, Causing Disability." *Ethics* 125 (2014): 88–113.
———. *The Minority Body: A Theory of Disability*. Oxford: Oxford University Press, 2016a.
———. "Reply to Kahane and Savulescu." *Res Philosophica* 93 (2016b): 295–309.
Bickenbach, Jerome E., Franziska Felder, and Barbara Schmitz. "Introduction: Rethinking the Good Human Life in Light of Disability." In *Disability and the Good Human Life*, edited by Jerome E. Bickenbach, Franziska Felder, and Barbara Schmitz, 1–18. New York: Cambridge University Press, 2014a.
——— (eds.). *Disability and the Good Human Life*. New York: Cambridge University Press, 2014b.
Bradford, Gwen. *Achievement*. Oxford: Oxford University Press, 2015.
Brock, Brian and John Swinton (eds.). *Disability in the Christian Tradition: A Reader*. Grand Rapids, MI: Wm. B. Eerdmans, 2012.
Brown, Christopher. "Friendship in Heaven: Aquinas on Supremely Perfect Happiness and the Communion of the Saints." In *Metaphysics and God: Essays in Honor of Eleonore Stump*, edited by Kevin Timpe, 225–248. New York and London: Routledge, 2009.
Campbell, Scott. "The Conception of a Person as a Series of Menta Events." *Philosophy and Phenomenological Research* 73 (2006): 339–358.
Campbell, Stephen M. and Joseph A. Stramondo. "The Complicated Relationship of Disability and Well-Being." *Kennedy Institute of Ethics Journal* 27 (2017): 151–184.
Creamer, Deborah Beth. *Disability and Christian Theology: Embodied Limits and Constructive Possibilities*. Oxford: Oxford University Press, 2009.
Cross, Richard. "Impairment, Normalcy, and a Social Theory of Disability." *Res Philosophica* 93 (2016): 693–714.
Emma. "My Identity and How My Disability Defines Me." *SimplyEmma* (2017). www.simplyemma.co.uk/my-identity-how-my-disability-defines-me/.
Ehrman C. S. C., Terrence. "Disability and Resurrection Identity." *New Blackfriars* 96 (2015): 723–731.
Eiesland, Nancy. "Liberation, Inclusion, and Justice: A Faith Response to Persons with Disabilities." *Impact* 14 (2001–2002): 2–3.
Falwell, Jerry. *Strength for the Journey*. New York: Simon & Schuster, 1987.
Foster, John. *The Immaterial Self: A Defence of the Cartesian Dualist Conception of the Mind*. London: Routledge, 1991.
Frankfurt, Harry G. "Freedom of the Will and the Concept of a Person." *The Journal of Philosophy* 68 (1971): 5–20.
Gould, James Barton. "The Hope of Heavenly Healing of Disability, Part 1: Theological Issues." *Journal of Disability & Religion* 20 (2016): 317–334.
———. "The Hope of Heavenly Healing of Disability, Part 2: Philosophical Issues." *Journal of Disability & Religion* 21 (2017): 98–116.
Green, Adam. "Omnisubjectivity and Incarnation." *Topoi* 36 (2017): 693–701.
Harding, Susan. *The Book of Jerry Falwell: Fundamentalist Language and Politics*. Princeton, NJ: Princeton University Press, 2000.

Harris, John. "Is There a Coherent Social Conception of Disability?" *Journal of Medical Ethics* 26 (2000): 95–100.

———. "One Principle and Three Fallacies of Disability Studies." *Journal of Medical Ethics* 27 (2001): 383–387.

Jackson, Frank. "Epiphenomenal Qualia." *The Philosophical Quarterly* 32 (1982): 127–136.

Kahane, Guy. "Non-Identity, Self-Defeat, and Attitudes to Future Children." *Philosophical Studies* 145 (2009): 193–214.

Kahane, Guy and Julian Savelescu. "Disability and Mere Difference." *Ethics* 126 (2016): 774–788.

Korsgaard, Christine. *The Sources of Normativity*. New York: Cambridge University Press, 1996.

Leibniz, Gottfried Wilhelm. *Textes inédits*. Edited by Gaston Grua. Paris: Presses Universitaires de France, 1948.

Lewis, C. S. *Miracles*. New York: Collier Books, 1960.

Lim, Chong-Ming. "Reviewing Resistances to Reconceptualizing Disability." *Proceedings of the Aristotelian Society* 117.3 (2017): 321–331.

Lowe, E. J. *Subjects of Experience*. Cambridge: Cambridge University Press, 1996.

Ludlow, Peter, Yujin Nagasawa, and Daniel Stoljar (eds.). *There's Something About Mary: Essays on Phenomenal Consciousness and Frank Jackson's Knowledge Argument*. Cambridge, MA: MIT Press, 2004.

Martin, Michelle and Joyce Duriga. "Cardinal George Remembered for Close Relationship with God." *Catholic News Service*, April 28, 2015. www.catholicherald.com/news/cardinal_george_remembered_for_close_relationship_with_god/.

Maslow, A. H. "A Theory of Human Motivation." *Psychological Review* 50 (1943): 370–396.

Mattlin, Ben. "Valuing Life, Whether Disabled or Not." *Opinion, National Public Radio*, December 7, 2005. www.npr.org/templates/story/story.php?storyId=5042181?storyId=5042181&t=1541155443435.

McMahan, Jeff. *The Ethics of Killing: Problems at the Margins of Life*. Oxford: Oxford University Press, 2002.

———. "Causing Disabled People to Exist and Causing People to Be Disabled." *Ethics* 116 (2005): 77–99.

Merricks, Trenton. 2009. "The Resurrection of the Body." In *The Oxford Handbook of Philosophical Theology*, edited by Thomas P. Flint and Michael C. Rea, 476–490. Oxford: Oxford University Press, 2009.

Mullins, R. T. "Some Difficulties for Amos Yong's Disability Theology of the Resurrection." *Ars Disputandi* 11 (2011): 24–32.

Olson, Eric T. *The Human Animal: Personal Identity Without Psychology*. New York: Oxford University Press, 1997.

Palmer, Ellis. "How I Saw Stephen Hawking's Death as a Disabled Person." *BBC News*, 16 March 2018. www.bbc.co.uk/news/world-43418251.

Parfit, Derek. *Reasons and Persons*. Oxford: Clarendon Press, 1984.

Paul, L. A. *Transformative Experience*. Oxford: Oxford University Press, 2014.

Ratcliff, Ace. "Stephen Hawking's Disability Wasn't Something to 'Overcome.'" *Huffington Post*, March 15, 2018. www.huffingtonpost.com/entry/opinion-ratcliff-hawking-ableism_us_5aaa8c5ee4b045cd0a6f6f2d.

Schechtman, Marya. *The Constitution of Selves*. Ithaca and London: Cornell University Press, 1996.

Schramme, Thomas. "Disability (Not) as a Harmful Condition: The Received View Challenged." In *Disability and the Good Human Life*, edited by Jerome E. Bickenbach, Franziska Felder, and Barbara Schmitz, 72–92. New York: Cambridge University Press, 2014.

Singer, Peter. "Ethics and Disability: A Response to Koch." *Journal of Disability Policy Studies* 16 (2001): 130–133.

Stoner, Ian. "Ways to Be Worse Off." *Res Philosophica* 93 (2016): 921–949.

Stump, Eleonore. *Wandering in Darkness: Narrative and the Problem of Suffering*. Oxford: Oxford University Press, 2010.

———. "Atonement and the Cry of Dereliction from the Cross." *European Journal for Philosophy of Religion* 4 (2012): 1–17.

———. "That Was Then, This Is Now." *Glancing Thoughts: Solemnity of Christ the King* (November 25, 2018). http://liturgy.slu.edu/ChristKingB112518/reflections_stump.html.

———. "Life After Death and the True Self." Unpublished manuscript.

Swinburne, Richard. *The Evolution of the Soul*. Oxford: Oxford University Press, 1997.

———. "Why the Life of Heaven Is Supremely Worth Living." In *Paradise Understood: New Philosophical Essays About Heaven*, edited by T. Ryan Byerly and Eric J. Silverman, 350–362. New York: Oxford University Press, 2017.

Thalberg, Irving. "Hierarchical Analyses of Unfree Action." *Canadian Journal of Philosophy* 8.2 (1978): 211–226.

Thomson, Judith Jarvis. "People and Their Bodies." In *Reading Parfit*, edited by Jonathan Dancy, 202–229. Oxford: Blackwell, 1997.

Timpe, Kevin. "An Argument for Limbo." *The Journal of Ethics* 19 (2015): 277–292.

———. "Defiant Afterlife—Disability and Uniting Ourselves to God." In *Marginalized Identities, Peripheral Theologies: Expanding Conversations in Analytic Theology*, edited by Michelle Panchuk and Michael C. Rea. New York: Oxford University Press, forthcoming.

Toy, Mitchell. "#RIPStephenHawking." *Twitter* (2018). https://twitter.com/mitchelltoy/status/973774076803248128?lang=en.

Van Dyke, Christina. "Aquinas's Shiny Happy People: Perfect Happiness and the Limits of Human Nature." In *Oxford Studies in Philosophy of Religion: Volume 6*, edited by Jonathan Kvanvig, 270–292. Oxford: Oxford University Press, 2015.

van Inwagen, Peter. "The Possibility of Resurrection." *International Journal for Philosophy of Religion* 9 (1978): 114–121.

Watson, Gary. "Free Agency." *Journal of Philosophy* 72.8 (1975): 205–220.

Wendell, Susan. *The Rejected Body: Feminist Philosophical Reflections on Disability*. New York and London: Routledge, 1996.

Williams, Bernard. "The Makropulos Case: Reflections on the Tedium of Immortality." In *Problems of the Self*, edited by Bernard Williams, 82–100. Cambridge: Cambridge University Press, 1973.

Williams, Scott. 2018. "Horrendous-Difference Disabilities, Resurrected Saints, and the Beatific Vision: A Theodicy." *Religions* 9 (2018): 1–13.

Woodward, Holly. "My Disability Isn't a Negative, It's a Part of Me." *Huffington Post*, September 27, 2016. www.huffingtonpost.co.uk/holly-woodward/my-disability-isnt-a-negative_b_12192006.html.

Yong, Amos. *Theology and Down Syndrome: Reimagining Disability in Late Modernity*. Waco, TX: Baylor University Press, 2007.

———. "Disability and the Love of Wisdom." *Ars Disputandi* 9 (2009): 54–71.
———. "Disability Theology of the Resurrection: Persisting Questions and Additional Considerations—A Response to Ryan Mullins." *Ars Disputandi* 12 (2012): 4–10.
Zimmerman, Dean W. "The Compatibility of Materialism and Survival: The 'Falling Elevator' Model." *Faith and Philosophy* 16 (1999): 194–212.

10 Disabled Beatitude

Kevin Timpe

This chapter is an extension of an earlier article, "Defiant Afterlife—Disability and Uniting Ourselves to God." My primary aim there was to push back against a common theological view which holds, even if unreflectively or uncritically, that union with God in the afterlife requires that individuals with disabilities will have those disabilities 'cured' or 'healed' prior to heavenly union with God.[1] To this end, I developed an argument for the possibility of redeemed individuals retaining their disabilities in the eschaton (i.e., in beatitude) and nevertheless enjoying complete union with God (and through God to others). In the present paper, I show not just that it is possible for there to be disability in heaven, but that there are considerations in favor of 'disabled beatitude.'

Methodological Issues

Before I summarize in greater detail my earlier argument for why there could be disabilities in heaven or address the considerations in favor of thinking there will be heavenly disabilities, let me first address three methodological considerations that ought to shape theological or religious philosophical reflection on disability.[2]

First, the present paper is admittedly a part of speculative theology. There are, so far as I can tell, no normative commitments about whether there will be disability in heaven binding on the Christian philosopher, even the Christian philosopher who takes seriously the Christian tradition as an epistemic source for boundaries. None of the first seven ecumenical creeds, for instance, mention disability.[3] And while the boundaries of Catholic theology are not set entirely by the *Catechism of the Catholic Church*, it is interesting that there is no single mention of 'disability' or 'impairment' in such a document which seeks to distill specifically Catholic theology. Similarly, to take another example, neither 'disability' nor 'impairment' is mentioned in any of the three primary Reformed confessions—the Belgic Confession, the Heidelberg Catechism, and the Canons of Dort—which are described as "revealing the contours of historic Christian teaching from a Reformed perspective" (Billings 2013, 10).

So it looks like Christian theology in general as well as more specific theological accounts of the Christian faith leave open what we ought to think about disability in the eschaton. While I think there are dangers that may arise when doing speculative theology, I don't think those dangers entail that we ought not do it. In fact, I think that the second methodological consideration to which I turn in the next paragraph gives us reason to engage in theological speculation specifically about disability.

Second, our theological vision can shape our communal practices. This certainly happens with official dogmatic theology, as when Catholics participate at least weekly in the Mass because

> the Church obliges the faithful to take part in the Divine Liturgy on Sundays and feast days and, prepared by the sacrament of Reconciliation, to receive the Eucharist at least once a year, if possible during the Easter season. But the Church strongly encourages the faithful to receive the holy Eucharist on Sundays and feast days, or more often still, even daily.
> (*Catechism of the Catholic Church* 2003, section 1389)

This isn't, of course, to say that such admonishments are always followed. One could fail to have one's practices reflect the theology that one confesses. The present point is simply that one's official theology often does, and should, shape one's practices. And what is true of dogmatic theology can also be true of speculative theology. Much American evangelical theology is shaped by speculative commitments regarding eschatology in ways that, for instance, lead them to be less likely to recycle than are other parts of the American public.[4]

My earlier paper is part of a growing literature which shows how theological beliefs about disability shape the Church's behavior toward those with disabilities, often with the result of excluding them from full participation in the Church. There I mention, for example, how John Calvin's views about both disability and the Eucharist led him to exclude individuals with cognitive disabilities from participating in the Eucharist. For Calvin, the Christian life "cannot be said to be well ordered and regulated unless in it the Holy Supper of our Lord is always being celebrated and frequented" (Calvin 1954, 48). As we'll see below, Calvin thought that individuals with cognitive disabilities are prohibited from the Eucharistic table, and thus seem excluded from 'the well ordered and regulated' Christian life. The past few decades have seen numerous scholars further explore how misguided views about the nature of disability and the value of lives with disabilities have negatively shaped Christian practices (Yong 2011; Hull 2014; Clifton 2018; Eiesland 1994; Ben Conner 2012; Wilder 2016; Reinders 2008; Swinton 2012; Brock forthcoming). In one of the influential books in this area, *The Disabled God*, theologian Nancy Eiesland explores how the history of excluding individuals with disabilities from the Church is often the result of theological reflection on disability:

> Three themes—sin and disability conflation, virtuous suffering, and segregationist charity—illustrate the theological obstacles encountered by people with disabilities who seek inclusion and justice within the Christian community. It cannot be denied that the biblical record and Christian theology have often been dangerous for persons with disabilities.
>
> (Eiesland 1994, 74)

Elsewhere, I've discussed some of the ways that problematic assumptions about the nature of disability have led the Church to mistreat individuals with disabilities both in the past and in the present (Timpe 2018).

Furthermore, Christian life is communal (see, e.g., Wolterstorff 2018; Cuneo 2016; Smith 2016), which connects with the third methodological consideration I want to mention. I think it's important to keep in mind that theology and disability are inherently social. That theology is an inherently social or communal enterprise ought to be obvious. But beyond just the communal nature of theological inquiry, Christian communities live out their theology in social ways. For instance, it was Dietrich Bonhoeffer's view of the social nature of Christian life that led him to support the Bethel community and structure his *Life Together* (Bonhoeffer 1954; see also Wannenwetsch 2012). Disability is also communal, both in terms of some of its causes and effects (Timpe 2019). The social nature of disability is also closely connected with social models of disability, including the influential recent Value-Neutral Model defended by Elizabeth Barnes (Barnes 2016, especially ch. 3).[5] Unlike other proponents of social models of disability, Barnes doesn't endorse the impairment/disability distinction that is often associated with the social model of disability. According to this distinction, while impairment is physical (i.e., biological or physiological), disability is "something imposed on top of our impairments by the way we are unnecessarily isolated and excluded from society. Disabled people are therefore an oppressed group" (Barnes 2012, 14).[6] Barnes rejects this distinction, in part because it pushes the question of 'what is disability?' back into the question of 'what is impairment?' She instead just talks about disability, which in her view still has an inherently social dimension. Eyler also calls into question the distinction as problematic: "The social model has a long life in Disability Studies research, but some scholars have questioned its effectiveness, primarily because the model forces the binary opposition of 'impairment' and 'disability' in ways that at times seems rather misleading" (Eyler 2010, 5). Shelley Lynn Tremain argues in a different direction that impairment itself is socially constructed, and thus argues against the traditional social model of disability built on the disability/impairment distinction (Tremain 2017).

While the details differ, those views that reject strongly individualist medical models of disability insist that there's a central social element to being disabled.

Making Space for Disability in the Eschaton

My earlier "Defiant Afterlife—Disability and Uniting Ourselves to God" sought to do three things.[7] It begins by briefly surveying how Christian theological reflection on disability has eschatological implications for individuals with disabilities. It then explores a number of recent treatments of the relationship between disability and eschatology, criticizing those extant accounts. The paper culminates in an argument for the possibility that at least some disabilities can be retained in the afterlife in a way that doesn't detract from the beatific vision[8] of the redeemed.

Given that the majority of disabilities are acquired rather than congenital, I don't think that all disabilities are essential to the personal identity of those who have them. Just as there are individuals who come to acquire a disability in a way that doesn't threaten their identity, so too it is possible for some individuals to cease to have a disability in a way that doesn't threaten their personal identity. However, I think we have good reason to think that many of the accidental or contingent features of our identities are such that we'll keep them in the eschaton. There are aspects of our identities that, even though not essential to us, will remain as part of who we are into the afterlife. Even if it's literally true that in heaven people 'will neither marry nor be given in marriage,' it will still be the case that my identity is shaped by the contingent experiences that are part of my ongoing relationship with my spouse. Furthermore, while being a parent is only a contingent part of my identity, stripping me of the relationship I have with my children in the afterlife would involve a needless, damaging, and perhaps even unjust change to my identity. So too with some disabilities.

Whether a person retains a disability in the resurrection or not, I think, depends on whether it involves what Barnes calls 'bad-difference' or 'mere-difference.' Those views which hold that "disability is by itself something that makes you worse off [are] 'bad-difference' views of disability" (Barnes 2016, 55; while she sometimes refers to *the* bad-difference view and *the* mere-difference view, each should be understood as a family of views, much as the problem of evil is really a family of related problems) while mere-difference views are those according to which having a disability doesn't by itself or automatically make you worse off. This way of drawing the contrast, she notes, is "rough-and-ready" (Barnes 2016, 55) for her purposes, but it should be sufficient for present purposes as well. Furthermore, the connection between the disability and the difference in well-being is important for differentiating bad-difference from mere-difference disabilities. It is consistent with a rejection of a bad-difference view that individuals with disabilities are in fact worse off than non-disabled individuals, insofar as that difference was caused by social structures or ableism. Furthermore, there can be bad effects of disabilities that would still exist in the absence of ableism. But those same disabilities might allow for other goods that are perhaps unique to or even just more common for those with the disability. So the question is whether the effects caused by disability are net-negative in that they are "counterfactually stable—disability would have such effect even in the absence of ableism" (Barnes 2016, 60).

I grant that if there are any disabilities that involve bad-difference or would interfere with a person's complete union with God, then Christian conceptions of heaven are such that those disabilities will not be present there given the nature of heavenly beatitude.[9] But these disabilities would be removed prior to the eschaton not *just* because a disability is present *simpliciter*, but rather because the specific disability prevents the perfection of the union with God characteristic of the beatific vision. For any disability that does not involve bad-difference or which does not intrinsically interfere with union with God, then that particular reason why it could not be present in heaven is absent.[10] On the view I've developed, there may be some disabilities that can be retained in the afterlife in a way that doesn't impair the beatific vision, even if there are others that may not have a place in our eschatology because they detract from a person's flourishing.[11] And I sought to give a number of examples that plausibly could be understood in this way. I concluded "Defiant Afterlife" by saying that we need not think, as Augustine does, that there is a problem with individuals being such that they "shall rise again in their deformity, and not rather with an amended and perfected body" (Augustine, *Enchiridion*, ch. 87: "The Case of Monstrous Births").

Extending the Account

It's one thing to say that some disabilities *could be* present in the beatific vision. It's quite another to say that we have reason to think that some disabilities *will be* eschatologically present. The present section seeks to give some admittedly speculative reasons to think that there will be some disabilities in heaven.

Incarnational Reasons

I begin with a few arguments that there will be disability in the eschaton that draw on the Incarnation that I think fail. Some theologians of disability argue that the resurrected Christ himself was disabled, thereby establishing the possibility of eschatological disability.[12] Nancy Eiesland's influential *The Disabled God*, mentioned earlier, is perhaps the best example. Speaking of Jesus's post-resurrection appearance to the disciples in Jerusalem recounted in Luke 24, Eiesland writes:

> Here is the resurrected Christ making good on the incarnational proclamation that God would be with us, embodied as we are, incorporating the fullness of human contingency and ordinary life into God. In presenting his impaired hands and feet to his startled friends, the resurrected Jesus is revealed as the disabled God.... The disabled God is not only the One from heaven but the revelation of true personhood, underscoring the reality that full personhood is fully compatible with the experience of disability.
> (Eiesland 1994, 100)

Here Eiesland thinks of Jesus as having impaired hands and feet from the crucifixion, as well as a disfigured side. But she doesn't specify what the disability is that God has.[13] She appears to endorse the impairment/disability distinction, discussed in the previous section, that is at the core of the social model of disability. In chapter 1 of *The Disabled God*, she allows that someone could have an impairment and not be disabled if they haven't been "single[d] out for differential treatment" or "shaped primarily by exclusion" (Eiesland 1994, 24). Presumably the impairment involved in the post-crucified Jesus would be loss of functioning that results from the damage to his hands (and feet and side) caused by the nails. And then presumably Jesus would be disabled in virtue of the differential treatment and exclusion resulting from the crucifixion. But it's not clear that the resurrected Christ actually does have a loss of functioning from the wounds imposed by the crucifixion; after the crucifixion and resurrection, Jesus is able to break bread (Luke 24:30), walk (Luke 24:15), and cook fish and eat (Luke 21:9). So what is the relevant impairment that remains after the wounds are healed? It's not clear. And remember that on Eiesland's view even if an impairment can be specified, having an impairment is not sufficient for having a disability.[14] Will the Incarnate Christ be singled out for differential treatment or shaped primarily by exclusion in the eschaton? Presumably not.

Theologian Amos Yong doesn't endorse explicitly Eiesland's line of thinking in his recent book *The Bible, Disability, and the Church*. As with his earlier *Theology and Down Syndrome*, Yong thinks that continuity of identity between the pre- and post-mortem life requires some disabilities to be present in the afterlife.[15] He also holds that rejecting heavenly disability would contribute to normate biases[16] that undervalue lives with disabilities:

> If there are no disabilities in the life to come, then that implicitly suggests that our present task is to rid the world of such unfortunate and unwanted realities.... If disability is a reflection of the present,

> fallen, and broken order of things, the redemption of this world and its transformation into the coming eon will involve the removal of all symptoms related to the tragic character of life dominated by sin [including disability].
>
> (Yong 2011, 118ff.)

If creaturely disability in heaven would counter such normate biases, even more so would a disability assumed or acquired in the Incarnation. Yong doesn't explicitly make this point. But he does make the weaker claim that the second person of the Trinity fully enters into the experience of disability in the Incarnation. According to Yong,

> Jesus need not have qualified for a disability license plate in order to enter into the existence of people with disabilities because, as I have been arguing throughout this volume, disability is not only an individualized, biological/medical experience but also a social phenomenon of oppression, marginalization, and exclusion. According to this definition, Jesus entered into the experience of disability fully in his suffering, persecution, and the execution at the hands of others. Thus, he is able to identify with people who have disabilities as one who has shared their ostracism 'in every respect.'
>
> (Yong 2011, 126)

And while Yong doesn't go so far as to say that because of the scars, Jesus has a disability or even an impairment, he does argue that they indicate the importance of "the continuities between the historical and eschatological bodies" (Yong 2011, 129) which, he thinks, gives us reason to think that we'll have the same continuity in our eschatological bodies. But all that requires is the marks or consequences of and not the disabilities themselves; and the same could be true of Jesus.[17]

Social Reasons

There are social reasons that, while I don't think they are decisive, give us some reason to think that there will be disabilities in heaven.[18] First, consider the roles that disability identity and disability pride can play in a person's life in the present life. Many people's experiences and life-projects get folded into their self-understanding and identities in such a way that, barring reasons for thinking they can't be part of one's heavenly identity, we might think will be retained. If these experiences and life-projects are not only good (as I think often is the case with respect to disability identity and disability advocacy) but also part of their lived love for God, then these goods could be folded into the goods found in heaven. Suppose, for instance, that so long as a desire isn't mis-ordered, it is good for us to get "the desires of our heart" (Stump 2010). If retaining their disability as part of their self-understanding or self-identity is among the desires of a person's heart, then perhaps God has a reason to retain a person's disabilities as part of God's act of loving them. Furthermore, these goods need not just attach to the good for the individual with the disability. Many social practices can connect individuals without disabilities (or with other disabilities) to an individual in such a way that matters for the common and not just individual good, as evidenced by the *L'Arche* communities. Disability pride, for instance, can motivate advocacy work aimed at justice and can strengthen the union and solidarity that people have with disabled individuals.

While I think that there's something important about these social reasons, the issues surrounding both proper pride and solidarity are complex. I think there are two less complicated lines of argument for the claim that there will, in fact, be disability in heaven. The first of these has to do with specific features of particular disabilities. The second has to do with those features of creation that make possible disability. I consider each of these in turn.

Specific Disabilities

My work on disability is shaped by what Manuel Vargas calls "the standard of naturalistic plausibility":

> on a standard of naturalistic plausibility the account requires something that speaks in its favor beyond mere coherence with the known facts. . . . We seek a theory that has something to be said for it, in light of what we know about the natural world.
>
> (Vargas 2013, 58)

My work on disabilities aims to satisfy what I refer to as the Principle of Minimal Agential Realism, which is structured on Vargas's standard of naturalistic plausibility:

> Make sure, when constructing a theory of agency, that the kinds of powers, capacities, and outputs posited by that theory could, for all we know, be had by us.[19]

To see how a particular disability might contribute to the good of the agent or community in the eschaton, consider the case of Williams syndrome. Williams syndrome is caused by a deletion on the long arm of chromosome 7 (more specifically, it's a deletion in 7q11.23). Individuals with Williams syndrome typically have a number of physical features, including a characteristic facial appearance; heart or blood vessel problems, such as supravalvular aortic stenosis; hypercalcemia (elevated blood calcium levels); and joint laxity or joint stiffness. While some of these conditions can be problematic (e.g., hypercalcemia can cause pain and interfere with the heart's functioning), their associated risks would presumably be absent from the resurrected body.

But consider instead some of the social and emotional effects of Williams syndrome, which plausibly are not problematic. Many individuals with Williams syndrome exhibit a unique range of social and interpersonal characteristics, including:

- unique intensity and duration of attention to people
- hypersociability
- heightened intensity of social interaction
- strength in interpreting non-verbal behavior
- excessive friendliness to others, including strangers
- higher than normal degrees of empathy and emotional sensitivity (Niccols 2012; Mervis et al. 2003; Morris 2000; Filder et al. 2007. In addition, some evidence suggests a similar strength in young children with Down syndrome; see Fidler 2005; Kasari 1995)

These characteristics can lead to increased motivation for interpersonal interaction and closeness.

Fidler et al. refer to the "complementary aspect of primary *intersubjectivity* (i.e., the ability to respond in synchronous ways to other people's emotional displays" as "emotional responsivity" (Fidler 2007, 194). The relative likelihood, defined as the ratio of proportions of individuals displaying the characteristic in question between groups, of positive interpersonal affective social behaviors ranged from 1.4 to 14.3 in favor of those with Williams syndrome, leading the researchers to conclude that children with Williams syndrome have increased performance with regard to emotional responsivity toward others (Fidler 2007; interestingly, this increase "did not seem to translate into improved performance in other areas of social functioning, in particular social decision-making" [202; see also 204]). Another study found that children with Williams syndrome are also more likely to seek interaction with other persons rather than with inanimate objects than are children without the condition (Mervis et al. 2003, 263). While the above two studies focused on toddlers with Williams syndrome, the cluster of interpersonal characteristics has been found to a significantly greater extent among individuals with Williams syndrome than any comparison group, and this "evidence regarding this profile has been obtained primarily from older children, adolescents, and adults" (Mervis 2003, 245).

Some researchers suggest that there can be a cost to the heightened social interaction and interpersonal focus characteristic of Williams syndrome which can be detrimental in certain situations that require attention to non-routine surroundings. In these cases, the hypersociality and increased focus on persons rather than other environmental features can "significantly reduce their opportunities to learn about the world" (Mervis 2003, 263). But these constraints need not be present in the afterlife, given the perfected nature of heaven (see the discussions in Timpe 2019; Pawl and Timpe 2009; Pawl and Timpe 2017). It's not the case, for instance, that one will run the risk of tripping and falling in heaven because one is too busy talking with Saint Cecilia and not paying enough attention to one's peripatetic environment.

Or consider 'hyperfocusing,' the (relative) inability to shift attention from particular preferred or agent-engaging tasks to other activities that is clinically well-known in both Autism Spectrum Disorders (ASD) and Attention-Deficit/Hyperactivity Disorder (ADHD) (see Ozel 2014; regarding ASD, there's reason to think that it isn't a unified condition but rather a cluster of conditions related by "family resemblance" [Cushing 2013, 22]; see also McGuire 2016, 21). Research suggests a link between hyperfocusing and the tendency among autistics[20] and persons with ADHD to perseverate; hyperfocus is also connected with the reasons that autistics participate in stimming (i.e., repetitive self-stimulatory or stereotypic behaviors). Hyperfocus, perseveration, and stimming have all been linked to executive function impairments in individuals with ASD (Lopez 2005; Ridley 1994; Turner 1997)[21] and ADHD (Corbett 2009). While the etiology of autism isn't known (Firth 2008), many researchers think that executive function deficits are only part of the etiology of ADHD (Corbett 2009). There is a very high comorbidity between having ASD and ADHD, though the degree of comorbidity ranges greatly by study, varying from 37% to 85% (see Leitner 2014 for a discussion). Even apart from the comorbidity, there are a variety of reasons to see common behavioral features between individuals with ASD and those with ADHD.[22]

Joseph Straus suggests that hyperfocus among autistics plays a positive role in autistic culture and, were it not for social conventions that dispose people against stereotypically autistic behaviors, could positively contribute to even wider-ranging communities (Straus 2013). Similarly, Jami Anderson recounts the story of Virginia Bovell, the mother of an autistic son, who thinks that autism gives her son "a kind of rapture. . . [and] access to a kind of rapture" that neurotypical people do not have access to (as quoted in Anderson 2013, 129). While the exact nature of the union with God in the beatific vision is contestable (see Van Dyke 2014), it will involve as a central element awareness of and union with God. A frequent objection to the possibility of an endless post-mortem paradisiacal state involving beatitude is that such a state would eventually become boring, or dull (Williams 1973; Fischer and Mitchell-Yellin 2014; Kagan 2012, ch. 11; Riberiro 2011; Bortolotti and Nagasawa 2009). While I'm inclined to think that the boringness worry can be avoided in other ways (Pawl and Timpe 2017; Silverman 2017), note that the greater one's ability to hyperfocus the less bite the boringness worry has. And even if the ability to hyperfocus isn't required for beatitude without risk of ennui or tedium, having such an ability would provide another way to secure a good that is at the heart of beatitude, and thus would contribute to the perfection of such a state.[23]

Though his focus is on how certain traits that often accompany autism, including hyperfocus, can be strengths for leadership within congregates, Grant Macaskill develops a line of argument that could support my own. Macaskill argues that autistics have goods to offer religious communities that could benefit from their leadership. Some of these goods are at least in part a function of their being autistic:

> our perception of leadership qualities is often based on natural properties of commodity or capital (perceived 'wisdom') that are effectively negated by Paul at the beginning of 1 Corinthians. Reflecting on the place that those with ASD might have in leadership invites us to reflect on whether we are drawn to those who possess a certain set of natural qualities or personality traits and whether our values are, in fact, subconsciously biased toward normality. The possibility that we overlook the capacity that those with ASD may have for leadership because they may lack such qualities is one that we must consider. . . . Properly considered, however, churches can value the unique insights and strengths of those with ASD and, in the process, can reflect upon their own residual biases.
> (Macaskill 2018, 32f. and 37)

Suppose that Macaskill is correct. Given the nature of the one body that is the Church, holding that none of the gifts that contribute to the goodness of local congregations could contribute to the goodness of the perfected Church in the eschaton is an instance of the normate biases that disability theologians like Yong argue we need to reject in our theology. Along these lines, theologian Benjamin Conner argues that Deaf Gain can contribute not just to communicative strategies, but to the fullness of the body of Christ (Conner 2018, ch. 3).

Some individuals in the neurodiversity movement make claims that can be seen as supporting the case for disabled beatitude. Drawing on the neurodiversity movement and with an eye toward the neurological underpinnings of the characteristics under discussion, Jami Anderson suggests that

> rather than regarding autistic neurological structures as 'defective' or 'disordered,' one should regard autistic neurology as worth valuing because each neurological structure contributes to the collective variety of human neurological diversity, in much the same way that each culture contributes to cultural diversity and each of the hundreds of

>   human languages makes a valuable contribution to human linguistic diversity.
>
>   (Anderson 2013, 127)

Anderson also suggests that the superior memory, a common splinter trait, that many autistic individuals have is "advantageous and highly valuable" (Anderson 2013, 131 note 7). While Anderson doesn't have eschatological beatitude in mind here, her point could be applied to this new context as well.[24] And similar considerations could be made for other claims about neurodiversity.

Admittedly, the disabilities discussed here are neither necessary nor sufficient for the characteristics related to those conditions that I've suggested could contribute to the beatific vision. Williams syndrome is neither necessary nor sufficient for the heightened social interaction and interpersonal focus characteristic of that condition. Neither autism nor ADHD are either necessary or sufficient for the ability to hyperfocus on particular tasks. But one need not think that a characteristic is necessary or sufficient for a good in order to think that the characteristic in question could contribute positively to the beatific vision. Being married sometimes helps individuals understand the importance of personal contribution to the good of a larger social group, but it's surely neither necessary nor sufficient for such a realization. Singing songs of praise is neither necessary nor sufficient for worship. Nevertheless, surely the history of having been married to another can contribute to that part of the realization of the social nature of the goods involved in the beatific vision, just as singing songs of praise can contribute to beatified corporate worship as part of our perfection union with God.

So there may be goods related to disability that positively contribute to the beatified state. In light of the history of undervaluing the lives of individuals with disabilities, it's important to note there that the positive justification for beatified disability is a good that goes to the individual with that disability. If the good from the disability in heaven benefits the community, it should do so by either being neutral or positive for the individual. The good here then isn't merely communal or other-focused. Richard Swinburne has argued that in some cases it is the 'good of being of use' that justifies another person's suffering:

> Now note another great good—the good of our life serving a purpose, of being of use to ourselves and others. . . . Just as it is a great good freely to choose to do good, so it is also a good to be used by someone else for a worthy purpose (so long, that is, that he or she has the right, the authority, to use us in this way). Being allowed to suffer to make possible a great good is a privilege, even if the privilege is forced on you.
>
>   (Swinburne 1996, 101f.; see also Swinburne 2004, 259–262)

As Swinburne later clarifies, God has the right to allow an individual to suffer even if the suffering doesn't benefit the individual, so long as their life is overall good (Swinburne 1999, 235; for a dissenting view see Stump 2010). On Swinburne's view, it is not unjust for God to use an individual's suffering instrumentally for the good of others without her consent in a way that justifies it. Given this, Swinburne would surely agree that if there is a heavenly good contributed by a disability, it need not be a good for the individual.[25] But not so on my view. There is data that suggests that communities do, in fact, experience goods from the inclusion of individuals with disabilities. There's evidence, for instance siblings of individuals with Down Syndrome show more empathy and a higher degree of caregiving behaviors than do siblings of typically developed children (Feniger-Schaal 2012, 340). Nevertheless, as Aaron Cobb and I have argued, the good that justified an evil of being the goods that could justify a bad-different disability (if such there are) shouldn't be understood as merely communal goods (such as 'the good of being of use'). Our view requires that the good involved is good for the individual, even if it also a good for the community (see Cobb and Timpe 2017).

General Conditions That Make Disability Possible

The previous section considered potential heavenly goods that could come from specific disabilities. But there may yet be other goods that are served not by the disabilities themselves, but by the conditions that make disability possible. To see the difference here, consider Michael Murray's work on the problem of divine hiddenness. Murray distinguishes between two kinds of theodicies:

> There are two distinct species of free-will theodicies. . . . The first type of free-will theodicy argues that one of the consequences of endowing creatures with free-will is that these beings have the option to choose evil over good. As a result, it is impossible that God actualize a world such that there are both free beings and also no possibility of those beings undertaking evil actions. I call theodicies of this type *consequent free-will theodicies*. They are 'consequent' in the sense that evil is to be accounted for in terms of the conditions that arise as a consequence of the existence of free-will in our world.
> (Murray 2009, 284)

While most free-will theodicies are of this sort, Murray's response to the problem of divine hiddenness takes another form:

> The theodicy that is important here argues that there are certain *antecedent* conditions that must necessarily hold or fail to hold if beings endowed with freedom are to be able to exercise this freedom in a

morally significant manner.... This argument strategy thus contends that certain antecedent conditions must obtain if free creatures are to be able to exercise their freedom in the most robust sense. And since there is good reason for creating creatures who can exercise their freedom in this fashion, there is good reason to create the necessary antecedent conditions which would allow for such exercising of freedom.

(Murray 2009, 284)

I'm not presently seeking to give a theodicy, much less a free-will theodicy. Given that I don't think that all disabilities are bad-differences, I don't think that their existence demands a theodicy.[26] Rather, it's the distinction between *consequent* and *antecedent* approaches that is of interest here. Notice that the potential goods of beatified disability in the previous section are consequent goods. Now I want to suggest that there may also be antecedent goods that also contribute to thinking that among the heavenly goods are beatified disabilities.

To see what I have in mind, consider the general features of creation that make at least some kinds of disability, namely congenital disabilities, possible.[27] The diversity and variation within life is best explained by an evolutionary account involving genetic mutation via sexual reproduction. Genetic variation made possible by mutation and natural selection gives rise to new forms, and thus the diversity, of life. If sexual reproduction with genetic variation due to mutation is, indeed, the correct explanation for biodiversity, then presumably God had a reason or reasons for creating according to such a process. As theologian John Haught argues, we have reason to think that the biological processes that allow for the emergence and evolution of life "are woven everlastingly into the kingdom of heaven" (Haught 2010, 53; see also Collins 2009). This evolutionary drama, he continues, "consists, at the very minimum, of the intensification of creation's beauty, a beauty that, to Christian faith, is everlastingly sustained and patterned anew within the life of God" (Haught 2010, 72). One need not agree with the details of Haught's account, of course, to think that the general claim that there is good reason for God to have created via an evolutionary account involving genetic mutation (see De Smedt and De Cruz forthcoming, especially ch. 2). It's precisely this way of understanding life that gives us reason to think that disability is an inherent part of actual human embodiment.[28] And if there is good reason for creating according to that process, there is good reason to create the necessary antecedent conditions that would allow for disabilities that are the result of genetic mutation (e.g., Williams syndrome or 2p15-16.1 microdeletion syndrome). Theologian Shane Clifton makes clear that while "God could have created things differently, setting up a universe without pain, suffering, and death, and without disability," had God created in such a way it would be a creation without many of the goods that the world actually involves (Clifton 2018, 39).

Conclusion

Many people might be surprised to think that there could be disability in the eschaton. But remember that many of the medievals thought they needed to defend the presence of females in heaven. Thomas Aquinas, for instance, considered it necessary to argue against those who "hold that among the bodies of the risen the feminine sex will be absent" (*SCG* IV, 88.1). In response, Aquinas asserts that

> the [purported] frailty of the feminine sex is not in opposition to the perfection of the risen. For this frailty is not due to a shortcoming of nature, but to an intention of nature. And this very distinction of nature among human beings will point out the perfection of nature and the divine wisdom as well, which disposes all things in a certain order.
> (*SCG* IV, 88.3)

Aquinas's point about the distinction between the sexes in human nature[29] can also be seen as applying to the diversity of the sexes, which serves the antecedent reasons considered above.[30] And then, by reasons parallel to Aquinas's reasoning about sex, one can think that the possibility of disability isn't due to a shortcoming of human nature, but rather a reflection of human nature as created by divine wisdom, which disposes all things in a certain order—namely beatitude. Those who think that no disability could contribute to beatitude in this way seem to understand all disabilities as involving bad-differences. And if one thinks that they are, we're back to the normate biases that we have good reason to reject.

While there may be certain goods that particular disabilities rule out, they don't always rule them out as uniformly as we may think. As Campbell and Stramondo point out,

> these features are multiply realizable, and most disabilities cut off only certain avenues for achieving such goods. The blind person may not be able to enjoy the paintings of Monet, but she can certainly appreciate beauty through the work of Tolstoy and Chopin. The paraplegic can always take a casual roll though the park and can engage in a range of competitive athletic events.
> (Campbell and Stramondo 2017, 157)

Furthermore, there is reason to think that the entire range of abilities isn't needed for perfect happiness. Do humans have to be sensitive to all wavelengths of light in order to be able to achieve beatitude? Do they also need to be able to have those aesthetic experiences that involve sonar or radar? We need not answer these questions in the affirmative. If human beatitude required our enjoyment of all goods, it would require rejecting human finitude. As Campbell and Stramondo write,

> since we do not judge the lives of nondisabled people to be impoverished when they fail to partake in every means of attaining every good in life, it is inconsistent and unreasonable to make a similar judgement about the lives of disabled people.
> (Campbell and Stramondo 2017, 158; see also Silvers 2003, 479 and Amundson 2005)

Speaking of the good that is her son Jack's life, Hillary Yancey makes clear that we don't need to think of lives with disability as good only despite the disability: "I can't believe God is a God who makes that gift [a human life, Jack] good *despite* its difference. God makes it good *because* of them, *in the midst* of them. God makes that life good" (Yancey 2018, 146f.). And the perfection of the human good is made perfect in the beatific vision.[31]

Notes

1. My work on disability in philosophy of religion has much in common with that of theologian Amos Yong, who has a similar motivation. While I disagree with Yong on various details, I share with him the desire to articulate an 'eschatological vision' which affords disability a place in humans' perfected union with God in the beatific vision (Yong 2007, 266).
2. The religious tradition I'll be working from is the Christian tradition. This is perhaps non-ideal for a volume that seeks to 'broaden the boundaries' of contemporary philosophy of religion, given that contemporary philosophy of religion in the English-speaking world predominately works with and very often simply assumes a Christian theology. Nevertheless, that is the tradition both that I am most familiar with and with which I identify. And so I'll work within it. It seems to me, however, that much and perhaps even most of what I say here could be endorsed by those working with the Islamic tradition, as well as by those working within those forms of Judaism that affirm the bodily resurrection.
3. For a discussion of the specific role of the earliest seven ecumenical creeds and why they are authoritative in the Christian tradition, see Pawl 2016, particularly ch. 1.
4. See Barna's study here: www.barna.com/research/a-new-generation-of-adults-bends-moral-and-sexual-rules-to-their-liking/. In 2013 megachurch pastor Mark Driscoll indicated no need to care for the environment since "I know who made the environment and he's coming back and going to burn it all up." Contrast this with the view of ecology promoted by Pope Francis in *Laudato Si'*.
5. Here is Barnes on the social model:

   > According to the social model, disability is the disadvantage produced by social prejudice against certain types of persons (persons with impairments). . . .

Disability *just is* the negative net effects of having an impairment in a society that discriminates against those with impairments.
(Barnes 2016, 25)

And disability Tom Shakespeare argues there's no agreement on what the social model actually is; see Shakespeare 2018.
6. This social model of disability, and the underlying impairment/disability distinction on which it draws, was originally advocated by UPIAS (the Union of the Physically Impaired against Segregation) in 1976. It has become extremely influential, both academically and politically. It is now codified, for instance, in the World Health Organization's *International Classification of Impairment, Disability, and Handicap*.
7. For a suggestion that disability could have been present in the Garden of Eden as well as in heaven, see Cooreman-Guittin 2018.
8. The phrase 'beatific vision' obviously has sighted overtones that could be seen to be ableist. While recognizing this, given the historical use of the phrase I'll continue to use it, but making it explicit here that 'vision' may be used metaphorically and may not require the sense of sight.
9. I think this conditional is relatively uncontroversial. What is more controversial, however, is whether the antecedent is ever fulfilled. I've argued in a number of places that not all disabilities involve bad-difference, nor do all disabilities mean that the person who has them fall below the relevant limit such that simply in virtue of having that disability their union with God is impaired. But I am open to this being the case for some disabilities; see Timpe and Cobb 2017; Timpe forthcoming-b.
10. If there are disabilities that accidentally interfere with one's union with God, then presumably the feature that leads to that accidental feature would be removed. For instance, if there is a disability that in some cases leads to one's community interfering with one's union with God, as is plausibly the case many times for autistics, then one's community could be perfected so that it no longer has that impact.
11. Given that I don't think there is a single thing that *is* disability, I'm completely comfortable with thinking that different disabilities need to be treated in different ways in our philosophical and theological accounts, including our accounts of heaven. See Timpe forthcoming-a.
12. Richard Cross argues that the incarnate Christ, both pre- and post-resurrection, is impaired, though not disabled. Cross differentiates between impairment and disability as follows:

> impairment is dependence; disability is the failure of the environment—be it the physical environment or the activities of other human agents—to provide the conditions for provide [*sic*] for opportunities for dependence necessary for flourishing. So, strictly speaking, human persons are intrinsically impaired, but not disabled.
> (Cross 2011, 657 note 28; see also 650)

13. There's also a trinitarian worry here for Eiesland's view. Even if it's true that the Incarnate Christ is disabled, it doesn't follow that God is disabled, given that not everything that is true of the Incarnate Christ in virtue of being true of his human nature is also true of the divine nature. See Pawl 2016.
14. For a related discussion of the marks of disability, specifically those caused by martyrdom, see Williams 2018, particularly 4f. For other criticisms of Eiesland's view, see Monteith 2005, 66f. and Creamer 2004, 260f. It may be

that we're identified by the marks of impairment, such as scars from crucifixion or martyrdom, without having the impairments in question themselves.
15. It's sometimes unclear what sense of 'identity' Yong has in mind. For my evaluation of Yong's argument on this point, see Timpe 2020.
16. Yong describes normate biases as "the unexamined prejudices that non-disabled people have toward disability and toward people who have them" (Yong 2011, 10). So understood, normate biases are closely related to ableism, as Yong himself notes (Yong 2011, 11f.). See also Scuro 2017; Goodley 2014.
17. In Timpe 2020, I discuss how Yong's view involves "retain[ing] their phenotypical features in their resurrection body" (Yong 2007, 282) but that doesn't entail retaining the disability itself; see especially section 3.2. Yong also calls for a "disability-informed theological anthropology. . . [in which] people with disabilities are . . . accepted, included, and valued members of the human family regardless of how they measure up to our economic, social, and political conventions" (Yong 2011, 180, 182). And taking the incarnation seriously, even if that doesn't mean attributing disability to the incarnate Christ, contributes to such an anthropology.
18. I'm grateful to Robin Dembroff, Hilary Yancey, and Mike Rea for getting me to think about these social reasons.
19. The Principle of Minimal Agential Realism is structured parallel to Owen Flanagan's "Principle of Minimal Psychological Realism," in Flanagan 1991, 34. See Timpe 2019, 18.
20. The vast majority of autistics prefer identity-first language to person-first language. See also McGuire 2016, ch. 5.
21. However, the executive function profile associated with ASD and that associated with ADHD differ, even if the two conditions have some similarities in terms of behavior; these differences suggest distinct executive function profiles.
22. For a summary of the modeling, biological pathways, and neuroanatomical correlates, see Corbett 2009. Corbett et al. suggest that individuals with both ASD and ADHD "may represent a distinct phenotype in autism that requires further study" (218).
23. I must also admit that it's not obvious that all of the executive function issues involved with ASD would have the positive impact in the afterlife that I'm considering here.
24. For another discussion of how disability can contribute to the goodness of the Church, see Yong 2011, 94f.
25. While Swinburne might allow for extrinsic goods to come from disability, he would deny the claim that there is an intrinsic good that comes from a disability.
26. What may be required is a theodicy for the social and personal harms that humans cause those with disabilities to suffer, but those could presumably be addressed with one's standard responses to the problem of moral evils.
27. I focus on human disability even though there is also disability, both acquired and congenital, among non-human animals. Insofar as I'm inclined toward a version of animalism, according to which humans are a particular kind of animal (and essentially so), I see the prevalence of disability across the spectrum of animals to reinforce the points I make here.
28. There are two ways I see this line of argumentation being resisted. First, one might think that since disability involves bad-difference, pre-fall human bodies could not have had disabilities as originally created. This seems to be Augustine's view when he says that "whatever deformity was in it [the body], and served to exhibit the penal condition in which we mortals are, should

be restored in such a way that, while the substance is entirely preserved, the deformity shall perish" (*City of God* 22: 19, 561). This line of thought has already been rejected. Second, one could think that all disabilities are the result of the fall even if they don't involve bad-difference. But if disability doesn't involve bad-difference, why think sin is relevant to its explanation?

29. Of course, we have good reasons to think that biological sex isn't nearly as binary as Aquinas thought it was. Aquinas's reasoning in the *SCG* may also give us reason to think that various intersexed conditions will also be present in heaven. See Merrick 2011 for a similar discussion.

30. Theologian John Hull, who is also blind, makes this connection. For Hull, theological reflection on disability can expand our theological understanding. And

> the same is true in some ways of feminist theology. It was a man's Bible and a man's church and women were made to feel that they had to put feminine characteristics behind them and act like a man, although even that was scarcely permitted. . . . When we consider disability theology as a kind of frontier theology [which refers to the ways that theology "seeks to interpret some area of human life which lies outside Christian faith, or which seems at first sight to lie outside" (54)], we discover that disability itself is not a problem. What faith does is to grasp people with disabilities and pull them into the body of Christ, where, as Paul says, the parts that were sometimes looked down on are now given the highest honours.
>
> (Hull 2014, 96f.)

31. I'm thankful for comments from Aaron Cobb, Jason Eberl, Blake Hereth, Hud Hudson, John Swinton, and Hillary Yancy. This paper also benefited from comments by Robin Dembroff and Mike Rea on Timpe 2020.

References

Amundson, Ron. "Disability, Ideology, and Quality of Life: A Bias in Biomedical Ethics." In *Quality of Life and Human Difference*, edited by Ryan Wasserman, Jerome Bickenbach, and Robert Wachbroit, 101–124. Cambridge: Cambridge University Press, 2005.

Anderson, Jami L. "A Dash of Autism." In *The Philosophy of Autism*, edited by Jami L. Anderson and Simon Cushing, 109–142. Lanham, MD: Rowman & Littlefield, 2013.

Anderson, Luvell and Ernie Lepore. "Slurring Words." *Nous* 47 (2013): 25–48.

Augustine. *The City of God*. Translated by Marcus Dods. Laschberg: Jazzybee Vergal Jürgen Beck, 2017.

Barnes, Colin. "Understanding the Social Model of Disability: Past, Present, and Future." In *Routledge Handbook of Disability Studies*, edited by Nick Watson, Alan Roustone, and Carol Thomas, 12–29. New York: Routledge, 2012.

Barnes, Elizabeth. *The Minority Body: A Theory of Disability*. Oxford: Oxford University Press, 2016.

Billings, J. Todd. "Introduction." In *Our Faith: Ecumenical Creeds, Reformed Confessions, and Other Resources*. Grand Rapids, MI: Faith Alive, 2013.

Bonhoeffer, Dietrich. *Life Together*. New York: HarperCollins, 1954.

Bortolotti, Lisa and Yujin Nagasawa. "Immortality Without Boredom." *Ratio* 22.3 (2009): 261–277.
Brock, Brian. *Wondrously Wounded: Disability, Theologically Reconstituted*, forthcoming.
Calvin, John. "Articles Concerning the Organization of the Church and of Worship at Geneva Proposed by the Ministers at the Council, January 16, 1537." In *Calvin: Theological Treatises*, edited by J. K. S. Reid. Philadelphia: Westminster Press, 1954.
Campbell, Stephen M. and Joseph A. Stramondo. "The Complicated Relationship of Disability and Well-Being." *Kennedy Institute of Ethics Journal* 27 (2017): 151–184.
Catechism of the Catholic Church, 2nd ed. New York, NY: Doubleday, 2003.
Clifton, Shane. *Crippled Grace: Disability, Virtue Ethics, and the Good Life*. Waco, TX: Baylor University Press, 2018.
Collins, Robin. "Divine Action and Evolution." In *The Oxford Handbook of Philosophical Theology*, edited by Thomas P. Flint and Michael C. Rea, 241–261. Oxford: Oxford University Press, 2009.
Conner, Benjamin T. *Amplifying Our Witness: Giving Voice to Adolescents with Development Disabilities*. Grand Rapids, MI: Wm. B. Eerdmans, 2012.
———. *Disabling Mission, Enabling Witness*. Downers Grove, IL: IVP Academic, 2018.
Cooreman-Guittin, Talitha. "Could Adam and Eve Have Been Disabled? Images of Creation in Catholic Religious Education Textbooks in France." *Journal of Disability & Religion* 22 (2018): 89–95.
Corbett, Blythe A., Laura J. Constantine, Robert Hendren, David Rocke, and Sally Ozonoff. "Examining Executive Functioning in Children with Autism Spectrum Disorder, Attention Deficit Hyperactivity Disorder and Typical Development." *Psychiatry Research* 166 (2009): 210–222.
Creamer, Deborah Beth. "The Withered Hand of God: Disability and Theological Reflection." Ph.D. thesis. Denver: Iliff School of Theology and the University of Denver (Colorado Seminary), 2004.
Cross, Richard. "Disability, Impairment, and Some Medieval Accounts of the Incarnation: Suggestions for a Theology of Personhood." *Modern Theology* 27.4 (2011): 639–658.
Cuneo, Terence. *Ritualized Faith: Essays on the Philosophy of Liturgy*. Oxford: Oxford University Press, 2016.
Cushing, Simon. "Autism: The Very Idea." In *The Philosophy of Autism*, edited by Jami L. Anderson and Simon Cushing, 17–45. Lanham, MD: Rowman & Littlefield, 2013.
De Smedt, Johan and Helen De Cruz. *The Challenge of Evolution to Religion*. Cambridge: Cambridge University Press, forthcoming.
Eiesland, Nancy L. *The Disabled God: Toward a Liberatory Theology of Disability*. Nashville, TN: Abingdon Press, 1994.
Eyler, Joshua R. "Introduction: Breaking Boundaries, Building Bridges." In *Disability in the Middle Ages: Reconsiderations and Reverberations*, edited by Joshua R. Eyler, 1–8. New York: Routledge, 2010.
Feniger-Schaal, Rinat, David Oppenheim, Nica Koren-Karie, and Nurit Yimiya. "Parenting and Intellectual Disability: An Attachment Perspective." In *The Oxford Handbook of Intellectual Disability and Development*, edited by Jacob

B. Burack, Robert M. Hodapp, Grace Iarocci, and Edward Zigler, 334–348. Oxford: Oxford University Press, 2012.

Fidler, Debbie J., Susan L. Hepburn, David E. Most, Amy Philofsky, and Sally J. Rogers. "Emotional Responsivity in Young Children with Williams Syndrome." *American Journal on Mental Retardation* 112 (2007): 194–206.

Fidler, Debbie J., Susan L. Hepburn, and Sally J. Rogers. "Early Learning and Adaptive Behavior in Toddlers with Down Syndrome: Evidence for an Emerging Behavioral Phenotype?" *Down Syndrome: Research and Practice* 9 (2005): 37–44.

Firth, Uta. *Autism: A Very Short Introduction*. Oxford: Oxford University Press, 2008.

Fischer, John Martin and Benjamin Mitchell-Yellin. "Immortality and Boredom." *The Journal of Ethics* 18.4 (2014): 353–372.

Flanagan, Owen. *The Varieties of Moral Personality: Ethics and Psychological Realism*. Cambridge, MA: Harvard University Press, 1991.

Goodley, Dan. *Dis/ability Studies: Theorising Disablism and Ableism*. New York: Routledge, 2014.

Haught, John F. *Making Sense of Evolution: Darwin, God, and the Drama of Life*. Lexington, KY: Westminster John Knox Press, 2010.

Hull, John M. *Disability: The Inclusive Church Resource*. London: Darton, Longman, and Todd, 2014.

Kagan, Shelly. *Death*. New Haven: Yale University Press, 2012.

Kasari, Connie L., S. Freeman, Peter Mundy, and Marian D. Sigman. "Attention Regulation by Children with Down Syndrome: Coordinated Joint Attention and Social Referencing Looks." *American Journal on Mental Retardation* 100 (1995): 128–136.

Leitner, Yael. "The Co-Occurrence of Autism and Attention Deficit Hyperactivity Disorder in Children—What Do We Know?" *Frontiers in Human Neuroscience* 8.268 (2014): 1–8.

Lopez, Brian R., Alan J. Lincoln, Sally Ozonoff, and Zona Lai. "Examining the Relationship Between Executive Functions and Restricted, Repetitive Symptoms of Autistic Disorder." *Journal of Autism and Developmental Disorders* 35 (2005): 445–460.

Macaskill, Grant. "Autism Spectrum Disorders and the New Testament: Preliminary Reflections." *Journal of Disability & Religion* 22.1 (2018): 15–41.

McGuire, Anne. *War on Autism: On the Cultural Logic of Normative Violence*. Ann Arbor, MI: University of Michigan Press, 2016.

Merrick, Teri. "Can Augustine Welcome Intersexed Bodies into Heaven?" In *Gift and Economy: Ethics, Hospitality and the Market*, edited by Eric R. Severson, 188–198. Newcastle upon Tyne: Cambridge Scholars Publishing, 2011.

Mervis, Carolyn B., Colleen A. Morris, Bonita P. Klein-Tasman, Jacquelyn Bertrand, Susanna Kwitny, Lawrence G. Applebaum, and Catherine E. Rice. "Attentional Characteristics of Infants and Toddlers with Williams Syndrome During Triadic Interactions." *Developmental Neuropsychology* 23 (2003): 243–268.

Monteith, Graham W. *Deconstructing Miracles: From Thoughtless Indifference to Honouring Disabled People*. Glasgow: Covenanters, 2005.

Morris, C. A. and Carolyn B. Mervis. "WS and Related Disorders." *Annual Review of Genomics and Human Genetics* 1 (2000): 461–464.

Murray, Michael. "Coercion and the Hiddenness of God." In *Arguing About Religion*, edited by Kevin Timpe, 282–294. New York, Routledge, 2009.

Niccols, Alison, Karen Thomas, and Louis A. Schmidt. "Socioemotional and Brain Development in Children with Genetic Syndromes Associated with Developmental Delay." In *The Oxford Handbook of Intellectual Disability and Development*, edited by Jacob A. Burack, Robert M. Hodapp, Grace Iarocci, and Edward Zigler, 254–274. Oxford: Oxford University Press, 2012.

Ozel-Kizil, Erguvan T., Ahmet Kokurcan, Umut Mert Aksoy, B. Bicer-Kanat, Direnc Sakarya, G. Bastug, Burcin Colak, Umut Altunoz, Sabri Kirici, Hatice Demirbas, and Bedriye Oncu. "Hyperfocusing as a Dimension of Adult ADHD." *European Neuropsychopharmacology* 24 (2014): 707–708.

Pawl, Timothy. *In Defense of Conciliar Christology: A Philosophical Essay*. Oxford: Oxford University Press, 2016.

Pawl, Timothy and Kevin Timpe. "Incompatibilism, Sin, and Free Will in Heaven." *Faith and Philosophy* 26.4 (2009): 396–417.

———. 2017. "Paradise and Growing in Virtue." In *Paradise Understood: New Philosophical Essays*, edited by Eric J. Silverman, 97–111. Oxford: Oxford University Press, 2017.

Reinders, Hans S. *Receiving the Gift of Friendship: Profound Disability, Theological Anthropology, and Ethics*. Grand Rapids, MI: Wm. B. Eerdmans, 2008.

Riberiro, Brian. "The Problem of Heaven." *Ratio* 24.1 (2011): 46–64.

Ridley, R. M. "The Psychology of Perseverative and Stereotyped Behavior." *Progress in Neurobiology* 44 (1994): 221–231.

Scuro, Jennifer. *Addressing Ableism: Philosophical Questions via Disability Studies*. Lanham, MD: Lexington Books, 2017.

Shakespeare, Tom. *Disability: The Basics*. New York: Routledge, 2018.

Silverman, Eric J. "Conceiving Heaven as a Dynamic Rather Than Static Existence." In *Paradise Understood: New Philosophical Essays*, edited by Eric J. Silverman, 13–29. Oxford: Oxford University Press, 2017.

Silvers, Anita. "People with Disabilities." In *The Oxford Handbook of Practical Ethics*, edited by Hugh LaFollette, 303–327. Oxford: Oxford University Press, 2003.

Smith, James K. A. *You Are What You Love: The Spiritual Power of Habit*. Grand Rapids, MI: Brazos Press, 2016.

Straus, Joseph. "Autism as Culture." In *The Disability Studies Reader*, edited by Lennard J. Davis, 4th ed., 460–484. New York: Routledge, 2013.

Stump, Eleonore. *Wandering in Darkness: Narrative and the Problem of Suffering*. Oxford: Oxford University Press, 2010.

Swinburne, Richard. *Is There a God?* Oxford: Oxford University Press, 1996.

———. *Providence and the Problem of Evil*. Oxford: Oxford University Press, 1999.

———. *The Existence of God*, 2nd ed. Oxford: Oxford University Press, 2004.

Swinton, John. *Dementia: Living in the Memories of God*. Grand Rapids, MI: Wm. B. Eerdmans, 2012.

Timpe, Kevin. *Disability and Inclusive Communities*. Grand Rapids, MI: Calvin Press, 2018.

———. "Moral Ecology, Disabilities, and Human Agency." *Res Philosophica* 96 (2019): 17–41.

———. "Defiant Afterlife." In *Marginalized Identities, Peripheral Theologies: Expanding Conversations in Analytic Theology*, edited by Michelle Panchuk and Michael Rea. Oxford: Oxford University Press, 2020.

———. "Denying a Unified Concept of Disability." Forthcoming-a.

———. "Emotion, Executive Dysfunction, and Agency: Can Emotional Disability Impair an Agent's Likelihood of Virtue?" In *Becoming Good: New Philosophical Essays in Aid of Virtue Formation*, edited by Scott Cleveland and Adam Pelser, forthcoming-b.

Timpe, Kevin and Aaron D. Cobb. "Disability and the Theodicy of Defeat." *Journal of Analytic Theology* 5 (2017): 100–120.

Tremain, Shelley. *Foucault and Feminist Philosophy of Disability*. Ann Arbor: University of Michigan Press, 2017.

Turner, Michelle. "Towards an Executive Dysfunction Account of Repetitive Behaviour in Autism." In *Autism as an Executive Disorder*, edited by James Russell, 57–100. Oxford: Oxford University Press, 1997.

Van Dyke, Christina. "Aquinas's Shiny Happy People: Perfect Happiness and the Limits of Human Nature." In *Oxford Studies in Philosophy of Religion*, edited by Jon Kvanvig, vol. 6, 269–291. Oxford: Oxford University Press, 2014.

Vargas, Manuel. *Building Better Beings: A Theory of Moral Responsibility*. Oxford: Oxford University Press, 2013.

Wannenwetsch, Bernd. "'My Strength Is Made Perfect in Weakness': Bonhoeffer and the War over Disabled Life." In *Disability in the Christian Tradition*, edited by Brian Brock and John Swinton, 353–369. Grand Rapids, MI: Wm. B. Eerdmans, 2012.

Wilder, Courtney. *Disability, Faith, and the Church: Inclusion and Accommodation in Contemporary Congregations*. Santa Barbara, CA: Praeger, 2016.

Williams, Bernard. "The Makropulos Case: Reflections on the Tedium of Immortality." In *Problems of the Self*, 82–100. Cambridge: Cambridge University Press, 1973.

Williams, Scott. "Horrendous-Difference Disabilities, Resurrected Saints, and the Beatific Vision: A Theodicy." *Religions* 9.2 (2018): 1–13.

Wolterstorff, Nicholas. *Acting Liturgically: Philosophical Reflections on Religious Practice*. Oxford: Oxford University Press, 2018.

Yancey, Hilary. *Forgiving God: A Story of Faith*. New York: Hachette Book Group, Inc., 2018.

Yong, Amos. *Theology and Down Syndrome: Reimaging Disability in Late Modernity*. Waco, TX: Baylor University Press, 2007.

———. *The Bible, Disability, and the Church*. Grand Rapids, MI: Wm. B. Eerdmans, 2011.

11 When Personhood Goes Wrong in Ethics and Philosophical Theology

Disability, Ableism, and (Modern) Personhood

Scott M. Williams

"Let it be known that by 'particular substance' [*meriken ousian*] (that is, a peculiar [*idiken*] [substance]) we wish to signify nothing other than the individual [*atomon*], that is, a person [*prosopon*]."
—Gregory of Nyssa[1]

"A person [*persona*] is an individual substance of a rational nature."
—Boethius[2]

"The heretic says, 'Every individual nature is a person [*persona*].' . . . [But I say that] there are many individual natures that are not also a person [*persona*], for example, [individuals of] inanimate natures and [individuals of] irrational natures."
—Rusticus the Deacon[3]

"A person [*persona*] is an incommunicable existence of a rational nature."
—Richard of St. Victor[4]

"'Person' [*persona*] signifies an intellectual substance that is an incommunicable hypostasis."
—Henry of Ghent[5]

"*Self* is that [incommunicable] conscious thinking thing . . . which is sensible, or conscious of Pleasure and Pain, capable of Happiness or Misery, and so is concern'd for it *self*, as far as that consciousness extends. . . . *Person*, as I take it, is the name for this self."
—John Locke[6]

"The traits which are most central to the concept of personhood . . . are . . . Consciousness . . ., Reasoning (the *developed* capacity to solve new and relatively complex problems); Self-motivated activity (activity which is relatively independent of either genetic or direct external control); The capacity to communicate, by whatever means, messages of an indefinite variety of types, that is, not just with an indefinite number of possible contents, but on indefinitely many possible topics; The presence of self-concepts, and self-awareness, either individual or racial, or both."
—Mary Anne Warren[7]

Introduction

This chapter is about personhood in relation to ethics and to conciliar Christian theology, and how concepts of personhood may discriminate against profoundly cognitively disabled human beings. (By 'conciliar Christian theology' I mean the Christian theology that is articulated in, or endorsed by, the first seven ecumenical councils.)[8] I believe we can learn several things about personhood by looking at these two topics together. By examining ancient and medieval concepts of personhood and some modern conceptions of personhood we gain a better grasp of the variety of concepts and what substantive work they were intended to do. By becoming familiar with (part of) the history of concepts of personhood we are better situated to appreciate and judge the theoretical work that these concepts were intended to do and what consequences they have in ethical and theological theorizing.

In the first section I tell a select history of moral philosophers theorizing about personhood and discuss these in relation to human beings with profound cognitive disability. I focus on John Locke, Immanuel Kant, and Mary Anne Warren. In the "When Personhood Is Discriminatory" section I argue that concepts of personhood, especially modern concepts of personhood, are typically used in a manner that discriminates against human beings with profound cognitive disabilities. I give two arguments against discriminatory uses of personhood, the Moral Shift Argument and the Argument against Exclusive Personhood. Although the Moral Shift Argument is deductively valid, it probably has little persuasive power over those who do not share the moral belief that profoundly cognitively disabled human beings are equal members of the moral community. However, the Argument against Exclusive Personhood has more argumentative force because it denies the claims that personhood is "self-evident" and that it is "obvious" to everyone.

In the following section I survey a select history of concepts of personhood in order to establish the claims that concepts of personhood are not self-evident and are not obvious to everyone. This history of personhood goes back to ancient and medieval Christian theorizing and debating about personhood. It shows that concepts of personhood are not "self-evident" but rather are theoretical posits that are posited in theory construction in order to explain certain putative theological facts. Given that personhood is a theoretical posit and is not "self-evident," moral philosophers who aim to determine the extent of the moral community on the basis of a supposedly "self-evident" concept of personhood are not justified in doing so. Moreover, given the Argument against Exclusive Personhood, philosophical theologians who wish to articulate models of the Trinity or Incarnation that are consistent with the seven ecumenical councils will find that they, like moral philosophers, are not justified to assume, or to insist on, modern personhood for their models of the Trinity or Incarnation. My overall conclusion, then, is that modern personhood is bad for ethics and unnecessary for conciliar ecumenical Christian theology.

A Story About Moral Personhood

According to Ruth Mattern, John Locke developed a concept of personhood in his attempt to articulate a demonstrative science of ethics. Locke found other notions inadequate to the task of a demonstrative science. Locke finds the notion of 'man' to be insufficient because it is unclear. Locke asked, "if several Men were to be asked, concerning some odly-shaped Foetus, as soon as born, whether it were a Man, or no, 'tis past doubt, one should meet with different Answers" (cf. Locke 1975, III.vi.27; cited in Mattern 1998, 265). (It is significant to note Locke's apparent ableism that is at the root of his rejection of the view that one's being a human being is sufficient for membership in the moral community.) Given the apparent inadequacy of the notion of "man" (or 'human'), Locke moves on to different notions, namely that of "moral man" and a "rational self" or "person":

> One difference between the concept of *moral man* and the concept of *rational selves* is that the former, as Locke explicates it, implies corporeality while the latter does not. This difference allows Locke to include incorporeal rational beings within the scope of the concept of moral agents. Since he believes that there are actually incorporeal agents, namely angels, this difference is probably an advantage from his point of view.
> (Mattern 1998, 273 note 14)

What Locke is after is the class of beings who are moral agents, namely those who deliberate by means of universal signs, make moral decisions, and can be held morally and legally responsible for their actions.

Locke stipulates that the term 'person' is a forensic term. If something is a person, then it has moral and legal standing (Mattern 1998, 274–275). Locke claimed that a person is an "incommunicable consciousness" that implies that one can remember what oneself did in the past and that one is aware of what oneself intends to do. From these it follows that one can be held morally and legally responsible for one's intended actions. For Locke, a person is a self, that is, a self-conscious being. It is important to recognize that Locke borrows from the theological tradition the term 'incommunicable' in his account of personhood. Unfortunately, Locke did not give a fine-grained analysis of incommunicability (like Duns Scotus) but left it unanalyzed. It makes sense, however, that given the forensic context in which he develops his notion of a person, that all he needs is an indefinite concept of a non-shareable stream of self-consciousness for what is required for moral and legal responsibility.

Like Locke, Kant makes personhood a relevant feature in his ethical theory. For Kant, something is either a person or a thing. Persons have intrinsic moral standing and things have extrinsic moral standing relative to persons who own them. A 'person' has moral dignity such that it is "above all price" (Kant 2008, 42, 4:434–435). A person is a rational being; and, a person or rational being "belongs as a member to the kingdom of ends when he gives universal laws in it but is himself subject to these laws" (G 4:433). And, "Rational nature is distinguished from the rest of nature by this, that it sets itself an end" (G 4:437). A person is distinct from things because a person causes certain kinds of activity, that is, "set[ting] itself an end." These passages suggests that one is a person only if one actually sets a universal law. This implies that personhood is like an event. However, in other passages Kant concedes that infants and children are persons even without making universal ends for themselves (cf. Kant 2017, 6:280–281, 70). It seems to me that Kant holds this because of the plausibility that human children typically come to be abstract reasoners when they become mature adults. If that is right, then their moral value depends on their future abstract reasoning, and not merely on their capacity for abstract reasoning. Should one factually never come to use one's capacity for abstract reasoning, then we can doubt their personhood. In sum, Kant could be clearer on the necessary conditions for personhood.

A more recent moral philosopher, Mary Anne Warren, has stipulated five conditions for moral personhood. I quote her in full because I believe her analysis fairly well represents many modern notions of personhood and the claim that personhood is self-evident. Her discussion of personhood is formulated in an ethical discussion of the morality of the abortion of human fetuses. What I want to focus on is her proposed account of personhood and its implications for profoundly cognitively disabled human beings. She writes:

> I would like to suggest an alternative way of defining the moral community, which I will argue for only to the extent of explaining why it is, or should be, self-evident. The suggestion is simply that the moral community consists of all and only *people* rather than all and only human beings; and probably the best way of demonstrating its self-evidence is by considering the concept of personhood, to see what sorts of entity are and are not persons, and what the decision that a being is or is not a person implies about its moral rights.
> (Warren 2010, 437)

Here we find the claim that personhood is, "or should be, self-evident." What does this imply? What is required for a concept of personhood to be "self-evident"? While there are different philosophical analyses of what is required for self-evident concepts (propositions), it is likely that what

Warren means is that her exclusive association between her concept of personhood and the moral community is "obvious" to her. This exclusive association is not self-evident in itself, but it is obvious to individuals like Warren. Nonetheless, Warren suggests that if one understands her criteria for personhood, then one must believe that this concept of personhood is the exclusive basis for membership in the moral community.

Warren gives her criteria for personhood that is the exclusive basis for membership in the moral community as follows:

> I suggest that the traits which are most central to the concept of personhood, or humanity in the moral sense, are, very roughly, the following:
>
> 1. Consciousness (of objects and events external and/or internal to the being), and in particular the capacity to feel pain.
> 2. Reasoning (the *developed* capacity to solve new and relatively complex problems).
> 3. Self-motivated activity (activity which is relatively independent of either genetic or direct external control).
> 4. The capacity to communicate, by whatever means, messages of an indefinite variety of types, that is, not just with an indefinite number of possible contents, but on indefinitely many possible topics.
> 5. The presence of self-concepts, and self-awareness, either individual or racial, or both.
>
> Admittedly, there are apt to be a great many problems involved in formulating precise definitions of these criteria, let alone in developing universally valid behavioral criteria for deciding when they apply. But I will assume that . . . we . . . know approximately what (1)–(5) mean, and that [we are] also able to determine whether or not they apply. . . . All we need to claim, to demonstrate that a fetus is not a person, is that any being which satisfies *none* of (1)–(5) is certainly not a person. I consider this claim to be so obvious that I think anyone who denied it, and claimed that a being which satisfied none of (1)–(5) was a person all the same, would thereby demonstrate that they had no notion at all of what a person is—perhaps because he had confused the concept of a person with that of genetic humanity. If the opponents of abortion were to deny the appropriateness of these five criteria, I do not know what further arguments would convince them. We would probably have to admit that our conceptual schemes were indeed irreconcilably different, and that our dispute could not be settled objectively.
>
> I do not expect this to happen, however, since I think that the concept of a person is one which is very nearly universal (to people). . . .

> Now if (1)–(5) are indeed the primary criteria of personhood, then it is clear that the genetic humanity is neither necessary nor sufficient for establishing that an entity is a person. Some human beings are not people, and there may well be people who are not human beings. A man or woman whose consciousness has been permanently obliterated but who remains alive is a human being which is no longer a person; defective human beings, with no appreciable mental capacity, are not and presumably never will be people; and a fetus is a human being which is not yet a person, and which therefore cannot coherently be said to have full moral rights.
>
> (Warren 2010, 438)

There are several things to note. First, Warren stipulates several higher-order cognitive achievements, namely (2)–(5), as conditions for personhood. Given that these stipulated conditions exclude profoundly cognitively disabled human beings from the moral community, we need to be especially careful. In the next section I develop the Argument against Exclusive Personhood in order to show that Warren does not successfully establish these as necessary conditions for membership in the moral community.

Second, in condition (5) Warren claims that having a racial concept and awareness of oneself as having a race, may be sufficient for one's being a person. There is much to be said about this. In the metaphysics of race we find three general views. Some metaphysicians are eliminativists about race; 'race' is nothing but a false belief we can have about ourselves or others. Some metaphysicians hold that race is a social construction; being a certain race consists in being treated and interpreted in a certain way by social practices, institutions, and conventions. Other metaphysicians hold that race is a natural kind that is discoverable through biology (Ney and Hazlett 2014). If Warren's claim is paired with eliminativism, then her stipulation is that one must have a false belief about oneself in order to be a person. This is an undesirable consequence for Warren's position because it implies that self-delusion is perhaps sufficient for one's being a person. If eliminativism is true, does it follow that personhood is a self-delusion? If her claim is paired with social constructionism, then her stipulation is that one must live in a society that makes racial distinctions and one is aware of which 'race' one is categorized in by one's society. On this view, then, an individual who does not live in such a society would not satisfy this criterion for personhood. This too is an undesirable consequence for Warren's position because it implies that many individuals can fail to be persons because they are unlucky enough to live in a society without racial social constructions. Whether one lives in a racial society seems irrelevant to sorting individuals into persons and non-persons. Lastly, if Warren's claim is paired with biological realism about race, then her stipulation is that one must have biological concepts in order to acquire a racial concept and apply that concept to oneself. Again, this is an undesirable consequence for Warren's position because it implies that individuals who have not studied biology and do not have a biological concept of race nor apply such a concept to themselves, might not count as persons. It seems arbitrary to stipulate that one can fail to be a person if one is not lucky enough to have studied biology, have racial biological concepts, and apply such a concept to oneself. Consequently, Warren's appeal to a racial self-concept seems implausible (or at least too narrow), given eliminativism, social constructionism, or biological realism about race. On a charitable reading, it seems that Warren stipulated racial self-concepts for personhood because she sought after an example of an individual's intrinsic properties and supposed that awareness of one's own intrinsic properties may be sufficient for personhood.

Third, Warren takes it as "obvious" to herself that if an opponent disagrees with her criteria for personhood, then that opponent simply does not have the concept of personhood. Warren's appeal of her concept of personhood's being obvious to her is noteworthy. Surely one can understand Warren's concept of personhood, and remain in doubt, or reject, her exclusive association of these as necessary conditions for personhood. When I narrate a history of personhood in the third section, it will be shown that personhood is neither "obvious" to everyone nor "self-evident" considered in itself. It is particularly significant to observe Warren's strong confidence in exclusively associating these five conditions with personhood. So, third, Warren appeals to the strong way that these five conditions seem to her as a basis for exclusively associating these five conditions with personhood. This is different than claiming that this concept of personhood is self-evident. On one analysis, a self-evident concept or proposition is one that meets four conditions: it is clear and distinct, it is ascertained by careful consideration, it is consistent with other self-evident truths, and it attracts general consensus (cf. Sidgwick 1967, 338). But Warren's criteria for personhood doesn't meet this standard.

Warren concedes that her account of personhood lacks "precise definitions of the criteria." This concession decreases our confidence that her concept of personhood meets the first condition for being self-evident. It might well be that Warren ascertained her concept of personhood by careful consideration; still, it is more likely that she is reporting her intuitions about personhood (what is "obvious" to her). But this differs from careful consideration—one would think that one should consult the history of concepts of personhood in order to be careful. If one were ignorant of the history of personhood, then arguing for a normative concept of personhood without careful attention to the history suggests that the proposed concept of personhood was not arrived at by sufficiently careful consideration. So, Warren's concept of personhood does not meet the second consideration either. It may well be that her concept of personhood is consistent with other self-evident truths, so I pass this condition by. Does Warren's proposed concept of personhood attract a general consensus? She claims that it is "very nearly universal." But no evidence for its near universality is given. Furthermore, if it is very nearly universal, then we should find that not only do human beings today understand and believe this concept of personhood but so too do human beings who happen to not exist currently. Universal consensus should be understood not only among the living but also among the dead. The history of personhood that I discuss in the third section shows that Warren's claim that her concept is "very nearly universal" is false. Her concept of personhood was, in fact, a recent development in western European philosophy. It is hardly "universal"; it is closer to a minority position in terms of the democracy of the living and the dead. Warren's claim that her concept of person is "very nearly universal" not only merits suspicion, but we should emphatically deny that it is true. From all this it follows that Warren's concept of personhood is not self-evident.

In the next section I argue that the situation is this: while it may be true that Warren's notion is shared today by many human beings, this is not in itself a good reason to accept it as *normative*. After all, there are several concepts shared by many human beings today that should not be taken as normative, for example, racist concepts and ableist concepts.

When Personhood Is Discriminatory

Warren points out that her concept of personhood excludes many human beings from the moral community, e.g., human fetuses, human babies, and many cognitively disabled human beings. (It should be noted that there is a parallel with Locke regarding those human beings that are not typical. Warren denies membership in the moral community for human fetuses, infants, and the profoundly cognitively disabled, despite acknowledging their humanity. Locke is skeptical about the humanity in cases of an "odly-shaped Foetus" that has just been born.) Warren also points out that her concept of 'personhood' includes some non-human animals. I find the exclusion of human fetuses, babies, and many cognitively disabled human beings from the moral community, on the basis of Warren's criteria for personhood, to be obviously and deeply morally disturbing. Others may find the exclusion of human fetuses less obviously morally disturbing than the exclusion of many cognitively disabled human beings. In any case, for many the disjunct is true, that is, the exclusion of human fetuses or human babies or profoundly cognitively disabled human beings from the moral community is morally disturbing. In what follows I limit myself to the case of profoundly cognitively disabled human beings.

Those who believe that profoundly cognitively disabled human beings are equal members of the moral community may reject Warren's concept of personhood in several ways. In the spirit of a G.E. Moore shift, they can put this rejection in the form of a modus tollens. For Moore, the existence of the external world is much more likely than the argument for external world skepticism. Likewise, for those who believe that profoundly cognitively disabled human beings are equal members of the moral community will find their membership in the moral community much more likely than Warren's normative concept of moral personhood. I call this the 'Moral Shift Argument':

1. If Warren's concept of moral personhood is correct, then profoundly cognitively disabled human beings are not equal members of the moral community.
2. But profoundly cognitively disabled human beings are equal members of the moral community.

Therefore,

3. Warren's concept of moral personhood is not correct.

This argument is persuasive to those who believe Premise (2) to be more likely than its negation. But those who do not believe Premise (2) to be more likely than its negation will obviously not find this argument persuasive. I want to give an argument that they would find more persuasive. This argument mirrors an argument that Eva Feder Kittay has given (cf. Kittay 2016, 728–730). I will argue that it is unjustified to exclude human beings that are profoundly cognitively disabled from the moral community. Their exclusion is unjustified. The idea that leads to this conclusion is that one goes wrong in making an unjustified *exclusive* association between two sets of properties, namely, the exclusive association between being a modern person and being an equal member in the moral community. On my view, Warren is unjustified to claim that her five conditions are exclusively associated with membership in the moral community because this exclusive association is a species of discrimination that is irrational or unwarranted.

In what follows I turn to Eva Kittay's analysis of the structural similarity between racism and ableism in order to explain my contention that Warren makes a discriminatory exclusive association between her concept of personhood and equal membership in the moral community. Kittay argues that the basic structure of racism is the same as the basic structure of ableism. This basic structure is discriminatory. So, we ought to condemn ableism just as we condemn racism. According to Kittay the way racism works is as follows. A racist individual, e.g., a white supremacist, values or desires certain properties, say the property of being white. The white supremacist also makes an exclusive association between the property of being white and other desired properties such as being intelligent, moral, or trustworthy. So, for a white supremacist,

When Personhood Goes Wrong in Ethics   273

someone is intelligent, moral, or trustworthy only if one is white. But what reasons are there for making an *exclusive* association between e.g., being white and e.g., being intelligent, moral, or trustworthy? There are no good reasons for this *exclusive* association. After all, there are many, many counterexamples; there are many intelligent, moral, and trustworthy individuals who are not white. And there are many who are white who fail to be intelligent, moral, and trustworthy individuals. The desirable properties of being intelligent, or being moral, or being trustworthy, are not exclusive to those who are white. Nevertheless, the white supremacist insists that these desirable properties are exclusive to those who are white, and refuses to acknowledge that there are any counterexamples. The refusal to acknowledge these counterexamples is irrational because the refusal is not based on any good reasons; instead, it is based on a discriminatory preference in favor of those who are white.

Kittay contends that racism is not simply the privileging of one's own group over other groups, but also depends on the type of group in question. Some groups are 'primal' in the sense that they are defined by extrinsic relations. A family is a primal group; individuals are in a family because they are in certain extrinsic relations like *being the parent of*, *being the child of*, *being the sibling of*, etc. In contrast, there are 'constituted groups' that are defined in terms of intrinsic properties that each member has. For example, the group of wise human beings is constituted by all the individual human beings who each have the intrinsic property of being wise. Kittay argues that we should understand the structure of racism to be that there is an assertion that only members of a certain 'constituted' group *should* be associated with certain desirable properties. If an individual human being does not have the relevant the intrinsic properties, then that individual *should* be excluded from having any of the desirable properties. A racist's key move is to claim that there is an exclusive association between a 'constituted' group and the desirable properties. Kittay comes to this analysis of racism by comparing racism and ableism; she writes,

> But seeing racism through the prism of disability adds the insight that rather [than] being predicated on group membership, racism is the exclusive claim to *a set of desirable inherent properties*—that is to say, *the characteristics or intrinsic properties that those in power judge to be desirable and want for their exclusive possession.* To conceive of racism in this fashion throws into doubt the idea that providing full moral status based on human species membership, which is a relation or primal kind membership, is necessarily pernicious, and that the solicitude that we give to the cognitively disabled (to the extent that they are treated with solicitude at all) is akin to racism. Furthermore, it is constituted groups who determine and claim

> exclusive possession of desirable traits that underpin both racism (the denigration of others without these properties) and ableism (which denigrates those who stand outside a singular norm of the human).
> (Kittay 2016, 719)

Kittay is responding to Peter Singer and Jeff McMahan, who claim that basing moral standing on species membership is akin to racism. Singer calls this speciesism. Their reason for associating racism and speciesism is that in both cases one simply prefers one's own group over other groups. But on Kittay's analysis racism and speciesism do not have the same structure. She contends that a speciesist does not posit that there is an *exclusive* association between one's group and a set of desired properties (in this case, the property of moral standing). Moreover, a speciesist does not need to base moral standing on intrinsic properties but can base moral standing on an individual's extrinsic relations (i.e., family relations). But a racist posits an exclusive association between a set of intrinsic properties (i.e., a constituted group) and desirable properties (e.g., the property of moral standing). Kittay concludes that speciesism and racism do not have the same structure.

Furthermore, Kittay argues that racism and ableism do have the same structure. Like a racist, an ableist exclusively associates a set of intrinsic properties with what is *normatively* human. For example, an ableist with regard to vision exclusively associates visual experience with a normative human life. This ableist excludes human beings that lack visual experience from the group of those human beings with a normative human life. But what is the ableist's basis for this exclusive association? While different ableists can give different answers, at the root of it all an ableist simply prefers that a 'normal' or good human life requires visual experience. There are complicating factors, however. Some environments are more hospitable to human beings with visual experience than those who are blind. This is an extrinsic or environmental or consequentialist consideration. The anti-ableist should concede that some environmental factors can make, e.g., a blind person's life harder than someone who is not blind. Many of these environmental factors are constructed by human society, and so can (in principle) be intentionally changed. But even more, there are some situations in which being blind is an advantage; for example, it is more difficult for those who are blind to be racist than it is for a sighted individual. However, my discussion about normative human lives is not about environmental or consequentialist considerations, but about whether certain intrinsic properties should be included or excluded from the normative human life. The ableist contends that some intrinsic properties, e.g., being sighted, should be exclusively associated with the normative human life. Given this, disabled human beings are excluded from the normatively human on the basis of the ableist's preferences, preferences that are not well supported, and so are unjustified.

Kittay argues that moral standing should be based on extrinsic relations (family relations) and not on intrinsic properties. But I worry that this stipulation is implausible because surely an individual human being must have some intrinsic properties in order for that individual human being to have some extrinsic relations. Put roughly, if Sally is the mother of Tom, surely Sally is a human being and so too is Tom, and that the extrinsic relations 'mother of' and 'son of' explanatorily presuppose their having such an intrinsic property. I think Kittay can get around this worry. We can enumerate properties that are more specific than 'being human.' But which properties are required for being human? Kittay says that there is a moral danger in the project of trying to identify these fine-grained properties and then basing moral standing on a set of those intrinsic properties. It is morally safer to base moral standing on extrinsic relations (family relations) than engaging in an inquiry and debate about the correct set of fine-grained intrinsic properties. So, one way to respond to the worry is to add to Kittay's position the claim that whatever fine-grained intrinsic properties are required for one's having the relevant extrinsic family relations, it is morally hazardous to claim that all of these fine-grained intrinsic properties are necessary conditions. Instead, we should say that the *disjunction* of all of these fine-grained intrinsic properties is sufficient for having these extrinsic family relations. For example, if two parents have three children, one child has a straight nose and a low IQ, another child has a round nose and an average IQ, and the third child has a stubby nose and a high IQ, each is a child of these parents. Each individual human being has intrinsic properties, and these are sufficient for being the child of these parents. While each child has different intrinsic properties, some set of disjuncts is sufficient for having extrinsic family relations. We should not worry too much about a certain disjunct (e.g., whether one can earn a certain minimal score on an IQ test in a given year). We should accept a long disjunction that is sufficient for equal membership in the moral community. As Kittay puts it,

> Sorting ourselves by intrinsic properties such as rationality is morally more hazardous than accepting a group membership that acts like a family. Like a good family whose strength grows as we take care of each other, we value each other equally as members of one family. Doing so does not preclude, and is entirely consistent with treating members of other families (in the case of species members, the many species with whom we co-occupy the world) respectfully.
> (Kittay 2016, 739–740)

Here Kittay offers an additional argument against ableism. It is morally *more risky* to base moral standing on a stipulated set of intrinsic properties like rationality than to base moral standing on primal group membership. Historically, it is the case that positing human moral standing on the basis of some constituted group often is motivated by an exclusive and discriminatory bias, and so this way of demarcating the moral community is unjustified. It is morally safer, and so better, to base human moral standing on primal group membership. (Note that Kittay is explicit that respect for non-human animals is consistent with a basis for moral standing being one's primal group. This basis is sufficient, but not necessary, for moral standing.)

Kittay's argument from moral safety can be construed as a version of the Moral Shift Argument with which I began this section. Akin to Premise (2) of the Moral Shift Argument, she assumes the equal moral standing of all human beings on the basis of extrinsic family relations. But someone like Mary Anne Warren would contend that Premise (2) is not obvious, not to her at least. Warren would not find Kittay's claim obvious because Warren exclusively associates moral standing with her own concept of moral personhood. Given this exclusive association, Warren would find Kittay's argument from moral safety to be counterintuitive.

What is needed, then, is an argument that challenges Warren's exclusively associating membership in the moral community with her concept of moral personhood. One way to develop this argument is to mirror what Kittay says about the structural similarities between racism and ableism. The argument contends that Warren's exclusively associating her concept of moral personhood with equal membership in the moral community has the same structure as racism and ableism. Consequently, Warren's exclusive association is unjustified.

Warren prefers and values certain cognitive achievements, namely (1)–(5): consciousness, reasoning, self-motivated activity, capacity to communicate about lots of things, and having self-concepts. She exclusively associates these with membership in the moral community. One has moral standing if and only if one has (1)–(5). But why should we exclusively associate moral standing with the conjunction (or even disjunction) of (1)–(5)? Why not claim that the *disjunction* of (1), or (2), or (3), or (4), or (5), or many more properties e.g., *being the child of*, is sufficient for membership in the moral community? (I claim that this disjunction is sufficient, but not necessary, because other species surely are members of the moral community as well.) Warren does not provide any non-question-begging reasons why we should accept her exclusive association between moral standing and the *conjunction*, or even the disjunction, of (1)–(5). She claims that her concept of moral personhood is "self-evident" and obvious, and on the basis of its being self-evident and obvious one should accept Warren's exclusive association. She writes,

> The suggestion is simply that the moral community consists of all and only *people* rather than all and only human beings; and probably the best way of demonstrating its self-evidence is by considering the concept of personhood, to see what sorts of entity are and are

When Personhood Goes Wrong in Ethics 277

not persons, and what the decision that a being is or is not a person implies about moral rights.

(Warren 2010, 437)

But the obviousness of her moral concept of personhood is precisely what is in question. It is in question (in part) because once we become acquainted with the history of concepts of personhood, as surveyed in the third section below, we realize that personhood is neither self-evident nor obvious. This history of personhood makes us aware that personhood is a term of art that was developed for specific Christian theological purposes, and later for forensic purposes having to do with moral responsibility. To claim that one's modern concept of personhood is obvious to oneself is not a good reason to accept it as the basis for moral standing. Warren needs to argue for the exclusive association between moral standing and this modern concept of moral personhood especially in a dialectical context in which the opponent is familiar with the history of concepts of personhood, the opponent does not find a modern concept of personhood to be obvious, and the opponent is worried that Warren's concept of personhood is shaped by her own ableist assumptions.

In what follows I give the argument against Warren's exclusive association with numbered claims in order to avoid misunderstanding. Call this the 'Argument against Exclusive Moral Personhood':

1. If Warren has successfully exclusively associated a set of properties (which is her concept of personhood, (1)–(5)) with the moral community, then Warren has a good reason for this exclusive association.
2. If Warren's reason for the exclusive association is that the exclusive association is self-evident, then Warren has a good reason for making this exclusive association.
3. If Warren's reason for this exclusive association is a good reason, then what it is to be a person is self-evident.
4. But, what it is to be a person is not self-evident. Warren's concept of personhood is not self-evident because

    4.1. she does not give a fine-grained analysis of personhood, and so it is not clear or distinct;
    4.2. she was not sufficiently careful in considering what personhood is because of inattention to the history of concepts of personhood;
    4.3. the history of personhood shows that personhood as a distinct general category was likely invented by Boethius in the early 500s, and,
    4.4. from a historical point of view Warren's concept of personhood is not the consensus view but it is a relatively recent minority position that has attracted lots of attention.

5. Given (3) and (4), it follows (by modus tollens) that Warren's reason for this exclusive association is not a good reason.
6. Given (2) and (5), it follows (by modus tollens) that Warren's reason for this exclusive association is not self-evident.
7. Given (1) and (5), it follows (by modus tollens) that Warren has not successfully exclusively associated a set of properties with the moral community.

The Argument against Exclusive Moral Personhood targets Warren's claim that her criteria for moral personhood are self-evident. There are different concepts of personhood. If we exclusively associated the moral community with one of these other sets of intrinsic properties for personhood, then the extension of the moral community would be different than in the case of Warren's concept of personhood. Why accept Warren's criteria for personhood in the first place? It seems to operate in a backwards manner. Warren starts with (what Kittay calls) a "constituted group" and because she prefers it or desires it or understands it, she exclusively associates membership in the moral community with it. But it is not self-evident why this "constituted group," as opposed to a different group constituted by other criteria for personhood, should be exclusively associated with the moral community. It seems to me that Warren has a discriminatory assumption: if one is in my preferred (or valued or understood) constituted group, then one is a member of the moral community. Warren puts all those that she understands to be similar to herself with regard to cognitive ability in the moral community; those that are not similar enough to her with regard to cognitive ability are excluded from the moral community. This is an ableist position and it is structurally the same as racism, as analyzed by Kittay.

A Select History of Personhood

In the Argument against Exclusive Personhood, claims 4.2, 4.3, and 4.4 refer to a history of personhood. In what follows I give a brief telling of this history (which I have written about in more detail elsewhere; cf. Williams 2019; Williams forthcoming for details on the rationality condition for 'persona'). This history of personhood shows several things. First, it shows that 'persona' or 'person' is a theological term of art that was developed for the purpose of Christian theorizing about the Trinity and Incarnation. Second, Boethius likely invented personhood (that is, the exclusive association of 'persona' with 'rationality') for these theological purposes. Third, the evidence considered supports the claim that Greek theologians did not have, and did not take themselves to need, personhood for theorizing about the Trinity and Incarnation; personhood as a distinct general category was an invention in Latin Christian theology. Fourth, Greek theologians debated the metaphysics of the Trinity and

Incarnation just as the Latin theologians did; but what the Latins added to the discussion is a rationality condition for 'persona.' Fifth, although Latin theologians accepted Boethius's rationality condition with modifications, it did little to no work in any Latin theologian's theorizing about personhood in relation to the Trinity or Incarnation. Just as the Greeks contended, Latin theologians on the whole treated rationality as an irrelevant add on to the definition of a 'persona' or person. Given this history, it is striking that Warren takes it as obvious, and even a self-evident truth, that personhood requires rationality as articulated through her conditions (1)–(5).

On the basis of (purported) revelation, ancient and medieval Christians believed that there is one God and there are three who are this one God. There is God the Father, God the Son, and God the Holy Spirit. They are one God, but they are not the same in every way. For example, only God the Son became incarnate as a human being (so the Christmas story goes), lived a human life, performed miracles, taught disciples, was the victim of capital punishment on a cross by the Roman government, and rose again from the dead on the third day. There are many other details, but it suffices to report that conciliar Christians believe that there is one God, that there are three who are this one God, and some things are true of one of these that are not true of others of these (cf. Pope St. Agatho 1899, 330). Some Greek-speaking Christian theologians, namely St. Basil of Caesarea or his brother St. Gregory of Nyssa (there is disagreement over which initially posited these terms), developed some vocabulary to help Christians articulate what they believed (Cross 2002; Zachhuber 2014. I agree with Cross's interpretation; cf. Williams 2019). The stipulation is that the Greek terms 'ousia' and 'hypostasis' should not be thought of as synonymous as some Greeks had contended but rather that they signify and refer to different things (cf. Basil of Caesarea 1961, 197–227). Their theological posit was the following. 'Ousia' should be understood to signify and to refer to a real common nature or essence. An 'ousia' is a mind-independent thing that is shared among individuals. An 'ousia' is an immanent universal that is predicated distributively of individuals. 'Hypostasis' should be understood to signify and to refer to an individual of a nature. An individual is a unique collection of attributes, namely an 'ousia' and individuating properties. Given this stipulation between 'ousia' and 'hypostasis' the claim is that if one wished to understand what Christians mean by the divine triad or trinity, they should say that there is just one divine 'ousia' and three divine 'hypostaseis'; e.g., God the Father and God the Son are numerically the same divine 'ousia' but not numerically the same divine 'hypostasis.' The Father's individuating properties are 'being unbegotten' and 'begetting.' The Son's individuating property is 'being begotten' and the Holy Spirit's individuating property is 'proceeding from' the Father. The divine 'hypostaseis' are distinct explanatorily prior to any relation they may have to creatures (e.g., God the Son's being united hypostatically with an individual human nature).

To some Latin and Greek-speaking theologians, e.g., Jerome, this stipulation seemed counterintuitive. Jerome had thought that 'ousia' and 'hypostasis' were synonymous and that if these Greek-speaking theologians required him to confess three 'hypostaseis,' then he thought he was being asked to confess three divine 'ousiai' or natures, which he took to be heretical (Jerome 1956, 308–311). Jerome was happy to confess three divine 'personae' (persons) but hesitant to confess three divine 'hypostasis.' Jerome gives little indication about what a 'persona' is other than that it is something that subsists. When we turn to the famous Latin-speaking theologian Augustine we find someone perplexed by the Latin church teaching that there are three divine 'personae' (persons). Augustine was unclear about what the term 'persona' signified (Augustine 1968, 255–267). The fact that it was not clear shows that it required clarification.

Among later Greek-speaking theologians, such as Severus of Antioch and Leontius of Byzantium, we find more fine-grained analyses of Basil or Gregory's stipulation about 'ousia' and 'hypostasis.' What prompted these analyses was the belief that God the Son, a divine 'hypostasis,' became incarnate and not the divine 'ousia' as such. (For references and discussion, see Williams 2019.) Severus interpreted Basil (or Gregory) as positing a collectivist account of universals such that 'ousia' is a collection made up of particulars, and a 'hypostasis' is a particular of an 'ousia.' On this reading 'ousia' is predicated collectively; and so each 'hypostasis' is a *part*icular (as opposed to an individual). Moreover, Severus stipulated an additional condition for 'hypostasis': the mark of 'hypostasis' is actual existence. A 'hypostasis' is an actually existing particular of an 'ousia.' And an 'ousia' is a collection of actually existing things, i.e. 'hypostaseis.' With this analysis to hand, Severus claimed that Christ is a composite nature that actually exists, and denied that Christ is two natures each of which has its own actual existence. Severus worried that if we say that there are two actual existences in Christ, a divine existence and a human existence, then this implies the condemned heresy of Nestorius according to which there is a divine hypostasis and a human hypostasis who are united by honor and being worshipped, but not united metaphysically. Severus proposed that Christ has one composite nature that is one actual existence.

Leontius of Byzantium strongly disagreed with Severus on several fronts. Leontius contends that Severus was wrong to interpret Basil or Gregory as positing a collective universal for the divine 'ousia' and wrong to posit that the mark of a hypostasis is actual existence. First, the divine 'ousia' and the human 'ousia' are immanent universals that are predicated distributively. Second, the mark of a 'hypostasis' is not actual existence, but rather 'what is in itself,' i.e. the ultimate subject of predication. This implies that a 'hypostasis' is what is complete in itself and not a part of something else. In effect, Leontius reversed Severus's metaphysics. When applied to the Christology, Leontius holds that Christ's individual human nature's existence is not identical to his divine nature's actual existence. What Leontius comes up with is a theory of the Incarnation according to which Christ has an individual human nature that is not itself a 'hypostasis' even though the individual nature has its own actual existence. What Christ's individual human nature lacks such that it is not itself a 'hypostasis' is that it exists in a divine hypostasis; it is not 'what is in itself,' instead it is predicated of a divine 'hypostasis.'

There was another dispute between miaphysites like Severus and neo-chalcedonians like Leontius: does Christ have one will or two wills? The dispute about the number of wills more or less followed the same line of argument about the metaphysics of 'ousia' and 'hypostasis.' The miaphysites argued that Christ has one composite will, and the neo-chalcedonians (notably Maximus the Confessor) argued that Christ has two wills—a divine will and a human will. The miaphysites worried that if we can count Christ's wills, then this implies that there are two 'hypostaseis.' If there are two wills, then this is equivalent to Nestorianism. Leontius, a neo-chalcedonian, contended that number does not imply division (i.e., numerically distinct 'hypostaseis'). Leontius argued that if number as such implied division into hypostaseis, then it would be false to claim that an individual human has numerically distinct attributes. But, an individual does have numerically distinct attributes, even though it is the same individual that has these numerically distinct attributes. Consequently, we can claim that Christ has two wills and this does not imply two separate 'hypostaseis.' There is one hypostasis who is the ultimate subject of the divine will and of a human will.

What this survey suggests is that among Greek-speaking theologians the dispute over the metaphysics of the Incarnation involved different metaphysical models of universals and individuals and how those different models interacted with theological beliefs about the Incarnation. What we do not find among Greek-speaking theologians is an invocation of a distinct category of personhood having to do with rationality in order to settle the dispute. Nevertheless, these disputes run close to what we might consider disputes about the metaphysics of personhood. There is discussion of the ultimate subject of predication, the same ultimate subject of different predicates at different times, and discussion of intellect and will. The key thing to observe is that there is no general category that captures 'rational beings'; instead, there is discussion of individuals of the divine being, and an individual with a divine nature and a human nature. 'Rationality' piggybacks on the sorts of natures under discussion; it does not feature as a property that is distinct from a natural kind (as John Locke would suppose). These disputes are in the neighborhood of personhood, but there is no distinct category of personhood here.

It is in the Latin-speaking world that personhood became a distinct category. While there were discussions of 'persona' in the Latin-speaking world before Boethius (Brouwer forthcoming), it was Boethius who stipulated one general definition of 'persona' that applies to all putative cases of a person. In his *Treatise against Eutyches and Nestorius* Boethius tries to resolve the metaphysical disagreements about the Incarnation by defining 'persona' using genus and differentia. He claimed that a 'persona' or person is an "individual substance of a rational nature" (Boethius 1997a, 85). With regard to a 'rational nature,' all that Boethius says for us to understand how he is using the term is:

> Now from all this it is clear that person cannot be predicated of bodies which have no life (for no one ever says that a stone has a person), nor yet of living things which lack sense (for neither is there any person of a tree), nor finally of that which is bereft of mind and reason (for there is no person of a horse or ox or any other of the animals which dumb and without reason live a life of sense alone), but we say there is a person of a human, of God, of an angel.
> (Boethius 1997a, 85)

In this context in which he is defining 'persona' he does not provide any list of necessary conditions for what has a 'rational nature' other than by ostension, namely whatever a human, God, or an angel have, that sets them apart from all else. Nevertheless, the truthmaker for being rational is the disjunction of these three natural kinds; rationality is not distinct from these natural kinds as Locke would later suppose (cf. Locke 1975, 187–188).

In his *Consolation of Philosophy* Boethius discusses rationality such that it implies one's capability for abstract thought (that is, cognition of universals), deliberation, and free choice. While these may seem to be conditions required for all putatively rational beings, Boethius denies that God is rational and instead affirms that God is intellectual. This means that God does not require investigation or deliberation for knowing what God knows, or judging what God judges, or willing what God wills (Boethius 1997b, 417).[9] So, it is not clear what exactly we are supposed to understand from Boethius's ostensive definition of 'rationality.' It might be that Boethius included 'rational' in his definition of 'persona' because he supposed there was something similar between a divine nature and a human nature. Given that God the Son happened to assume a human nature, Boethius supposed that what Christ is one of is an individual with a 'rational nature.'

Boethius also says that when one ascribes personhood ('persona') to an individual, one is ascribing dignity to that individual, that is, "the term [hypostasis] has been applied to thing of higher value [*melioribus*], in order that in some way what is more excellent might be distinguished" (Boethius 1997a, 91). While having a "higher value" is not included in his definition of 'persona,' Boethius associates "higher value" with 'persona' in his overall discussion of 'persona.' He goes so far as to say that the Greeks used the term 'hypostasis' to ascribe "higher value" to rational beings. It is important to note two things here. First, we have evidence from Greek theologians like Gregory of Nyssa (and later Greek theologians like Leontius of Byzantium and John of Damascus) that falsifies Boethius's claim about the Greeks; Gregory's 'hypostasis' refers to any individual of any nature whatsoever. 'Hypostasis' as such is not associated with what has a "higher value." Second, it is likely that Boethius adds "higher value" to personhood because he was already committed to the claim that all rational beings, whether humans, angels, or God, have a "higher value" than non-rational beings. Given all this, we can understand Boethius's overall account of a 'persona' to be the conjunction of rationality (from a part of the definition of 'homo'), individuality (from the Greek use of 'hypostasis'), and "higher value" (from a comparison between rational and non-rational beings).

What the foregoing shows is that Boethius's proposed definition of a 'persona' is embedded in a Christian theological debate about the Incarnation, that he did not posit any detailed necessary conditions for 'rationality,' and that he associated "higher value" with rationality in his overall discussion of personhood.

Not very long after Boethius wrote *Treatise against Eutyches and Nestorius*, its proposal about personhood was criticized by other Latin-speaking theologians. One of the earliest critics was Rusticus the Deacon. In his dialogue *Contra Acephalos*, which was written between 553–564 CE, Rusticus interacts with a miaphysite opponent (likely Severus of Antioch) about the metaphysics of the Incarnation. In it he discusses what is meant by the term 'persona.' Rusticus has his opponent say that "every individual nature is a person" (Rusticus 2013, 39).[10] It is important to note that this definition reflects Basil of Caesarea's (or Gregory of Nyssa's) account of 'hypostasis'; for Basil (or Gregory), there is, e.g., a hypostasis of a man, of a horse, etc. 'Hypostasis' refers to an individual of any nature whatsoever. It does not exclude non-human or non-rational animals. Rusticus replies to this proposed definition of 'persona' by saying that "there are many individuals of a nature that are not also persons, such as what are inanimate and irrational" (Rusticus 2013, 39).[11] In reply, the miaphysite opponent says that

> there is much to say about this, even if it is *not aptly related to* this which is proposed. But letting go of the other things, I define the proposition in this way: every person is an individual and rational nature.
>
> (Rusticus 2013, 40)[12]

Two things should be noted. First, the opponent disagrees about exclusively associating 'persona' with rationality but allows it here for the sake of argument. Second, Rusticus has his opponent give what is equivalent to Boethius's definition of 'persona.' Rusticus goes on to criticize this definition of 'persona' on the basis of a theological counterexample (Rusticus 2013, 40, ln. 1234–1240). He worries that if this definition were accepted, then Christians would say that the one divine nature is a person. But no Christian ought to believe that, according to orthodox Christians. So, there is something missing in Boethius's definition of 'persona.' What Rusticus takes to be missing is 'subsistence.' Subsistence is the term for being an ultimate subject of predication that implies being a whole (and not a part of a whole). Later, Richard of St. Victor argues that 'subsistence' is uninformative and that we need a better concept for the theological explananda, namely 'incommunicable existence' (cf. Richard of St. Victor 2013, 144–145, 162–163). Richard's revision was widely accepted in the Latin theological tradition, though it was clarified further by (e.g.,) John Duns Scotus (cf. Cross 2005, 159–163; see also Adams 2005, 15–52).

There are two points that we can take from Rusticus's discussion of the Incarnation. First, he bears witness to Boethius's Latin theological innovation of exclusively associating personhood with rationality for he represents his miaphysite (Greek-speaking) opponent as not being familiar with this concept and not wishing to accept it because of its seeming irrelevance to the theological discussion at hand. There is good reason for this. Gregory of Nyssa explicitly claimed that 'hypostasis' applies to different species of animals, e.g., this man, this horse. Leontius of Byzantium echoes this in saying that 'hypostasis' applies to e.g., this horse, this ox, this man; John of Damascus even applies 'hypostasis' to olive trees. There was no need for the invention of personhood as such for the Christological debates so far as the Greek-speaking theologians were concerned. What they thought was needed was a distinction between an individual and a shareable nature. Second, Boethius and Rusticus accept a definition of 'persona' that requires rationality to be relevant to the definition of 'persona.' Rationality is a specific difference of 'persona.' Nonetheless, neither Boethius nor Rusticus provide any list of necessary conditions for all rational beings according to genus and differentia. In the Christological context they give only ostensive definitions of rationality. I suspect they give only ostensive definitions because the details are irrelevant to their theological inquiry.

What we find in later Latin theological reflection about personhood and the Incarnation supports my suggestion that rationality plays almost no role in these ancient and medieval concepts of personhood. For example, Richard of St. Victor criticizes Boethius's definition of personhood on the basis of the same theological counterexample that Rusticus gave. Richard corrects Boethius's definition saying that a divine person is an *incommunicable existence* of the divine nature, thereby replacing Rusticus's term "subsistence" with "incommunicable existence." But even more, Richard thinks the rationality condition is too narrow to be put in the general definition of 'persona.' When writing about the divine persons, Richard replaces 'rationality' with the 'divine nature' (cf. Richard of St. Victor 2013, 162–163) because the details about cognition, knowledge, and volition, are not relevant for our coming to have the appropriate theological concept of 'persona.' Although Richard believes that 'persona' implies a rational nature, he indicates that details about 'rationality' are not essential to the definition of 'persona.' Like Boethius, Richard holds that the extension of the term 'rational' includes the divine nature, angelic nature, and human nature.

Later, theologians like Thomas Aquinas and William of Ockham do not discuss any details about rationality when discussing the metaphysics of the Incarnation with regard to 'persona.' God the Son is one 'persona' who assumes an individual human nature (cf. Adams 2005, 36–39; Ockham 1991, 272–273). The individual human nature assumed in the Incarnation is not itself a 'persona' because it is ontologically united with, and depends on, a divine 'persona.' While God the Son's individual human nature is a truthmaker for the proposition that Christ's human nature is an individual rational being, it is not a truthmaker for the proposition that this individual human nature is a 'persona.' This shows that for scholastic theologians rationality is necessary but not sufficient for 'persona.' This is quite different than Warren's modern concept of personhood, according to which rationality is necessary and sufficient if we formulate rationality according to Warren's conditions (2)–(5). But in the Greek theological tradition, 'rationality' is not even a component in the definition of a 'hypostasis,' and so isn't even a necessary condition. 'Rationality' was absent in the Greek theological tradition and peripheral in the Latin theological tradition because details about rationality were not directly relevant.

When we compare this history of personhood to the development in the 19th and 20th centuries of social models of the Trinity, we find different concepts of personhood.[13] Social models of the Trinity (or Incarnation) assume and insist on a modern concept of personhood along the lines that Warren stipulates (cf. Hasker 2013, 19–25). Instead of positing that a 'hypostasis' or 'persona' is explanatorily prior to any cognitive acts, including higher-order cognitive acts, advocates of a social model of the Trinity assume that to be a person requires not only incommunicable mental powers (e.g., intellect and will), but also incommunicable mental acts, including higher-order cognitive acts (cf. Williams 2017, 343–344; see also Barth 2004, 357–358). This concept of personhood has led to the emergence of Social Trinitarianism. If philosophical theologians did not assume a modern concept of personhood—an assumption that does not derive from any authoritative conciliar documents—then social Trinitarianism would lose its obviousness or self-evidence. Still, there is an independent argument for a modern conception of personhood for Trinitarian theology, that is, what I've elsewhere called the Argument from the Essential Indexical 'I.' But I have argued that this argument fails to establish its conclusion. The Argument from the Essential Indexical 'I' concludes that a divine *person* requires numerically distinct and *incommunicable* mental powers. But I've given an alternative model of the Trinity that undermines the claim that personhood requires that a divine individual have numerically distinct and *incommunicable* mental powers (Williams 2017, 336–339). Moreover, I've argued (elsewhere) that a modern concept of personhood is inconsistent with authoritative conciliar sources (Williams forthcoming unpublished). Given these two objections against the use of modern personhood in Trinitarian theology, philosophical theologians who are working on the Trinity (or Incarnation) and who aim for consistency with the authoritative conciliar councils can no longer appeal to its seeming obviousness, or the argument from essential indexical 'I,' as conclusive reasons for insisting on a modern concept of personhood in theorizing about the Trinity (or Incarnation).[14]

Can Personhood Be Saved?

It is like a wild-goose chase in trying to identify exactly the right fine-grained criteria for personhood—especially in our context in which we have rather fine-grained analyses of psychological and cognitive activities as detailed in the International Classification of Functioning (ICF) by the World Health Organization. How does one know when one has found the right set of properties? In the case of ancient and medieval Christian theorizing about the Trinity and Incarnation, philosophical theologians found an explanans for their specific explananda. There was a target that guided the stipulated criteria for 'persona,' here taken as equivalent to 'hypostasis.' In the case of Locke, he needed a concept that explains when someone can be held morally and legally responsible; that is, what does it take to be a moral agent? (This is different than asking about membership in the moral community because moral agency need not exhaust the membership of the moral community; there can be moral patients who are not (currently) moral agents, e.g., a profoundly cognitively disabled human being and some non-human animals.) In both cases, the explananda guided the search for the right explanans. These ways of going about 'personhood' make sense.

However, Warren is in a different situation. She is after whatever seems self-evident to her regarding personhood. There is not a specific explanandum that guides her investigation into personhood. Instead, she begins with her (supposedly) "self-evident" concept of personhood and then exclusively associates it with membership in the moral community. There is a significant gap between her concept of personhood and its exclusive association with the moral community, and nothing bridges the gap. I suspect she was somewhat aware of this problem when she writes in passing, "Admittedly, there are apt to be a great many problems involved in formulating precise definitions of these criteria" (Warren 2011, 438).

Those familiar with story about ancient and medieval concepts of personhood may contend that a Boethian concept of personhood (or any later Latin medieval variation of it) is inclusive of all human beings, and so is better than modern conceptions of personhood like Warren's for moral theory. Boethius's concept of personhood, namely an individual substance of a rational nature, is underdetermined with regard to the rationality condition, and so every individual human (excluding Christ's individual human nature) could count as a person. While I agree with the goal of saying that all human beings are equal members of the moral community in addition to some non-human species, I do not believe this is a good way to get there. If one goes this Boethian route, then one faces two challenges. First, Boethius claimed that personhood can only be predicated of humans, angels, and God. But what should prevent us from including some non-human animals in the category of personhood, and so as members of the moral community? Boethius gives an ostensive definition of the rationality condition that excludes non-human animals from personhood. This would be a morally risky foundation for a moral theory because it simply asserts that e.g., human beings are persons and non-human animals are not persons. If personhood bestows membership in the moral community and we assume Boethius's concept of personhood, then this conjunction entails that non-humans are not members of the moral community. In effect, the Boethian route has the same dialectical challenge as the Moral Shift Argument. Just as one might believe that the Moral Shift Argument begs the question, one might believe that Boethius's ostensive definition of the rationality condition begs the question about who is inside and who is outside the moral community.

The second challenge for the Boethian route is indirect. Why should we use Boethius's concept of personhood for ethical theorizing when it was posited as a response to the metaphysics of the Incarnation? Boethius was not trying to identify a concept that picks out all and only those who are members of the moral community. What justification have we for appropriating Boethius in this way, other than on the basis of a modern preference for exclusively associating personhood with membership in the moral community? All things considered, we should not take the Boethian route in moral theorizing without having a good argument that his concept, stipulated for another purpose in another context, can do the work it is put to in another, and very different, context.

Conclusion

Moral philosophers should be wary of appealing to personhood as a self-evident starting point for developing an ethical theory or for adjudicating ethical questions. Moreover, philosophical theologians should be wary of assuming a modern concept of personhood for theorizing about the Trinity or Incarnation. Making this assumption leads to positing models of the Trinity or Incarnation that are inconsistent with the ecumenical Christian councils. If a philosopher of religion does not share the evaluative criterion that a model of the Trinity or Incarnation should be consistent with the ecumenical councils, then there remains other worries such as consistency with Jewish monotheism (cf. Williams 2017, 321–322).

My overall conclusion is that philosophers are not justified to use personhood as a basis for membership in the moral community (because it is discriminatory), and philosophical theologians are not justified to assume modern personhood in doing constructive conciliar Christian theology (because better alternatives are readily available). Personhood, modern or Boethian, is bad for ethics and unnecessary for conciliar Christian theology.

Notes

1. Gregory of Nyssa 1958, 23, ln. 6–8; trans. Richard Cross 2002, 406.
2. Boethius 1997a, 84, ln. 4–5.
3. Rusticus the Deacon 2013, 39, ln. 1223, 1226–1227.
4. Richard of St. Victor 1958, 186–190. This definition is an aggregate of what Richard says in these passages.
5. Henry of Ghent 2014, 56, ln. 333–334.
6. John Locke 1975, 341, ln. 14, 16–18; 344, ln. 18; 346, ln. 24.
7. Mary Anne Warren 2011, 438.
8. I mean the same thing that Timothy Pawl 2016, 11–14 means by 'conciliar.'
9. "But reason belongs only to humankind, as intelligence only to the divine."
10. Ln. 1213: "Omnis natura indiuidua persona est."
11. Ln. 1226–1227: "Multae indiuiduae sunt naturae, quae non sunt etiam personae, sicut inanimatorum et irrationabilium."
12. Ln. 1224–1226: "Multa quidem de hoc dicere est, etsi non apte ad id quod propositum est. Ego uero cetera praeteriens, propositionem definio sic: omnis indiuidua et rationalis natura persona est."
13. I discuss problems with social Trinitarianism from a patristic and scholastic point of view in Williams 2017, 321–346.
14. Williams 2017, 321–346.

References

Adams, Marilyn McCord. "What's Metaphysically Special About Supposits? Some Medieval Variations on Aristotelian Substance." *Proceedings of the Aristotelian Society, Supplementary Volumes* 79 (2005): 15–52.

Augustine. *De Trinitate*. Edited by W.J. Mountain and Fr. Glorie. Turnholt: Brepols, 1968.
Barth, Karl. *Church Dogmatics: Volume I: The Doctrine of the Word of God*, 357–358. New York: T&T Clark, 2004.
Basil of Caesarea. *Letter 38*, 197–227. Cambridge, MA: Harvard University Press, 1961.
Boethius. *Contra Eutychen et Nestorium*. Edited by H. F. Stewart, E. K. Rand, and S. J. Tester. Cambridge, MA: Harvard University Press, 1997a.
———. *The Consolation of Philosophy*. Cambridge, MA: Harvard University Press, 1997b.
Brouwer, René. "Funerals, Faces, and Hellenistic Philosophers: On the Origins of the Concept of Persons in Rome." In *Persons: A History*, edited by Antonia Lolordo. Oxford: Oxford University Press, 2019.
Cross, Richard. "Gregory of Nyssa on Universals." *Vigiliae Christianae* 56 (2002): 372–410.
———. *Duns Scotus on God*. Burlington, VT: Ashgate, 2005.
Gregory of Nyssa. "Ex Communibus Notionibus." In *Gregorii Nysseni Opera Dogmatica Minora*, edited by F. Mueller, vol. III.1. Leiden: Brill, 1958.
Hasker, William. *Metaphysics and the Tri-Personal God*. New York: Oxford University Press, 2013.
Henry of Ghent. *Summa (Quaestionum Ordinarium)*. Edited by G. A. Wilson and G. J. Etzkorn. Leuven: Leuven University Press, 2014.
Jerome. *Letter 15 "To Pope Damasus."* Louisville: Westminster John Knox Press, 1956.
Kant, Immanuel. *Groundwork of the Metaphysics of Morals*. Edited by Mary Gregor. Cambridge: Cambridge University Press, 2008.
Kant, Immanuel. *The Metaphysics of Morals*, revised edition. Edited by Lara Denis and Translated by Mary Gregor. Cambridge: Cambridge University Press, 2017.
Kittay, Eva Feder. "Deadly Medicine: Project T4, Mental Disability, and Racism." *Res Philosophica* 93.4 (2016): 728–730.
Locke, John. *An Essay Concerning Human Understanding*. Edited by Peter H. Nidditch. Oxford: Clarendon Press, 1975.
Mattern, Ruth. "Moral Science and the Concept of Persons in Locke." In *Locke*, edited by Vere Chappell. Oxford: Oxford University Press, 1998.
Ney, Alyssa and Allan Hazlett. "The Metaphysics of Race." In *Metaphysics: An Introduction*, edited by Alyssa Ney, 259–278. New York: Routledge, 2014.
Pawl, Timothy. *In Defense of Conciliar Christology: A Philosophical Essay*. New York: Oxford University Press, 2016.
Pope St. Agatho. "Epistola Prima Ad Augustos Imperatores." In *Patrologia Latina*, edited by J. P. Migne, Paris, 1863, vol. 87, 1165D–1168A. Translated by Henry R. Percival as "The Letter of Agatho, Pope of Old Rome, to the Emperor [. . .]." In *The Seven Ecumenical Councils of the Undivided Church*, 330. Edinburgh: T&T Clark, 1899.
Richard of St. Victor. *De Trinitate*. Edited by Jean Ribaillier. Paris: Vring, 1958.
———. *On the Trinity*. Translated by Ruben Angelici. Eugene, OR: Cascade Books, 2011.
Rusticus the Deacon. *Contra Acephalos*. Edited by Sara Petri. Turnhout: Brepols, 2013.

Sidgwick, Henry. *The Methods of Ethics*, 7th ed. London: Palgrave Macmillan, 1967.
Warren, Mary Anne. "On the Moral and Legal Status of Abortion." In *Applied Ethics: A Multicultural Approach*, edited by Larry May, Kai Wong, and Jill Delston, 5th ed., 360–366. Boston: Prentice Hall, 2010.
William of Ockham. *Quodlibetal Questions*. Translated by Alfred Freddoso and Francis E. Kelley. New Haven: Yale University Press, 1991.
Williams, Scott M. "Unity of Action in a Latin Social Model of the Trinity." *Faith and Philosophy* 34.3 (2017): 321–346.
———. " 'Persons' in Ancient and Medieval Christian Theology." In *Persons: A History*, edited by Antonia Lolordo. Oxford: Oxford University Press, 2019.
———. Personhood, Ethics, and Disability Before and After Original Sin." In *Disability in Medieval Christian Philosophy and Theology*, edited by Scott Williams. New York: Routledge, forthcoming.
———. "In Defense of a Latin Social Trinity: Response to William Hasker." Unpublished.
Zachhuber, Johannes. *Human Nature in Gregory of Nyssa: Philosophical Background and Theological Significance*. Leiden: Brill, 2014.

Section V
Sex, Gender, and Race

12 Marriage, Reproduction, and the Incarnation
What Could Jesus Do?

Eric T. Yang and Stephen T. Davis

Introduction

It has been customary among Christians to hold that Jesus Christ did not take a spouse, did not have children, and did not engage in sexual activity.[1] The canonical Gospels certainly report no such things. But some recent historians and archeologists have challenged this view. For instance, in 2012 Harvard historian Karen King brought to public attention a fragment from a fourth-century Coptic gospel that included the inscription, "Jesus said to them, 'My wife,'" which led some to believe that Jesus had been married. Another example comes from Simcha Jacobovici and Barrie Wilson's (2015) book *The Lost Gospel*, which purports to expose evidence that Jesus was married to Mary Magdalene and had children. These ideas also appear in popular culture, such as Dan Brown's book (and the resulting film) *The Da Vinci Code*. However, most historical scholars have impugned the authenticity of these findings.[2] Even King has recently concluded that the discovered fragment is likely a forgery.

We will not be addressing this historical debate but will assume the standard view regarding Jesus's marital and parental status. We are, however, aware of some Christians who find the idea of Jesus engaging in sexual activity, being married, or having children as impious or somehow demeaning of Christ's divinity, and we want to take this concern seriously. There are two related questions that should be distinguished:

1. Would it have been *morally impermissible* for an incarnate God to take a spouse, to engage in sexual relations, or to biologically reproduce?[3]
2. Would it have been *(overall) unfitting*[4] for an incarnate God to do so?

In this paper, we'll attempt to answer both of these questions. Regarding (1), we consider some possible reasons for answering that question in the affirmative, but we conclude that these reasons are weak. However, this issue does raise the question of why we should think that such activities are morally permissible for an incarnate God, and, as we will argue, how one answers that question depends on which theory one holds with respect to God's ethical standards.

But even if it is morally permissible for an incarnate God to engage in sexual relations or have a wife and children, one may still wonder about (2). After a brief discussion on the notion of fittingness, we'll look into considerations for why it may seem fitting for an incarnate God to engage in such activities. In the end, however, we argue that it would not have been *overall* fitting for Jesus to do so, especially given the actual circumstances of the time and the location of the incarnation and its subsequent effects. Given that it is overall unfitting, we should expect not to find an incarnate God who did engage in such activities, which accords with the dominant view of historical scholarship on Jesus's marital and parental status.

The Question of Moral Permissibility

As far as we know, no academic scholar has offered an argument for the moral impermissibility of Christ engaging in sexual activity or having a wife or children. Nevertheless, we have noticed an almost knee-jerk reaction against the very idea of it. When King's fragment and Jacobovici and Barrie's book came out, there was a storm of popular-level responses on blogs and social media seeking to refute the alleged claims. On some occasions, there seemed to be an implicit assumption or concern that it is somehow unbecoming or unacceptable for Jesus to have engaged in such things.

One motivation for this popular reaction may be due to a quasi-Gnostic impulse by some Christians, where the body or bodily desires are regarded as inherently bad whereas the spiritual or spiritual desires are regarded as inherently good. This may yield tendencies towards Docetism in Christology, where Jesus was truly divine but only appeared to be human. Additionally, some Christians also understand St. Paul's use of '*sarx*' or 'flesh' to mean sin-nature (which is evident in some of the earlier NIV translations of the Bible), which is often associated with the physical body and its desires—and this is so even though most biblical scholars do not interpret '*sarx*' in this way (Russell 1993). This negative attitude towards the body or the physical should not hold much weight, however, since traditional Christianity maintains that God created a good world, and that human beings are created in the image of God (which we take to include both mental and physical aspects). Moreover, Jesus is clearly depicted in the Gospels as eating and drinking, even to the point where some of his contemporaries worried that he was a drunkard (or at least associated too closely with those who were). So the quasi-Gnostic impulse should be rejected by Christians.[5]

Another reason for the negative reaction to Jesus having a wife or engaging in sexual activity may come from strictly Roman Catholic quarters, in particular in the defense of celibate priests. Catholic theologian Max Thurian (1993) claims that since Christ never married, "His life is valid justification for the vocation to celibacy." The mandate of priestly celibacy is no doubt controversial, but the claim is that holding to a celibate Christ appears to provide some support for priestly celibacy given that Christ serves as an example or model for priests. This will of course be unpersuasive for those who reject the requirement of celibacy for clergy. Moreover, there may be other reasons for endorsing priestly celibacy (which Thurian and other Catholic theologians have offered) which does not rely upon Christ's celibacy.

Lastly, we have heard of reactions to the claim that Christ engaged in sexual activity as somehow treating the incarnate God's behavior in a way similar to the ancient Greco-Roman gods, who are recorded as having performed sexual activities and sired demi-god children through the usual biological means (as well as having divine children through non-biological means—such as Athena springing forth from Zeus's head). Clearly much of the sexual activities of Zeus and the other gods were morally unacceptable, so perhaps it would also be unacceptable for Christ. But the problematic elements between the relations of the Greek gods and humans need not have been present had Christ engaged in such activities. The morally reprehensible aspects include sexual assault and violation of human dignity against the human victims of the gods. But it does not follow that loving sexual activity is thereby precluded.

The source of the worry, as we diagnose it, appears to be the feeling of unease when it comes to discussing sexuality and divinity. But if sexuality is part of God's creation, which is good, then such a feeling of unease is not warranted, especially with a lack of a compelling reason. Moreover, one might have to be more nuanced in the claim that Christ engages in sexual activity. For the incarnate God could only do so in his human nature—just as he eats and drinks by way of his human nature and not his divine nature. Now his human nature (understanding 'nature' in a concrete way)[6] has biological reproductive features, and his employment of those features should not be any more problematic than his employment of his cardiovascular or gastrointestinal features.

Perhaps, then, the main response to the popular-level worry is to "get over it"—to get over what we are not accustomed to conjoining in our thoughts. However, there is a more pressing issue, which is understanding exactly why it would be morally permissible for an incarnate God to engage in sexual activity, which we turn to next.

What if God's Ethical Standards Are the Same as Ours?

In order for us to assess whether it is morally permissible for God to engage in sexual activity, we have to answer what makes any act morally permissible or impermissible for God. That is, we have to ask what the ethical standards are for God. God's ethical standards are either the same as ours or they are different. Let us take each possibility in turn.

Suppose God's ethical standards are the same as ours, or at least that they overlap considerably with ours. For many Christians, some of the basic moral rules are found in the Ten Commandments and the teachings of Jesus, and it would be morally impermissible to violate any of those moral injunctions. Or one might opt for a particular moral theory—such as divine command theory, Kantian ethics, utilitarianism, virtue exemplarism, etc.—such that moral obligations are grounded in God's commands, or the good will, or more pleasurable or less painful outcomes, or moral exemplars, etc. If God's ethical standards are the same as ours, then God would perform a wrong action provided that he violated the norm that arises from whichever theory is true of our moral obligations.

With the particular case of sexual activity, marriage, and reproduction, whatever the ethical standards are for humans with respect to these activities would then apply to God. In order to assess this, we need to know what is morally permitted with respect to these activities. Some philosophers have argued that sexual activity must only occur among monogamous married partners or that complete satisfaction of sexual fulfillment must be coital.[7] Under this view, had Christ engaged in sexual activity without being married or reached complete sexual satisfaction outside of coitus, then Christ would have acted wrongly (which would be incompatible with the claim that he was morally perfect). However, other philosophers claim that sexual activity need not only occur between married couples or that complete satisfaction need not occur only through coitus.[8]

The difficulty, then, of knowing what is morally permissible for an incarnate God to perform depends on figuring out what is morally permissible for anyone with regards to some action. Nevertheless, since we are assuming that Christ is God incarnate, whatever the conditions are for some action being morally permissible, we can state that Christ did not do anything that was morally impermissible.[9]

That said, by most ethical standards, engaging in sexual intercourse, getting married, and having children are not intrinsically morally wrong. And they are not intrinsically immoral according to Christian doctrine. Humans can be involved in these activities provided that they abide by the relevant moral requirements (whatever they may be). If so, then Christ could have licitly engaged in sexual intercourse, married, and had children as long as he did not violate any moral obligations or perform a morally prohibited act.

There is a possible objection: does it follow that because it is not morally wrong for a human being to have sexual relations, take a spouse, and have children, then it is not morally wrong for an incarnate God to do so? This is a complex issue, especially since we are dealing with the concept of a morally perfect being. For some have argued that God must always do what is best or what is in the class of best actions (Rowe 2004). Thus, even if God incarnate violates no binding moral rule in engaging in sexual activity or taking a spouse, it does not follow that this would be one of the morally best things to do.

In response to such a concern, one might argue that a morally perfect being need not always do what is best or that there is neither a best action nor class of best actions (Plantinga 1974). Or one might argue that it is part of the class of best actions for an incarnate God to take a spouse, have sexual relations, or have children (though we have a hard time seeing how the case for this might go). However this is answered, the burden appears to be on the objector who claims that it is not the best for God to marry or have children. After all, what appears to us as the best state of affairs may not in fact be so. For example, we might suppose that the actual world is the best or is among the best worlds, yet it appears to contain horrifying evils, ones that we might not have initially included in our description of the best worlds. Yet if such a world is in the class of best worlds—perhaps because it contains the incarnation and the atonement (Plantinga 2004)—then we should not be troubled by considerations that make it appear as though it is not (at least without further reflection). God may have outweighing reasons for creating a world with horrifying evils, though we may not know what those reasons are.[10] Similarly, God may have outweighing reasons for taking on a spouse that are unknown to us. So this worry seems to us to be misplaced (or at least inadequately developed).

What if God's Ethical Standards Are Different Than Ours?

There is an easier way out of the above worry, which is to claim that the ethical standards for God are not the same as ours—that the set of moral injunctions that apply to God is disjoint from the set of moral commands that apply to human creatures. In that case, what is morally impermissible for us may not be morally impermissible for God.

Recently, Mark Murphy (2014, 2017) has offered such a view. When moral goodness is ascribed as a property of God, it is often assumed that such a notion includes an orientation towards the welfare of other sentient beings. From this assumption, some conclude that a morally good being (as far as able) prevents anything that would significantly undermine creaturely well-being unless there were strong reasons for not doing so. However, Murphy has rejected this conception of God, instead arguing that a perfect being is not required to promote creaturely well-being.[11] One reason is that given the maximal intrinsic value of a perfect being, every possible world with a perfect being would have no difference in value. So, the promotion of creaturely well-being does not increase the value in a world, and thus a perfect being cannot be required to perform any act that promotes creaturely well-being or prevents any setback to creaturely well-being.

What follows is that the ethical standards for God are entirely different from ours (which is compatible with the view that God has no moral obligations). The moral obligations that apply to us do not impose the same requirement for God, especially if God need not act in such a way as to promote creaturely well-being. So it would be morally wrong for one human being to steal someone else's car or to command another person to slaughter an innocent bystander, but under Murphy's view, it would not be morally wrong for God to take someone's car or to command bringing about the death of an innocent individual.

One need not adopt Murphy's account to make this claim, for a similar view regarding the non-overlapping ethical standards between God and human beings may also follow from certain forms of divine command theory.[12] In response to the criticism against God's moral goodness which arises from God's command to the Israelites to destroy every living being in the land of Canaan, William Lane Craig attempts to defend God's moral perfection by adopting a view in which the ethical standards for God and for humans do not overlap. According to Craig,

> [s]ince God doesn't issue commands to Himself, He has no moral duties to fulfill. He is certainly not subject to the same moral obligations and prohibitions that we are. For example, I have no right to take an innocent life. For me to do so would be murder. But God has no such prohibition. He can give and take life as He chooses.
> (Craig 2007)

Under divine command theory, moral obligations are grounded in God's issuing of commands. Since God commands that we do not steal or murder each other, such actions are morally impermissible for us. However, no such commands are made to God since God is the giver of the moral law and not the recipient, and thereby no action is morally forbidden for God.

Whether one adopts Murphy's approach or Craig's version of divine command theory, the ethical standards for God are unlike ours, and hence what is morally wrong for us may be morally permissible for God. Thus, an incarnate God that has the property of being morally perfect would have no moral prohibition against any action that undermines creaturely well-being since there would be no decrease in the total value of the world, even if he were to engage in actions or permit events that diminish the well-being of human creatures. We therefore cannot assert that any sexual activity is morally impermissible for God, and the same is true for getting married and having children. So, if the ethical standards for God are different, it follows that Christ could have engaged in various activities that are morally wrong for us, such as have multiple spouses or have children out of wedlock (on the assumption that these are morally impermissible for us).

We should note that we do not endorse these views which maintain that the ethical standards for God are wholly unlike ours. It seems to us that the practice of God making covenants with human beings in effect morally binds God to act in certain ways and not in others. Moreover, the biblical claim that "it is impossible for God to lie" (Hebrews 6:18) seems to us to make little sense unless it is morally wrong for God to lie. However, it is worth making perspicuous that stating what is morally permissible for God depends on what one's account of morality is for God, and the laxity of Murphy and Craig's approach allows one to claim (quite easily) that sexual activity, marriage, and having children are morally permissible for incarnate God—though it also implies that many other activities that are illicit for humans may be morally licit for God.

The approaches discussed so far have been taking moral obligations as fundamental, whether these are moral obligations that apply to both humans and God or whether there are different sets of obligations for each. They also begin by stating what such obligations are and then claim that a perfect being is one who does not violate any of them (and for Craig's view, there need not be any such obligation). However, Linda Zagzebski has proposed another account of God's relation to morality that reverses the priority. Instead of stating what moral duties there are that God must follow, divine motivation theory begins with an exemplar and the motives or emotions of that exemplar.[13] What is morally fundamental, then, is a moral agent or exemplar. So an act is morally wrong just in case a moral exemplar would characteristically have an adverse motive or emotion towards that act in relevantly similar circumstances.

God does not act based on what God first regards as a good outcome or right action, but God's actions are expressive of God's own nature, in particular God's motives. Zagzebski thinks this moral framework can help with certain versions of the problem of evil. The problem is often stated in a way that invokes the concept of a morally perfect being, where such a being would not permit setbacks to creaturely well-being without strong reason, and since there doesn't appear to be any strong reason, the presence of significant setbacks (such as horrifying suffering) makes the existence of a morally perfect (and omnipotent) being less likely. For Murphy, since God need not promote creaturely well-being, God is off the hook. For Zagzebski, the problem lies in the framework which starts with certain moral duties (such as the obligation to promote creaturely well-being) that a morally perfect being must then follow. But divine motivation theory does not start with duties but rather with the emotions of exemplars. What is morally bad or morally wrong is grounded on the emotions of a moral exemplar such as God. Since God does not appear to be wholly averse to the presence of significant setbacks to creaturely well-being (since there is horrifying suffering in our world), there isn't an obligation for God to prevent such setbacks.

The proponent of divine motivation theory, then, will have an answer similar to Murphy's on the question of whether it is morally permissible for an incarnate God to engage in sexual activity or have a wife or children. If an incarnate God is not characteristically averse to or has no negative emotions towards such activities, then God would not be performing a morally wrong act by undertaking such activities. But unlike Murphy's view, divine motivation theory allows for overlapping ethical standards for God and humans while claiming that certain activities related to sexual activity and reproduction are not morally impermissible for God.

We even have reason for thinking that an incarnate God would have positive attitudes towards these activities. Christ clearly had positive emotions towards children and rebuked those who attempted to keep children away from him. And since marriage, and its consummating act of sexual union, is a covenant that Christians claim has been established by God, then it would be odd to think that an incarnate God would have negative attitudes toward these things.

Answering the question of what is morally permissible for God is a complex issue, leading to questions about whether God has similar ethical standards as we do. From the theories examined so far, we have no reason for believing that it would have been morally impermissible for an incarnate God to have engaged in sexual activity, been married, or had children. Some of these views will maintain that he could have done so (morally speaking) only if he played by the same moral rules that we do. Other views claim that he would have done nothing wrong by doing so, and that he could have even engaged licitly in activities that would have been morally impermissible for us. So even if, contrary to current historical scholarship, Christ engaged in sexual activity, took a spouse, or biologically reproduced, he would have done nothing morally wrong. He could engage in all these acts while still being divine. Hence, the popular-level worries against somehow discovering that an incarnate God had engaged in such activities are misguided. The historical question is interesting, and there is as of yet no reason to doubt the historical consensus regarding Christ's non-marital or non-parental status. But even if new evidence shows up that is contrary to the current historical consensus, there is no worry here—at least with respect to whether an incarnate God has done anything morally wrong.

The Question of Fittingness

We now turn to our second question, whether it would be fitting for an incarnate God to engage in sexual activity, take a spouse, or produce children. There are different notions of fittingness,[14] and we mean by 'fitting' something along the lines of what was meant by medieval philosophers in their use of the term *convenientia*. What is fitting, in the sense at issue, is what is appropriate or proper given the relevant conditions of some circumstance. But that term also appears to connote various other aspects, such as beauty, harmony, suitability, expectation, probability, etc. A course of action for God is fitting provided that such an action makes the most sense, or is the most harmonious with background knowledge, or is what we would expect given God's nature and the situation at hand, etc. For our purposes, it may be enough to proceed with a rough-and-ready sense of what is appropriate or fitting for God (or any rational agent) to do. However, examining some of the different medieval conceptions might be useful in answering our question regarding what is fitting for an incarnate God to do.

Medieval philosophers, such as Anselm and Aquinas, appealed to considerations pertaining to fittingness to explain why God performed certain actions, such as becoming incarnate or making atonement for human beings. But there is an open question regarding the relation between fittingness and truth. Even Anselm concedes that fittingness does not entail truth. But consider the following passage from Anselm:

> Does not this seem to be a sufficiently necessary reason that God ought to have done the things we say: that the human race—such a precious work of God—had utterly perished, and that it was not fitting that God's purpose for human beings should be completely annihilated, and that his purpose could not be brought to fulfillment unless the human race were liberated by its Creator himself?
> (Anselm 1997, I.4)

Even if fittingness does not entail truth, the above passage claims that unfittingness entails falsity—that is, an unfitting course of action strictly implies that God would not undertake that course of action (Flint 2009, 99).[15]

Anselm's account of (un)fittingness focuses on eliminating possible courses of action for God. He also makes the distinction between what is *fitting* and what is *most fitting* (Flint 2009, 101).[16] Anselm holds that if it is most fitting for God to perform such action, then it follows that God does perform that action. Though even this account appears to have worrisome consequences, such as yielding a problematic modal collapse where every true proposition turns out necessarily true (Flint 2009, 104–107).

There is, however, another way to construe fittingness, which follows closer to Aquinas's approach. Here is one way to interpret Aquinas's account of fittingness:

> For Thomas *convenire* refers primarily to the bringing together of various things: *convenire*, to come or bring together. At a key point early in the argument, Thomas makes this understanding explicit:

"A means is the more appropriate [*convenientior*] for an end, as it brings together [*concurrent*] more assets towards the end" (*ST* 3.46.3). A logic based on God's purposes underlies Christ's passion, which we may appreciate by understanding how this act is the most fitting way to achieve that end—that is to say, how it brings about the most effects ordered towards that end. This understanding of fittingness is decisive for Thomas: the way in which a particular act is preferable to another by bringing about more effects which themselves contribute towards the goal of that act.

(Johnson 2010, 305)

What is fitting for God to do, then, is a matter of what would bring about the greatest number of desired effects. It is not to say that God is required to bring about the greatest number of desired effects, and so like Anselm, Aquinas maintains that fittingness does not entail truth. But given God's goals, what is fitting is what would contribute to bringing about more effects related to that goal.

For this chapter, we will adopt Aquinas's approach to fittingness. So, when we ask whether it is fitting for God to engage in sexual relations, marry, or have children, we are asking whether doing so would bring about a greater number of desired effects. If it would, then that is overall fitting for God to do; and if it does not, then that is overall unfitting for God to do.[17] As we'll argue, there are considerations of fittingness that favor God's engaging in these activities. However, we conclude that there are more desired effects in God not engaging in these activities, and hence it is overall unfitting for God to have undertaken such activities. If fittingness is connected with expectation or probability, then the overall unfittingness of Christ engaging in sexual activity or getting married gives us reason to expect that Christ would not have done so—just as the current evidence suggests.

Reasons Favoring Fittingness

What are some desired effects that favor an incarnate God to engage in sexual activity and procreation? Let us assume a classical conception of God. From this conception, a preincarnate God arguably does not know what it is like to be limited in space, to have only finite knowledge, or to be tempted by worldly goods. However, by becoming incarnate, God acquires first-person knowledge of what it is like to be contained in a certain region, not to know everything (and to grow in wisdom), and to be tempted by food and comfort given a lengthy period of hunger and physical discomfort.[18] Prior to the incarnation, God had only third-person knowledge of these experiences, but there is great value in God acquiring first-person knowledge of these experiences. Thus, it would also be valuable for God to know what it is like to experience marital and parental activities and the associated human goods involved. There is great value in knowing what it is like to fall in love with another, make vows of commitment, consummate that union through sexual intimacy, and share with one's partner the joint activity of loving one's progeny. So, acquiring first-person knowledge of these valuable experiences provides some reason for God to engage in these activities.

However, some may claim that God need not actually engage in these activities to have first-person knowledge of them. For God may have the property of omnisubjectivity, which is "the property of consciously grasping with perfect accuracy and completeness the first-person perspective of every conscious being" (Zagzebski 2008, 232). It is often assumed that God does not know what it is like to be me. However, even humans are able to somewhat understand the perspective of another via empathy, such that one experiences the emotion of another person. That is, if one empathizes with a person's grief over the loss of a loved one, then the empathizer experiences that emotion (or one very similar to it). One *totally* empathizes with another if she is in a "state of representing all of another person's conscious states including their beliefs, sensations, moods, desires, and choices, as well as their emotions," and *perfect total* empathy "includes a complete and accurate representation of all of another person's conscious states" (ibid., 241). If God has perfect total empathy for every conscious being, then God has omnisubjectivity. An omnisubjective being would not have to engage in sexual, marital, or reproductive activity in order to know what it is like to experience these activities, especially if such a being perfectly and accurately represents those experiences for herself. Therefore, the above reason for the fittingness of an incarnate God to engage in sexual activity wouldn't apply to God if God has omnisubjectivity.

But even if God already knows what these experiences are like, there is great value in God sharing the full human experience, including mundane marital and parental activities that are part of our daily joys and struggles. Even in human relationships, there is value in participating in an activity that one is familiar with but with different companions. One might already know what camping is like with one friend, but there is great value in sharing that experience with another friend. By possessing omnisubjectivity, God therefore already knows what it is like to be sexually intimate with someone or to be a parent, but sharing in that experience with us by actually engaging in them can yield a deeper sense of fellowship and mutual understanding.[19]

Consider the following biblical passage: "For we do not have a high priest who is unable to sympathize with our weaknesses, but one who in every respect has been tempted as we are, yet without sin" (Hebrews 4:15). If God has the property of omnisubjectivity, then he empathizes with us maximally, and so is consciously aware of our weaknesses. The passage also states that Christ has been tempted as we have been, and there are unique temptations with respect to sexual relations, marriage, and parenthood. By being involved in a romantic relationship, Christ could have been tempted by bouts of jealousy. By being a parent, Christ could have been tempted to neglect his children when there were competing goods, such as working as a carpenter or teaching his disciples. Similar temptations are ones that those of us involved sexually with others or who have children deal with on a regular basis. Experiencing these temptations not only would have allowed an incarnate God to share in the full range of human experiences, but it also would have provided for us an exemplar who demonstrated through his own life how we are to manage through these temptations.

Reasons Favoring Unfittingness

It is clear that there are some considerations that make it fitting for an incarnate God to engage in sexual activity, marry, or have children, for it is a desirable effect for God to know what it is like to undergo these experiences or for God to share in a wider range of human experiences that do not involve sin. Nevertheless, we will argue that there are outweighing considerations that favor the unfittingness for an incarnate God to engage in these activities, especially in the actual circumstances in which God decided to become incarnate. Therefore, we conclude that it would be overall unfitting for God to be sexually intimate with another partner, take a spouse, or reproduce.

Suppose Jesus had taken a spouse and consummated that union. It seems likely that in first-century Palestine that the partner of Christ would have been attributed an elevated status, perhaps regarded on a level much higher than would be merited or appropriate. Although we think multiple incarnations by divine beings are possible,[20] we have no reason to believe that Christ's partner would have been a divine person (that is, that such a human nature was assumed by a divine person). Moreover, given that sexual relations are unitive acts in which the persons involved are united biologically, psychologically, spiritually, etc., one might expect a strong temptation on the followers of Christ to worship that partner, thereby increasing the likelihood of idolatry (leading to the violation of the command that one should not worship anyone but God).[21,22]

For similar reasons, it would be unfitting for Christ to procreate since the incarnate being's progeny would also be subject to the increased likelihood of idolatry or being given an inappropriate elevated status, again on the assumption that the child remained merely human. There already exists in popular imagination conspiracy theories related to the bloodline of Christ. Now imagine that Christ really did have biological successors, none of which were divine. When candidates for a messianic figure were killed off or defeated, followers of that figure often turned to that individual's family member to follow subsequently as the next messianic candidate. So, if Jesus had a child, we might expect a turn away from Christ at his death and a turn to the child as the next messianic figure, which goes against orthodox Christology that Christ is the anointed one and true king of God's people. Therefore, given how followers of the Messiah might well have acted in that time period, there likely would be undesirable effects had Christ married or had children.[23]

Another reason why sexual relations and reproduction would have been unfitting for an incarnate God has to do with the circumstances of the Christian church in the first two centuries. Imitation of Christ was taken extremely seriously, to the point that many early Christians were willing and perhaps even overly zealous to be martyred in order to share in Jesus's self-sacrifice. For example, Ignatius of Antioch appeared quite eager to imitate in Christ's suffering, and this appears to be true also of Polycarp. Hence, we find a theme of *imitatio Christi* running throughout some strands in the early Church approach to Christian living (Moss 2012). If Jesus were married or had children, then there may have been many who might have been tempted to elevate the status of marriage or parenthood, and this could yield the consequence of some denigrating those who are single or without children.[24] However, the quality of discipleship is not necessarily related to one's marital or parental status.[25]

In addition, when considering what activities are fitting for an incarnate God to perform, we must take into account God's purpose for the incarnation, which we take to be primarily soteriological—to accomplish the redemption and reconciliation of human beings to God. So, although there is nothing wrong with getting married, engaging in intercourse, or having children, such activities and their accompanying roles might have detracted Christ from his soteriological mission.[26] St. Paul, in 1 Corinthians 7, maintains the moral permissibility of marriage and sexual relations while claiming that it is better to avoid these activities when one is concerned with the work of the Lord. Married individuals and parents have divided interests, while unmarried persons can concentrate much more single-mindedly on the work of the Lord (1 Corinthians 7:32–34), and so *a fortiori* does this hold for Christ.

Part of Christ's soteriological mission involved fulfilling Jewish prophecies (when he read from the prophet Isaiah in Luke 4 and declared the fulfillment of the year of the Lord's favor), overturning legal and ceremonial systems that harmed individuals (especially the poor and the oppressed, such as the injunction against divorce which would have likely harmed women in that society since they would have likely become destitute), and ultimately save people through his death and resurrection. It is hard to imagine how one could be a good or exemplary spouse or parent while trying to accomplish these tasks, especially since his interaction with political and religious rulers often put Christ in harm's way (or at least raised the threat of harm). It is even recorded how difficult it was for his mother and his family members to get close to him, and Jesus appears aloof with respect to them given the need of the people to whom he was ministering (Matthew 12:46–50). Finally, his soteriological task culminated in his death, his resurrection, and to his bodily ascension. Thus, his soteriological mission would have resulted in leaving behind a widow and an orphan had Christ been married and reproduced.[27]

Had circumstances been different or had God decided to become incarnate in a different place or time, it might have been more fitting for God to have taken a spouse, engaged in sexual activity, or biologically reproduced. If the cultural tendencies were not such that followers of a messianic figure would elevate the status of close family members, then the temptation to elevate the status of Christ's spouse or child might have been removed or kept to a minimum. Or had the situation of the early Church not focused on *imitatio Christi*, perhaps the unwarranted elevation of marriage or parenthood could be avoided. Then under these circumstances, it might have been more fitting for an incarnate God to engage in these activities. So fittingness is somewhat relative; it depends on the local and temporal context.

We have seen, then, that there are considerations of fittingness in favor of an incarnate God engaging in sexual activity, taking a spouse, and reproducing. However, we have also raised considerations for its unfittingness. To be clear, we take overall fittingness to be estimating which action would result in more desired effects, hence the reasons in favor of an overall fitting action need not be so strong as to defeat the reasons against—hence, it is possible for an incarnate God to do something that is not overall fitting, for God may have good reasons for doing so. But in our estimation, there seem to be more desired effects with respect to God's ultimate goal that can be achieved if Christ does not undertake these activities, and hence it is overall fitting for Christ not to do so.

Overall Fittingness vs. Most Fittingness

Since fittingness is associated with probability or expectation, we conclude that the overall unfittingness for Christ to engage in sexual relations or have a spouse or child should yield historical evidence that accords with this expectation. And indeed, current historical scholarship favors the standard view that Christ remained celibate. But one may worry about the possibility of the current historical consensus being mistaken. Even if it is, this would not undermine the historicity of the New Testament documents (since they are silent about it), nor would it undermine the divinity of Christ since we have argued that such activities are morally permissible for an incarnate God. But would the overturning of the historical consensus threaten our case that such activities are overall unfitting?

For the Anselmian approach to fittingness, it is not a problem since all these considerations may merely be showing what is fitting for God, not what is most fitting for God, which would entail truth since God does what is most fitting. But if one is only providing a case for what is fitting, then it is possible to find an outcome contrary to what one expects. However, given the concerns raised against Anselm's approach (in Flint 2009), we opted for a Thomistic account of fittingness.

We take overall fittingness not to be decisive in the sense that it entails that God does what is overall fitting (so we take overall fittingness to be distinct from what is most fitting). It was overall fitting that the atonement was accomplished through the death of Christ on the cross (and his resurrection), but it was not necessary such that the atonement could have been accomplished by other means. But the desirable effects of such an atonement (as enumerated by Aquinas in *Summa Theologiae* III, Q. 46, a. 3–4) makes it overall fitting. Hence, what is overall fitting is what is more probable. For example, it may be more probable that a loaded die (skewed towards landing on '6') land on '6,' but it may land on another number, and doing so would not imply that the die is not loaded. So, we have argued that there are more desirable effects if Christ does not engage in sexual activity or have a spouse or child, but there are also some desirable effects if Christ does so. Choosing on the basis of producing a desirable effect is not irrational for an agent, and hence Christ would have been rational in choosing to engage in sexual activity. The historical consensus turning out wrong, then, does not threaten our case that it is overall fitting for Christ not to engage in such activities, for what is overall fitting is not what is most fitting.

Conclusion

Our conclusion is that it was morally permissible for an incarnate God to have sexual relations, take a spouse, or biologically reproduce. Historical fascination with overturning current consensus regarding Christ's marital or parental status, then, should not be threatening for traditional Christians who maintain an orthodox Christology. Either Christ engages in such activities but remains within the parameters of our moral laws (on the assumption that the ethical standards for God and humans overlap with respect to sexual activities) or that any of those activities are licit for God since God has different ethical standards. Thus, there need be no knee-jerk reaction to dismantle the case that contradicts the historical consensus of Christ's marital or parental status. We should take each historical evidence on its own and weigh it on its own merits, and not with the impulsive need to overturn it.

We have also concluded that it is overall unfitting for Christ to have engaged in these activities, and thus we expect the evidence to be as it actually is, that Christ was celibate. But since we take what is overall (un)fitting to be probabilistic (unlike the Anselmian notion of what is most fitting), the overturning of the historical case would not go against our view that it is overall fitting for Christ not to engage in these activities.

Now much of what we have been arguing in this paper has been rather speculative. This is inevitable when investigating counterfactual situations, especially concerning what God would or wouldn't do. We are open to being corrected where we have erred. But in the spirit of this volume, we do not expect to have given the last word on this matter, but we hope that this is only the beginning of a discussion on these matters which have been mostly neglected in the philosophy of religion.

Notes

1. We should note that in this paper, we assume orthodox Christology as defined by the ancient creeds. That is, we hold that Jesus Christ was God incarnate, one person with a human nature and a divine nature.
2. For one example of serious critique, see Richard Bauckham's "Assessing *The Lost Gospel*," which he posted online as a series of refutations of Jacobovici and Wilson's theory. His critique can be found online at: http://markgoodacre.org/BauckhamLostGospel-full.pdf
3. In this chapter, we will assume that such activities will in some cases be morally permissible for mere human beings (i.e., non-divine human beings), and so we will assume for the sake of argument the denial of anti-natalism (with regards to the moral permissibility of biological reproduction).
4. We define 'fitting' and 'overall fitting' below.
5. Some of the creeds were formulated to rule out such impulses, thereby giving Christians even more reason to reject this line of reasoning. We thank Kevin Timpe for this point.
6. It is typical to construe Christ's natures as either abstract or concrete. An abstractist approach treats the natures as abstract properties whereas a concretist approach treats the natures as concrete entities, typically a soul-body composite for the human nature of Christ. For more on this distinction, see Plantinga 1999.
7. For those who defend this position, see Pruss 2012 and Lee and George 2014.
8. For a defense of this view, see Corvino 2013. Of course, Corvino rejects the theological assumptions of Christians. But if his arguments are correct and if the ethics of an incarnate God overlaps ours, then the boundaries of what is morally permissible for an incarnate will be drawn differently than the boundaries set by the Catholic philosophers cited in endnote 7.
9. There are some complications. If one had strong antecedent reason to believe that Christ is divine, then if it were discovered that Christ did have sexual activity outside of marriage, then such a fact may serve as a defeater for the claim that such an activity is morally impermissible for anyone. Or one might be strongly convinced that sexual activity outside of a monogamous marriage is morally impermissible, so one may conclude that we will never come across strong reasons or evidence to suppose that Christ did do so. And perhaps it is this conviction that yields the knee-jerk reaction against Christ having engaged in such activities that we discussed in the previous section.
10. One way of taking this approach would be adopting skeptical theism. For more on skeptical theism, see Bergmann 2009 and Dougherty 2014.

Marriage, Reproduction, and the Incarnation 309

11. Murphy's key distinction is between *requiring* reasons and *justifying* reasons (2017, 59), where a justifying reason for S to perform action A makes that action a rational option for S (though S's not performing A would also be rational), whereas a requiring reason for S to do A makes not doing A irrational for S. And Murphy argues that a perfect being would only have justifying reasons for promoting creaturely well-being, not requiring reasons.
12. For one example, inspired by an Ockhamist approach, see Adams 1999.
13. Zagzebski 2004, 309. According to her theory, we can pick out moral exemplars even without knowing the necessary and sufficient conditions for being a moral exemplar (similar to those who claim that we can pick out water without knowing it is made up of H2O). Zagzebski argues that moral exemplars are picked out by the emotion of admiration (and by reflection). For more on her theory, see Zagzebski 2017.
14. Our meaning of 'fitting' is different than a familiar term used in current ethical/metaethical discussions. For more on the latter concept, see Howard 2018.
15. Flint 2009 also shows that Anselm may have held the stronger principle that unfittingness entails impossibility, which would make fittingness equivalent to possibility, which may not be an adequate conception.
16. The distinction between what is fitting and what is most fitting appears to be similar to Murphy's 2014 distinction between *justifying* reasons and *requiring* reasons, respectively.
17. Kevin Timpe has raised the worry that this account of overall fittingness may collapse into what is most fitting, for if God has more reasons to do x than y, then God will do x. However, we maintain that Aquinas's approach leaves open God doing y. Suppose God has reasons R1 and R2 for doing x but only reason R3 for doing y. So doing x is overall fitting given that it would produce greater number of desired effects (e.g., whatever reason cited in R1 and R2). However, God may still do y, and if God were asked why, God would cite R3. Having a greater number reasons or a greater number of desired effects does not guarantee that that action will be performed.
18. Of course this is not God's main reason for becoming incarnate, though we think it may serve as a valuable good in favor of doing so. Moreover, if one maintains that God is omnirational (in the sense found in Pruss 2013), then God does act partly on this basis.
19. Some may want to claim that God exercises some restraint here. For example, we have heard that Dallas Willard held a view such that although God could know all true propositions, he intentionally withholds knowledge of some things for the good of creatures (or something along these lines). Similarly, God might be able to represent every first-person perspective but may withhold from doing so in some cases.
20. See Pawl 2016 and Aquinas 1947, *Summa Theologiae* III, Q.3, a. 7.
21. Kevin Timpe raises the worry that in the incarnation, there is a union of the divine nature and the human nature, but that we don't worship the human nature. But since that union is greater than the union of marriage, why worry about worshiping Christ's partner? However, this comparison appears inapt, since we would argue that we don't worship natures but rather worship the person Christ, who has both a divine and human nature. Moreover, the idolatrous outcome is only probabilistic—it is not guaranteed or entailed.
22. Blake Hereth raises the concern that our reasoning may count against Jesus picking disciples, especially since there was some temptation to elevate the disciples. Historically, the only disciples elevated were the clear successors or those associated with miraculous deeds. Moreover, we are indeed asserting that given the cultural milieu of first-century Palestine, the probability of

idolatry occurring appears significantly higher for a divine being taking a spouse than for a divine being taking on students. We are, of course, open to correction here.
23. Additionally, Christ marrying or having children may exhibit a problematic form of favoritism, thereby making such acts unfitting. We thank Blake Hereth for this point.
24. There exists, even now, in some Protestant circles, a problematic view of those who are in church ministry and who are single or who have no children (despite Paul's claim otherwise in 1 Corinthians 7), and this problem may have been aggravated had Jesus taken on a family.
25. No doubt that some may argue that Jesus's remaining single and celibate has yielded some problematic effects such as the controversy surrounding priestly celibacy. However, it does not appear that the status of being single as such has been elevated, whereas we think that Christ's being married would have elevated that status as such—especially since getting married would have been something that he had to go out and do, whereas remaining single doesn't require going out and doing something (and it's harder to argue for the case that because Christ didn't do A, then not A-ing is a better thing).
26. Of course Christ engaged in activities that appear not to have detracted from his soteriological mission, such as eating at feasts and going to weddings. However, we believe there is a big difference between these more mundane activities and the activities of marriage and reproduction since these add the social roles that Christ would have had to play, such as being a husband or father, along with the attending obligations that come with such roles. Whereas eating, drinking, and attending parties do not come with a significant social role with significant obligations.
27. We think that Christ's death was the overall fitting means of accomplishing atonement. However, some may claim that Christ's death was neither necessary nor overall fitting. If so, then the result of leaving a young widow or an orphan may not be applicable (had Christ lived a typical life and died a natural death). We thank Blake Hereth for raising this point.

References

Adams, Marilyn McCord. "Ockham on Will, Nature, and Morality." In *The Cambridge Companion to Ockham*, edited by Paul Spade, 245–271. Cambridge: Cambridge University Press, 1999.

Anselm. *Basic Writings*. Edited and translated by Thomas Williams. Indianapolis: Hackett Publishing Company, Inc., 1997.

Aquinas, Thomas. *Summa Theologiae*. Translated by the English Dominican Province. London: Benzinger Bros., 1947.

Bergmann, Michael. "Skeptical Theism and the Problem of Evil." In *Oxford Handbook of Philosophical Theology*, edited by Thomas P. Flint and Michael C. Rea, 375–399. Oxford: Oxford University Press, 2009.

Corvino, John. *What's Wrong with Homosexuality?* Oxford: Oxford University Press, 2013.

Craig, William Lane. "Slaughter of the Canaanites." 2007. www.reasonablefaith.org/question-answer/P10/slaughter-of-the-canaanites.

Dougherty, Trent and Justin McBrayer. *Skeptical Theism: New Essays*. Oxford: Oxford University Press, 2014.

Flint, Thomas. "Fittingness and Divine Action in *Cur Deus Homo*." In *Metaphysics and God: Essays in Honor of Eleonore Stump*. edited by Kevin Timpe, 97–111. New York: Routledge, 2009.

Howard, Christopher. "Fittingness." *Philosophy Compass* (2018).

Jacobovici, Simcha and Barrie Wilson. *The Lost Gospel*. New York: Pegasus Books, 2015.

Johnson, Adam. "A Fuller Account: The Role of 'Fittingness' in Thomas Aquinas' Development of the Doctrine of the Atonement." *International Journal of Systematic Theology* 12 (2010): 302–318.

Lee, Patrick and Robert George. *Conjugal Union: What Marriage Is and Why It Matters*. Cambridge: Cambridge University Press, 2014.

Moss, Candida. *Ancient Christian Martyrdom*. New Haven: Yale University Press, 2012.

Murphy, Mark C. "Toward God's Own Ethics." In *Challenges to Moral and Religious Belief: Disagreement and Evolution*, edited by Michael Bergmann and Patrick Kain, 154–171. Oxford: Oxford University Press, 2014.

———. *God's Own Ethics*. Oxford: Oxford University Press, 2017.

Pawl, Timothy. "Thomistic Multiple Incarnations." *Heythrop Journal* 57 (2016): 359–370.

Plantinga, Alvin. *God, Freedom, and Evil*. New York: Harper and Row, 1974.

———. "On Heresy, Mind, and Truth." *Faith and Philosophy* 16 (1999): 182–193.

———. "Supralapsarianism, or 'O Felix Culpa.'" In *Christian Faith and the Problem of Evil*, edited by Peter van Inwagen, 1–25. Grand Rapids, MI: Wm. B. Eerdmans, 2004.

Pruss, Alexander. *One Body: An Essay in Christian Sexual Ethics*. South Bend: University of Notre Dame Press, 2012.

———. "Omnirationality." *Res Philosophica* 90 (2013): 1–21.

Rowe, William. *Can God Be Free?* Oxford: Oxford University Press, 2004.

Russell, Walter. "Does the Christian Have 'Flesh' in Galatians 5:13–26?" *Journal of the Evangelical Theological Society* 36 (1993): 179–187.

Thurian, Max. "The Theological Basis for Priestly Celibacy." *Vatican* (2013). Accessed October 19, 2018. www.vatican.va/roman_curia/congregations/cclergy/documents/rc_con_cclergy_doc_01011993_theol_en.html.

Zagzebski, Linda. *Divine Motivation Theory*. Cambridge: Cambridge University Press, 2004.

———. "Omnisubjectivity." In *Oxford Studies in Philosophy of Religion: Volume 1*, edited by Jonathan Kvanvig, 231–248. Oxford: Oxford University Press, 2008.

———. *Exemplarist Moral Theory*. Oxford: Oxford University Press, 2017.

13 A Transfeminist Critique of Mormon Theologies of Gender

Kelli D. Potter

Introduction

In the philosophy of religion, we often focus on an abstract version of theism that excludes the particularities of different theistic sects. By abstracting in this way, we exclude the particular context and content of the various religious groups. This leads us to ignore the social and political significance of particular religious groups. The upshot is that philosophers rarely if ever engage particular traditions in terms of their sociopolitical consequences. One theistic religious group whose beliefs are quite unlike the philosopher's abstract version of theism is Mormonism.[1] Mormonism is philosophically interesting due to its commitment to a kind of materialism. Mormonism's materialism should pique the interest of feminist philosophers in particular since one feminist criticism of the theistic tradition is based on its denigration of matter and the body. Given its positive evaluation of the body, one might think that Mormonism would avoid feminist criticisms of traditional theism. However, this is not the case. Mormonism is quite patriarchal in its approach to gender. So, looking at Mormonism from the point of view of a feminist philosopher opens up new ground and is a good illustration of how philosophers of religion can engage more directly with particular religious denominations within the Abrahamic fold.

In addition to being quite patriarchal, Mormonism is notoriously anti-LGBTQ+. The connection between its patriarchy and its cisgender-heteronormativity is close. Whereas there have been several very compelling critiques of Mormonism's patriarchy (Toscano and Toscano 1990; Allred 1997) and its heteronormativity (Petrey 2011), the literature has yet to see a philosophical critique that looks at the theology from the point of view of a transgender person. In this chapter, I will present a transfeminist standpoint-theoretical critique of both orthodox and heterodox theologies of gender in the Mormon tradition. This involves an application of the methodology of feminist standpoint theory where, in lieu of starting from the standpoint of women, we start from the standpoint of transgender folk. I will argue that the various Mormon theologies of gender fail to do justice to a transgender point of view. Furthermore, I will argue that an interpretation of Mormon theology that is friendly to trans folk is not hard to find. Moreover, my analysis will reveal the way in which the LDS commitment to patriarchy, heteronormativity, and cis-normativity hang together, implying the intersectionality of the oppression of women, queer, and trans folk.

Standpoint Theory

To begin, we need to get clear about what feminist standpoint theory is and how it can be applied in the context of religious belief. Standpoint theory in general originated in the Marxist philosophical tradition (Ellis and Fopp 2001). In that tradition, one's standpoint in society determines how one perceives society. A standpoint is composed of the intersection of the various groups of which one is a member. So, for example, black women will have a different standpoint from both white women and black men.

Not only does everyone have a standpoint that affects how they see the world, but some standpoints are dominant and others are marginalized. Those that occupy marginalized standpoints often have the capacity to perceive things about society that are hidden from those that enjoy the dominant standpoint. To put it another way, dominant standpoints will tend to obscure reality to the extent that manufacturing consent for the dominance of certain groups requires ignoring important aspects of society. For example, a white person might not easily recognize the ways that our culture employs negative stereotypes of black people or that there are iterative microaggressions in the form of white (and dominant) discourse. Once we are aware of the existence of such racist phenomena, it is hard not to reject them. By contrast, marginalized standpoints possess a kind of epistemic privilege with respect to seeing the reality of society. It's *not* that they have an automatic ability to see things more objectively; it's that they occupy a position that is both inside (because they are members of the group) and outside (because they are dominated within the group) the institutional structures of society and this gives them an advantage; they possess a "double-consciousness" (Du Bois 1903). Upon thoughtful reflection and collaboration with others that also have marginalized or dominated standpoints, those that occupy such standpoints can approximate a more impartial view of society. One consequence of this is that when we are discussing issues of oppression, the perspective of the oppressed must be privileged over that of the oppressor.

Clearly, standpoint theory can apply to different identity groups, including but not limited to, class, race, sexual orientation, gender, etc. So, it is not surprising that many feminist scholars have adopted a broadly standpoint-theoretical approach. Clearly, women are uniquely placed to understand the reality of the gender regime and how it is used to dominate them. Examples of those that have taken a standpoint-theoretical approach are Sandra Harding in the philosophy of science and Pamela Sue Anderson in the philosophy of religion.

Feminist standpoint theory has come to involve a particular methodological approach. It is one that recognizes the embodied nature of the cognizing subject and incorporates this in its critique of the dominant epistemology. First, standpoint theory advocates that we interrogate the basic assumptions of the dominant conceptual scheme, showing to what extent it is based on arbitrary factors arising from the standpoint of those that dominate. Second, standpoint theory advocates that we build an alternative scheme from the standpoint of those that are marginalized. The goal of standpoint epistemology is to come to have a less partial viewpoint via a critique of the dominant standpoint. Sandra Harding calls this 'strong objectivity' (1991). Pamela Sue Anderson describes strong objectivity as follows:

> [S]trong objectivity is comprised of two main motives: first, the new subjects move outward to shift away from the privileged subject's standpoint to think from the lives of others; second, the subjects move backward—reflexively—to re-examine the basic background beliefs of their own originally privileged position as a subject of knowledge. The goal of these moves toward objectivity is not to achieve absolute truth nor impartial knowledge, but to gain less partial knowledge than the subject has from his or her [sic] privileged perspective on reality. Instead of justifying true belief and refuting skepticism in the manner of conventional epistemology, feminist standpoint epistemologists aim to gain knowledge by scrutinizing the credentials of knowledge-claimants and putting knowledge-claims under communal criticism from the perspective of the outsider.
>
> (1998, 131)

So, according to Anderson, standpoint methodology involves interrogating the background beliefs and concepts of the dominant standpoint. This is justified because, according to standpoint theorists, much of our knowledge is embodied and situated in a material context, where the material context includes systematic relationships of power. Anderson calls this "moving backward" because it involves an investigation into the preconditions of our cognitive framework or, as she puts it, "our basic background beliefs." In addition to "moving backward," Anderson identifies a process of "moving outward." This involves a conscious inclusion of the perspectives of marginalized groups for the purpose of constructing a framework that empowers and liberates those who are dominated.

Transfeminism

So, what does it mean to call my argument a *trans*feminist critique? Before answering this question, I must introduce some terminology for those unfamiliar with transgender issues. Someone is *transgender* just in case they do not identify with (or identify exclusively) with the gender/sex they were assigned at birth. Some, but not all, transgender persons have *gender dysphoria* as identified the DSM V (Parry 2013). This is the subjective sense of misalignment between one's sense of one's self and the sexual characteristics of one's body and/or the social roles associated with a gender/sex assignment. This condition is not considered delusional or paraphilic, despite past theories to that effect (Serano 2010). The proper treatment for gender dysphoria involves therapy and what is called 'medical transition' (Bockting and Goldberg 2006; WPATH 2011, 2016). Medical transitioning involves hormone replacement therapy (HRT) and (sometimes) various types of surgeries (including, but not limited to, genital reconstruction surgery). People that identify with the gender assigned them at birth are called *cisgender* or just *cis*. *Cissexism* is the marginalization of and/or domination over transgender individuals. *Transmisogyny* is the double nature of a trans woman's oppression at the intersection of femininity and being trans. Not all transgender people identify within the gender binary (i.e., the existence of male and female categories that are mutually exclusive and collective exhaustive). Some identify as *non-binary*, i.e, outside or between the usually mutually exclusive and collectively exhaustive categories of male and female. Finally, we say that anyone that is both cisgender and heterosexual is *cishet*.

Given this terminological background, we can say that transfeminism attempts to address issues that arise from cissexism as well as from transmisogyny. Given the LDS Church's political activities regarding the LGBTQ+ community, including official church policies concerning transgender individuals, it is vitally important for transgender Mormons and their allies to develop a standpoint critique of orthodox LDS theology. This standpoint critique involves two steps: (1) a critique of the dominant theological paradigm and practice showing how it arbitrarily excludes the trans community (this is Anderson's moving backward) and (2) a presentation of an alternative theology that starts from the position of trans folk (this is Anderson's moving outward).

Moving Backward

Mormon theology is well known for taking an extremely anthropomorphic approach to the concept of God. In Mormonism, the Father and the Son are (separately) embodied (Paulsen 1995–1996). The physical status of the Holy Ghost is not as clear. However, the LDS Scripture *The Doctrine and Convenants* claims that "all spirit is matter" (The Church of

Jesus Christ of Latter-day Saints 2018, section 131, verse 4). Moreover, in some sense, it would be correct to say that Mormonism is polytheistic, since it is definitely committed to the existence of many Gods. Indeed, in Joseph Smith's well-known "King Follett Discourse" he went so far as to say that God (the Father) was once like us and we will become like him (Larsen 1978). We are the same kind of being that God is but we are earlier on in the process of development. Moreover, Latter-day Saints believe that there is a Mother in Heaven as well. And so, while traditional Christianity usually interprets the gendered terminology as strictly metaphorical or analogical when applied to God, Mormonism takes it literally. God the Father is a male, with a male's body and God the Mother is a female with a female body. Of course, it is not entirely clear what this means. But for many Latter-day Saints it means that in the next life some of us will enjoy sexual relations, as do our Heavenly Parents. And these sexual relations will produce spiritual offspring who will then go on to live mortal lives of their own (Petrey 2011).[2]

So, orthodox LDS theology of gender is rooted in an extreme version of theistic anthropomorphism. However, an explicit statement of the implications of this anthropomorphism for gender wasn't made by the church until the church released "The Family: A Proclamation to the World" in 1995, which states in part,

> All human beings—male and female—are created in the image of God. Each is a beloved spirit son or daughter of heavenly parents, and, as such, each has a divine nature and destiny. Gender is an essential characteristic of individual premortal, mortal, and eternal identity and purpose.

In the premortal realm, spirit sons and daughters knew and worshipped God as their Eternal Father and accepted His plan by which His children could obtain a physical body and gain earthly experience to progress toward perfection and ultimately realize their divine destiny as heirs of eternal life. The divine plan of happiness enables family relationships to be perpetuated beyond the grave. Sacred ordinances and covenants available in holy temples make it possible for individuals to return to the presence of God and for families to be united eternally.

> The first commandment that God gave to Adam and Eve pertained to their potential for parenthood as husband and wife. We declare that God's commandment for His children to multiply and replenish the earth remains in force. We further declare that God has commanded that the sacred powers of procreation are to be employed only between man and woman, lawfully wedded as husband and wife.
> (The Church of Jesus Christ of Latter-day Saints 1995b)

One striking claim in this document is that gender is an essential and eternal characteristic of who we are. What does this claim mean? It could mean that genders are objective and eternally existing universals. But it seems more likely that this claim about gender being eternal is about our spiritual essences. Unlike traditional Christianity, Latter-day Saints believe that in some sense we have always existed, although the exact nature of our premortal spiritual existence is a matter of great controversy (McMurrin 1959, 49ff.). So, perhaps these spirits are supposed to have a gendered nature that doesn't change. To me, this seems to be the most plausible interpretation of what is meant by the claim that gender is eternal. However, the claim remains ambiguous without further clarification.

The "Proclamation" (as it is now called) was released in the midst of a legal battle in Hawaii concerning gay marriage (The Church of Jesus Christ of Latter-day Saints 1995a). The LDS Church played a significant role in that court case and needed theology to justify their advocacy on political matters. One goal of the Proclamation was to give a theological basis for rejecting the legalization of gay marriage. There were, of course, other goals for this document; but it is clear that opposition to gay marriage was one of the motivations (1995a).

Let's consider how this justification runs. Human beings are Gods in embryo and part of being a God is being in a procreative, heterosexual, and eternal marriage. So, it might seem that, since being a God is the telos of being human and being a God requires being in a heterosexual union, homosexual marriage is contrary to the human telos. Of course, this inference requires that we also assume that monogamy is in force in this life and in the next. Given the LDS Church's historical practice of polygamy, it is not clear that they can really make this assumption. However, polygamy is another can of worms that I want to ignore for the purposes of this paper. So, I will grant the assumption of normative monogamy.

Now, the reason for the claim that gender is eternal is clear: if one's gender could change, then a heterosexual marriage could become a homosexual one, and vice versa. The line between the two would be blurred and this would problematize heteronormativity. Moreover, a member of the church that was assigned 'female' at birth might come out as a trans man and petition to be ordained to the priesthood. This is very dangerous because it threatens the LDS Church's patriarchal system of governance. It seems clear that the LDS commitments to patriarchy, heteronormativity, and cis-normativity are intertwined. The latter two are a necessary condition for maintaining the patriarchy, which gives cishet men the power to control the direction of the church. However, the existence of trans folk is not ruled out by the Proclamation as it stands, even given the most common interpretation identified above. To show this, I will turn to view the issue from the perspective of a trans person.

Moving Outward

In order to illustrate how a transfeminist interpretation of Mormon theology can emerge from within the tradition, I will consider the 2014 documentary *Transmormon* directed by Torbern Bernhard. This film follows the coming out story of trans woman Eri Hayward, who was also raised as a Mormon in Utah. In this short film, we hear from Eri and her parents about their Mormon faith, Eri's transgender journey, and how the two relate. She talks about the pain and suffering she experienced being raised as the wrong gender, suffering that started very early in her life. Her dad tearfully relates the story of how Eri told her parents about her fantasy in which she would cut off her penis hoping her parents would find her to take her to the hospital in time to save her life. This is when, her father relates, he realized that they had to find help for her. Of course, the medical and therapeutic communities have discovered that the best way to help trans folk is to validate their identity and help them to medically transition, if they so choose. And so, these obviously orthodox parents made the decision to help Eri affirm her true self, including taking her to Thailand to get gender confirmation surgery (2014).

From the perspective of Eri and her family, the theology of the Proclamation doesn't really exclude trans women and men, since Eri's spirit is obviously female and eternally so, despite the gender mismatch with her 'male' body. Indeed, in one scene, her dad describes how he would be surprised to get to the afterlife and see that Eri is male, since he is so firmly convinced that her spirit is female. Notice that this understanding is perfectly consistent with the second (more plausible) interpretation of the claim that gender is eternal. In fact, it is even consistent with the claim that one's gender cannot change. Eri could say that her gender has not changed; she was female all along, even when she was forced to live as a male. Nevertheless, despite this seeming coherence with the proclamation, LDS policy continues to exclude anyone that has undergone gender confirmation surgery from full participation in the church (The Church of Jesus Christ of Latter-day Saints 2010). We see clearly that trans women and men raise a significant issue for Mormon practice, since the former's authenticity can be described in ways that fit into the orthodox LDS narrative. In fact, the very idea that the spirit is gendered almost begs for the possibility of a mismatch with the (biologically sexed) body. Why isn't this a possibility?

Eri's father is an orthodox Mormon and his response to the dissonance caused by Eri's trans status is an orthodox one in the sense that he is trying to stay within the heteronormative framework of the church. He would prefer that Eri be a trans woman interested in boys (and thus, heterosexual) than a femme gay boy.³ But, once we pull on the thread here, the fabric starts coming apart. For, as mentioned above, once trans women and men are accepted, then some members' sexual relationships that were once sanctioned by the church (even ones that involved temple marriages) would suddenly become taboo because they would go from being heterosexual to homosexual. And these couples could easily protest that this change in the legitimacy of their relationships would be quite arbitrary.

Of course, the trans narrative of having a woman's spirit/soul in a man's body (or vice versa) is a familiar one in the trans community (Prosser 1998). For some trans folk, this narrative doesn't fit with their sense of what it means for them to be trans. However, for others, it is a very useful metaphor. Given the purpose of the Proclamation, it is rather surprising that the anonymous authors of that text didn't anticipate how the idea of a gendered spirit would fit very well with this common trans narrative. This is a good example of the phenomenon described by standpoint epistemologists in which the viewpoint of those in dominant positions obscure features of reality from their view.

One might imagine a Mormon apologist expressing something like the following: "Perhaps we do need to recognize that our theology does indeed allow for the possibility of binary trans folk, but not non-binary folk. And since it remains the case that they cannot be in homosexual relationships, this will have implications for their relationships. So, for example, if a trans woman that was living as a man was, during that time, married to a woman, then that marriage would have to be declared void once she transitioned."

There are a couple problems with this apologetic. First, this wouldn't explain the policy that excludes those that have had gender confirmation surgery. Second, accepting binary trans folk leads to accepting non-binary trans folk. The reason is that the basis of being trans is similar in both cases—i.e., one doesn't feel entirely comfortable in one's gender assignment. Such subjective feelings are a matter of degree and, thus, the difference between binary and non-binary trans folk is a difference of degree. If we are going to trust trans men and trans women about their gender identity, then we should also trust non-binary folk. And so, heading down this path of transgender acceptance might lead to the undermining of the binary presupposed by the patriarchal approach to church governance.

Rather than accepting binary trans folk, I think that the orthodox Latter-day Saint is more likely to argue as follows: "Clearly, 'gender is eternal' means that we all have the same gender in this life that we had in the previous life. That is, it *means* that there cannot be a mismatch between the gender of one's spirit and that of one's body and that there is no mismatch between your gender in mortality and your gender in pre-mortality or the afterlife." But why not just say that? At this point, the fact that the homophobic and sexist tail is wagging the theological dog becomes pretty obvious. It is quite clear that extant Mormon theology, including the Proclamation, could be interpreted to be consistent with someone's being transgender and yet it is also clear that this is not how it is being interpreted in practice.

Of course, the LDS Church has a strict ecclesiastical hierarchy and the people at the top are the texts' primary interpreters. So, Eri's father's understanding of the Proclamation is trumped by the interpretation that is accepted by the church leadership. And, more importantly, Eri's testimony that she is a woman is trumped by the leadership's interpretation of the Proclamation. So, the LDS Church's current interpretation of the Proclamation tells transgender members to deny their subjective experiences about themselves. Yet this is also a church that tells its members to accept their subjective feelings about the truthfulness of the gospel. Latter-day Saints believe that they can receive personal revelation in the form of the witness of the Holy Ghost about the truthfulness of doctrines and practices of the church and also about the choices they should make in their personal lives. So, it would be natural for a transgender Latter-day Saint to claim that she knows via the witness of the Holy Ghost that her spirit is female despite the typically male biology of her body. Nothing in the history of Mormon theology or even in the (more recent) Proclamation rules this out. The only thing that rules it out is the official church policy of barring full membership to those that get gender confirmation surgery. So, it seems clear that this policy has no solid ground in the theology and, thus, is arbitrary.[4]

LDS orthodoxy doesn't find itself forced by unequivocal revelation from God to reject transgender folk and yet it continues to do so. But why interpret the Proclamation so as to exclude them unless it is motivated by a desire to uphold heteronormativity? Orthodox Mormons are not *forced by* their theology to reject gays and trans folk; instead, they are *forcing* their theology to reject queer and trans folk. This is why the standpoint of trans members is so important for the perception of the arbitrariness of the anti-queer agenda in LDS Mormonism.

Interestingly, the theology developed from Eri's perspective is similar to the approach in some Mormon feminist theology, which has often accepted a broadly essentialist and binary approach to gender. To see this, let's situate Mormon feminism in terms of the broader feminist movement within Abrahamic theism. Feminist philosophy of religion has rejected the androcentric theology (largely developed by men) of the theistic traditions. In part, this means that the concept of God was associated with the concept of disembodied reason, where this implies the exclusion of emotion. This notion of dispassionate and disembodied reason is associated with masculinity while passion and embodiment are associated with femininity. These connections are then used by this tradition to justify patriarchy. But this approach to reason and the nature of divinity is a mistake, according to feminist philosophers and theologians. There is no such thing as a disembodied knower, emotion and reason are not diametrically opposed, and different contexts give rise to different ways of seeing the world (e.g., see Anderson 1998, 127ff.).

So clearly embodiment plays an important role in the feminist approach to philosophy of religion. Given that Mormonism embraces God's embodiment and the materiality of spirit (The Church of Jesus Christ of Latter-day Saints 2018: Section 131, Verse 4), it would seem that it is tailormade for a feminist approach. And indeed, Mormon feminist theologians such as Margaret Toscano recognize this strength in Mormonism. Consider the following quotation from her well-known coauthored book *Strangers in Paradox*,

> A theology of a God of flesh and glory provides a model preserving binary opposites but refusing to favor one component over the other or to link the so-called less favorable component with the female. If God is both body and spirit, then we may believe that both are equally necessary and valuable.
>
> (1990, 47–48)

However, it is also clear that Toscano embraces the gender binary, where this is the assumption that each person has one and only one of the two genders: male and female. The passage continues,

> For us God is not only flesh and glory but also male and female. We disagree with those who assert that avoiding sexism means picturing God as being beyond gender and sexuality. A picture of God beyond all categories and relations encourages the very spirit/matter dichotomy which has denigrated women and sex. In our view the more salutary doctrine is one that sees God as spirit and body, male and female. For this reason, we have come to accept both a male God and a female God each of whom is simultaneously transcendent and immanent.
>
> (1990, 48)

Notice that until the last sentence this is compatible with a non-binary, but nevertheless gendered God. But the last sentence seems to commit Toscano to the view that the Gods and each of us has one and only one gender, where the options are only male and female exclusively (i.e., the binary). This view is problematic once someone accepts the possibility of a binary trans person. For example, I am a binary trans woman. The difference between someone like myself and a transgender person that is non-binary is a matter of degree. In fact, when I first came out, I came out as non-binary due to some ambiguity in my feelings. Over time, after socially and beginning to medically transition, I realized that my feelings were predominantly on the female side of the spectrum. But these feelings are a matter of degree. And so, the validation of binary trans folk inevitably leads to the validation of non-binary folk as well.

This shouldn't be a surprise. Once we focus on the body and its subjectivity, we leave the realm of the binary and enter the realm of the analog. Connecting gender to one's sexual embodiment cries out for a linear approach to gender rather than a binary approach. A Mormon feminism that takes embodiment seriously should reject the gender binary and should, instead, allow that being male and female is a matter of degree with various combinations being possible in a similar way to biological sex. Moreover, as Riki Lane has argued, the biological is in constant flux, it is open ended, and unpredictable (Lane 2009).[5] The emerging dynamic picture of living organisms doesn't fit well with the claim that gender is eternal as it was interpreted earlier on in this chapter. Indeed, it seems to suggest that we might consider sex and gender to be subject to constant change due to the impermanent nature of embodiment. Starting from the position of non-binary trans folk, the Mormon emphasis on divine and human embodiment can be quite affirming. It's all a matter of degree with bodies and this is exactly what many non-binary individuals feel applies to gender.

To her credit, Toscano's views have progressed significantly since she coauthored *Stranger in Paradox*. In a more recent paper, she seems to develop a more non-binary-friendly position. She states,

> In this paper I will argue for the importance of diversity and valuing the wide variety of gender and sexual identities and expressions that are evident in the history of human cultures. I will also argue for the importance of male and female as biological, theological, social, and linguistic categories. I do not believe that divine perfection lies either in moving beyond the male female binary, or in moving beyond bodies that are sexed and gendered. But I also believe that we need to see all categories as fluid and that we need to increase our categories. Let me be clear at the outset because I do not want to be misunderstood.
> (2014)

In addition to feminist approaches to Mormon theology of gender, some have looked at the Mormon theology of sex and gender from a queer point of view. In particular, Taylor Petrey has explored the possibility of a "post-heterosexual" interpretation of Mormon theology of sex and gender (2011). Petrey shows that the textual and interpretative support for view that we are "procreative" in the afterlife is rather thin (2011, 108–114). In particular, although terms like 'spirit birth' and 'spirit children' are used in Mormon theology to describe our existence in our premortal existence, it is not clear from any scriptural text that a spiritual birth must be the product of some kind of spiritual sexual reproduction. Instead, Petrey argues that

> [A] theory of sexual difference that claims to be rooted in "nature" is always already heterosexual, thus concealing its political import. One must be aware that the binary division between male and female, taken to be on the order of not only nature, but also God's will, has as its goal the sanctification of heterosexual sex. There must be strict gendered correspondence between a spirit and a body, it is believed, because of God's providence over creation. This view of the premortal gendered spirit is often put to use against transsexuality and intersexuality.

The problem with this view arises in explaining not only the real experiences of transgender persons, but also the existence of intersexed persons whose bodies resist categorization in the gender binary. Anne Fausto-Sterling has suggested that as many as five "sexes" occur in nature. The idea of a natural or inherent binary sexual difference in LDS discourse makes a legible "sex" the prerequisite to personhood, rendering the differently sexed "accidents of nature" illegible as children of God and divine potentials. (2011, 122).

Instead of thinking of gender as an essential and eternal aspect of human nature, Petrey seems to lean toward Judith Butler's (1990) approach to gender:

> The contingency of "gender identity" here reveals that it is not, in fact, "natural" at all but rather must be maintained and enforced juridically. Gender is constantly at risk of failing to correspond to the sexed body. As Judith Butler explains, "There is no gender identity behind the expressions of gender; that identity is performatively constituted by the very 'expressions' that are said to be its results." The idea that gender is performed, not possessed, reveals just how unstable it is as a category for defining people. Such a view—that gender is something that develops, or is achieved—suggests that there is no true or false gender, nor one that coheres with a precultural "nature."
> (2011, 124)

Of course, Butler's understanding of gender is incompatible with the Proclamation. But Petrey's point is that there is an alternative way that Mormon theology might go on queer and trans issues, by rejecting the idea that gender is an essential and eternal part of our nature as human beings. From a standpoint-epistemological point of view, the Butlerian approach to gender certainly does justice to intersex and non-binary trans individuals. This is an argument in favor of it.

However, it is not as clear that a Butlerian approach to gender can do justice to trans individuals that identify *within* the gender binary. In particular, it seems that a Butlerian approach to gender doesn't do justice to the experience of gender dysphoria. As mentioned above there are two aspects to gender dysphoria: (1) discomfort regarding social roles and expectations associated with a particular gender and (2) discomfort regarding the primary and secondary sex characteristics of one's body. Clearly, (1) can be alleviated, in large part, by helping the dysphoric person to see the contingency of these gender roles. It is (2) that leads the medical/clinical community to recommend medical transitioning. These feelings of dysphoria about one's body don't just go away. As mentioned above, it leads to the 'wrong body' narrative. Transgender biologist and activist Julia Serano describes her feelings in the following way:

> Perhaps the best way to describe how my subconscious sex feels to me is to say that it seems as if, on some level, my brain expects my body to be female. Indeed, there is some evidence to suggest that our brains have an intrinsic understanding of what sex our bodies should be. For example, there have been numerous instances in which male infants have been surgically reassigned as female shortly after birth due to botched circumcisions. . . . Despite being raised female and appearing to have female genitals, the majority of such children come to identify as male.
>
> (2016, 80)

The performative model of gender advocated by Butler and many others in queer theory just doesn't do justice to this experience since, on such a view, gender is disconnected almost entirely from the body and its subjectivity. However, for many trans folk gender is, in fact, connected to the body in a way that transcends contingent performative structures. Gender dysphoria reveals a lacuna in the cis imagination. If Serano is right that there is such a thing as a subconscious sex that accounts for the subjective sense of body-gender misalignment, then it would follow that cis folk have this subconscious sense as well, but fail to notice it. It's harder to notice one's comfort than it is to notice one's discomfort. The binary trans experience with gender dysphoria reveals something about the nature of gender that is not captured by the performative model of gender.

As with the body, feelings of dysphoria are analog, not digital. Some trans folk experience very intense body dysphoria, others have only mild dysphoria, some have intermittent dysphoria, and some have no dysphoria at all. Different trans individuals might experience body dysphoria with respect to different body parts. And these subconscious inclinations (Serano 2016, 77ff.) are not just about visual appearance but about emotional states and tactile sensation as well. Dysphoria reveals how gender—social construct though it may be—is tethered to aspects of our biological existence. It seems that taking gender dysphoria (of type 2) into account in our re-thinking of Mormon theology of gender leads us to the view that gender is tethered to our experience of our bodies, bodies that also manifest a variety of sexual characteristics. Mormon theology's emphasis on the body as well as the importance of subjective experience in religious devotion dovetails well with this approach. It wouldn't be quite right to say that gender is analog, but it would be right to say that the 'stuff' to which our construction of gender is tethered is analog and hence allows for a variety of different constructions of gender.

At this point, one might ask, should an advocate of this analog approach to gender accept the Proclamation's claim that gender is eternal? Perhaps surprisingly, I don't think that the answer to this question matters since the claim itself can be interpreted in so many different ways. For example, as we saw above, one could interpret it to be about Platonic universals and this would say nothing about anyone's particular gender: masculinity and femininity exist as Platonic ideals and yet we all have a mixture of these characteristics to varying degrees. That is, although Gender is eternal, gender isn't. Or one could agree that gender is eternal and claim that gender is an eternal multi-dimensional spectrum. The interesting question isn't whether to accept or reject the language of the Proclamation. The interesting question is whether there is a non-arbitrary rationale for interpreting it in an anti-trans manner.

Let me summarize my arguments. Given that one purpose of the Proclamation was to give a non-arbitrary reason to reject gay marriage, there is a loophole in the document. The loophole is that the language of the document is logically consistent with the valid existence of binary trans folk. And, furthermore, one cannot accept the valid existence of binary trans folk without problematizing the sexual orientation of their relationships, including marriages. Of course, this is not how the document is interpreted by the leaders of the LDS Church, but their interpretation lacks a further rationale. It is circular and hence arbitrary: the document is supposed to justify the LDS anti-LGBTQ+ stance and yet one must assume an anti-LGBTQ+ stance in order to interpret it properly. Once we accept the possibility that binary trans folk exist, it is hard to see a principled reason not to slide further down the slope to accept non-binary trans folk, since the basis for trans folk's identities are their subjective feelings and such feelings are a matter of degree. Moreover, the importance of embodiment in Mormonism—both in physical and subjective terms—suggests again that gender is a matter is degree and not a binary structure. The LDS claim to have a theological justification for their anti-LGBTQ+ stance fails.

Conclusion

The dominant theological paradigm in Mormonism is employed to reject all that fall outside the norms of the cishet-patriarchy embodied in LDS practice. However, this paradigm cannot function as it is intended to do, since it doesn't really justify the exclusion of a trans woman like Eri. Eri's existence problematizes the orthodox theology of gender. But also, reflection on her perspective raises the possibility of an alternative Mormon theology of gender that recognizes gender to be much more complicated than the cisgender person might imagine. The Mormon trans community is in a unique position to stand as insiders/outsiders that can articulate an alternative theological view of gender that is LBGTQ+ inclusive.

Notes

1. Although the term 'Mormon' sometimes applies to all the various religious sects that originate with Joseph Smith, I will use it in this paper to apply to the Church of Jesus Christ of Latter-day Saints. I will also follow the common practice of using 'LDS' to refer to the church or its beliefs.
2. For more on this issue of the role of procreation in Mormon theology see Blaire Ostler 2016.
3. There is a history of anti-queer psychologists that thought of transitioning as a way of curing homosexuality. The problem is that this ignores the portion of transgender folks that are homosexual (Serano 2016, 115ff.).
4. Of course, a typical criticism of basing gender identity on one's subjective sense of one's gender is that such a feeling could be a delusion. Indeed, someone with schizophrenia might very well feel that they are an extraterrestrial and yet this feeling doesn't make it true. Although schizophrenia is widely recognized to be a delusional condition, this isn't true about transgender patients with gender dysphoria. Delusion is not one of the symptoms of gender dysphoria according to the DSM V. Moreover, anyone that talks to trans folk about their feelings and beliefs about themselves can easily see that it is not a delusion. Trans folk are not deluded about the biological characteristics of their bodies. They are not deluded about what gender/sex they were assigned at birth. They merely claim that something is not right about this assignment. Even if they were wrong about that, it would not be a delusion. Finally, the delusion argument usually relies on the assumption that the facts about one's gender are determined by biology, where the latter provides the factual basis for gender. But the Mormon approach to gender undercuts this since they allow that gender transcends the biological and is a matter of spiritual constitution instead. On what basis could they claim that a trans person is deluded without basing it on biology?
5. See also Roughgarden 2004.

References

Allred, Janice. *God the Mother, and Other Theological Essays*. Salt Lake City, UT: Signature Books, 1997.
Anderson, Pamela Sue. *A Feminist Philosophy of Religion: The Rationality and Myths of Religious Belief*. Oxford: Blackwell Publishers, 1998.
Bockting, W. O. and J. M. Goldberg. "Guidelines for Transgender Care." *International Journal of Transgenderism* 9.3–4 (2006).
Butler, Judith. *Gender Trouble: Feminism and the Subversion of Identity*. New York: Routledge, 1990.
The Church of Jesus Christ of Latter-day Saints. "Church Opposes Same-Sex Marriages." *Church News* (1995a).
———. "The Family: A Proclamation to the World." 1995b. Accessed August 30, 2018. www.lds.org/topics/family-proclamation.
———. *Church Handbook of Instructions: Book 1, Stake Presidencies and Bishoprics*. Salt Lake City, UT: The Church of Jesus Christ of Latter-day Saints, 2010.

———. "The Doctrine and Covenants of the Church of Jesus Christ of Latter-day Saints." 2018. Accessed August 31, 2018. www.lds.org/scriptures/dc-testament/dc/131?lang=eng.

Du Bois, W. E. B. *The Souls of Black Folk: Essays and Sketches*. Chicago: A.C. McClurn & Co, 1903. Accessed April 15, 2019. www.bartleby.com/114/1.html.

Ellis, Bob and Rodney Fopp. "The Origins of Standpoint Epistemologies: Feminism, Marx and Lukacs." TASA 2001 Conference, The University of Sydney (2001), 13–15.

Harding, Sandra. *Whose Science? Whose Knowledge? Thinking from Women's Lives*. Ithaca, NY: Cornell University Press, 1991.

Lane, Riki. "Trans as Bodily Becoming: Rethinking the Biological as Diversity, Not Dichotomy." *Hypatia* 24.3, *Transgender Studies and Feminism: Theory, Politics, and Gendered Realities* (Summer, 2009): 136–157.

Larsen, Stan. "The King Follett Discourse: A Newly Amalgamated Text." *BYU Studies* 18.2 (1978): 1–18.

McMurrin, Sterling M. *The Philosophical Foundations of Mormon Theology*. Salt Lake City, UT: University of Utah Press, 1959.

Ostler, Blaire. "Sexuality and Procreation." 2016. Accessed August 30, 2018. www.blaireostler.com/journal/2016/3/22/broadening-our-understanding-of-sexuality-and-procreation.

Parry, Wayne. "Gender Dysphoria: DSM-5 Reflects Shift in Perspective on Gender Identity." 2013. Accessed August 31, 2018. www.huffingtonpost.com/2013/06/04/gender-dysphoria-dsm-5_n_3385287.html.

Paulsen, David. "The Doctrine of Divine Embodiment: Restoration, Judeo-Christian, and Philosophical Perspectives (Intro): Part I: Restoration of the Doctrine of Divine Embodiment." *Brigham Young University Studies* 35.4 (1995–1996).

Petrey, Taylor. "Toward a Post-Heterosexual Mormon Theology." *Dialogue: A Journal of Mormon Thought* 44.4 (2011): 106–141.

Prosser, Jay. *Second Skins: The Body Narratives of Transsexuality*. New York: Columbia University Press, 1998.

Roughgarden, Joan. *Evolution's Rainbow: Diversity, Gender, and Sexuality in Nature and People*. Berkeley, CA: University of California Press, 2004.

Serano, Julia. "The Case Against Autogynephilia." *International Journal of Transgenderism* 12.3 (2010): 176–187.

———. *Whipping Girl: A Transsexual Woman on Sexism and the Scapegoating of Femininity*, 2nd ed. Berkeley, CA: Seal Press, 2016.

Toscano, Margaret. "The Gender of God, and the Diversity of Human Sexuality Margaret Toscano." Panel Presentation, Sunstone Symposium, 2014.

Toscano, Margaret and Paul Toscano. *Strangers in Paradox: Explorations in Mormon Theology*. Salt Lake City, UT: Signature Books, 1990.

Transmormon. Directed by Torben Bernhard. OHO Media, 2014.

WPATH. World Professional Association for Transgender Health. "Standards of Care." 7th ed., 2011.

———. "WPATH Policy Statements: Position Statement on Medical Necessity of Treatment, Sex Reassignment, and Insurance Coverage in the U.S.A." 2016.

14 Heavenly (Gendered) Bodies? Gender Persistence in the Resurrection and Its Implications

Hilary Yancey

Introduction

On Sally Haslanger's (2000a,b, 2012) view of gender, a fully just society would lack men and women. While Haslanger does suggest that there might be "non-problematic" new genders compatible with full justice (2000, 51), she defines the concepts 'man' and 'woman' as a type of participation in an unjust system. One is or functions as a woman by being marked for systematic subordination along some dimension because of "observed or imagined" bodily features "presumed to be evidence of a female's biological role in reproduction" (Haslanger 2000; see also Haslanger 2012, ch. 7 and 8). Similarly, one is or functions as a man by being marked as a target for systematic privilege as a result of some observed or imagined bodily features presumed to evince the male's biological role in reproduction (Haslanger 2012, 230). Such a view of gender is partly motivated by goals in Haslanger's *ameliorative project*. Rather than focus our inquiry on what gender *is* (what the concept tracks), Haslanger urges us instead to attend to what we want gender concepts to *do* in social and political life. As she puts it, we should ask "how we might usefully revise what we mean for certain theoretical and political purposes" (Haslanger, 2012, 34; see also Haslanger 2005).

Other contemporary views of gender also take gender to be a socially constructed property and more particularly one that can be eliminated with no loss of personal identity, whether metaphysical, attributive, or psychological. In fact, many of these views are advanced in part to show how we might best understand gender so as to eliminate it in the pursuit of justice.

In this paper, I want to consider a different question, prompted by consideration of the Christian doctrine of resurrection: will resurrected persons be gendered? More particularly, would justice *require* that God eliminate, rather than maintain, gender for resurrected persons? I argue that justice does require gender persistence in the resurrection. God does not merely choose to resurrect persons who are gendered; God must do so in order to accomplish the justice promised in the resurrection itself.

First, I argue that a Christian picture of resurrection requires not only a new age of complete justice but also a final (and full) rectification of injustices suffered in earthly life. The visions of healing the nations found in Revelation suggests that we should take the kingdom to be one in which past injustices are made right *in addition to* inaugurating a new and fully just kingdom. This suggests that a Christian picture of resurrection requires us to consider not only the fact of post-mortem survival but also that resurrected persons are subjects of rectification.

One might also think that this rectification is plausibly part of accounting for the problem of evil. For instance, Marilyn McCord and Stewart (1989) argue that to adequately answer horrendous evils, God must be good to the agents who experience them in such a way as to integrate that evil into the narrative of the person's life such that they no longer wish the evil away. She claims, "How could God do it [defeat horrendous evils]? So far as I can see, only by integrating participation in horrendous evils into a person's relationship with God" (Adams and Sutherland 1989, 307).

One type of injustice that requires rectification, I argue, is injustice suffered because of (to use Miranda Fricker's [2007] term) identity prejudice. I then argue that in order for justice to be fully restored to someone who suffered under this kind of identity prejudice, that person must bear the relevant property in receiving rectification for the injustice they have suffered. I consider and reply to some objections to this view. I argue that the resurrected person's features, *especially* those once cited as justifying *unjust* discrimination, are seen as worthy of celebration. Amos Yong suggests that what should persist in resurrected persons are "features that emerge from and express human identities across the lifespan" (Yong 2012, 5). Gender, I argue, is such a feature. And given how it plays this role, doing justice in the resurrection requires that it persist.

After presenting these reasons, I argue in the third section that Haslanger's particular account of at least traditional genders is incompatible with the picture of resurrected persons that I have sketched above. I then turn to the consideration of what our thinking about resurrection might reveal about the nature of gender as a property. This section of the paper aims to outline the logical space rather than endorse a definitive view of gender. Therefore, I consider my argument about justice and resurrection in light of thinking gender as an accidental property as well as thinking it an essential property. I also consider the relationship of biological sex and gender, and the relationship more generally of gender and the human body. My argument about gender and the resurrection here is not committed to the claim that gender is binary. While it is compatible with my view to think of gender as such, it is equally compatible to think of it as a degreed property or one that admits of multiple gender identities and gender fluidity. I consider some candidate accounts of gender that seem most promising for accommodating the resurrection case, including Charlotte Witt (2011), Natalie Stoljar (1995), and Jennifer McKitrick

(2015). My aim is to show how considering gender persistence in the resurrection might provide new insight into what gender is.

The Metaphysics of the Resurrection

Contemporary discussions in philosophy of religion about the doctrine of resurrection have largely focused on its metaphysical possibility, given different views of the human person, rather than on particular properties that might or might not persist in resurrected bodies. Philosophers like Peter van Inwagen (1978) give an account of the human person on which bodily resurrection is possible. Kevin Corcoran notes that both Christian dualists and Christian materialists face the problem of explaining "how a body that apparently falls apart and ceases to exist can nevertheless put in an appearance in the Heavenly City" (Corcoran 2002, 1). And Lynne Rudder Baker notes that accounts of the resurrection must go beyond a weak sense of survival: "the relation between a person here and now and a person in an afterlife must be identity" (Baker 2007, 339). Baker claims that the best metaphysics can do is give a picture of the human person that makes such resurrection possible (Baker 2007, 340); I think an equally important, but still modest task, for metaphysicians considering resurrection is to give an account of the kind of properties a resurrected person must have to satisfy diachronic identity across death. In this I follow Andrei Buckareff and Joel Van Wagenen's observation: attempts to give a plausible account of identity persistence in resurrection should be equally attentive to the types of bodies we must have and, more generally, the types of properties required for the persistence of the resurrected person's earthly identity (Buckareff and Van Wagenen 2010, 124).[1]

Interestingly, early Christian writers on the resurrection *did* discuss the persistence of some properties in our resurrected persons, including bodily properties. Some, like Pseudo-Justin in *On the Resurrection* or Irenaeus in *Adversus Haersus* argued that the dead must rise with a perfected—specifically a non-disabled or infirm—body (see Moss 2011, 1004–1005).[2] Augustine claimed that we would persist in having sexually differentiated bodies,[3] as did Aquinas (*Summa Theologiae* Supplement, Q. 81, a. 3),[4] though neither thought we would experience sexual desire or engage in sexual activities, at least not as it is understood in the present context.[5] Augustine also argued that at least some martyrs' scars that resulted from their martyrdom persist in the resurrection, even as glorified (see Upson-Saia 2011). While some have argued that we should not speculate about resurrected bodies or persons, given Paul's admonition that the resurrection is a mystery, where "this perishable body must put on imperishability, and this mortal body must put on immortality" (1 Corinthians 15:53),[6] there is a strong Christian tradition of seeking to better understand these mortal bodies *in the light of* resurrection considerations.

According to Christian doctrine, the general resurrection of the dead ushers in a new age that includes both a final judgment and a final (and full) rectification of the injustice suffered in this life. Consider this passage from Revelation:

> Then I saw "a new heaven and a new earth," for the first heaven and the first earth had passed away, and there was no longer any sea. . . . And I heard a loud voice from the throne saying, "Look! God's dwelling place is now among the people, and he will dwell with them. . . . He will wipe every tear from their eyes. There will be no more death or mourning or crying or pain, for the old order of things has passed away." He who was seated on the throne said, "I am making everything new!"
> (Rev. 21:1, 3–5)

One might read this as saying that injustice is not rectified, but merely eliminated: God creates a new heaven and a new earth in which there is *no longer* any injustice but that does not answer past injustices. However, a few passages later, St. John continues, "Then the angel showed me the river of the water of life. . . . On each side of the river stood the tree of life, bearing twelve crops of fruit, yielding its fruit every month. And the leaves of the tree are for the healing of the nations" (Rev. 22:1–2). The visions of healing the nations suggests that we should take the kingdom to be one in which past injustices are made right in addition to inaugurating a new and fully just kingdom. This suggests that a Christian picture of resurrection requires us to consider not only the fact of post-mortem survival but also that resurrected persons are subjects of rectification.

Indeed, as Aquinas points out when discussing the resurrection in his *Supplement* to the *Summa Theologiae*,

> According to Romans 2.15, 16, "In the day when God shall judge" each one's conscience will bear witness to him and his thoughts will accuse and defend him. And since in every judicial hearing, the witness, the accuser, and the defendant need to be acquainted with the matter on which judgment has to be pronounced, and since at the general judgment all the works of men will be submitted to judgment, it will behoove every man to be cognizant then of all his works.
> (*Summa Theologiae* Supplement, Q. 87, a. 1)

Here Aquinas considers the necessity of our knowledge of our own sins for the effectual working of the judgment itself. In the next article, Aquinas goes on to consider whether *everyone* will know everyone else's actions as good or evil, and concludes that this too must be the case if the judgment is to be recognized *as* just by all who witness it.

Importantly for the purposes of this paper, the relevant moment (while not assuming it lasts for any specified amount of chronological time) under consideration is the general resurrection and the final judgment. Given the way I will argue about the relationship between resurrection and injustice (and rectification), it is possible that at some point past the final judgment, in the midst of the new heavens and the new earth, gender or other personal properties are transformed. But, for the sake of the judgment itself, and what I argue that judgment and rectification must accomplish, gender must persist at least through that time.

Consider, too, how the author of the letter to the Hebrews notes that

> God is not unjust; he will not overlook your work and the love that you showed for his sake in serving the saints, as you still do. And we want each one of you to show the same diligence so as to realize the full assurance of hope to the very end.
>
> (Hebrews 6.10–11)

Here we are exhorted to trust the *justice* of God in seeing and accounting for earthly labor in the resurrection. Presumably, part of this exhortation includes enduring the suffering of injustices while working "for his sake" (that is, righteously) in part because of the hope assured in the resurrection that such suffering is made right.[7]

The notion that the resurrection involves a rectification of injustice is also found in some prominent treatments of the problem of evil. Marilyn McCord Adams (1986) argues that if we are to reconcile horrendous evil with the goodness of God, God must be good to agents who experience horrendous evil so as to *integrate* the evil into the narrative of the person's life, even to the point where the person no longer wishes the evil away. She claims, "How could God do it [defeat horrendous evils]? So far as I can see, only by integrating participation in horrendous evils into a person's relationship with God" (Adams and Sutherland 1989, 307). Similarly, Eleonore Stump argues in *Wandering in Darkness* that "a person's suffering is defeated by a benefit that goes primarily to her, that outweighs her suffering, and that could not be gotten just as well without the suffering" (Stump 2010, 455). At least one way that God can be good to believers in this integrating way is in the resurrection: resurrection life involves a new intimacy with God previously unexperienced by believers. So plausibly the resurrection (and the life that follows) *answers* certain types of injustice and suffering and not only in a global but also in a particular way to particular persons.

Restoring Gendered Injustices

Here is a reasonable condition for rectifying injustice: one must appropriately direct the rectificatory activity towards the person who suffered the injustice. This is key to what Stump argues about a benefit's being able to defeat suffering—such a benefit must go "primarily" to the sufferer. Suppose that Tom injures Thomasina deliberately, but their mother requires that Tom do another sibling's chores (perhaps Tim's). Plausibly, this is not a case of rectification because the person who receives the restoration is not the person who suffered. It may be a case in which injustice is punished (Tom must do someone's chores) but not a case where Thomasina experiences a Tom's making right his injustice *against her*. It need not be the case, however, that the rectificatory activity is identical with a punishment of some kind. What is critical to rectification is that it directly involves, insofar as that is possible, the injured person. Imagine that Tom steals Thomasina's valuable heirloom necklace. Suppose he is caught and punished by the state (say, he is forced to serve a year in prison) and he is required to restore the necklace to Thomasina (or, in the event that's impossible, pay her the value of the necklace). The component of this outcome that involves the *rectification* of Tom's unjust taking of Thomasina's necklace is his restoring it to her. Given how the resurrection is described not only in terms of the elimination of injustice but also the restoration and healing of injustices, this kind of restoring, rectifying activity is what primarily concerns us.

In some cases, such direct restoration is impossible in *this* life. If you swindled my elderly grandmother's fortune and she dies before you repay it, you might repay my father as her descendant. But importantly, my father 'stands in' for my grandmother, receiving *on her behalf* a rectification that is properly due to her. In the case of the resurrection, however, God's activity in the general resurrection makes it possible for direction restoration between offenders and victims of injustice.

Some injustices, unlike the case of swindling fortunes, seem to involve our identity in more profound (and problematic) ways. Discrimination against a person based on an assumption of their membership in some specific class of persons—whether in the workplace, in police profiling, or in a college admissions process—is a category of this kind of injustice. Rosa Parks's treatment is one example; suffragettes' harsh treatment in the early 20th century is another. Some would also argue that hate crimes constitute gross injustices because they are founded on vicious assumptions about some particular property, like gender or race, and the group that possesses the property. In these cases, a person's bearing some relevant property (or being perceived to bear it) figure in the explanation of the injustice itself: it is impossible to explain discrimination without reference to the perceived identity of the individual against whom it is directed.

Gender is a feature that can ground injustices of the above type. In addition to discrimination and hate crimes, these injustices could include beliefs and attitudes held by others about the individual in question that are themselves grounded in judgments about that person *qua* woman *or qua* demi-boy (or *qua* other gender identities). Thus some particular woman is denied the right to attend medical school in the

18th century because she is judged to be in a class not considered worthy of equal educational opportunity. Or an individual in ancient Athens is forbidden from participating in the life of the polis because they are perceived to belong to a class considered insufficiently rational for such work.

In considering cases of epistemic—specifically testimonial—injustices, Miranda Fricker (2007) offers several paradigmatic examples of this type of injustice. Fricker's cases[8] centrally concern what she calls "credibility deficits," where hearers' prejudices against a group cause them to negatively assess a speaker's credibility. In particular, Fricker is concerned with prejudices about a person's identity—gender being a prime example. Consider this case, taken from Fricker's second chapter:

> One Egyptian woman, working in Cairo, said that when she is at a meeting and wants to make a suggestion about policy, she actually writes down the suggestion on a little piece of paper, surreptitiously passes it to a sympathetic male colleague, has him make the suggestion, watches it be well received, and then joins in the discussion from there. She adopted this policy after mounting frustration at the incredulous reception that her ideas typically got from her male colleagues when she presented them as her own. I think I am right in saying that her attitude was feisty resignation that this was how she got things done, and also perhaps that somewhere in the process she probably got more credit than was allowed to show on the surface. It was clear none the less that she was considerably disadvantaged by the prejudicial attitudes towards her word as a woman.
>
> (Fricker 2007, 47)

The case concerns the person's identity *as* a woman; she is unjustly treated by her colleagues because of her gender. Her colleagues in particular (whether consciously or unconsciously) make judgments about her competency or intelligence based on assumptions they have about women as a larger class of persons.

Now imagine this woman at the resurrection. Can she experience the rectification of these injustices without being gendered? To put it another way, we might imagine that the woman is, as a part of restored justice, now able to fully pursue (and succeed in) her ideas as her own—her intellectual property and innovation is respected, she is free to make contributions and suggestions without fear of prejudicial response—but she is no longer a woman. Something seems lacking. For it was not just for *any* unjust or prejudicial reason that she was once prevented from making such full contribution: it was for a specific property—the property of being a woman—in virtue of which she was prevented. Were her identity *qua* woman to be rendered invisible, such that those who previously discriminated against her no longer view their interactions with her as gendered, the full weight of the injustice against her is unhelpfully diminished. In a genderless state she would have been capable of pursuing her career without the relevant discrimination; so, in restoring justice to her, it matters that she bears the relevant property at least at the time that justice is restored.[9]

Consider a second example from Fricker's text. Suppose we have a woman in the early 19th century who cares deeply about political life. She is informed, desires to vote, and has unique ideas about governing the nation she loves. Fricker suggests that among the harms done by epistemic injustice to this woman by being excluded from political conversation is that she is "inhibited precisely in the development of an essential aspect of who she is" (Fricker 2007, 55). Fricker continues:

> Excluded from the trustful conversation of the only people apparently allowed to talk politics, is she not blocked from becoming, in some significant aspect, the person that she is? . . . Persistent testimonial injustice can indeed inhibit the very formation of self.
>
> (Fricker 2007, 55)

To press this intuition further, if we imagine that the woman devoted to political life was suddenly given the right to vote, *not* because women were understood as also meriting a voice in political affairs, but instead because the entire category no longer existed as significant, it seems reasonable to think that what the woman sought has not been fully achieved. Eliminating gender might get everyone the vote, but it fails to do justice to the very reasons that one of those groups was prohibited. It would fail to overturn the mistaken conclusion about women, which seems critical as part of undoing prejudicial injustices.

Another, though related, reason we might think that resurrected persons must be gendered is that they must be capable of recognizing themselves as the participants in the injustices that they suffered, so as to fully experience the restoration of justice. Gender is a means of recognition of oneself as the subject of one's own life. Amos Yong (2012) suggests with respect to the context of disability that what should persist in resurrected persons are "features that emerge from and express human identities across the lifespan" (Yong 2012, 5). While I have not yet tackled whether such features are essential or accidental in themselves, it is clear that some features have this role of expressing identity across our life. Gender, I argue, is such a feature. It is part of how we understand ourselves in relationships with others and with ourselves.

One might object here that this seems to unjustly (and perhaps contradictorily) require the persistence of *just one* identity in the case of persons with fluid or multiple gender identities. Suppose, for example, that an individual who has identified over the course of their life as both a demi-boy and a demi-girl was unjustly treated by a medical professional while identifying as a demi-girl. Suppose further that when that individual died, they strongly identified as a demi-boy. Is God required to resurrect them in only the demi-girl identity, to rectify the injustice they suffered? Other forms of prejudicial discrimination, such as ageism or some forms of ableism against temporarily disabled individuals, might pose a similar problem for my view.

Here is one possible reply: God does not require the individual to present or identify as a demi-girl, but does resurrect the person with the property of being capable of identifying with both, and the demi-girl gender property is there, albeit passively (not unlike our having the passive property of dancing a jig even while seated). And, importantly, God maintains the related bodily properties such that reconciliation between the medical professional who perpetrated the injustice, and the demi-boy who was once a demi-girl, is possible. Perhaps the specifications of bodily and psychological properties persisting into the general resurrection for a gender fluid person is more general than in a cisgender case. In order for there to be reconciliation, the relevant parties to the injustice must exist and must be capable of reaching a new understanding of each other and more particularly a new understanding of those individuals *as* bearers of the property once deemed inferior—and if genders ceased to exist altogether, and individuals cannot be identified as being the bearers of those properties, such reconciliation would not be possible. Reconciliation requires a new understanding of the property itself as well as the individual. So an elimination of the relevant properties would prevent the kind of reconciliation that seems to characterize the harmony or *shalom* of resurrected life.

It seems plausible that part of the relevant rectificatory activity of the general resurrection is the way that properties once considered worthless or even evil come to be understood—particularly by those who perpetrated injustice—as valuable. The resurrected person is a site where features once given as reasons for discrimination become celebrated, where the very reasons cited in defense of unjust treatment are redeemed as reasons, not for unjust treatment, but for admiration and praise.[10] As Amos Yong (2009) writes on the question of disability persistence in the resurrection: "Precisely because the meanings of our lives are constituted by but irreducible to our bodies, so also will the resurrected body be the site through which the meaning of our narratives are transformed (and that, eternally)" (Yong 2009, 283). And it is not enough, I think, for these individuals to recognize that a property *in general* is valuable, because the injustice was done not against the property per se but against some specific bearer of that property. It was not against *any* woman or *any* demi-boy that a person acted unjustly, but against *that woman* or *this demi-boy*. Those identities should be celebrated in the resurrection, not merely as abstract valuable identities, but as valuable in situ, in the very people who bear them.

In this section I have briefly sketched a reason to think that gender persists in the resurrection. I've argued specifically that some injustices are intrinsically gendered; they are constituted by prejudicial judgments about a person because of her gender. For such injustices to be truly rectified, the persons who experience these injustices must have the relevant properties used as discrimination. Without her gender persisting, a resurrected person couldn't receive a full restoration of the injustices done to her.[11]

Resurrected Gender on Sally Haslanger's Account

Among the more famous quotations in feminist literature is Simone de Beauvoir's claim that, "*On ne naît pas femme: on le devient*": "One is not born, but rather becomes, a woman" (de Beauvoir 2011, 330). Many scholars take de Beauvoir to be defining gender as the 'social meaning' of sex. Even if one doesn't endorse Beauvoir's view here, many (and perhaps most) scholars think that gender is a different property than sex. Specifically, some theorists argue that gender is nothing but the significances in social customs and expectations we give to supposed biological properties. For Haslanger and others, identifying gender as a socially constructed property (as opposed to a natural one) helps realize justice within oppressive regimes. If gender is constructed, it can be deconstructed so as to resist oppression. Haslanger's contention is that what we want the concept of gender[12] to do for us is appropriately pick out the social groups who have been subject to systemic subordination and oppression on the basis of particular bodily features. Consider her definition of a woman:

> S is a woman iff$_{df}$ S is systematically subordinated along some dimension (economic, political, legal, social, etc.), and S is "marked" as a target for this treatment by observed or imagined bodily features presumed to be evidence of a female's biological role in reproduction. (Haslanger 2012, 230)

Haslanger's definition is particularly interesting to consider in light of the argument from justice in Section II because she defines gender as nothing *but* a particular type of participation in an unjust system. To be a woman is to experience specific types of injustice(s), characterized by the presumption of certain bodily features as providing reasons for that unjust treatment. By identifying being a woman with the injustice of subordination, it would be impossible for God to do justice to individuals while maintaining their gender in the resurrection.

Moreover, on Haslanger's view gender is "to be understood first and foremost as social *groups* defined within a structure of social relations; whatever links there might be to identities and norms are highly contingent and would depend on the details of the picture" (Haslanger 2012, 244–245 emphasis added). The resurrection, however, does not seem to resurrect social structures or social groups. If it doesn't, then individuals in the resurrection couldn't bear gender properties, as understood in this sense. Haslanger allows for the persistence of biologically sexed bodies (male, female, and possibly a variety of other sexes; see Fausto-Sterling 1993), so one question that must be answered is whether the persistence of biologically sexed bodies would be sufficient to answer the arguments given above.

While she grants that we might still mark certain bodies as having particular (medical) entitlements, Haslanger concludes that "this need not have broad implications for psychological identity or everyday social interactions, for the 'sex' of bodies might not even be publicly marked" (Haslanger 2012, 245). Thus Haslanger's view also runs against the idea that gender in the resurrection would be necessary for the individual's recognition of herself *as* herself since on Haslanger's view "neither should we assume that membership in a gender will constitute one's personal or psychological identity to any significant degree" (Haslanger 2012, 244).

Haslanger's conception of gender and its relation to the achievement of justice requires that there are no women or men[13] (as she defines it in terms of being marked for subordination or privilege) when justice has been achieved. If Haslanger is right, then resurrected individuals would participate in justice in part by eliminating their genders. Whatever other properties might or might not persist, gender will not. And God, in bringing about resurrection (and the justice it entails), could not cause gender to persist.

One might raise the worry here that what I have been tracking in this paper is not gender at all, but merely biological sex. One might more specifically worry that the conditions for sufficient rectification of injustice can be met so long as our resurrected bodies persist with their biological sexes. A defender of Haslanger might respond to my argument by noting that on her view, while categories like "men" and "women" are eliminated, sex need not be. Haslanger goes so far as to argue that sex ought to be marked as significant at least insofar as the various sexes play different roles in reproduction. But if this is the case, one could argue that gender can easily be eliminated so long as biological sex is preserved. In the resurrection, our bodies would be sexed as they were on earth but without any of the unjust subordination that constitutes gender. One might also observe that Haslanger is open to constructing new, non-hierarchical genders. While this is true, and it might very well be that post-resurrection, new genders are either made or appreciated, it is still the case that, on my argument, both 'men' and 'women' need to exist as the genders they currently are for the purposes of rectification. Whether alternative genders emerge afterward is compatible with, but beyond the scope of, the present project.

Here is an alternative explanation: we have gotten the normative import of biological sex wrong, and thus part of the injustice perpetrated specifically against individuals of a particular biological sex is that we draw bad conclusions about what having that sex means in other areas. One might assume that having a female sexed body is connected with irrationality, or that having an intersexed body is connected to posing certain threats to others. One might argue that while there is such a thing as gender properties, they ought not be identified as those false normative judgments about biological sex. Rather, we might modify the implications of having a certain gender—returning a certain kind of 'good' significance to it—without requiring its elimination. It's interesting that on Haslanger's view the (generally) same class of individuals previously 'women' who were marked for unjust subordination will now *also* be marked as 'women' (or a different term) in order to preserve justice. Haslanger claims:

> Although from the point of view of justice, it would be irresponsible not to accord differences between our bodies some social meaning, it would also be irresponsible not to overturn the meanings we now assume to be natural and right.
>
> (Haslanger 2012, 269)

Again, one could accept this premise without identifying gender exclusively with the meanings certain biological properties have historically been assigned. We have gotten some normative facts about gender wrong; clearly, these norms will be corrected in the resurrection (part of doing justice is recognizing that women were equally rational, or that they should be considered citizens and thus accorded political rights). But revisions that aim to capture *true normative import* rather than false normative import need not entail that gender itself be eliminated. Such a goal can be accomplished on a different picture of gender than the one Haslanger offers, with the advantage that we do not need to think of gender as something we must eliminate.

Is Gender Accidental or Necessary?[14]

In this final section, I want to turn to consider the implications of the above arguments for thinking about what kind of property or feature gender is: namely, whether gender is accidental or necessary. I will first sketch some implications for the accidental picture of gender and then some implications for the necessary picture.

Accounts of gender as an accidental property could accommodate the argument that gender persists in the resurrection, and, given gender fluidity, we might have further reason to think gender is an accidental property. Clearly certain other accidental properties persist in Jesus's resurrected body—for example, the marks of the nails in his hands.[15] Thinking that a property persists in the resurrection does not entail that such a property *needs* to persist. But if this is the case, and the property is unnecessary for God to successfully raise that very person from the dead, then presumably God has some other reason for causing that accident to persist, while permitting others (say, eye color or the bruise I once had on my left elbow) to cease.

One could argue that having a gender in general is a *proper accident* of the human form, following something like Thomas Aquinas's account of proper accidents like risibility (the ability to laugh). (For a description of Aquinas's view of proper accidents, see Kerr OP 2015.) On this view, one's having a gender would be an accident that flows from the human essence. Perhaps God maintains all human beings' proper accidents in the resurrection.

The main downside to this kind of view is that it fails to do justice to how gender (and, arguably, other similar features)[16] differ from even proper accidents like our ability to laugh. The ability to laugh does not play the unifying role in our identity that gender does. And even if this feature of gender—that it plays such a unifying role—is an accidental feature of our communities, its relationship to our identity still warrants asking whether God has special reason to maintain it, as opposed to other accidental properties. Charlotte Witt argues that gender functionally unifies social roles for a given social individual, and this is what makes gender what she calls "uniessential" to an individual. She writes, "The intuition guiding my argument for gender essentialism is that the social roles associated with being a man and being a woman are organizing and unifying roles in the lives of social individuals" (Witt 2011, 77). I think this intuition is right, though I have some worries about Witt's particular account, which I discuss further below. Even if gender were considered something like a Thomistic "proper accident," one still needs to explain how it, unlike some other proper accidents, plays this unifying role and how that relates to resurrection identity.

Another possibility for those favoring the view that gender is an accidental feature but who are inclined to think gender persists in the resurrection is to claim that gender is *accidentally necessary*. Thus, while gender is in itself accidental, once I have some specific gender I must continue to be that gender. This seems to accord with intuitions like those of Amos Yong about disability. In a critical dialogue with Yong, Ryan Mullins takes the view that "a disability is an accidental, and not a necessary, property" (Mullins 2011, 27) and therefore need not be a feature of resurrected bodies. Yong replies: "But this ignores the fact that many of the 'accidents' that mark our lives—from chromosomal ones to speech impediments to living in a wheelchair for an extended length of time, etc.—shape our identities in indelible ways" (Yong 2012, 8). This seems congenial with the thought that properties like gender, once we have them, are necessary in this accidental way. They could have been otherwise; but once they are, they are that way necessarily.[17]

Natalie Stoljar (1995) suggests that gender might be accidentally necessary—"Perhaps, however, having the gender that I have, *once I have it*, is essential to me. On this view, if I change genders, I become a different person" (Stoljar 1995, 287). Stoljar advances a view of gender as a cluster concept necessarily linked to sex. Drawing on Wittgenstein's notion of a family resemblance, Stoljar claims that the concept 'woman' picks out a resemblance class of individuals. She suggests four elements in the concept 'woman': female sex (which includes chromosomal and anatomical features as well as other bodily characteristics), a range of phenomenological features, roles, and self-attributions and the attributions of others (Stoljar 1995, 283–284). This seems to me the most promising view accommodating both the intuition that gender is itself an accidental feature and the view that the gender we have is essential to our identity such that resurrected persons must have it.

What of accounts of gender whereby it is essential, rather than accidental? On first glance these views have the advantage of simplicity when it comes to explaining why any given gender persists in the resurrection: gender persists because gender is essential for identity—I cannot be the person that I am without it. What it means for me to be myself is in part explained by my having the gender that I do. But how could such an account go? Aristotle's own account of gender clearly does not take gender to be an essential property. As Gareth Matthews observes, Aristotle identifies male and female as accidental modifications to a common human form. "Later on [Aristotle] says that 'male and female are indeed modifications peculiar to "animal," not however, in virtue of its essence [kata ten ousian] but in the matter, i.e. the body'" (Matthews 1986, 22). One possibility is to revise Aristotle's account and make the case that metaphysical species are more finely individuated than biological species. Particularly, there are substantive forms of men and women (and perhaps other genders as well). Given the problems with Aristotle's own biological concept of the sexes (thinking, for example, that women were 'incomplete' men or that the transmission of the human form took place solely through the father's agency),[18] this might be an attractive alternative.

One problem with this view is whether *all* features that seem to possess the unifying features of gender as described earlier would be candidates for individuating forms. Would disabled bodies be substantive forms in their own right? This seems obviously false at least for acquired or temporary disabilities, given that acquisition (or loss) of a disability would result in the destruction of the (previously) non-disabled person. And we don't typically think that an individual goes out of existence when they become or cease to be disabled. Would different races be individual substantiating forms? There are problems to thinking that either of these properties ought to generate new forms—indeed, we might generally worry that the forms would become so fine-grained that they collapse into each individual person having their own substantial form.

Charlotte Witt (2011) offers an alternative neo-Aristotelian account of gender as an essential property. Witt argues that gender is uniessential to social individuals: a principle of functional unity of the various social roles that a social individual occupies. Witt distinguishes between the persistence conditions of biological organisms, human persons, and social individuals (see Witt 2011, ch. 3). Gender is uniessential to just one of these—the social individual. To be the social individual that I am, my gender is essential (but it is not essential to my being the same person). In seeking a principle of unity for these individuals, Witt writes,

> the kind of unity appropriate for social agents concerns how the various social roles an agent is responsive to and evaluable under are unified and integrated with one another so that what results is a normatively unified social individual or agent.
>
> (Witt 2011, 77)

That an individual is unified by her gender is not contingent on the individual feeling herself to be so unified (there is no requirement that an individual conceive of her gender as this normatively unifying property), but it is contingent in the sense of being contingent on social institutions, norms, and structures. Thus, Witt concludes her chapter, "viewing gender as uniessential to social individuals accomplishes both of these goals simultaneously, by developing a theory of relational essences that fits within a contingent, historical framework" (Witt 2011, 106).

Witt's view appears able to accommodate gender persistence in the resurrection so long as we suppose that social individuals are resurrected. But this would be an additional assumption, one that isn't entailed by thinking that persons are resurrected. Another reason I think Witt's account falls short is that it fails to sufficiently link gender to the body. Elizabeth Barnes argues for a moderate social construction picture of disability wherein disability is not merely a matter of how one is situated socially but also involves the presence of certain bodily features. She claims,

> the question of whether someone is disabled ought to be a question of what their body is (really) like. That is, whether someone is disabled is not merely a matter of how they are treated or how they self-identify. It's a matter of whether they in fact have particular objective bodily features.
>
> (Barnes 2016, 38)

Barnes continues:

> but the fact that these bodily features are important to us—the fact that they matter and are considered relevant to the classification

of someone as disabled—is due to the way we think about bodies, rather than some objective similarity between such bodies. And that's what it is, on my view, for disability to be socially constructed.

(Barnes 2016, 38)

Barnes here offers an important picture for our general framework of thinking about bodies and their relationship to identity. First, there is something about the body that seems to ground being disabled. But secondly, the significance of that bodily property is due to the way in which we think about the body. To apply this to gender, we might think that gender is not merely a question of social relationship (as on Haslanger's picture), but a mixed question both of certain bodily features *and* how those features interact with social relationships and judgments. Since Witt's account only makes gender essential to a social individual, it cannot account for the significance of the body in understanding gender, as accounts like either a modification to Aristotelian forms or some of the accidental property pictures can.

Conclusion

In this paper I argued that justice in the Resurrection requires gender to persist in resurrected persons. I have also argued that a Haslangerian account of genders where they are identified exclusively with respect to certain unjust social responses is incompatible with these reasons. Thus, to the extent that one is convinced that men and women do persist (and perhaps even other genders as well), one must either substantially modify Haslanger's view or be pressed towards a different picture of gender. I have drawn out some implications and challenges for thinking of gender as metaphysically accidental or essential property, based on how these views can accommodate the intuition that gender persists in the resurrection. To the extent that I have presented compelling reasons to think we will meet gendered persons in heaven, I hope to have shown that an adequate account of gender and its relationship to personal identity must be compatible with this intuition.

Notes

1. Note only should we be attentive to the type of bodies resurrection persons have, we should also be attentive to the other properties we think persons should have (whether these be relational properties or others not strictly bodily in kind). One might worry that I am here presupposing a particular picture of gender *as* a bodily property by linking my arguments in this paper to observations about the types of bodies we have in the resurrection. But what concerns me is the more general locus of attention in Buckareff and Van Wagenen, namely, the shift from asking about the possibility of resurrection according to different views of human persons and towards considerations of what properties are needed for identity persistence.

2. Moss importantly notes that the opponents against whom Pseudo-Justin writes are not themselves expressing a disability-positive view, though Pseudo-Justin himself, she notes, does think that *barrenness* will persist in the resurrection; see Moss 2011, 1006.
3. In his *City of God* (Supplement Q.81, a.3, *sed contra*), Augustine notes, "Those who are wiser, seemingly, who doubt not that both sexes will rise again."
4. "Moreover, this same diversity is becoming to the perfection of the species, the different degrees whereof are filled by this very difference of sex and quantity. Wherefore just as men will rise again of various stature, so will they rise again of different sex."
5. For an interesting consideration of Augustine on sexed bodies and sexuality in the resurrection, see Miles 2005.
6. All biblical citations are taken from the New Revised Standard Version (NRSV) unless otherwise noted.
7. The precise manner in which it is made right remains mysterious, and perhaps it ought to. My point here is merely to show that Christian Scriptures seem to make clear the expectation that the resurrection involves individual experiences of rectification for injustice and the restoration of justice.
8. These concern what Fricker calls identity prejudice. She defines this as a "prejudice relating to social identity," and observes that it can be expressed as "prejudice for or against people owing to some feature of their social identity." See Fricker 2007, 27–28.
9. As noted earlier, I do not claim that gender necessarily persists *ad infinitum* in the new heavens and the new earth. My argument more narrowly concerns the question of gendered bodies as they feature in the general resurrection at least to the point at which God's judgment is complete.
10. Haslanger notes that this kind of thinking is at least one option with respect to race (which she treats simultaneously with gender):

    > For members of subordinated races, their racial affiliation—as it has been constructed from within the group—is often not only a source of pride and value in their lives, but has provided resources to combat racial oppression. So if we are thinking about the possible future of race, one option is to build on these positive racial reconstructions, rather than the damaging structures of oppression.
    >
    > (2012, 264)

    I won't weigh in here on the metaphysical status of race; rather, I want to suggest that one possible alternative to eliminating gender would be to build on these more positive reconstructions at least of the normative *import* of gender features for individuals.
11. Both Kevin Timpe and Blake Hereth pressed my argument here, for which I am grateful. I am not wholly satisfied with the answer I put forth, though I offer one further thought. Perhaps the relevant requirement is a bit more general: one must still be *gendered* even if one is no longer the specific gender that one was at the time of the relevant discrimination. In the case of disability, suppose that Paul acquires a temporary disability and has tremors in his hand. Paul is fired from his job unjustly because of how his disability slowed him down during certain tasks. Then Paul's tremors cease. In heaven, does Paul need to have tremors again? Maybe not—but Paul needs to have hands; specifically, Paul needs to have the hand that had the tremors. This facilitates the specific kind of reconciliation I have in mind, where his former

boss looks upon the hand and recognizes that mistreatment of Paul, with *this* hand (even if it is not tremoring) was wrong.
12. Haslanger treats race and gender together in both her 2000, 2012. For my purposes I don't take up the question of race in this paper.
13. For Haslanger, there would also be no more races. For another view on race, see Andreason 2000.
14. In what follows, I am considering accident and essence in the sense of its contribution to something like what it means for a person to be that person as opposed to another. This is, I think, closer to both Aristotelian uses of "essence" and "accident" and more akin to definition, as Fine 1994 understands it.
15. I'm grateful to Alexander Pruss for this example.
16. Here I am thinking of features like race and (some) disabilities, though there is more work to be done to explore the analogies and dis-analogies between these various features.
17. For a helpful discussion of accidental necessity, see Freddoso 1982.
18. See Matthews 1986, 22. For this notion of females incomplete or mutilated males, see *On the Generation of Animals* 2.3 737a27 or *GA* 1.20 728a17, as cited in Matthews.

References

Adams, Marilyn McCord. "Redemptive Suffering: A Christian Solution to the Problem of Evil." In *Rationality, Religious Belief, and Moral Commitment: New Essays in the Philosophy of Religion*, edited by William Wainwright and Robert Audi, 248–267. Ithaca, NY: Cornell University Press, 1986.

Adams, Marilyn McCord and Stewart Sutherland. "Horrendous Evils and the Goodness of God." *Proceedings of the Aristotelian Society, Supplementary Volume* 63 (1989): 297–323.

Andreasen, R. O. "Race: Biological Reality or Social Construct?" *Philosophy of Social Science* 67 (2000): 653–666.

Appiah, Anthony. "'But Would That Still Be Me?' Notes on Gender, 'Race,' Ethnicity, as Sources of 'Identity.'" *The Journal of Philosophy* 87.10 (1990): 493–499.

Aquinas, Thomas. *Supplement* to the *Summa Theologiae*. Translated by the Fathers of the Dominican Province. London: Benziger Bros., 1947.

Bach, Theodore. "Gender Is a Natural Kind with a Historical Essence." *Ethics* 122 (2012): 231–272.

Baker, Lynne Rudder. "Persons and the Metaphysics of Resurrection." *Religious Studies* 43 (2007): 333–348.

Barnes, Elizabeth. *The Minority Body: A Theory of Disability*. Oxford: Oxford University Press, 2016.

Buckareff, A. and J. Van Wagenen. "Surviving Resurrection." *International Journal for Philosophy of Religion* 67.3 (2010): 123–139.

Corcoran, Kevin J. "Dualism, Materialism and the Problem of Post Mortem Survival." *Philosophia Christi* 4 (2002): 395–409.

de Beauvoir, Simone. *The Second Sex*. Translated by Constance Borde and Sheila Malovany-Chevallier. Vintage eBooks, 2011.

Fausto-Sterling, Anne. "The Five Sexes: Why Male and Female Are Not Enough." *The Sciences* 33 (1993): 20–24.

Fine, Kit. "Essence and Modality." *Philosophical Perspectives* 8 (1994): 1–16.
Freddoso, Alfred J. "Accidental Necessity and Power Over the Past." *Pacific Philosophical Quarterly* 63 (1982): 54–68.
Fricker, Miranda. *Epistemic Injustice: Power and the Ethics of Knowing*. Oxford: Oxford University Press, 2007.
Haslanger, Sally. "Feminism in Metaphysics: Negotiating the Natural." In *The Cambridge Companion to Feminism in Philosophy*, edited by Miranda Fricker and J. Hornsby, 107–126. Cambridge: Cambridge University Press, 2000a.
———. "Gender and Race: (What) Are They? (What) Do We Want Them to Be?" *Noûs* 34.1 (2000b): 31–55.
———. "What Are We Talking About? The Semantics and Politics of Social Kinds." *Hypatia* 20.4 (2005): 10–26.
———. *Resisting Reality: Social Construction and Social Critique*. Oxford: Oxford University Press, 2012.
Kerr, Gaven O. P. *Aquinas's Way to God: The Proof in De Ente et Essentia*. Oxford: Oxford University Press, 2015.
Matthews, Gareth B. "Gender and Essence in Aristotle." *Australasian Journal of Philosophy* 64.1 (1986): 16–25.
McKitrick, Jennifer. "A Dispositional Account of Gender." *Philosophy Studies* 172 (2015): 2575–2589.
Miles, Margaret R. "Sex and the City (of God): Is Sex Forfeited or Fulfilled in Augustine's Resurrection of the Body?" *Journal of the American Academy of Religion* 73.2 (2005): 307–327.
Moss, Candida. "Heavenly Healing: Cleansing and the Resurrection of the Dead in the Early Church." *Journal of the American Academy of Religion* 79.4 (2011): 991–1017.
Mullins, Ryan. "Some Difficulties for Amos Yong's Disability Theology of the Resurrection." *Ars Disputandi* 11 (2011): 24–32.
Stoljar, Natalie. "Essence, Identity and the Concept of Woman." *Philosophical Topics* 23.2 (1995): 261–293.
Stump, Eleonore. *Wandering in Darkness*. Oxford: Oxford University Press, 2010.
Upson-Saia, Kristi. "Resurrecting Deformity: Augustine on Wounded and Scarred Bodies in the Heavenly Realm." In *Disability in Judaism, Christianity and Islam*, edited by Schumm and Stoltzfus, 93–122. New York: Palgrave Macmillan, 2011.
van Inwagen, Peter. "The Possibility of Resurrection." *International Journal for Philosophy of Religion* 9.2 (1978): 114–121.
Witt, Charlotte. *The Metaphysics of Gender*. Oxford: Oxford University Press, 2011.
Yong, Amos. "Disability and the Love of Wisdom." *Ars Disputandi* 9 (2009): 54–71.
———. "Disability Theology of the Resurrection: Persisting Questions and Additional Considerations." *Ars Disputandi* 12.1 (2012): 4–10.

15 Limbo, Hiddenness, and the Beatific Vision (and Procreation, for Some, in the Life to Come)

David Worsley

Introduction

Grant that the final destination of a human person is either heaven, hell, or limbo.[1] Grant also that those who find themselves in heaven depart this life:

1. without the stain of original sin,[2] and
2. without unrepented mortal sin.[3]

That those who find themselves in Hell depart this life:

3. with or without the stain of original sin, and
4. with unrepented mortal sin.

Whilst those who find themselves in limbo depart this life:

5. with the stain of original sin, and
6. without unrepented mortal sin.

Following Kevin Timpe, I will take it that a person must exercise certain cognitive and volitional capacities in order either to remove the stain of original sin (by cooperating with God in some act of personal redemption)[4] or to commit mortal sin (see, for instance, Stump 2010; Timpe 2015).[5] Given the conditions for entry outlined above, and granting the theological claim that all (or all but one or two) postlapsarian human persons are born *already with* the stain of original sin, it seems possessing certain cognitive and volitional capacities is necessary for a person's entrance to either heaven or hell.[6] Thus, it might seem that limbo will be the final destination of (at least) those who leave this life without having ever having (or ever exercising) these capacities, for instance, those who die in early infancy.[7] However, whilst those who die in early infancy might find themselves in limbo *at some point*, why think this will remain their *final* destination?

Indeed, in a recently published paper, Kevin Timpe has argued that limbo, like Purgatory, may be an 'interim state.' He writes:

> if there are cases where individuals have not had an opportunity to be reconciled to God in the present life, then God will give those individuals an opportunity to do so in the next life.
>
> (2015, 283)

He terms this the 'Minimum Limbo Conclusion' (MLC), and explains that adopting MLC allows

> for a way that infants and those [who] are disabled and who, as a result, have lacked an opportunity to reconcile with God in the present life to have such an opportunity post-mortem. For those who have died prior to developing the capacities that would be needed to cooperate with God in their reconciliation, Limbo could function as a place wherein they develop those needed capacities and are then offered the opportunity to use them. This account of Limbo is an 'interim state' since; like purgatory, it will ultimately be empty.
>
> (2015, 291).

Whilst careful to distance this account from the traditional *limbus infantium*, Timpe describes this 'interim state' not as "a place of 'second-chances,' but rather a place of first-chances for those who were denied them in their terrestrial life" (2015, 283). This chapter serves to outline some implications I take to follow from Timpe's interim limbo.[8]

MLC, Freedom, and Union with God

To motivate the capacity component of his MLC, Timpe stipulates that those in heaven enjoy an unending union of love with God. God, however, cannot secure such union unilaterally; instead, it must be freely willed by both lover and beloved, with each exercising a certain degree of moral agency (Timpe 2015, 290). Timpe argues that the need for such agency rules out the possibility of theological or causal determinism in bringing about such union, concluding that the desired union can only obtain if both lover and beloved possess libertarian freedom of the will.[9] Furthermore, as the mere *possession* of libertarian freedom of the will is clearly insufficient for union with God, the possessor must also actually desire union with God, and must not be inhibited from uniting with God. Timpe takes both original and actual sin (and the guilt and shame that accompany them) to inhibit both a person's desire for and ability to unite with God. As a result, a freely willed personal redemption (some act of cooperation with God that eliminates the stain of original sin in a person, whatever this might be) is also required before

Limbo, Hiddenness, and the Beatific Vision 349

a person can join in a union of love with God.[10] However, as earlier noted, freely cooperating in this sort of personal redemption involves the exercise of certain complex cognitive and volitional capacities, capacities not all persons come to possess in this life.[11] So, rather than ruling out the possibility of a heavenly union with God for persons that do not come to possess such capacities in this life (and therefore, who die without committing mortal sin, but with the stain of original sin intact), Timpe suggests that it is precisely this opportunity to develop (and exercise) the capacities needed to freely cooperate in some act of personal redemption (or mortal sin), that is afforded to those in his interim limbo.

Although not expressed in so many words, I take Timpe to be putting forward something in the neighborhood of the following line of argument:

1. All persons have as their final destination either Heaven, Hell, or limbo.[12]
2. In order to enjoy an unending union of love with God in heaven, a person must freely will a personal redemption.[13]
3. In order to be permanently separated from God in Hell, a person must freely will some mortal sin.
4. Freely willing either personal redemption or mortal sin requires the free exercise of certain complex cognitive and volitional capacities.
5. In this life, there are some persons who do not come to possess the relevant cognitive and volitional capacities required to will either personal redemption or mortal sin.
6. All those who leave this life without possession (or exercise) of the cognitive and volitional capacities needed for freely willing either personal redemption or mortal sin find themselves in limbo (from 1, 2, 3, 4, and 5).[14]
7. If God could grant all those in limbo the relevant capacities needed for freely willing personal redemption (or mortal sin), and it is fitting for God to do so, then God will do so.[15]
8. God could grant all those in limbo the relevant capacities needed for freely willing personal redemption (or mortal sin).[16]
9. It is fitting for God to grant all those in limbo the relevant capacities needed for freely willing personal redemption (or mortal sin).[17]
10. Therefore, God will grant all those in limbo the relevant capacities needed for freely willing personal redemption (or mortal sin) (from 6, 7, 8, and 9).[18]
11. If an inhabitant of limbo comes to possess the relevant capacities needed for freely willing personal redemption (or mortal sin), and they exercise those capacities, they will leave limbo and end up in heaven (or hell).
12. It is inevitable that those in possession of the relevant capacities for freely willing personal redemption (or mortal sin) will (eventually) exercise them to freely will personal redemption (or mortal sin).[19]

13. Therefore, nobody will have limbo as their final destination (from 10, 11, and 12).

Whilst there is plenty that could be said about each of (1)–(13), I will limit myself to five observations that I take to follow from this line of reasoning. Those observations are as follows:

1. If union with God requires a freely willed personal redemption, those in limbo cannot (immediately) experience beatific revelation.
2. If those in limbo do not (immediately) experience beatific revelation, and they are embodied, their time in limbo will last longer than an instant.
3. If limbo is to be nobody's final destination, and if limbo lasts longer than an instant, the duration of time a person spends in limbo must have some non-arbitrary cutoff point. The best candidates for such a cutoff point are either the initial freely willed act of personal redemption[20] (or mortal sin), or some later death.[21]
4. If some later death is the best candidate for this non-arbitrary cutoff point, atonement for (at least) mortal sin must be possible in limbo. If it is fitting that atonement in this life is secured through an incarnational birth, so too might an incarnational birth (and so, the possibility of general procreation) be fitting in limbo.
5. Plausibly, if both procreation and death are possible in limbo, so too is infant death, and so, future iterations of limbo are also possible. Furthermore, if there is at least one future iteration of limbo, there could be unending iterations of limbo, and so, an unending increase in the number of those who join in union with God in heaven (and, possibly, Hell). If there is an unending increase in the number of those in heaven, there could be a corresponding unending (extensive) increase in the joy of all the inhabitants of heaven.

I'll take each in turn.

Limbo, Hiddenness, and the Beatific Vision

Can any flesh be added to Timpe's MLC bone? I think some can. Timpe's limbo is designed to elicit either some freely willed mortal sin or some freely willed personal redemption from those unable to will either in this life. As such, we may rule out theological determinism in limbo. And if determinism is ruled out, so too is any form of compatibilism.[22] God's determining that an inhabitant of limbo desire divine union would render impossible the sort of union that motivated this account of limbo in the first place. Thus, those in limbo must have the ability and the opportunity to reject God.

How might this observation prove clarifying? If the human will is understood as something akin to an appetite for goodness (as, traditionally, it has been taken to be; see Aquinas *ST* I–II, Q. 8, A. 1), and if God is the greatest good[23], were God to be revealed fully and completely to an inhabitant of limbo able to behold such revelation, it seems inevitable that this person would desire union with God.[24] In fact, they could not do other than desire union with God and God would have created them such that this be the case.[25] Certainly, were God to be so revealed, the beholder may find themselves wanting to want union with God, but such higher-order desire would only obtain in virtue of God's prior determination that it be so.[26]

If the ruling out of compatibilist accounts also eliminates the above-mentioned 'source-compatibilist' scenario, for Timpe's limbo to achieve what it sets out to do, God must be (to some extent) hidden from its inhabitants (see Murray 1993). With this, we are left with a situation analogous to that faced by both primal and original sinners.[27] In the case of the primal sinner, we learn from tradition that they were intellectually flawless, supremely happy, and morally good, yet they did not (or could not) behold this beatific vision—God withheld it from them, at least, initially.[28] In the case of the original sinner, Christian Scripture teaches that they too lacked a certain knowledge of good (and so, God) and evil (see Genesis 2:16–17, 3:4–7). Of course, this is not to say that God must remain completely hidden in limbo; in the case of both primal and original sin, each sinner knew of God that he existed, even if some knowledge of God's nature was withheld from them.[29]

Plausibly, then, if MLC is true, God must remain *to a certain extent* hidden from those in limbo. And this conclusion prompts another.

A Temporal Limbo

I have suggested that in Timpe's limbo, God must remain (at least partially) hidden, such that its inhabitants are not determined to desire divine union. This being the case, those in limbo must decide for themselves whether to join in union with the divine (and so, engage in some act of freely willed personal redemption). However, as the desire for union with God *follows* (logically, if not temporally) such deliberation, this volitional act cannot take place the very instant they find themselves in limbo.

If those in limbo are incorporeal (that is, they exist without a body), this decision will most likely occur in the very instant *after* their entrance into limbo (as incorporeal beings do not reason discursively, anything that they could come to know that might inform their decision, they will immediately know and immediately understand—there is therefore no development in such a limbo).[30] However, given that it is in part the lack of a certain *cognitive* capacity that saw said persons inhabit limbo, I find the prospect of an incorporeal limbo unappealing.[31] In any case, if those in limbo are corporeal (that is, with bodies and brains, and so, with the ability to develop or be granted the relevant cognitive capacities), this decision-making process must last longer than an instant. Because corporeal human beings are rational, they do reason discursively, and reasoning discursively takes time. Therefore, if those in limbo are embodied, they will be temporal (just as we are in this earthly life), not aeviternal (as the Christian tradition teaches angels are).

But if those in limbo are temporal, and limbo is to be nobody's final destination, the time a person spends there must have some (hopefully non-arbitrary) cutoff point. What might this be? At first glance, it seems there are two prime candidates for such a cutoff, either (1) the first point of decision (that is, the first mortal sin committed, or the first engagement with some act of personal redemption), or (2) that person's death.

Limbo, Duration, and Death

What of the first option, the cutoff for those in limbo being the point of their first decision? There are two ways this might work, each contingent upon whether those in limbo are granted the relevant cognitive and volitional capacities immediately (as the Christian tradition teaches happened with both primal and original sinners) or whether they develop them over time, as they might have done had their time on earth not been cut short.

If the relevant cognitive and volitional capacities are just granted to a person, such that they find themselves from the first moment of their time in limbo capable of choosing either mortal sin or some act of personal redemption, we might well expect each inhabitant to reason in the same way, at least initially.[32] Initial deviation in volition between the inhabitants of this limbo would imply either some sort of random chance event, or some divine manipulation (e.g., God giving some a greater cognitive capacity than others), rather than such a choice being the careful product of a moral agent's deliberative decision-making process.[33] Of course, it's possible that reflection on that person's own ante-mortem first-person experiences might account for these differences (for instance, their reflection on the sheer badness of sin, as it pertained to their death).[34] Presumably, however, the moral agent in limbo had little to no choice over such ante-mortem first-person experiences, and so, if these do decisively affect their volition, it seems they will still lack the requisite agency to have chosen otherwise.

Alternatively, the relevant cognitive and volitional capacities could develop over time, just as (in the case of an infant) they would have done had their earthly life not ended prematurely.[35] Indeed, this possibility is speculatively proposed by Timpe. He writes:

> it could be that [those in Limbo] are allowed to develop as normally as resurrection bodies allow and then be extended the opportunity

for union with God once their rational faculties are sufficiently developed.

(Timpe 2015, 288)

On this account, once the inhabitant of limbo has developed to a point where they can exercise the relevant cognitive and volitional capacities, they are afforded the opportunity to make a singular decision. However, if God is in some sense hidden from them, they will not have access to *all* relevant knowledge pertinent to this decision.[36] In addition to a certain level of ignorance concerning the divine nature, they will (at the very least) lack knowledge about what it is like to commit mortal sin and what it is like to be united to God. So, although able to exercise moral agency, they will be *immature* moral agents, ignorant of things important to their decision and still (presumably) stained by original sin.[37] Thus, even if they were to cooperate in some moral redemption, their desire for God may be considerably weaker than it could have been, with any union that follows correspondingly weaker than it could have been, too.[38] More troublingly, given an accompanying claim that those stained by original sin *will*, should they live long enough, sin, one might think it more likely than not that those in limbo will freely choose to commit some mortal sin before they choose any cooperative redemption. (For a fuller exploration into possible consequences of original sin, see Wyma 2004.)

Unlike the incorporeal primal sinner, but very much like the embodied original sinners, after developing the cognitive and volitional capacities necessary for moral agency, they *would have been able* to learn new information, to grow in desire, to make mistakes, and to change their minds. To take this first decision as final would amount to God denying the (immature) inhabitant of limbo these opportunities.

Plausibly then, just as in this life, God may afford those in limbo the opportunity to grow in desire, or change their minds, even after an initial decision has been made.[39] However, whilst in one sense attractive (after all, it is remarkably reminiscent of this life on earth!), such a state of affairs comes with its own set of problems. If limbo is to be nobody's final destination, this time for deliberation must eventually conclude (for it seems a person's desire for God could continue to grow indefinitely, or could indefinitely flip between desiring union with God and desiring to separate themselves from God).[40]

Such conclusion could, of course, be timed; a person in limbo could be given, say, 70 years, with whatever state their will is in once the 70 years has elapsed considered final. But timing such a decision definitely does strike me as arbitrary—what reasons might God have for this particular allotment? Would each person have the same amount of time (fairness dictates this probably ought to be the case)? Would this limit be known by the inhabitants of limbo? If so, how might knowledge that a decision really could be put off for years affect those in limbo?[41]

Alternatively, God could wait until a person had a certain level of desire for union with, or separation from God. However again, this seems somewhat arbitrary. What level of desire is considered 'enough'? Would the levels be made public knowledge? Could a person aim to develop merely just enough desire? If so, could they keep themselves from going just too far in one direction?[42] If so, perhaps limbo will be the final destination for its indecisive inhabitants!

Given these sorts of concerns, it seems to me the most plausible cutoff point just is as it is in this earthly life, namely, that person's death.[43] At the very least, one might think that if God has orchestrated such an arrangement in this earthly life, God might do so in limbo, too. But granting this, we are faced with a new problem. If the cutoff point extends beyond the point of first decision, such that those who commit mortal sin in limbo have the opportunity to repent, how are they to deal with the guilt and shame that might (as it does in this earthly life) accompany their sin? Presumably, some form of atonement must be possible in limbo. But if so, how are the inhabitants of this limbo to make amends?

Limbo, Atonement, and Procreation

Say that a person's habitation in limbo concludes with their death, rather than their first mortal sin (or their first desire for union with God). If they remain in limbo after committing a mortal sin, it seems, just as in this life, they might have the opportunity to efficaciously atone for their sin. Further, it seems reasonable to suppose that, just as in this life, God will make some form of atonement available to them (else, they would be damned to Hell as soon as some mortal sin has been committed).[44]

What form might such atonement take? Well, an inhabitant of limbo might offer a repentant apology for their mortal sin, but it would be surprising if this apology was alone sufficient to deal with the guilt and shame that accompanies it.[45] It is part of the Christian tradition that in this earthly life, something about the life, passion, death, or resurrection of Christ is (cooperatively) added to a person's repentant apology in order to make efficacious atonement for their sin. In this life, appropriate amends *cannot* be made without such divine cooperation. Now, this is not the place to explore the nature of such cooperative atonement, but it is, I think, appropriate to question whether Christ's earthly life, passion, death, or resurrection can be pled by those in limbo.

How, for instance, might those in limbo find out about Christ's work?[46] Wherever Timpe's limbo is, it isn't here,[47] so those in limbo could not discover what Christ had done from human testimony. Rather, God must reveal it to them some other way.[48] Of course, God could do this through some form of direct revelation (e.g., a booming voice from heaven reading out the gospels), but I'm not certain God's revealing such contextless historical information could convey, for instance, the same moral example that Christ's life had in this world, let alone God's specific care for those in limbo.[49] If it could, why do otherwise in this earthly life? Why not have Christ become incarnate elsewhere in the universe, with the gospels given later as glorified just-so stories?[50] Whatever the answer one might give to such questions, I imagine the same sort of response could be employed in defense of a further incarnation in limbo, too.

In any case, just as in this life, I see no reason to think God would not interact with the inhabitants of (a prolonged) limbo in much the same way he did in this earthly world, that is, on their level, in their context, in their language. And I think this extends to thinking about both the incarnation and the atonement, too. Take for instance Aquinas's model of the incarnation. On his account, multiple incarnations are explicitly possible.[51] Granting this, if in this life it is fitting for the second person of the Trinity to become incarnate, assuming all aspects of human life in order to effect some atonement, to provide a moral example, and to demonstrate God's love for those on the earth, one might think it fitting for the second person of the Trinity to do so in limbo, too.

How might God become incarnate in limbo? Well, if part of the rationale for Christ's birth includes his exemplary growth in wisdom and stature, and his assuming all aspects of human life, plausibly, this same rationale will also apply in limbo. That is to say, if Christ's birth was an essential aspect of his earthly incarnation,[52] if the second person of the Trinity is to become incarnate in limbo, procreation must be possible in limbo, too.[53]

Procreation, Death, and Multiple Limbos: Some Implications

So, if a person's time in limbo concludes with their death, and if procreation is possible in limbo, for all we know, infant death might be possible in limbo, too. And indeed, the same sort of rationale that motivated Timpe's limbo will very likely motivate future iterations of limbo as well. So, should an infant die in limbo before developing the cognitive and volitional capacities required either to commit mortal sin or to engage in some cooperative act of personal redemption, Timpe's MLC dictates that they will find themselves in a future iteration of limbo.[54] Furthermore, if death and procreation are possible in limbo, there is no reason to think they won't be possible in every future iteration limbo, too. Possibly, then, there could be unending iterations of limbo, with the inhabitants of each iteration of limbo departing for either Heaven, Hell, or a future iteration of limbo.[55]

Such a possibility has several significant implications. I would like to focus on just one, that pertaining to there being an unending increase in the number of saints in heaven. Take Aquinas's account of the heavenly beatific life. On his account of the beatific vision, God gives each inhabitant of heaven as much union as they desire (with the depth of their union corresponding to the degree of knowledge of the divine essence each has). However, once in heaven, this desire for God that has developed in this earthly life (or, possibly, in limbo) ceases to grow, remaining instead stable. Aquinas writes:

> Of those who see the essence of God, one sees Him more perfectly than another. This, indeed, does not take place as if one had a more perfect similitude of God than another, since that vision will not spring from any similitude; but it will take place because one intellect will have a greater power or faculty to see God than another. The faculty of seeing God, however, does not belong to the created intellect naturally, but is given to it by the light of glory, which establishes the intellect in a kind of "deformity." . . .
>
> Hence the intellect which has more of the light of glory will see God the more perfectly; and he will have a fuller participation of the light of glory who has more charity; because where there is the greater charity, there is the more desire; and desire in a certain degree makes the one desiring apt and prepared to receive the object desired. Hence, he who possesses the more charity, will see God the more perfectly, and will be the more beatified.[56]

On Aquinas's view, in order for a person to know anything, there needs to be a certain union between (1) an intelligible species (by which they know that thing) and (2) their power to know (under which they know that thing). However, a person cannot come to know an infinite God through a created, and therefore finite, intelligible species. So, at the beatific vision, God instead unites with a person's intellect, with God's very essence taking the role of the intelligible species (albeit one clearly not drawn from a created phantasm). Nevertheless, such union alone is still insufficient for knowledge, so God also gifts the saint the supernatural power to know God's essence. That is, at the beatific vision God also gives the beholder a created 'light of glory,' and God gives them as much of this light as they, through their love for God, desire.

On this view, the greater a saint's love of God develops in this life (or in limbo), the greater the degree to which they will know God in the beatific vision (and so, the more intense their beatific enjoyment will be). However, this power to know a person receives from God (this 'light of glory') must be commensurate with the desire that person has to know God. If one also grants, as Aquinas does, a contemplative heavenly existence, after beholding the beatific vision, it seems a person's desire to know God remains stable (that is to say, in a contemplative beatific afterlife, nothing could increase [or decrease] their desire for God). That saint has as much of God as they desire. The only thing that could cause them to desire more of God is a greater knowledge of God, but greater knowledge of God would only be possible if God gave them a power to know that was not commensurate with their current desire to know. No doubt, of course, God could give a person a greater power to know, but to do so would be to abrogate that person's freedom of will. The person

Limbo, Hiddenness, and the Beatific Vision 357

experiencing the beatific vision has exactly as much knowledge of God as they desire. God's unconsensual gift of a greater power to know would amount to God's giving a person more of him than they desire.[57]

Given the connection Aquinas draws between knowledge and joy, the *intensity* of joy a saint in heaven experiences must remain unchanged. However, whilst their joy might not grow any more intense, it can grow *extensively*, as each saint rejoices in the joy of other saints experiencing the beatific vision.[58] In Aquinas's exposition of the Apostles Creed, he notes of those in heaven that:

> Since each one will possess all good together with the blessed, and they will love one another as themselves, and they will rejoice in the others' good as their own. It will also happen that, as the pleasure and enjoyment of one increase, so will it be for all.
> (*Symbolum Apostolorum*, A. 12)

If my participation in the life of heaven extensively increases the joy of those who died generations before I was born, I see no reason why those joining the heavenly cohort from some later iteration of limbo might not also have the same effect on my extensive enjoyment in heaven. Plausibly, then, if unending iterations of limbo lead to an unending growth in the number of saints in heaven, the joy of each saint will likewise unendingly grow in extent in a way not possible if the number of saints in heaven was fixed.[59]

Conclusion

In this chapter, I have suggested a few ways in which Timpe's Minimum Limbo Conclusion might be developed. Starting with his emphasis on the importance of the libertarian freedom of the will of those in limbo, I have argued that if Timpe's limbo exists, in order for it to achieve the end hoped for, life for those in it will, plausibly, remain quite similar to our life on earth, with these similarities extending to both procreation and death. I noted that this raises the possibility of further, indeed, unending, iterations of limbo, with inhabitants of each iteration departing either to Heaven, Hell, or some further iteration of limbo. Finally, I suggested that this might have positive consequences for the life of heaven,[60] as (at least on Aquinas's contemplative account of the life of heaven) such an unending increase in the number of those in heaven will in turn lead to an unending increase in the extensive joy of all the heavenly saints.[61]

Notes

1. *Limbus infantium*, as neither *limbus patrum* nor purgatory are taken to be possible 'final' destinations. As will become apparent, although motivated by similar concerns, the version of Limbo discussed below is fundamentally different to the traditional Christian doctrine of *limbus infantium*. Unlike

the Limbo of this paper, the Limbo of tradition is indeed a final destination, and is often (but not always) associated with state of perfect natural (but not supernatural) happiness.
2. Whatever else this stain of original sin entails, I will take it that those who remain stained are in some sense unfit for union with God. For a helpful account of the doctrine of original sin, see Couenhoven 2013.
3. Following the catechism of the Catholic church, I take it that a sin is mortal if (1) the act of sin is grave, (2) the sinner has full knowledge of the sinfulness of the act, and (3) the will of the sinner fully and deliberately consents to the action.
4. I will leave the question of whether (infant) baptism is sufficient to remove original sin to one side in this paper. If it helps, assume the infant in question in this paper was not baptized prior to their premature death.
5. For both Stump and Timpe, the removal of original sin typically requires the exercise of a higher-order cognitive capacity (for instance, wanting to want to engage in an act of personal redemption). Whilst venial sin requires only lower-order capacity, mortal sin also requires a higher-order capacity. Unlike venial sin, the mortal sinner must have full knowledge of the sinfulness of their action, and they must fully consent (will to will) to the sinful action.
6. On this score, Timpe writes:

> I am here assuming that anyone separated from God via sin, either actual or original, is in need of redemption. And this predicament is true of all humans.
>
> (2015, 279)

7. For more on this possibility, see Pinsent 2016. Pinsent suggests that what those in Limbo lack is the capacity for "second-person relatedness to God." I will leave it an open question as to what might happen to those who had the capacity to freely will personal redemption but, prior to their death, lost this capacity.
8. Whilst Timpe's paper addresses both infants and those with severe cognitive disabilities, he also includes as candidates for Limbo those who died without ever having the opportunity to reconcile with God (regardless of cognitive or volitional capacity). In this chapter, I intend only to discuss the case of infants; however, I take it that the below discussion can be expanded to include all those Timpe includes in his Limbo.
9. Given this, God cannot just join in union with those who have not had the chance to choose such union, for instance, an infant. Rather, God must remain distant (or, to some extent, hidden) until the agent is capable of, and in fact does make, such a free choice.
10. Timpe uses the following summary to describe his position:

    1. Libertarianism is true; free will exists, but is incompatible with the truth of causal or theological determinism.
    2. All humans suffer from sin (actual or original).
    3. If a human suffers from sin, then unless she is reconciled to God, she is not fit for ultimate union with God in heaven (i.e., 'redemption').
    4. Only humans who are fit for heaven will experience union with God in heaven for all eternity.
    5. Free, sinful agents cannot be determined to be reconciled to God and experience full redemption.

    (Timpe 2015, 281)

11. At the very least, the capacity to comprehend one's apparent predicament.
12. For more on what such a state of Limbo might look like, see Pinsent 2016. On Pinsent's view, those in Limbo remain incapable of a certain sort of second-personal relatedness, and so experience attachment to God, but not union with or separation from God.
13. This should be properly understood as a person freely willing *cooperation with God* in some act of personal redemption (see Timpe 2015a for more on this point). For present purposes, I will not speculate on what such cooperation might look like or involve, except that it must be freely willed by the person. I use the term 'freely will a personal redemption' to capture this element of the cooperative act, and for ease of reading.
14. Where 1, 2, 3, 4, and 5 are all theologically motivated, if somewhat controversial, premises. Timpe notes that the will's 'free exercise' is, of course, especially controversial, given that there are many theists who deny libertarian freedom of the will.
15. God's granting such might come in the form of allowing a person to gradually develop such capacities, as they may have done in this earthly life, or could be given immediately to a person.
16. One might think (8) raises questions about personal identity, but these questions are, in at least the case of infants, unproblematic. It seems the infant in Limbo who never developed the relevant capacities needed for personal redemption, *would have* developed them, had their life not been cut short, and just as that development in their earthly life should not cause us to worry about their identity, neither should this (plausibly gradual) development in Limbo cause us to worry about their identity. This question of identity might be more problematic for those who want all relevant cognitive and volition capacities to be granted *immediately* to the inhabitant of Limbo.
17. Why might this be fitting? If the natural end of man is to be united with God, God would have created a creature whose natural end *could not* have been fulfilled, and such a state of affairs would be unfitting.
18. I take establishing this as a possibility to be the first part of Timpe's argument.
19. That it is inevitable does not mean it will inevitably happen quickly, although given that those in Limbo will have the stain of original sin, and so, a proclivity to sin, it might happen more quickly than if they did not.
20. Where upon this freely willed act of personal redemption, a person would then either leave Limbo for heaven, or, if not sufficiently unified, leave Limbo for Purgatory to complete the process of their unification.
21. To be clear, Timpe's paper does not discuss the possibility of death in Limbo. I mention it here just as a possibility.
22. This is a view Eleonore Stump takes issue with (see Stump 1996). She argues that libertarian freedom of the will is compatible with a person not having the ability to do otherwise; however, if her view genuinely does rule out alternative possibilities, such a view is source compatibilism in all but name.
23. Granting the coreferency of the transcendentals, if God is the greatest being, then God is also the greatest good.
24. Alternatively, those who are guilty and shamed (as, perhaps, all those in Limbo still with the stain of original sin might be) would be unable to behold God's self-revelation. Indeed, God's manifest presence would make Limbo a hellish experience for them. See Worsley, 2019 for a development of this claim. See Stump 2018 for a persuasive account of why a person's guilt or shame might prevent a person from experiencing (or being able to behold) this revelation of God.

25. Answering the question of whether God can be loved immediately in this life, Aquinas writes:

> the act of a cognitive power is completed by the thing known being in the knower, whereas the act of an appetitive power consists in the appetite being inclined towards the thing in itself. Hence it follows that the movement of the appetitive power is towards things in respect of their own condition, whereas the act of a cognitive power follows the mode of the knower.
>
> Now in itself the very order of things is such, that God is knowable and lovable for Himself, since He is essentially truth and goodness itself, whereby other things are known and loved: but with regard to us, since our knowledge is derived through the senses, those things are knowable first which are nearer to our senses, and the last term of knowledge is that which is most remote from our senses.
>
> Accordingly, we must assert that to love which is an act of the appetitive power, even in this state of life, tends to God first, and flows on from Him to other things, and in this sense charity loves God immediately, and other things through God.
>
> (*ST* I–II, q. 27, a. 4.)

26. God created the person's will as a desire for goodness and then was revealed to that person as goodness personified.
27. In the Christian tradition, the primal sin is typically associated with Lucifer's fall, whilst the original sin is associated with Adam's fall. Regardless of historical accuracy, I will use both terms with such tradition in mind.
28. Aquinas, for instance, writes:

> Therefore, the devil's first sin was that, to attain the supernatural happiness consisting of the complete vision of God, he did not elevate himself to God so as to desire with holy angels his ultimate perfection through God's grace. Rather, he wanted to attain his ultimate perfection by the power of his own nature without God bestowing grace, although not without God acting on his nature . . . the devil sinned not by desiring something evil, but rather by desiring something good, viz., ultimate beatitude, but not in a fitting manner, that is, not in such a way as to attain it by God's grace.
>
> (*De Malo* 16.3)

See Worsley 2016; Pini 2013; Hoffmann 2012.

29. Likewise, if this account of Limbo extends to those who knew nothing of God in this life, it would be strange for this ignorance to extend into their time in Limbo.
30. We learn in the Christian tradition that this was the case with the incorporeal primal sinner. See *ST* I. Q. 63, A. 6–8 and *ST* I, Q. 57, A. 3, ad. 2.
31. That is, Limbo ought to be a place where this cognitive capacity is either developed or granted for the first time. There is also a question of identity raised if those in Limbo are incorporeal. Is the incorporeal person in Limbo really the same person as either (say) the infant that died in this earthly life, or the bodily inhabitant of Heaven? See Van Dyke 2014a for more on this problem.
32. I take it that the same would be true if all inhabitants of Limbo were incorporeal.
33. Whilst it is true that those who come to develop such cognitive and volitional capacities in this life do not reason the same way the instant they develop these capacities, there is, I take it, an important distinction between such and

the inhabitants of the Limbo so described. Namely, those who develop such capacities in this life do so after a significant period of lived (if immature) experience, becoming aware of differing pleasures and pains. Those in this Limbo do not have this unique repository of experience to call upon. I thank Kevin Timpe for pushing this point.

34. In any case, I take this to be tricky, given that they (presumably) did not experience these pre-death situations with the self-awareness and cognitive capacity needed to appropriately reflect upon them, and, presumably (especially in the case of very young infants), they could do nothing about the situations they experienced.
35. If those in Limbo are expected to develop such relevant capacities over time, do those in starting out in Limbo begin their time there in the care of angels? Or incubators? I suspect not. Rather, I imagine the situation more closely likened to that presented in Genesis 2 and 3.
36. Thereby, plausibly, removing some culpability. For more on this, see Hebrews 6:4–6.
37. Of course, even if they were allowed to mature, so long as they remain unable to behold the beatific vision, they would remain ignorant of some things pertaining to the divine nature. Nevertheless, they would come to know more.
38. If Aquinas is right, a person receives as much power to know the divine essence as they desire, with the strength of this desire directly correlating with the degree of knowledge of God received. See *ST* I, q. 12, a. 7.
39. Indeed, Timpe notes in a footnote:

    > I am not saying that there can be only one opportunity for reconciliation with God in limbo, but there can be no second-chances if there is not a first-chance. And I am primarily interested here in limbo as giving at least a first-chance.
    >
    > (2015, 283)

40. Were this not to be the case, Limbo might turn into something akin to Hell, as those who have decided to separate from God wreak havoc on those undecided.
41. One can only imagine it would affect them in the same way it would affect us, if we were told for certain we had a limited and certain time left to live.
42. Reminiscent of the problems associated with the motivation behind the 'how close can I get to sinning without actually sinning?' question.
43. This would mark Limbo out as fundamentally distinct from Heaven, Hell, or Purgatory (where in each case, there is no death). As Kevin Timpe has noted in correspondence, this view is broadly analogous to reincarnation (albeit reincarnation in a different world).
44. Indeed, regardless of whether mortal sin is committed, it seems some form of atonement must be available in order to (cooperatively) deal with the stain of original sin.
45. Assuming, of course, that guilt and shame might manifest in Limbo as they do in this life.
46. Indeed, if those in Limbo are stained with original sin, there must be *some* historical connection between Limbo and this world explaining why the inhabitants of Limbo are stained with original sin (even if they have no first-person recollection of this life).
47. Unless we opt for some version of contemporaneous reincarnation.
48. Presumably those who may otherwise have had (in this life) the cognitive capacity to process and recall details concerning Christ's earthly life, death, and resurrection, would not find themselves in Limbo.

49. Those in Limbo would, presumably, be without any context by which to understand Christ's teachings, being in a position more intractable than that facing the Ethiopian eunuch of Acts 8:31. Further, God's demonstrating his love for some other world is likely to go only so far in demonstrating his care for those in Limbo.
50. Interestingly, Kierkegaard seems to think this scenario is not problematic. See Cockayne 2015 for a detailed analysis of Kierkegaard's argument.
51. See *ST* III, Q. 3, A. 7. See also Pawl 2014, 2019, for more on the possibility of multiple incarnations.
52. The incarnation was, after all, no mere theophany.
53. Just as the possibility of death in Limbo might separate it from Heaven, Hell, and Purgatory, so does the possibility of birth. I take it that were a child to be born in Heaven, they would either immediately experience the beatific vision (and so run into the same problems discussed in my first observation), or else they would be born peccable, raising the possibility of their being sin in heaven. Likewise, I take that were a child to be born in Hell, whatever the environment of Hell turns out to be like, said child would be quite unlikely (although perhaps still possible) to choose union with God. For these reasons, God may restrict procreation in each location. However, given the similarity between the Limbo under consideration and this present life, if procreation is permitted now, I see no further overriding reason why it might not be so in Limbo, too.
54. Indeed, for all we know, our own earthly life may just be one such iteration of Limbo, begun when just two persons died in infancy in some previous iteration!
55. If we grant Timpe's developmental model of Limbo, that is, that the requisite cognitive and volitional capacities are developed by a person in Limbo over time, one unlucky person might end up in multiple iterations of Limbo (although, presumably, they will only experience one birth).
56. *ST* I, Q. 12, A. 6.
57. With this in mind, Christina van Dyke notes:

   > Differences in our will's dispositions and affections that were formed over the course of our earthly lives thus appear to have a lasting effect. In the beatific vision, our wills rest in eternal and perfect enjoyment of the ultimate end, but the degree of that unchanging enjoyment depends on how we have disposed our wills in this life.
   >
   > (Van Dyke 2015, 275)

58. Some, like Christopher Brown, have argued that others in Heaven can help one know more of God, such that one's enjoyment grows in intensity, however this is not Aquinas's position. Brown writes:

   > enjoying God in the society of friends affords [someone in Heaven] more ways to see the beauty and goodness of God than before, i.e., not only from his own perspective as a 'foot' of Christ's body, but now also from the perspective of a 'hand,' 'eye,' 'ear,' etc. In other words, [one] can see God's essence not only through his own experience of God—naturally colored by his own life's journey, but also through the eyes of friends in Christ who saw a different aspect of God because of their own distinctive vocations, stories, and crosses.
   >
   > (Brown 2009, 240)

59. It seems procreation in Heaven ought to be ruled out, as any children born there would not have access to the beatific vision (if they did, they would not

be able to desire other than union with God, and so such union either cannot obtain, or would remain forever weak), and so could, in theory, commit mortal sin. And it seems to me that the life of Heaven ought to be incompatible with the presence of any mortal (or venial) sin.
60. One might think such a conclusion repugnant if this also unendingly increases the number of those in Hell. However, I'm not sure if this will prove as troubling to those who do not find the general idea of a populated Hell repugnant.
61. Of course, one might also take this conclusion to be a *reductio* of Timpe's Limbo. I would like to thank Blake Hereth and Kevin Timpe for their excellent comments on an earlier draft of this chapter.

References

Brown, Christopher. "Friendship in Heaven: Aquinas on Supremely Perfect Happiness and the Communion of the Saints." In *Metaphysics and God: Essays in Honor of Eleonore Stump*, edited by Kevin Timpe, 225–248. London and New York: Routledge, 2009.

Cockayne, Joshua. "Empathy and Divine Union in Kierkegaard: Solving the Faith/History Problem in Philosophical Fragments." *Religious Studies* 51.4 (2015): 455–476.

Couenhoven, Jesse. *Stricken by Sin, Cured by Christ: Agency, Necessity, and Culpability in Augustinian Theology*. Oxford: Oxford University Press, 2013.

Hoffmann, Tobias. "Theories of Angelic Sin from Aquinas to Ockham." In *A Companion to Angels in Medieval Philosophy*, edited by Tobias Hoffman, 283–316. Leiden and Boston: Brill, 2012.

Murray, Michael J. "Coercion and the Hiddenness of God." *American Philosophical Quarterly* 30.1 (1993): 27–38.

Pawl, Timothy. "Thomistic Multiple Incarnations." *The Heythrop Journal* 6 (2014): 359–370.

———. *In Defence of Extended Conciliar Christology: A Philosophical Essay*. Oxford: Oxford University Press, 2019.

Pini, Giorgio. "What Lucifer Wanted: Anselm, Aquinas, and Scotus on the Object of the First Evil Choice." In *Oxford Studies in Medieval Philosophy: Volume 1*, edited by Robert Pasnau, 61–82. Oxford: Oxford University Press, 2013.

Pinsent, Andrew. "Limbo and the Children of Faerie." *Faith and Philosophy* 33.3 (2016): 293–310.

Stump, Eleonore. "Libertarian Freedom and the Principle of Alternative Possibilities." In *Faith, Freedom, and Rationality: Philosophy of Religion Today*, edited by Daniel Howard-Snyder and Jeff Jordan, 73–88. Lanham, MD: Rowman and Littlefield, 1996.

———. *Wandering in Darkness: Narrative and the Problem of Suffering*. Oxford: Oxford University Press, 2010.

———. *Atonement*. Oxford: Oxford University Press, 2018.

Timpe, Kevin. "Cooperative Grace, Cooperative Agency." *European Journal for Philosophy of Religion* 7.3 (2015a): 223–245.

———. "An Argument for Limbo." *Journal of Ethics* 19 (2015b): 277–292.

Van Dyke, Christina. "I See Dead People: Disembodied Souls and Aquinas's 'Two-Person' Problem." In *Oxford Studies in Medieval Philosophy: Volume Two*, 25–45. Oxford: Oxford University Press, 2014.

———. "Aquinas's Shiny Happy People: Perfect Happiness and the Limits of Human Nature." In *Oxford Studies in the Philosophy of Religion: Volume Six*, edited by Jonathan Kvanvig, 269–292. Oxford: Oxford University Press, 2015.

Worsley, David. "Could There Be Suffering in Paradise? On the Primal Sin, the Beatific Vision, and Suffering in Paradise." *The Journal of Analytic Theology* 4 (2016): 87–105.

———. "(Affective) Union in Hell." *Religious Studies* 55.2 (2019): 261–278.

Wyma, Keith D. "Innocent Sinfulness, Guilty Sin: Original Sin and Divine Justice." In *Christian Faith and the Problem of Evil*, edited by Peter van Inwagen, 263–276. Grand Rapids, MI: Wm. B. Eerdmans, 2004.

16 Religious Racial Formation Theory and Its Metaphysics
A Research Program in the Philosophy of Religion

Sameer Yadav

Introduction

That race and religion have a long and sordid history in the US is not news to anyone in our society. Or rather, it is news to everyone, insofar as headlines about the latest racial unrest or expression of racist political attitudes regarding immigration, economics, war, and policing are often linked with white Christian culture, and particularly white evangelicalism.[1] Such alleged links warrant more than merely standing within the crossfire of political punditry directed from opposing poles on an overly simplistic ideological spectrum, or merely sidestepping the claims at issue. Rather, if we are going to understand and evaluate the merits of an intersection between Christian group identity and various forms of racism, what is needed is a research program. At present, however, the resources for identifying such a program and describing what it might consist in lays strewn across the landscape of many distinct academic disciplines, lacking any integrated framework that might coordinate them.

Religious studies scholars, historians and sociologists of religion, and theologians have suggested that there is an intimate relationship between the historically lived expression of Christian faith and practice and the creation and maintenance of a race-based ordering of society that systematically privileges whites over non-whites. But even though analytic philosophers of religion remain predominantly philosophers of *Christianity*—with the vast majority of these being philosophers who hold to some form of traditional Christian faith and practice—they have largely neglected the task of theorizing a race-religion intersection.[2] By and large, Christian philosophers of religion and analytic theologians seem to have supposed that such a task is a matter of religious ethics that belongs far downstream of the central metaphysical questions about what the religious realities are to which Christians ought to be ontologically committed, or what they ought to regard as knowable about such realities.[3] On the other hand, analytic philosophers outside of philosophy of religion working on the ontology of social categories such as gender, sexuality, and race have identified several controversial questions in the metaphysics of social reality that are upstream of the questions of applied ethics in an order of explanation (see, for example, Barnes 2016; Haslanger 2012). How we ought to inhabit, maintain, or revise these social categories depends at least in part on what they are and what they can do. But even when the focus of analysis is the peculiar manifestation of race-thinking in Western and North American society, analytic philosophers of race have had virtually nothing to say about its intersection with religion in general or Christianity in particular.

Given these lacunae, the goal of this chapter is modest. I shall not aim to offer any substantive theory of the race-religion intersection. What I seek to do in what follows is simply to draw together these distinct disciplinary contributions—social-historical, philosophical, and normative-theological—into a single integrated framework within which the resources of each can be brought to bear on the others. I call that framework "religious racial formation theory," and I claim that the work of specifying a determinate religious racial formation theory is not merely a sociological and historical task but a necessarily philosophical one. In the first section below, I gather together various historical, social scientific, and theological studies under a common banner of "religious racial formation theory" that suggests that there is an intimate connection between Western Christian faith and practice and a race-based social order of white supremacy. In the second section, I go on to show how religious racial formation theory thus understood remains necessarily indeterminate apart from the specification of its metaphysics. I then detail what sorts of metaphysical determinations are required in order to yield an adequate explanation of the intersection uncovered by the sociohistorical data summarized in the first section. Taken together, my outlining of a research program in religious racial formation theory and the issues and stakes of properly interpreting its metaphysics constitutes what Nathaniel Goldberg has called an act of "conceptual cartography"—i.e., a "practice of mapping how concepts generally (including philosophical views) relate conceptually (including logically and extralogically)" (Goldberg 2017, 123).

Religious Racial Formation Theory

Racial Formation Theory

As a basic methodological orientation for analyzing contemporary notions of race in the US Omi and Winant's influential sociological framework of "racial formation theory" (hereafter, RFT) provides a useful point of departure. The idea of "racial formation" according to Omi and Winant is "the sociohistorical process by which racial identities are created, lived out, transformed, and destroyed" (Omi and Winant 2015, 109). On their analysis, this process involves what Paul Taylor summarizes as both "semantic and structural aspects," which are really two sides of the same coin, or rather two discernible signals in a feedback loop, each one informing and shaping the other (Taylor 2013, 25).[4] The semantic side involves the sociohistorical process by which we "assign meaning to human bodies and bloodlines" and the structural side involves the process by which we "distribute social goods along the lines laid down by the resultant systems of meaning" (Taylor 2013, 24). Whenever "a previously racially unclassified relationship, social practice, or group" comes to acquire a racial meaning, that relationship, practice, or group has become "racialized" (Omi and Winant 2015, 111). Racial projects on Omi and Winant's approach, are just any particular human activities that can be accurately described as engaged in the semantic or structural side of creating, living out, transforming, or destroying racial categories—whether or not we recognize them as such. The various (and not always consistent) meanings of racial group membership that we now recognize and the distribution of social goods indexed to those meanings in our contemporary context are explicable as the result of some identifiable shifts in prior configurations of the semantics and structure of racial categories.

Because RFT understands racial categories in terms of whence they've come and where they are going, it naturally emphasizes "the *instability* of the race concept" as one that is "constantly made and remade in everyday life" (Omi and Winant 2012, 307; see also Moya and Markus 2010). As Taylor has recently noted, RFT has faced criticism for giving too central a place to the power of political authorities as the primary determining force behind the relevant semantic and structural shifts that have produced our contemporary conception of racial categories. In addition to worrying about this commitment to the "primacy of the political" in their sociological explanations (Omi and Winant 2012, 307), there have been those scholars specializing in the particular periods, social movements, or cultural dimensions that figure in Omi and Winant's account of the history of racial formation who have taken issue with various aspects of their narrative (see, e.g., Hesse 2016; Singh 2012). Finally, as a paradigm for understanding contemporary racial categories, RFT has been challenged by Joe Feagin's alternative sociological approach. Feagin takes Omi and Winant to give insufficient analysis of the underlying racism behind processes of racial formation in "the West,"[5] as well as obscuring the underlying *stability* of white supremacy as a consistent and durable frame that governs many diverse paths of racial formation (Feagin 2013; Feagin and Elias 2013). But as Taylor rightly notes, it is possible to take these sorts of worries on board not as reasons to reject RFT, but as "friendly amendments" (Taylor 2016). The most important contribution of RFT is more formal than material.

RFT takes a non-reductive and genealogical approach to the social construction of race. RFT is non-reductive insofar as claims that once racial categories have been created, their social meanings and effects cannot be understood in any fundamentally non-racial terms—like gender, sex, or class, race is a "master category" (Omi and Winant 2015, viii). RFT approaches race genealogically insofar as it seeks to understand the creation and development of the semantic and structural aspects of racial categories as endpoints of some discernible path of social change. For any given context in which racial categories have been constructed, a good answer to the question "what is race?" for that context consists in citing some prior stage of racial meanings and its social effects that gives rise to those of the target stage, and describing the mechanisms by which the former generates the latter. That approach is entirely compatible with many different and competing genealogies of racial categories and analyses of the relevant social forces that explain the relevant semantic and structural shifts. Taylor's more 'formalist' takeaway from Omi and Winant therefore gives us a conception of RFT that leaves all of this open.

Having distinguished the formal from material dimensions of RFT, it becomes possible to recognize a good deal of recent religious studies and theological scholarship as engaged in offering a substantive theory of racial formation in the US via colonial Christian Europe. According to this steadily growing literature, the semantics and structure of our racial categories have been most centrally determined by evolutions in the semantics and structure of Christian religious identity, from its earliest development to its subsequent European and contemporary American cultural expressions. This literature is not internally uniform—it treats many different periods, figures, and places and gives various and sometimes competing accounts of how Christianity contributes to creating or shaping the formation of Western racial categories and their systematic effects. Nevertheless, what unites it as a body of scholarly literature is that it offers non-reductive genealogical accounts of race and cites Christianity as a primary explainer of the creation or shifts in racial formation, requiring a fundamentally religious understanding of what race was as a key for understanding what it is in the European and North American context. In contrast to Omi and Winant's claim about the "primacy of the political" in racial formation, the class of literature grouped above as smaller scale components of an overarching RFT implies a "primacy of the religious."

Let's call this explanatory emphasis on Christianity in the formation of race *religious* racial formation theory, or RRFT. RRFT studies in ancient Christianity trace the birth of Western race-thinking to Christianity's departure from Judaism. RRFT studies in European and American colonial Christianity argue that formations of Christian group identity and formations of racial group identity in these contexts significantly intersect and exert a mutually determining influence on one another. Studies focusing on early modern to contemporary secular society have sought to show that while race has taken on a life of its own apart from its Christian religious patrimony, the life it now lives in some important sense continues to be sustained by an underlying framework structured by Christian faith and reflective of it, even if only implicitly.[6] The burden of the second section of this chapter ("The Metaphysics of Religious Racial Formation Theory") will be to demonstrate that an RRFT of this sort is ripe for philosophical exploration by philosophers of religion no less than philosophers of race. But in order to see how that might be, it will prove useful to have before us at least the rudiments of a substantive RRFT, a material specification of its form.

Religion in a Genealogy of Racial Formation

A comprehensive literature review is not possible here, much less an overarching account of how the various area and period studies in that literature might fit together into any overarching or composite genealogy that counts as a full blown genealogy.[7] I will therefore content myself with an illustrative sketch. As an organizing scheme, I'll borrow Paul Taylor's useful structure for the kind of story we find in mainstream RFT. Taylor identifies a wide-angled genealogical narrative of Western racial formation developing into what it is in the contemporary US context in four successive acts: the naturalizing of ethnic difference into distinct human kinds called "races," the rationalizing of white racial dominance, the politicization and decline in that dominance, and a less overtly coercive and "post-racial" mode of maintaining hierarchically arranged racial identities (Taylor 2013, 72). Each of these names a large-scale stage of development from the ancient world to the present that purports to explain how a contemporary semantics and structure of race in the US has come to be what it is. But while Taylor's summary offers a nice overview of a mainstream RFT, it is not an RRFT, for the simple reason that religion does not play a fundamental explanatory role as the primary mechanism of naturalization, rationalization, politicization, or post-racialization. Therefore, in order to suggest how an RRFT might go, I offer a modified narrative of Taylor's stages citing just a few relevant studies that purport to show the primacy of Christian group identity in an explanation of each of the four semantic and structural shifts.

Taylor follows many others in tracing the emergence of Western notions of race to a particular form of ethnocentrism widely exhibited as a general feature of many ancient societies. Whereas ethnocentrism consists in an "over-reading" of real and imagined out-group traits by an in-group and exaggerating their depth and extent of difference in order to assign negative meanings and social implications to out-group members in virtue of those differentiations, our now familiar Western notions of "race" emerged as a particular way that colonial European societies *naturalized* their ethnocentrism (Taylor 2013, 18–23). Taylor follows many others in tracing the birth of the naturalized notion of races to the 15th-century horse-breeding practices of Spain. The discovery of breeding as a way to target desirable traits and eliminate undesirable traits in horses was used to explain the lingering suspicions of Spaniards about the genuineness of Jewish and Moorish (Muslim) "conversions" to Christianity that accompanied their conquest and incorporation into imperial Christian culture. There was "still something deeply different about the *conversos* and the *moriscos*, something carried, as it were, in the blood" (Taylor 2013, 39). This "naturalization of social status is ... one of the key moments in the shift from anti-Judaism, a theological posture, to anti-Semitism, a race-based prejudice" (Taylor 2013, 39).

There are, however, scholars of early Christianity who offer significant evidence for placing this transition much earlier, arising from a mechanism much more centrally from Christian theology than discoveries drawn from horse breeding. For example, Matthew Thiessen argues that the form of religious group identity exhibited in the New Testament was already a naturalization of social status (Thiessen 2016). The Apostle Paul construes the Jew/Gentile distinction as precisely a distinction of God-ordained nature into two distinct human kinds distinguished by relations of bodily descent. The mode of Gentile inclusion into the privileged social status of the Jew made possible by Christ, on Theissen's reading, is one that imparts the "correct" relations of bodily descent requisite to divine favor by a means other than sexual reproduction—namely, by being given the "Spirit of Christ" who is the "Seed of Abraham" as a mechanism of transforming Gentile humanity into the correct *kind* of human, one requisite for salvation (Thiessen 2016, 105–160; see also Frederickson 2018, 26–28). The governing influence of the Spirit on the body, Paul held, can more effectively transform the nature of Gentile humanity than the mere "cosmetic surgery" of circumcision demanded by his "Judaizing" opponents (Thiessen 2016, 121). Moreover, Denise Kimber Buell's reading of second- and third-century Christian communities confirms at least the plausibility of Thiessen's proposal as a matter of reception history.[8]

Buell shows how early Christian uses of the 'ethnic' terms of peoplehood (*ethne*, *laos*, *genos*) suggests a kind of naturalized conception of Christians as a distinct 'kind' of human. Christians are, alongside Jews and various sorts of Gentile heathen, a 'new race' which was superior to both non-Christian and Jewish kinds, with conversion and baptism constituting not a *contrast* to relations of natural bodily descent but alternative (miraculous, or supernatural) *mechanisms* of bodily descent (see Buell 2005; Buell 2009a, 2009b). The conversion of Constantine and subsequent development of an anti-pagan, anti-Semitic imperial Christian culture in medieval Europe and early modern Spain thus represents not merely precursors to a racial anthropology, but developments within an already religious-racial anthropology (Heng 2018). That anthropology was not *replaced by* but rather *codified within* Liennaeus's 18th-century development (subsequently developed by Blumenbach) of the color-coded taxonomy of the four races and their aboriginal geographies (the white European, the yellow/brown Asian, red Amerindian, and the black African). As Willie Jennings has shown, during this evolution of naturalizing racial distinctions, "whiteness" and "Christian" were regarded as not merely contingently or accidentally connected, but rather as internally related and naturally "fitting" or suited to one another via a doctrinally well-developed Christian social imagination (Jennings 2010).

A second stage in the formation of racial categories is marked by a rapid acceleration in the *rationalization* of European white supremacy, which comes to pervade every register of society in Europe and its colonies by the time of the late 18th century. This is what Taylor refers to as the ascendency of a "high modern" or "classical racialist" regime in Europe and North America that would persist until the early 20th century (Taylor 2013, 37). It is marked by the widespread presumption of white superiority and dominance in the infrastructure and discourse of practically every social, political, and economic register from popular culture to the intellectual elite. Taylor follows many others in emphasizing the role of philosophical and scientific discourses in rationalizing the nature and role of white supremacy across these registers of European and North American society. Whereas Blumenbach had proposed the "monogenist" thesis that our common descent from Adam resulted in racial differentiation through the long-term exogenous impacts of climate, geography, and culture on breeding populations that separated races from one another by "insensible degrees," this came to be replaced by a Darwinian "polygenist" thesis proposing a fixed, rigid racial typology exhibited by the "one drop" rule (Taylor 2013, 40–42). But whereas Taylor characterizes scientific discourse as *replacing* religious discourse in the structure of racial rationalization, Terence Keel shows how the 19th-century polygenist thesis that stood behind the rigid delineation of races in the typological synthesis was "buttressed by Christian ideas about the supernatural origins of life, the stable heredity of racial traits, and the inherent order of nature" notwithstanding claims of scientific objectivity and a disavowal of reliance on biblical revelation (Keel 2018, 18). Keel further traces out many ways in which early 20th-century scientific developments of biological determinism about race play the same conceptual roles previously played by "the God concept" and a "theological view of nature" in earlier ways of fixing human typology (Keel 2018, 55–82).

Likewise, in *The Arrogance of Faith*, Forrest Wood documents how the mainstream in abolitionist and slaveholding reasoning alike arose out of a theological anthropology committed to both the genuine humanity of non-whites as made in the image of God and the inferiority of non-whites as requiring white governance for the sake of achieving a divinely ordained social order. Far from challenging these claims, abolitionists challenged the morality of slaveholding as a permissible practice predicated on them (Wood 1990, 237–244; Haynes 2015). It is precisely this theological common ground shared with their slaveholding brethren that motivates Reconstruction-era white Christians to prioritize reunification of white churches divided over abolition and explains widespread agreements among whites during Jim Crow segregation that miscegenation or "race-mixing" is a public health issue that violates God's natural order and thus requires criminalization by the state for the sake of a healthy population. The forms of social engineering motivated by scientific progress were guided by the social visions of divinely ordered human community cultivated in the racialist imagination of Christendom, abstracted to a greater or lesser degree from traditional and explicit Christian confession (Wood 1990, 20). In these ways, earlier forms of Christian theological reasoning about race were therefore not abandoned in favor of secular-scientific reasoning but rather mediated implicitly within scientific and political discourses.

The third shift in the meaning and function of 'race' in US society is marked by the decline of "classical racialism" through the politicization of racial categories that culminates in civil rights legislation and an official repudiation of a white supremacist regime. The scientific rationale for distinguishing racial types led to a hierarchy among whites with Anglo-Saxon descent being privileged over Celts and Slavs in the US and UK (Taylor 2013, 71). Since the first US naturalization statute only granted status to whites among "whites, blacks and Indians," there arose legal battles among non-Anglo-Saxon whites and Asian Indians fighting to establish that they ought to legally count as 'white'—the former generally succeeded and the latter generally failed (Taylor 2013, 45–57). But the ability to contend for ancestral whiteness among those who didn't 'look white' resulted in a break of racial rationalization from scientific definition making the 'free white person' a matter of what the 1923 Supreme Court decision in *US vs. Thind* calls "common understanding." But it was precisely 'common sense' intuitions of white supremacy that were undermined in public consciousness through witnessing the horrors of the Holocaust. The disciplinary development of the social sciences made possible the 1951 UNESCO statement, a high-profile repudiation of classical racialism as pseudo-science debunked by social science. These factors created needed traction for social and political resistance movements—including the American civil rights movement—to push Western nations to give up their colonies, and abolish apartheid-style systems of race-based labor exploitation (Taylor 2013, 73). As evidenced by, e.g., the 1965 Moynahin Report on *The Negro Family*, however, the "new racism" that emerged out of the rejection of the earlier pseudo-scientific polygenism represents a kind of fallback on the previous monogenism, with racial identity being a matter of "culture," now apparently divorced from theology and rooted in a social science (Taylor 2013, 75).

As Kelly Brown Douglas argues, however, "the narrative of Anglo-Saxon exceptionalism" that characterizes the politicization of race "is a religious narrative, be it the narrative of civil religion or Protestant evangelicalism" (Douglas 2015, 42). Douglas shows how the doctrine of Anglo-Saxon supremacy among white races and the resulting taxonomic contestations that Taylor cites were driven by the notion of whiteness as a *sacred possession*, a natural property "set apart" by God as holy and elect, chosen for a divine vocation (Douglas 2015, 3–47; see also Harris 1993). Douglas thus extends the same sort of argument we find in Keel about the implicitly Christian theological structure of racial reasoning and its effects. Douglas likewise analyzes secular social arrangements as structured by an underlying theological anthropology installed by our society's white Christian past that remains preserved in the institutions and discourses it put in place. In *Beloved Community*, Charles Marsh details the flip side, that the challenge to white supremacy in earliest civil rights movements was essentially a religious challenge to white Christian orthodoxy on the part of an alternative Christian social vision nurtured by the black church—one which likewise subsequently underwent a process of secular abstraction (Marsh 2005). As Keel claims regarding the scientific domain, so too for the political, Douglas and Marsh differently show how a movement away from the overt Christian reasoning in the secularization of racial discourse is one that retains its basic conceptual roles and structure.

Finally, Taylor identifies our present notion of racial categories as "postracial"—race is "aestheticized" and "flattened" to signify marks of "merely" ethnic and cultural differences appreciable in the absence of any affirmation or approval of white privilege (Taylor 2013, 76–77). Alongside this "multicultural" transformation of racial categories that now blocks the path to any mainstream claims of white supremacy, however, historically established and durable institutions built upon white supremacy have been adjusted rather than disbanded, being incentivized toward "minimizing the costs of maintaining themselves, by accommodating and co-opting resistance" (Taylor 2013, 76). The co-opting rather than crushing of dissent marks what Taylor describes as the shift from a predominantly violent and "dominating" rule of whites over non-whites by brute force to a predominantly "hegemonic" rule by consent (Taylor 2013, 76). Contemporary racial categories are thus tied to the dynamics of earlier racial projects in promoting racial disparities of white privilege while also being forced into new racial projects bound to less explicitly race-based discourses that nevertheless continue to track racial difference, such as the projects and discourses tied to class, nation, culture, ethnicity (Taylor 2013, 81–86).

Like Thiessen, Buell, Keel, and Douglas, J. Kameron Carter argues that the post-racial meaning and effects of our racial categories are driven by an inner logic that is distinctively Christian in vintage. Post-racial America is a kind of eschatological "afterlife" of classical racialism (Carter 2014). Vincent Lloyd similarly suggests a kind of "already/not yet" structure of Christian eschatology in which God's promised and idealized future of human peace and reconciliation has begun to be realized here and now in the racial reconciliation of American multicultural society as a witness to the world and in anticipation of a future fulfillment (Lloyd 2018, 198–215). Our national vocation of healing our past racial wrongs in anticipation of a genuinely multicultural age to come demands of us a particular form of discipleship; namely, one that accepts a post-racial disavowal and denial of classical racialism. But in much the way that Christian Smith and Michael Emerson describe of evangelical Christian church communities in America, secular society engages in its version of multicultural discipleship without any widespread evidence of a "cultural toolkit" capable of acknowledging, challenging, or uprooting racially coded patterns of advantage and disadvantage that persist.[9] Granting an ongoing power of a white supremacist past amounts to heresy of faith and practice. On Carter's account, it is not merely that the religious domain of Christian theology coincidentally happens to exhibit some isomorphism with a distinct secular domain of post-racial politics—rather, they are isomorphic precisely because, as in the past so too in the present, they do not name entirely distinct anthropological norms.[10]

It is easy to see in the above genealogy the lineaments of a research program: that of filling out particular narratives from each period and stitching them together into an evolutionary account of the entanglement of Christian religious identity with race. Less clear, however, is how the description of this entanglement might constitute a research program for *philosophers* of race and religion. It seems rather like the relevant work to be done is for historians, sociologists, and religious studies scholars to do—they are the ones best qualified to determine in what ways the proposed racial-religious intersection needs to be further substantiated, challenged, or developed. What is left for philosophers to work out? Quite a lot.

The Metaphysics of Religious Racial Formation Theory

Social Groups: Causal Histories and Constitution

Defining the explanatory scope and significance of an RRFT requires more than merely documenting genealogies of the sort sketched above. Beyond a social or intellectual history, we require a metaphysics that specifies what kinds of social realities 'Christianity' and 'race' purport to pick out in any given RRFT—as well as how the properties ascribed to each social category ground the explanatory claims an RRFT makes about the relationship between them. In the absence of this sort of theorizing, no amount of sociological or historical information will be sufficient to tell us either what an RRFT explains or what its purported mechanism of explanation is. A simple thought experiment can show

how an RRFT genealogy of the sort suggested above might nevertheless remain metaphysically underdetermined, and what sort of philosophical work is required to clarify its explanatory reach and power.

Suppose you are walking along the beach when down from the heavens descends a condensate mist. Much to your surprise, the mist speaks to you, informing you that it is an alien being with keen interest in human life forms, and particularly wishing to understand our apparently strange form of embodiment and locomotion. Directing you to the trail of footprints in the sand behind you, the alien observes that you seem to be leaving these markings behind as you move, and it requests an explanation of them. You might respond by giving the alien an account of the causal history that explains how these marks got there. This would include all manner of facts about the marks considered as impressions caused by the striking of your feet against the sand. This could get rather involved, including all the properties about you and this particular stretch of sand required to explain how impressions of just this sort came into being— e.g., your mass; the surface area of your foot; its angle, trajectory, and velocity in striking; the composition of the sand; its precisely patterned displacement; etc. Still, even with an exhaustive knowledge of this causal history—a comprehensive explanation of how these marks got here—the alien might nevertheless remain uninformed about *what the marks are*. It is consistent with knowing how these marks were made to remain ignorant of the fact *that they* are *footprints*, or of the relevant facts *constitutive* of being a footprint.[11]

Even when provided with the fact that these marks are called 'footprints' and a detailed understanding of how they were made, our alien could still sensibly wonder what it takes for anything to *count as* a footprint—must an impression left behind by a human have the same shape and patterns of sand displacement as these marks to count as a footprint? How different can they be and still be footprints? Must such marks be left behind by a human, or can other beings have footprints? Must the marks be made by displacing the surfaces struck by one's foot, or can impressions be made in other ways? Does it count as a footprint if its causal history does not include the striking of a foot at all but only something that *looks like* a foot has struck, like a foot-shaped rock? Do any ambulatory strikes on the ground which are not made by feet count? What if, e.g., they're made by objects with the *function* of a foot (e.g., prosthetics, peg-legs)? What is the subsequent status footprints in relation to the beings that made them? Suppose that the alien's misty embodiment is such that any condensation it leaves behind remains constitutive of its embodiment—are footprints likewise, it might reasonably wonder, extensions of a human body? Or do we have natural rights over them as 'belonging' to us? A mere causal history explaining where these marks in fact came from and how they were made—no matter how exquisitely detailed—answers none of these questions.[12] Of course, an account of what anyone's particular footprints are will necessarily *include* these facts about their causal history. But it will also go beyond them by assigning various roles to the facts provided by such a history that identify the contribution that they make to constitute these marks as the sort of thing they are.

When it comes to the social categories of Christianity and race in the West, we are in the position of the alien, and what an RRFT's genealogies of the sort I've summarized above succeed in giving us is for the most part a *causal history* of those categories. In some perhaps surprising ways it shows us how the meanings and functions of religious and racial group identity have evolved alongside one another in an intimate relationship. What it does not for the most part tell us, at least not in any careful or systematic way, is what constitutes a Christian group or a racial group at any given stage of an RRFT, and thus what the nature of the purported relationship is. While RRFT genealogies often purport to show how racial and religious group identities are presently constituted in light of their past, they do not tell us precisely what it is *about* their past that fixes their present constitution.

Epsteinian and Haslangerian Desiderata

More precisely, there are at least four features constitutive of social groups that RRFT studies of the sort I mention above fail to make fully explicit, each of which is necessary for properly interpreting the claims and consequences of that literature. Each of the four features belongs to a comprehensive framework for analyzing the metaphysics of social groups recently developed by Brian Epstein (2017).[13] On Epstein's framework, any kind of social group can be characterized as having four basic dimensions or 'profiles.' First, a 'construction profile' describes the criteria for identifying any group as belonging to some group kind. The job of such criteria is to tell us under what conditions a collection of individuals constitutes members of a social group of the relevant kind (whether a garage band, a faculty committee, or a race), and the conditions under which any group of that kind comes to exist or continues to exist. The point of elaborating this profile is that it provides us with sufficient information about the identity conditions of a given group-kind such that, for any two social groups, whether or not they are groups of the same or different kinds (Epstein 2017, 15). For example, what is it in virtue of which ancient Christians and modern whites both count as 'races' on an RRFT while, say, ancient Buddhists, do not?

Second, Epstein distinguishes an 'extra essentials' profile that determines what features beyond the identity criteria of membership in and persistence of a group-kind are necessary for making any group of that kind what it is, e.g., the rights, obligations, permissions, powers, and abilities conferred by or upon the group or its members as such. Sometimes these sorts of features are criteria of membership in a group-kind and hence features of a construction profile. For example, perhaps having some minimal threshold of visual acuity is a criterion for membership in the group of commercial airline pilots. In such cases, one cannot give sufficient identity conditions for any group's being a group of this kind apart from a reference to the relevant visual ability. In other cases, however, it might be that certain rights, powers, etc. are *essentially associated* with a group-kind without being criteria for the identity conditions for being a group of that kind. Epstein cites the example of being able to give sufficient identity and persistence conditions for any group's constituting a marriage that can be satisfied with reference to "signing papers, or going through a ceremony," etc. and without reference to "the many other powers and limitations, rights and obligations" that may nevertheless be essential properties associated with "married people" as the particular kind of social group it is (Epstein 217, 28).

Third, Epstein identifies an 'anchor' profile that determines *why* any group has the construction profile it does, such as the events, institutions, conventions, etc. that fix the facts about what counts as the identity conditions and essential characteristics for that kind of group (Epstein 2017, 36–39).[14] Like added essentials, the anchors that establish what will count as a social group of a particular kind may or may not belong to other profiles as well. Conceivably, some particular kind of group K might have anchors responsible for its coming about as the kind of group it is which are also features constitutive of the identity of K or essential characteristics of K. On the other hand, there might be anchors that explain why K has the identity conditions or necessary characteristics it does, while not forming any part of those identity conditions or necessary characteristics. For example, it might be that Constantine's conversion is among the anchoring features that put in place the identity conditions for colonial Christendom, even if Constantine's conversion is neither constitutive of membership in colonial Christendom or an essential characteristic of it.

The construction profile constitutive of colonial Christendom as a kind of Christian social group and its added essentials could have been just what they are even if many of the contingent historical circumstances that were in fact responsible for configuring those profiles as they are had been very different. Perhaps the contribution of Constantine's conversion in fixing various features of the construction profile might just as well have been fixed by some other counterfactual circumstance, like Nero's conversion. In such cases, a group-kind's anchors might belong to what Epstein distinguishes as its 'accident' profile, which determines the properties of a group that might be salient for understanding a group without being essentially defining of its identity or essentially characteristic features (Epstein 2017, 39–40). Whereas some anchoring features of a given group-kind might also be included in an accident profile in this way, there are a host of other merely accidental features associated with a

378 *Sameer Yadav*

particular kind of social group that are not constituent in any of the other profiles but nevertheless crucial for understanding that group-kind. If we are seeking to assess how the causal histories or genealogies of any given set of social groups determine what those groups are and how they relate to one another, we can do so by analyzing what role these genealogical facts play in filling out each of these profiles of those groups.

The genealogical facts conveyed by an RRFT can therefore be analyzed according to the particular kinds of roles they play in explaining what makes Western Christian social groups or racial groups the particular kinds of groups that they are.[15] For example, we can read Thiessen and Buell to imply that a Christian theology that unites a doctrine of divine election to ancestral lineage as a taxonomy for distinguishing human kinds is an anchor for Western racial identity—such a theology puts into place a distinction of human kinds determined by bodily descent as an identity condition constitutive of membership for racial groups. But unlike the Constantine example above, a Christian theology of election is not an *accidental* anchor but an *essential* one, insofar as it fixes the identity conditions for race by itself forming part of identity conditions for racial group membership in its construction profile. Some genealogical facts might thus contribute essentially to Western Christian or racial group belonging by contributing simultaneously to its construction, added essentials, and anchor profiles, with others figuring in two or only one of these profiles, or in none of them as an accident of the relevant kind of group formation. A metaphysics of RRFT minimally involves resolving ambiguities in the Epsteinian roles played by the details of its proposed genealogy.

A comparative analysis of Epstein's profiles for both Christian and racial kinds of social groups for any given period identified in an RRFT can reveal the precise respects in which the social categories of Christianity and race *intersect*. The kind of intersection of Christianity and race proposed by an RRFT can be construed as any overlap between Epsteinian profiles exhibited by both kinds of groups—a description of the way in which the anatomy of one group-kind is constituent in the anatomy of the other. Differing ways of resolving the many ambiguous explanatory roles played by the facts in an RRFT's genealogy therefore result in substantially different theories of the race-religion intersection implied by an RRFT. Thus, for example, perhaps a feature essentially associated with racial group belonging (as defined by its added essentials profile) is also a necessary condition of Christian group membership (as defined by its construction profile). In that case, since the relevant feature (in different ways) explains what makes both racial and Christian group identities what they are, it marks a kind of *essential intersection* in those identities. Alternatively, perhaps there are necessary conditions of racial group identity (features of its construction profile) that are also accidents of Christian group-kinds, important but merely contingent manifestations of Christian group identity. In that case, it marks a non-essential or *accidental intersection* in those identities. The nature and manifestations of intersectional identities implied by the various proposed stages of an RRFT are therefore potentially complex, and they can admit of different kinds and greater and lesser degrees of essential or accidental overlap with one another.[16] While many RRFT scholars have supplied the materials suggestive of a race-religion intersection, precisely what sorts of intersection are implied remains for the most part under-analyzed.

What makes such an Epsteinian metaphysics of the religious-racial intersection proposed by an RRFT a useful thing to have? Its usefulness consists in helping us who are the inheritors and perpetuators of these identities to evaluate what we have made and continue to make of ourselves, racially and religiously. Raced identities in our society are inextricably bound up with the moral wrongs of *racism*. As Sally Haslanger has observed, part of the point of a theory of race is *diagnostic*, to identify the sites of moral malignancy within the development of a social body, where such diagnoses are oriented by antecedent norms of social 'wholeness' or 'health' and oriented toward the *amelioration* of racism (Haslanger 2012, 239–240). By identifying the wrong-making features of race-based meanings and effects along the particular paths of racialization by which racial group identity itself has been created, transformed, or destroyed, an RFT can motivate proposals for an amelioration of racism by way of whatever sort of *reconstruction* or *destruction* of these processes is called for by its diagnosis.[17] As a species of RFT, an RRFT proposes, minimally, that there are features of Christian group identity that form the anchors of contemporary racial group identity—initially fixing its identity, membership, and persistence conditions—including its various *racist* conditions of hierarchy, dehumanization, and asymmetric distribution of social and political goods. It therefore raises the question of what sort of diagnosis and amelioration of racism might be required in our making and re-making of the race-religion intersection.

Does a Christian religious constitution of race on an RRFT diagnosis, plus our antecedent commitment to anti-racism imply a *destruction* or merely a *reconstruction* of contemporary Christian group identity? If merely a reconstruction, then what sort is called for? Likewise, are the wrongs of racism constitutive of racial identity per se, or are they associated characteristics or accidents of that identity which might be revised while leaving racial identities and their criteria of group membership (criteria of e.g., whiteness, blackness, etc.) intact? (See, for example, Linda Martín Alcoff's defense of retaining and reforming rather than dissolving whiteness as a social identity in Alcoff 2015.) All this depends entirely on the details of our analysis of the metaphysics of one or both of the constituents of a race-religious intersection. For example, to know just what anti-racism implies for Christian group identity, we need to know whether the relevant features of Christianity that anchor the racist features of contemporary racial group identities are essential or accidental anchors of Christian group identity. If essential, are they also constitutive of Christian group identity as features of its construction profile, or essentially associated with Christianity in virtue of comprising one's permissions, obligations, abilities, etc. qua Christian?

These normative questions, while crucially important for deciding who and what we ought to become, cannot be answered either by means of an RRFT genealogy alone, or from any armchair moralizing apart from an Epsteinian type of analysis of that genealogy. It might seem, however, like answering those questions consists simply in assigning the empirical information given by historians and sociologists to the metaphysical profiles Epstein identifies, against the background of a general normative commitment to the moral badness of race-based social hierarchy or privilege. In that case, the required metaphysics of RRFT seems to reduce to the task of cataloging genealogical facts, perhaps followed by a disapproving gesture and handoff to political policy makers or community organizing to address the racism we uncover. If that were so, we might be forgiven for regarding that task as a mere clarification of what historians, sociologists, religious studies scholars ought to be doing to develop their accounts more rigorously and what sort of analysis religious and secular ethicists and activists ought to be working from to effect social change—in neither case would such cataloging amount to much of a substantive philosophical program.

But giving a fully specified RRFT involves a good deal more than merely sorting genealogical facts into some categories that display their basic structure guided by a general moral and political interest in understanding racial wrongs. Epsteinian description and Haslangerian normative orientation are both radically underdetermined. They give us broad structural desiderata for a normatively oriented metaphysics of RRFT but without actually specifying the metaphysical and normative shape that any such theory ought to take. For the remainder of this essay, I'll briefly outline some competing ways of theorizing each of these matters. Given the merits of the sociological and historical work of religious studies scholars and theologians summarized in the first part of this essay, these philosophical challenges represent a substantive but heretofore untapped research agenda for philosophers of religion.

Construction of the Race-Religion Intersection: Three Theories

First, an Epsteinian construction profile of 'race' and 'Christianity' for any given stage of an RRFT aims to specify the criteria by which we can individuate these group kinds and thus determine if and when any group counts as a racial group or a Christian group, thereby enabling us to say when either group has been created, transformed, or destroyed. But even on the assumption that the identity conditions of the racial group kinds we are interested in are socially constructed—i.e., that they are fixed by socially constituted anchors—there remain substantial debates over what sorts of identity conditions these are, and hence what sorts of social anchors were required to fix their content. A genealogical story of RRFT can be made consistent with various incompatible theories about this, yielding significantly different roles for Christianity to play in an RRFT explanation of its contribution to Western race and racism.

Recall, for example, RRFT claims of the sort made by Keel, Douglas, Carter, and Lloyd above, according to which a Christian theological anthropology and eschatology in some sense continues to operate within secular social arrangements, such that the semantics and structure of race within secular notions of e.g., political community, sovereignty, multicultural ideals—while abstracted from their overtly religious contexts—remain in some sense manifestations of Christian faith and practice. Such claims are best interpreted as saying that the relevant features of Christian faith and practice are not only *anchors* for a post-racial semantics and structure of race, but also essential features of it, whether individuating features of how it is constructed or added essentials. But whether that claim is correct or what it would mean for it to be correct might radically differ depending on what theory of social categories we rely on to specify the construction and added essentials profiles of 'race' for any given stage of the genealogy. I'll mention three of the most prominent options.[18]

On Ásta's account, social categories like 'race' are defined by the possession of social properties, e.g., the property of *being white*, or (more generally) the property of *being raced*. An individual's being a member of a social category thus consists in their possessing the relevant social property. What it is for any person S to possess a racial property P, Ásta claims, is just for some persons, groups, or entities with institutional authority or communal standing—under some contextually appropriate circumstances—to implicitly or explicitly *confer* the racial status of *being P* on S by way of some publicly expressed act, attitude, or behavior, in an attempt to perceptually track some set of base properties (such as bodily appearance, ancestry, culture, experience, etc.), resulting in some corresponding determination of S's enablements, obligations, etc. (Ásta 2018, 104). The meaning and effects of, e.g., *being white* thus necessarily depend on one's being *perceived* or *judged* as white, and *what whiteness is* for any given context reduces to some authoritative subjective conferrals that stipulate what whiteness is in that context. If this is right, then showing that features of Christian religious identity (or features essentially associated with it) are constituent in *being white* in secular society amounts to showing that those features are constituent in the perceptions or judgments of contemporary secular institutional and communal authorities—a highly implausible assumption on its face. At best, the Christian past of these categories seem best relegated exclusively to the anchor profile.

We might, however, dispute the view that membership in social categories is determined by any subject attitudes or their conferrals of the relevant social properties, and instead take a view more like Sally Haslanger's or Charles Mills's, both of whom regard social categories as *objective social structures* that, while anchored by the attitudes and actions of subjects, may persist and configure various social properties possessed by an individual without anyone's having conferred it on that individual (Mills 1998, 47–66; Haslanger 2012, 235–238). Rather than dwelling on the (important) differences between their particular accounts, what they share is an analysis of the criteria for belonging to a racialized group that can be satisfied by individuals apart from anyone's particular propositional attitudes toward them, much in the way that, e.g., "a given economic state can be a recession, even if no one thinks it is, and even if no one regards *anything* as a recession or any conditions as sufficient for counting as a recession" (Thomasson 2003, 276; cf. Khalidi 2015, 99). Likewise, if what 'whiteness' is and does as a social category is consistent with a good deal of explicit and implicit ignorance on the part of the institutional and communal authorities who perceive and judge individuals to be white, then it becomes more plausible to regard its historically Christian anchors to also constitute features of its construction or added essentials profiles.

One reason that objective social-structural accounts yield an increased relevance and plausibility of building the theological anthropologies of a Christian past into our present construction of race is that they are more permissive about the principle of unity that determines what race is for any given context—beyond merely shared attitudes and perceptions, it allows other kinds of shared continuities with the past to serve as defining features of what race is now, such as shared functional roles or patterns of social organization. Still, both sorts of accounts define race as a social property in virtue of which those who possess that property resemble one another and hence belong to the same group-kind. Theodore Bach has characterized this approach as a social version of an outdated biological model of species membership—one in which species kinds are defined 'phenetically' by resemblances between members rather than 'phylogenetically' by reproductive and replicative lineage (Bach 2016, 196). Likewise, Bach commends defining social categories phylogenetically as essentially social and historical, rather than biological, modes of replication and reproduction.[19] Theorizing the construction profile of race as an replicative natural kind with an historical essence yields an 'ontogenetic' account of group membership. The property of *being white* would thus be analyzable in terms of the replicative processes in virtue of which being white participates in an identifiable historical lineage of whiteness. If this is the right sort of account to give, then the claims that Keel, Douglas, Carter, and Lloyd make about the continued contemporary relevance of Christianity to a secularized construction of race become even more plausible than they were on the sorts of accounts offered by Haslanger or Mills.

Working out what sort of theory of the identity conditions for 'race' that an RRFT ought to adopt thus represents a substantial undertaking with significant stakes for our understanding of the semantics and structure of race as a Christian category. But successfully defending any such theory of race would only account for half of the intersectional relation an RRFT posits, since it would not tell us how we ought to understand Christianity as a *racial* category. Specifying this half of the proposed intersectional relation would require working out a theory of the identity conditions for 'Christianity,' which we might likewise develop according to a conferralist, objective structural, or socially ontogenetic analysis in order to determine whether the anchors Christianity supplied (or now supplies) for racial group identity were (or are) essential or accidental features of a Christian group identity. Moreover, just as in the different possibilities for theorizing race, just which of these types of theories we adopt for Christian group identity will have non-trivial differences in the type of intersection an RRFT can claim to demonstrate and the kind of diagnosis of religiously grounded racism it is capable of giving us.

Norms of Amelioration for the Race-Religion Intersection

A final site of fruitful philosophical theorizing demanded by an RRFT is that of determining its normative orientation. It might seem that making our legitimate moral and practical interests in a metaphysics of the race-religion intersection a *criterion* for the correctness of that metaphysics distorts the truth-aimed character of that enterprise. If there is such a thing as 'getting it right' with respect to what Christianity and race historically and presently refer to as social categories and how they are entangled in our context, then it seems to follow that requiring an account of them conform to our political interests can threaten to distort that account. Elizabeth Barnes is right to observe, however, that Haslanger's arguments for an ameliorative criterion is best understood not as a test of whether we have correctly analyzed the social categories that are the referents of our theory, but rather a test of whether our analysis has the capacity to identify and explain the features of social phenomena that prompted our theorizing in the first place (Barnes 2017). We cannot know to what extent a metaphysics of RRFT 'saves the appearances' with respect to Christianity and race unless our theory incorporates those appearances in what it analyzes and explains—which centrally includes moral and political phenomena of race-based inequalities with historical and contemporary ties to our society's religious history.

A question that Haslanger does not adequately address, however, is just what sort of normative framework to utilize for an ameliorative analysis and explanation of social categories.[20] If we are seeking to understand what those categories are in order to determine what they *ought* to be, then we will need to specify what constitutes their wrong-making features and what sorts of proposed revisions to them would count as ameliorating them. Both of these matters, however, are bound to be controversial and subject to reasonable disagreement about the legitimacy of the ameliorative aims that constrain our metaphysical theorizing. Suppose, for example, that we can establish that a minimally sufficient ameliorative RRFT is committed to some generally anti-racist moral norms such as the equality and dignity of all human persons, and a right to freedom from coercive race-based restrictions to one's autonomy. Still, these moral norms might be grounded in radically different sorts of ways depending on the background beliefs within which they are embedded, and that in turn might dictate distinct kinds of diagnoses and social visions for an 'ameliorated' race-religion intersection that is supposed to guide an RRFT. At the broadest level, two questions can help us to distinguish normative theory types for an ameliorative RRFT: first, will such a theory aim at a *theological* or *non-theological* kind of amelioration? Second, should the theorist adopt an *ideal* or *non-ideal* theory of amelioration?

A theological RRFT is one taken up by Christians whose group membership implicates them in the wrong-making features of the race-religion intersection, and whose anti-racist ameliorative interests might thus be aimed at reconstructing or recreating Christian social groups. In that case, theological background beliefs about—and ontological commitments to—e.g., God, divine creation and providence, sin, salvation, the church, and eschatology (the final state toward which Christians take God to be guiding creatures) might figure into both the diagnosis and the remedy of racism uncovered by an RRFT and theological facts might enter into an explanation of both *why* we ought to reconstruct racial and religious identities in conformity with principles of human dignity, equality, etc. as *religiously grounded* norms, and an explanation of what reconfigurations of our current social categories would best serve to exemplify those norms. An RRFT can reveal that it is much harder to be 'anti-racist' in one's theology than Christians, and especially Christian philosophes and theologians, have often assumed.[21] For example, if it turns out from our Epsteinian analysis of the essential features of Christianity qua social category that it requires some notion of God's electing of a special people as a 'new humanity' through whom human salvation is made available to the rest of the world, then this would place some radical revisionary demands on a theologically ameliorative RRFT not confronted by a non-theologically ameliorative RRFT.

A second important philosophical debate for determining the normative orientation of an RRFT metaphysics is the debate between 'ideal' and 'non-ideal' theory. The distinction between ideal and non-ideal theory in an approach to theorizing about the demands of justice stems from worries that political philosophers have expressed about the Rawlsian picture as presented in *A Theory of Justice*, but have subsequently expanded to embrace the wider question of how our theorizing about the norms of social and political community ought to relate to our practical interests in their implementation (Stemplowska and Swift 2014). Generally, ideal theorists suppose that the philosophical task consists or ought to consist primarily in first identifying what such communities ideally ought to be like—the best possible or thinkable norms of social or political ordering—and then utilizing that ideal standard as a standard for deriving the demands for social reconstruction imposed on us by the way our social reality is presently configured. Non-ideal theorists, on the other hand, are either skeptical that we can have anything like an ideal theory, and/or suspicious that relying on a purported social ideal as a norm of social reconstruction will result in furthering oppressive social arrangements or creating new ones (Anderson 2009, 135).

Laura Valentini helpfully distinguishes three distinct and separable debates that tend to go under the banner of the ideal/non-ideal debate, all of which confront our theorizing of the proper norms guiding a metaphysics of the race-religion intersection (Valentini 2012). First, we might construe the debate in terms of the kind of compliance presupposed in our theorizing about what the race-religion intersection ought to be. Ideal-compliance theorists would thus aim to specify what the Christianity-race intersection would look like when *all* the relevant agents in society are *fully compliant* with the demands of justice. An ameliorative RRFT thus describes its constituent social categories in terms of their partial compliance or non-compliance as compared with how those categories would look under the conditions of full compliance. Non-ideal-compliance theorists, on the other hand, "doubt that a theory designed under conditions of full compliance can take us very far in understanding what is required of us in conditions of partial compliance" (Valentini 2012, 655). A second form of 'idealizing' in theorizing the demands of justice that orient an RRFT has to with the relative degree to which we take contingent factual considerations to be relevant for identifying what a just political or social community looks like in the first place. Thus, 'utopian' ideal theorists either eliminate or as much as possible eliminate considerations about contingent social, historical, or material constraints on a specification of just community, whereas 'realistic' non-ideal theorists take the stipulation and incorporation of contextually contingent constraints to be important or necessary desiderata for giving such a specification (Valentini 2012, 656–660). Finally, Valentini identifies a distinction between the guiding role given to 'transitional' versus 'end-state' norms of social ordering in specifying what a reconstructed race-religion intersection requires of us. Ideal-end-state theorists advocate the development of a long-term or final vision to guide our evaluation of what counts as legitimate political and social goals that might contribute to transitioning who and what we are toward that end state. Non-ideal transitionalist theorists, on the other hand, hold that we do not require and need not rely on the specification of any such end-state goals in order to determine transitional states that move us toward *better* reconfigurations of the social categories we have constructed and currently maintain (Valentini 2012, 661–662).

While we might approach an RRFT as a species of ideal theory or non-ideal theory in any of the above three ways, each will have different consequences for identifying the relevant wrong-making features of the race-religion intersection for ameliorating racism and the role of Christianity in anchoring it. Moreover, whether or not one takes a theological approach to RRFT might place different philosophical pressures on us to adopt various sorts of configurations of ideal and non-ideal theory. For example, various theological background beliefs about the existence of the church as an eschatological social reality, or the obligations of agents as judged in light of full compliance with divine commands, or the contingent and material social and historical features of earthly life as unnecessary constraints to be abstracted away from our vision of a heavenly utopia might all be unique motivations that propel theologically ameliorative RRFTs toward ideal theory. Or, perhaps there are likewise theological grounds for rejecting these motivations in preference of a non-ideal theoretic approach to a theologically ameliorative RRFT.

Conclusion

Heretofore, the literature in race and religion has given very little attention to the philosophical tasks implicit in theorizing the intersection implied by RRFT genealogies or the demands imposed by an anti-racist social vision in our use of those genealogies. The historical, social scientific, and theological literature proposing a race-religion intersection is an insufficient guide for interpreting or assessing its explanatory and normative significance. What I have attempted above is to offer just that sort of guidance. An Epsteinian paradigm supplies us with the requisite desiderata for a metaphysics while a Haslangerian ameliorative paradigm supplies us with the requisite desiderata for the legitimate social and political goals that such a metaphysics ought to help us achieve. Offering a substantive Epsteinian analysis oriented by a substantive normative framework, however, confronts us with various competing and non-trivial differences in theory-choice about the nature of the social categories involved and whether we ought to take a theological or non-theological and an ideal or non-ideal approach to them. My aim has not been to navigate these difficult questions of theory-choice, but rather to show how they are coordinated in the philosophy of religion's contribution to an interdisciplinary project on race and religion in the US. As with precious little else in philosophy, the stakes of getting our metaphysical and normative theories right are high—both for Christians and non-Christians—just insofar as we wish to know what sort of people we are and what sort we ought to become.

Notes

1. See, for example, www.washingtonpost.com/news/acts-of-faith/wp/2016/11/23/the-racist-roots-of-white-evangelicalism-and-the-rise-of-donald-trump/?noredirect=on&utm_term=.7597db337557 and www.huffingtonpost.com/entry/white-evangelicals-race-immigration-diversity_us_5bda1fb1e4b019a7ab5a04be.
2. Elsewhere I offer some reasons this might be the case. See Yadav forthcoming. One reason for this neglect may be the ways that philosophers tend to abstract away from their lived experiences. For further development of that point, see Michelle Panchuk's contribution to this volume.
3. As I've often heard it expressed, if there is any such complicity of Christianity in racism, this is merely a contingent and accidental feature of Christianity, and hence not central to understanding what Christianity essentially is or claims. The presumptuousness of this dismissal should become evident below.
4. For the notion of a social "looping effect" see Hacking 1996, 351–383.
5. The designation of the "Western world" is itself a product of the European cultural way of carving up the world that was constituent in its sociohistorical processes of racial formation. See Said 1979.
6. Following *Galatians* 2:20 we might say of race that "the life that it now lives in the flesh it lives by faith in the Son of God."
7. For a recent account that differs in some ways to mine, see Hill-Fletcher 2017.
8. Whether Thiessen's reading is best understood as representing Paul or Paul's later reception history is a question I leave open.
9. See Emerson and Smith 2001, 76–83; for an analysis of the 'rationalized Christianity' that stands behind the secular construction of the 'self,' see Taylor 1989, 234–247.
10. If therefore the notions of post-racial sainthood and eschatological political community are theological 'analogies,' then for Lloyd and Carter they are, we might say, "analogies of being," in Aquinas's sense.
11. I am here extending an example discussed by Epstein 2016, 153–155.
12. Or suppose that our alien possesses satisfactory answers to all of these questions. It may nevertheless sensibly wonder: are these *necessary and sufficient conditions* for anything's being a footprint, or are footprints more loosely natured sorts of things, constituted in terms of, e.g., a syndrome of properties? Which conditions for anything's being a footprint are a matter of social convention and which aren't?
13. The primary object of explanation in Epstein's framework is the social group *kind*, rather than their individual and unique instances. In the present case, the question is what constitutes Christianity and race as the relevant kind (or kinds) of social groups constituent in an RRFT.
14. I agree with Jonathan Shaffer that it is best to characterize anchors as a species of grounds, but nothing I say here or below necessarily turns on that debate. See Shaffer forthcoming.
15. My talk of essential and accidental features/properties of a social group is analogous to Anderson's notion of constitutive vs. contextual goals of a practice; cf. Anderson 1995.
16. Moreover, we can distinguish this sort of *category* intersectionality from a category *exemplification* intersectionality, which consists in an inseparability

not necessarily between the social categories themselves, but only an inseparability in the way they come together in the individual who exemplifies them. For an analysis of the metaphysics of what I'm calling "exemplification intersectionality" as a kind of ontological and explanatory priority of the joint-exemplification of social properties, see Bernstein (unpublished). On my analysis, category intersectionality entails exemplification intersectionality but not the reverse.

17.
> To recognize that race is historically and politically constructed is . . . to acknowledge our power, both collective and individual, to transform the meaning of race. We created this meaning-system and the social order it supports. We can change it as well.
> (Omi and Winant 2012, 16)

18. Khalidi 2015 distinguishes between kinds of social kinds depending on how they answer to two determinations: (a) Does the social kind's *existence* depend on any subjective attitudes? (b) Does *membership* in the kind depend on any subjective attitudes? Type 1 social kinds answer "no" to both (while nevertheless depending on subjective attitudes towards other things). Type 2 answers "yes" to (a) and "no" to (b), and Type 3 answers "yes" to both. The three theories of race I consider below are instances of, respectively, a Type 3, Type 2, and Type 1 on the Khalidi scale.
19. For Bach's application of this view to the category of gender, see Bach 2012, 231–272. Indeed, Bach's view best approximates the RFT claim that race just 'is' its historical path of racialization. For another way of theorizing this idea, but one that proposes eliminating race-talk in favor of racialization-talk, see Hochman 2017.
20. Although Haslanger identifies the regulative role for a background picture of "*eudaimonia*" or more generally what we take to be "cognitively valuable for us *as a group*" in guiding our knowledge pursuits, she bypasses any substantive argument on behalf of her preferred picture, which centers on the value of autonomy in our agency (Haslanger 2012, 361).
21. Namely, it is not a simple or straightforward matter to discern how the wrong-making features of racial group identity supervene on ontological commitments expressed in traditional Christian doctrines and practices.

References

Alcoff, Linda Martín. *The Future of Whiteness*. Malden, MA: Polity, 2015.

Anderson, Elizabeth. "Knowledge, Human Interests, and Objectivity in Feminist Epistemology." *Philosophical Topics* 23.2 (1995): 27–58.

———. "Toward a Non-Ideal, Relational Methodology for Political Philosophy." *Hypatia* 24.4 (2009): 130–145.

Ásta. *Categories We Live By*. New York: Oxford University Press, 2018.

Bach, Theodore. "Gender Is a Natural Kind with a Historical Essence." *Ethics* 122 (2012): 231–272.

———. "Social Categories Are Natural Kinds, Not Objective Types (and Why It Matters Politically)." *Journal of Social Ontology* 2.2 (2016): 177–201.

Barnes, Elizabeth. *The Minority Body: A Theory of Disability*. New York: Oxford University Press, 2016.

———. "Realism and Social Structure." *Philosophical Studies* 174 (2017): 2417–2433.

Bernstein, Sara. "The Metaphysics of Intersectionality." Unpublished. https://www3.nd.edu/~sbernste/MOI.pdf.
Buell, Denise. *Why This New Race? Ethnic Reasoning in Early Christianity.* New York: Columbia University Press, 2005.
———. "God's Own People: Specters of Race, Ethnicity and Gender in Early Christian Studies." In *Prejudice and Christian Beginnings*, edited by Laura Nasrallah and Elisabeth Schussler Fiorenza, 159–190. Minneapolis: Fortress Press, 2009a.
———. "Early Christian Universalism and Modern Racism." In *The Origins of Racism in the West*, edited by Miriam Eliav-Feldon, Benjamin Isaac, and Joseph Ziegler, 109–131. New York: Cambridge University Press, 2009b.
Carter, J. Kameron. "Post-Racial Blues." Qideas.org lecture, December 4, 2014. www.youtube.com/watch?v=5yxlSlbqOmQ.
Douglas, Kelly Brown. *Stand Your Ground: Black Bodies and the Justice of God.* New York: Orbis, 2015.
Emerson, Michael and Christian Smith. *Divided by Faith: Evangelical Religion and the Problem of Race in America.* New York: Oxford University Press, 2001.
Epstein, Brian. "A Framework for Social Ontology." *Philosophy of the Social Sciences* 46.2 (2016): 146–167.
———. "What Are Social Groups? Their Metaphysics and How to Classify Them." *Synthese* (2017): 1–34.
Feagin, Joe. *The White Racial Frame: Centuries of Framing and Counter-Framing*, 2nd ed. New York: Routledge, 2013.
Feagin, Joe and Sean Elias. "Rethinking Racial Formation Theory: A Systemic Racism Critique." *Ethnic and Racial Studies* 36 (2013): 931–960.
Hill-Fletcher, Jeannine. *The Sin of White Supremacy: Christianity, Racism and Religious Diversity in America.* New York: Orbis, 2017.
Frederickson, Paula. *When Christians Were Jews.* New Haven: Yale University Press, 2018.
Goldberg, Nathaniel. "History of Philosophy and Conceptual Cartography." *Analytic Philosophy* 58.2 (2017): 119–138.
Hacking, Ian. "The Looping Effects of Human Kinds." In *Causal Cognition*, edited by Dan Sperber, David Premack, and Ann James Premack, 351–383. Oxford: Oxford University Press, 1996.
Harris, Cheryl. "Whiteness as Property." *Harvard Law Review* 106.8 (1993): 1707–1791.
Haslanger, Sally. *Resisting Reality: Social Construction and Social Critique.* New York: Oxford University Press, 2012.
Haynes, Stephen. "Distinction and Dispersal: Folk Theology and the Maintenance of White Supremacy." *Journal of Southern Religion* 17 (2015). http://jsreligion.org/issues/vol17/haynes.html.
Heng, Geraldine. *The Invention of Race in the European Middle Ages.* New York: Cambridge University Press, 2018.
Hesse, Barnor. "Preface: Counter-Racial Formation Theory." In *Conceptual Aphasia in Black: Displacing Racial Formation*, edited by P. Khalil Saucier and Tyron Woods, vii–xii. London: Lexington Books, 2016.
Hochman, Adam. "Replacing Race: Interactive Constructionism About Racialized Groups." *Ergo* 4.3 (2017): 61–91.

Jennings, Willie James. *The Christian Imagination*. New Haven: Yale University Press, 2010.
Keel, Terence. *Divine Variations: How Christian Thought Became Racial Science*. Stanford: Stanford University Press, 2018.
Khalidi, Muhammad Ali. "Three Kinds of Social Kinds." *Philosophy and Phenomenological Research* 90.1 (2015): 96–112.
Lloyd, Vincent. *Religion of the Field Negro: On Black Secularism and Black Theology*. New York: Fordham, 2018.
Marsh, Charles. *The Beloved Community: How Faith Shapes Social Justice from the Civil Rights Movement to Today*. Cambridge, MA: Basic Books, 2005.
Mills, Charles. *Blackness Visible*. Ithaca, NY: Cornell University Press, 1998.
Moya, Paula and Hazel Rose Markus (eds.). *Doing Race*. New York: Norton, 2010.
Omi, Michael and Howard Winant. "Racial Formation Rules: Continuity, Instability, and Change." In *Racial Formation in the Twenty-First Century*, edited by Daniel Martinez HoSang, Oneka LaBennett, and Laura Pulido, 302–331. Los Angeles: University of California Press, 2012.
———. *Racial Formation in the United States*, 3rd ed. New York: Routledge, 2015.
Said, Edward. *Orientalism*. New York: Vintage Books, 1979.
Shaffer, Jonathan. "Anchoring as Grounding: On Epstein's *The Ant Trap*." *Philosophy and Phenomenological Research* (forthcoming).
Singh, Nikhil. "Racial Formation in an Age of Permanent War." In *Racial Formation in the Twenty-First Century*, edited by Daniel Martinez HoSang, Oneka LaBennett, and Laura Pulido, 276–301. Los Angeles: University of California Press, 2012.
Stemplowska, Zofia and Adam Swift. "Rawls on Ideal and Nonideal Theory." In *A Companion to Rawls*, edited by John Mandle and David Reidy, 112–127. Oxford: Wiley-Blackwell, 2014.
Taylor, Charles. *Sources of the Self: The Making of the Modern Identity*. New York: Cambridge University Press, 1989.
Taylor, Paul. *Race: A Philosophical Introduction*, 2nd ed. Malden, MA: Polity, 2013.
———. "What Is Philosophical Race Theory?" Modern Critical Theory Lecture Series at the University of Illinois, October 25, 2016.
Thiessen, Matthew. *Paul and the Gentile Problem*. New York: Oxford University Press, 2016.
Thomasson, Amie. "Foundations for a Social Ontology." *Protosociology* 18–19 (2003): 269–290.
Valentini, Laura. "Ideal vs. Non-Ideal Theory: A Conceptual Map." *Philosophy Compass* 7.9 (2012): 654–664.
Wood, Forrest. *The Arrogance of Faith: Christianity and Race in America from the Colonial Era to the Twentieth Century*. Boston: Northeastern University Press, 1990.
Yadav, Sameer. "Toward an Analytic Theology of Liberation." In *Marginalized Identities, Peripheral Theologies: Expanding Conversations in Analytic Theology*, edited by Michelle Panchuk and Michael Rea. New York: Oxford University Press, forthcoming.

Contributors

Joshua Blanchard is Visiting Assistant Professor of philosophy at Oakland University in Rochester Michigan. He received a PhD in philosophy in 2018 from the University of North Carolina at Chapel Hill and an MA in philosophy from Brandeis University. He received a BA from the University of Michigan at Ann Arbor. He has published articles in *Ethical Theory & Moral Practice*, *Philosophical Studies*, and the *European Journal for Philosophy of Religion*.

Joshua Cockayne is a Lecturer at the Logos Institute for Analytic and Exegetical Theology at the University of St. Andrews. Joshua's research focuses on issues of spirituality, spiritual practice, and ecclesiology in analytic theology. He completed his PhD at the University of York for work on Kierkegaard and the spiritual life. He has published articles in *Religious Studies*, *Faith and Philosophy*, *The British Journal for the History of Philosophy*, and *Zygon*. His book on Kierkegaard and Christian spirituality will be coming out in 2020 with Baylor University Press.

Dustin Crummett is a Postdoctoral Researcher at the Ludwig Maximilian University of Munich working as part of a project on the philosophy of animals in the Islamic world. Crummett specializes in political philosophy, ethics, and philosophy of religion, and in particular focuses on questions concerning egalitarianism, animal ethics, and the nature and content of divine obligations to creatures. Crummett's work has appeared in venues including *Oxford Studies in Philosophy of Religion*, *Res Publica*, *Faith & Philosophy*, */Ergo/*, and several edited volumes.

Stephen T. Davis is the Russell K. Pitzer Professor of Philosophy, Emeritus, at Claremont McKenna College. He is the author or editor of some 17 books and over 80 academic articles. He mainly writes about the philosophy of religion, Christian thought, and analytic theology. His books include *Christian Philosophical Theology* (Oxford University Press: 2009), *After We Die: Theology, Philosophy, and the Questions of Life after Death* (Baylor University Press: 2015), and *Rational Faith: A Philosopher's Defense of Christianity* (InterVarity Press: 2017).

Contributors

Helen De Cruz holds the Danforth Chair of Philosophy at Saint Louis University. Her publications are in empirically informed philosophy of cognitive science, philosophy of religion, social epistemology, and metaphilosophy, including *Religious Disagreement* (Cambridge University Press, 2019) and *A Natural History of Natural Theology* (with Johan De Smedt, MIT Press, 2015). Her overarching research project is an investigation of how humans engage in thinking about abstract domains such as theology, mathematics, and science, what it means for limited, embodied beings like us to think about these topics, and what epistemic conclusions we can draw from this.

David Efird is a Senior Lecturer in philosophy at the University of York. He received his DPhil from the University of Oxford, and his research focuses on the philosophy of religion and analytic theology. In addition, he is a priest in the Church of England.

Blake Hereth is a PhD Candidate in philosophy at the University of Washington. Ze has defended animal immortality in *Heaven and Philosophy* (2018), animal universalism in *Paradise Understood: New Philosophical Essays on Heaven* (2017), and afterlife justice for transgender persons in *Hinder Them Not: Centering Marginalized Voices in Analytic Theology* (forthcoming).

Kirk Lougheed is a PhD Candidate in philosophy at McMaster University where he specializes in epistemology and the philosophy of religion. He is currently most interested in questions about peer disagreement and about the axiological status of the existence of God. He is editor of the forthcoming volume, *Does God Matter? Four Views on the Axiology of Theism* (Bloomsbury).

Michelle Panchuk is an Assistant Professor of philosophy at Murray State University. Her current research is situated at the intersection of philosophy of religion, trauma theory, and feminist philosophy, with a particular focus on giving a philosophical account of religious trauma. Prior to coming to Murray State, Michelle held a postdoctoral research fellowship in the Center for Philosophy of Religion at the University of Notre Dame. Her other interests include metaphysics, medieval philosophy, and philosophy of race.

Faith Glavey Pawl is a Research Fellow at the Logos Institute for Analytic and Exegetical Theology at the University of St. Andrews, and teaches philosophy at the University of St. Thomas in Minnesota. Her research focuses on issues concerning animals and the environment in philosophical theology, especially in the Thomistic tradition.

Kelli D. Potter is Associate Professor of philosophy and Associate Director of religious studies at Utah Valley University. She has published articles in *Dialectica*, *Faith and Philosophy*, *The International Journal* of *Philosophy of Religion*, and *Dialogue: A Journal of Mormon Thought*. Her current research focuses on the philosophical significance of heterodoxy.

Kevin Timpe holds the William H. Jellema Chair in Christian Philosophy at Calvin College. His recent books include *Disability and Inclusive Communities* (2018), the *Routledge Companion to Free Will* (2017), and *Free Will and Theism* (2016). In addition to philosophy of religion, Timpe's scholarly work focuses on philosophy of disability, metaphysics, and virtue ethics.

Scott M. Williams (DPhil, University of Oxford) is Assistant Professor of philosophy at the University of North Carolina Asheville. He publishes in the areas of medieval theology and philosophy, philosophy of religion, and philosophy of disability, and is editing the book, *Disability in Medieval Christian Philosophy and Theology* (Routledge, forthcoming) and coediting a special issue (forthcoming) of the journal *Theo-Logica* on 'Conciliar Trinitarianism.' Prof. Williams is also writing a book on the Trinitarian theology of Henry of Ghent.

David Worsley is an associate lecturer in the department of philosophy at the University of York, UK. He holds a BA in politics, philosophy, and economics, an MA in political philosophy, an MA in philosophy, theology, and ethics, and a PhD in philosophy, all from the University of York. His research interests are in philosophy of religion and analytic theology.

Sameer Yadav (ThD, Duke Divinity School) is Assistant Professor of religious studies at Westmont College. He is a systematic and philosophical theologian who works on Christian mysticism, religious experience, and race and religion. Sameer is author of *The Problem of Perception and the Experience of God* (Fortress Press, 2015) and a number of articles in edited volumes and journals on various topics such as the nature of doctrine, Scripture, divine hiddenness, liberation theology, and mystical experience in religious epistemology.

Hilary Yancey is completing her PhD in philosophy at Baylor University. Her research interests focus in metaphysics, philosophy of disability, philosophy of biology, and medical ethics. She enjoys teaching philosophy to all ages and advocating for inclusive spaces, particularly schools.

Eric T. Yang is an Assistant Professor in the department of philosophy at Santa Clara University. He received his PhD in philosophy at the University of California, Santa Barbara. His research areas are primarily in metaphysics, philosophy of religion, and philosophy of mind, though he occasionally dabbles in epistemology, value theory, and Chinese philosophy.

Index

ableism 245, 266, 272–276, 336
Adams, Marilyn McCord xi, 150, 173, 195, 332
Adams, Robert Merrihew 223–224
agnosticism 38–39, 48
Alcoff, Linda Martin 379
Alston, William 108–111, 163–165, 168, 174
ameliorative project 71, 328, 379, 383–386
Anderson, Jami 250–252
Anderson, Pamela Sue 314–315
Andow, James 35
Anglo-Saxon 372–373
animal awareness argument 15
animal cognition 167, 172–173, 178
animal gods 16, 184, 190, 192
animal incarnations *see* incarnation, animal
animal universalism *see* universalism, animal
animals 14, 142, 145–147, 151–156, 164–165, 167, 169–179, 198, 200, 202, 258n27; non-human 13, 19, 141–145, 149, 152, 157–159, 163, 183–184, 189–190, 193, 196–199, 201–202
Anselm of Canterbury 195, 301–302, 307
Anselmianism *see* theology, perfect being
Appearance View 16, 199–200
Aquinas, Thomas 163–164, 174, 183, 197, 214, 216, 231n14, 255, 285, 301–302, 307, 330–331, 340, 351, 355–357, 360–361
Argument against Exclusive Moral Personhood 18, 265, 269, 277–278
atonement 42, 57, 60–61, 68–69, 102, 297, 301, 307, 350, 354–355
attention-deficit/hyperactivity disorder (ADHD) 250, 252

autism 101, 250–252
autonomy 103, 145, 160n6, 384
Avrahami, Yael 97, 102, 116

baboons. 169–171, 176–177
Barnes, Elizabeth 17, 55, 58, 63, 213, 215–216, 243–245, 342–343, 383
beatific vision 17, 21, 145, 214, 233n31, 244–245, 250–252, 256, 257n8, 351, 356–357; *see also* heaven
beliefs xiii, 49–50, 113, 133, 172, 175; background 12, 114–115, 314, 384; M-beliefs 164–165, 168, 179n3; religious 7, 11, 40, 48, 52, 108
beneficence argument 14, 142–144, 147–148, 150–151, 156–157
Benton, Matthew 166
bias 9, 32, 63–65, 67–68, 88, 276; against religious belief 87; implicit 52, 57; masculinity and purported lack of 45; *see also* normate biases
bioethics 35
Boethius 264, 277–279, 282–285, 287
Bradford, Gwen 217
Bradley, Ben 147–148
Brison, Susan 55
Buckareff, Andrei 330, 343n1
Burchard, Melissa 55, 58
Butler, Judith 323–324

Calvin, John 242
Carter, J. Kameron 373–374, 381–382
cartography, conceptual 21, 366
Cheney, Dorothy 169–170, 176–177
Christianity *see* religion, Christian
cis-normativity 313, 317
cissexism 315
clarification, task of 4–5
Clough, David 196–197

Coakley, Sarah 33
Compensation Argument 14, 142–143, 145, 154–156
Conciliar Christian Theology 18, 265–266, 288; *see also* Pawl, Timothy
Cone, James 16, 60–62, 195–196
Corcoran, Kevin 330
corvids 175
Craig, William Lane 298–299
credibility defects 51, 71, 82, 90
Creegan, Nicola Hoggard 16, 196
creeping things *see* animals, non-human
Crenshaw, Kimberlé 31

Dawes, Greg 4
death 14, 120, 147, 149–150, 152, 218, 254, 298, 330–331, 350, 352, 354–355, 357; Jesus's 196, 305–307, 310; smell of 102, 115; survival of 141, 145, 151, 156–157, 183
Descartes, René 31, 34
desires 115, 190, 234; animal 147–150; bodily 294; and disability 225, 233; of the heart 247–248; higher-order 21
de Waal, Frans 170, 175–176, 198
Dionysius the Areopagite 103–104
disability 16–17, 55, 65–66, 68, 101, 212, 214, 223–224, 229, 241–248, 253–254, 256, 340–343; 'bad-difference' 216, 244; cognitive 16, 204n18, 242, 265, 273, 358n8; in heaven 17, 254–255, 336; 'mere-difference' 17, 216, 244; optionality view of 224; physical 17, 212–216, 218–226, 228–229, 235n39; unilateral elimination view of 215; unilateral retention view of 220; vs. impairment 243
discrimination 159, 329, 333, 335–336; against fawns 193; racial 60
diversity 3, 7, 9, 18, 40, 51, 255, 322
Divine Asymmetry 185, 189
divine hiddenness 21, 60, 253, 350
Divine Love Argument 14, 142, 150–152, 154
'divine reversals' 13, 120–121, 123–124, 127, 133–134
Dotson, Kristie 42–43, 56, 58, 64–67
Douglas, Kelly Brown 372–373, 381–382
Draper, Paul 1, 7, 9, 33
Durkheim, Émile 172

Eiesland, Nancy 17, 66–67, 223, 242–243
Eilan, Naomi 111
Elimination View 17, 215–216, 224
Emerick, Barrett 72
emotion 24, 11, 55, 57, 59, 62–64, 66–68, 71, 72–73, 100–101, 103, 106, 110–111, 161, 166–167, 176–177, 180, 249, 299–300, 303, 309, 320, 324
epistemic credit 45, 65, 334
epistemic humility 11, 69, 71–72
epistemic injustice 11, 12, 35, 41, 45, 56–57, 64, 70, 74, 80, 86, 90, 93, 94, 95, 335
epistemic violence 56, 63, 64, 65, 70, 74
Epstein, Brian 376–377, 380
Epsteinian profiles 378–379, 384, 386
Equal Power Presumption 187–188, 193
Ertz Yisrael 120, 125–127
ethics 18, 62, 73n1, 83, 132, 150, 164, 265–266, 288, 296, 308n8, 365; applied 58, 121, 131, 183, 366; bioethics (*see* bioethics); sexual (*see* sexual ethics)
ethnocentrism 369
eucharist 101, 242
evangelicalism 22, 365, 373–374
exclusion 10, 18, 37, 39, 46–47, 50–51, 60, 246–247, 271–272
experience, lived 3, 31, 35, 37–38, 50, 57, 59–65, 67–69, 73
experience, mystical 108–111, 165, 169; religious 11–13, 33, 79–80, 82–93, 97–98, 101, 107–116, 163, 165, 169, 173–174, 178, 202; transformative (*see* transformative experience)
experimental philosophy 34–35

fairness, maximal 16, 187–191, 193
feminism 31, 49, 312–314, 322, 337
feminist epistemology 79, 93
feminist philosophy 10, 32, 41, 55, 58, 62, 312, 320–321
focus group study 10, 32, 34–41, 43–44, 46–50
Franciscan knowledge *see* knowledge, of persons
Francis of Assisi 174–175, 178
Fricker, Miranda 11, 45, 64, 70–72, 79–82, 90–92, 329, 334–335

Index

gender 3, 10, 19–20, 31, 33–34, 40, 43–45, 50–52, 56–58, 80, 127–131, 133, 312–343; gender identity 63–64
gender dysphoria 315, 323–324
gender oppression *see* oppression, gender
genealogy of race 369, 374–375, 378, 380–381
Goldberg, Nathaniel 21, 366
Goodall, Jane 171
Gould, James Barton 215, 224
Graves, Shawn 146–152, 157–158
Green, Adam 12, 98, 111–112
Gregory of Nyssa 98–99, 102, 264, 279–280, 283–284
Griffioen, Amber Leigh 9, 23n12

Hadewijch 33–34
Hanson, N. Russell 98, 113
Harding, Sandra 49, 314
harm 37, 46–47, 51, 60, 64, 66, 80–82, 86–89, 155–156, 196, 219–220, 234–235, 305
Harm Avoidance Argument 14, 142, 146–150
Harris, Harriet 5, 8
Haslanger, Sally 20, 58, 63, 328–329, 337–339, 343, 366, 379–380, 382–383
Hauerwas, Stanley 220–221, 235n40
'Hauerwas's dictum' 221
Hawking, Stephen 211–213
heaven 14, 16–18, 21, 33, 101, 103–104, 106–107, 124, 129, 145, 149, 151–153, 156–158, 212–221, 223–225, 229, 241, 244–248, 250, 252–255, 316, 331–332, 343, 347–350, 355–357; *see also* beatific vision
Held, Shai 122
hell 20, 347, 349–350, 354–355, 357
Hereth, Blake 14, 141, 146–147, 149–152, 154, 155–158
hermeneutical injustice 11, 72, 79–80, 82, 89, 91–92
heteronormativity 20, 191, 312–313, 317, 320
heterosexuality 19, 56, 159, 197, 317, 319, 323
historical theology 5–6; *see also* theology
Hobson, Peter 166–167
human value 80, 222, 242, 267, 283
hyperfocus 250–252
hypostasis 264, 279–286

ideal theory vs. non-ideal theory 384–386
identity, group 21, 365, 369–370, 377–378, 380, 383; numerical 17; personal 32, 35, 221, 224, 248, 328, 330, 334, 341; religious 52–53, 368, 374, 376; social 71, 80; theoretical identity vs practical identity 17, 222–224, 228–229; *see also* intersectionality
ignorance 64–65, 67–68, 71–72, 353; reliable 56, 63, 65, 70
immortality. 83, 147, 156–157
incarnation 17, 19, 21, 202, 245–247, 265, 278–279, 281–288, 297, 301, 305, 350, 355; animal 199–200; multiple 183; fittingness of 197
Incarnation Argument 16, 195–197, 201
Injustice, epistemic *see* epistemic injustice
Insole, Christopher 5, 24, 25, 26
intersectionality 31, 33, 45, 313; category vs. exemplification 313, 387n16
intuitive knowing 11, 83–85, 92–93
Isaac of Ninevah 154, 162
Islam 7, 37, 41, 43, 45, 256, 346, 391

Jaggar, Alison 75
Jennings, Willie 371, 390
Jesus 12, 17, 19, 61, 101, 124–125, 128–129, 136, 184, 196–197, 199, 213, 224–225, 246–247, 293–294, 304–305
Judaism *see* religion, Judaism
John, Tyler M. 24, 146, 162, 206
justice xiii, 20, 65, 71, 72, 126–127, 132, 134, 145, 157–158, 160, 200–201, 205, 216, 218, 237, 243, 248, 313, 323–324, 328–329, 332, 334–335, 337–340, 343–344, 384, 385, 389–390; hermeneutical *see* hermeneutical injustice
justification, task of 4–5

Kant, Immanuel 265, 267
Keller, Lorraine 169
Kittay, Eva Feder 18, 55, 62–63, 71, 272–276, 278
Knepper, Timothy 3, 5–7, 22
knowledge, perceptual 14; Franciscan (*see* knowledge, of persons); intuitive 11, 83–85, 92–94, 96; of persons 14–15, 166, 169, 180n9; propositional 15, 59, 165–166, 169

Korsgaard, Christine 222
Kummer, Hans 171

LDS Church 20, 23, 313, 315–318, 320, 323, 325–327; see also theology, Mormon
Leontius of Byzantium 280–281, 283–284
Lewis, C.S. 201, 229
LGBTQ+ 46, 128, 312, 315
limbo 21, 235n42, 347–357
liturgy 103–104, 106–107, 110, 242; see also worship
lived experience see experience, lived
Lloyd, Vincent 373–374, 381–382
Locke, John 18, 264–267, 271, 281–282, 286
Loftus, John 1–2
Longino, Helen 49
Lycan, William 108

Macaskill, Grant 251
MacDonald, Scott 4–5
Manne, Kate 58
Mary, and what she didn't know 15, 59, 166, 226–227
masculinity 44–45, 320, 325
materialism 145, 312, 330
Matthews, Gareth 341
Mattlin, Ben 218–219, 221
M-beliefs see beliefs, M-beliefs
McCall, Thomas 6
McMahan, Jeff 62, 222, 274
Medina, José 45, 70
membership 16, 189–190, 200, 268–269, 271–276, 278, 287–288, 320, 367, 376–379
Mills, Charles 58, 200, 382–383
mind-reading see knowledge, of persons
Minimum Limbo Conclusion (MLC) 348, 350–351, 355
minorities 31–32, 35, 39, 41, 50–51; religious 10, 36–37, 39, 41–42, 94n14
Mizrahi, Moti 6–7, 203n12
monogenism 371–372
monotheism 7. 288; social 191–192; strict 191–192
moral agency 141, 197–198, 286, 348, 353
moral community 18, 55, 62, 267–269, 271–272, 275–276, 278, 286, 287–288

Moral Shift Argument 18, 265, 272, 276, 287
moral standing 143–144, 160, 267, 274–277
moral value 267, 283
Mormonism see theology, Mormon
Moses 121, 129
Mullins, Ryan 340
Murphy, Mark 144, 150, 297–300
Murray, Michael 253–254
mystical experience see religious, experiences, mystical

narrowness of philosophy of religion see philosophy of religion, narrowness of
naturalism 12, 50, 89–90, 92–93
neurodiversity 251–252
New Atheists, the xii, 12, 86
New Testament 6, 102, 121, 124, 127–130, 133–134, 370
Nichols, Ryan 1, 9, 22n3, 33
normate biases 18, 246–247, 251, 255, 256n16
nowhere see oppression, of men

olfaction see olfaction, religious experience
Omi, Michael 366–368
ontology, social 22, 58, 365
oppression 13, 31, 159, 197; animal 200, 205n25; epistemic 10, 56; gender 317; of men (see nowhere); systems of 61, 344; of women 313, 315

Palmer, Ellis 212
Panksepp, Jak 177–178
Parker, Rebecca 60–61, 68
Patriarchy 20, 312–313, 327, 320
Paul, Laurie 59, 72, 94n9, 226, 228
Paul, the Apostle 97, 102–103, 155–116, 124, 213, 251, 294, 305, 330, 370
Pawl, Timothy 199, 250, 288n8
perception 98, 100, 111–116, 163, 165; non-sensory 109; sense 12, 83, 98, 104, 168; spiritual 101, 105, 164–165, 167–169, 174, 179
personal identity see identity, personal
personhood 18, 246, 264–272, 276–279, 281–288, 323; medieval approaches to 265, 284, 286–287; modern approaches to 18, 265, 267, 272, 277, 285–288

philosophical practice xii, 2, 10–11, 31–32, 34–35, 37–38, 50, 52, 56, 59, 71, 81, 93, 107, 134, 172
philosophy of race *see* race, philosophy of
philosophy of religion x–xi, xii–xiii, 1–11, 13–14, 16, 18–19, 21–23, 31–41, 43–52, 55–61, 64–65, 67–70, 72–74, 79, 93, 98, 107–108, 141, 164, 166, 256, 308, 312, 314, 320–321, 330, 365, 380, 386; Christian 1, 4, 6, 8–9, 21, 23, 33, 241, 365, 384; crisis of 2; narrowness of x, xii–xiii, 5, 6–10, 22, 33, 40, 98, 108
physicalism 226–227
Plantinga, Alvin 1, 195, 297
polytheism 191–192
Power Argument 16, 185–190, 192, 201–202
Preexistence View 16, 199–201
prejudicial stereotypes 81, 87
privilege 9–11, 20, 22, 49, 66–67, 70, 73, 102, 175, 197, 199–201, 252, 313–314, 328, 338, 365, 372–373, 380
problem of evil 9, 13, 37, 42, 46–47, 51, 57–58, 60, 141, 143, 145–146, 165, 183, 203, 244, 258, 297, 299, 329, 332
Proclamation, the 20, 316–317, 319–320, 323, 325
procreation 20–21, 302, 316, 326, 347, 350, 354–355, 357, 362

qualitative research 35, 37, 50

race 10, 21–22, 33–34, 341, 365, 381, 386; philosophy of 56, 58, 61, 269–270, 344n10, 369, 374, 378, 381–383; theology and 365–366, 374, 378–379, 383–386; semantics and structural aspects 369–373; racial formation theory 366–368, 376, 378–381, 383; *see also* white supremacy
racial formation theory 367, 369, 371; *see also* religious racial formation theory
racial politicization 369, 372
racial rationalization 371–372
racism 18; *see also* white supremacy
Ratcliff, Ace 212–213
Rea, Michael xi, 98, 110–116, 146, 154

redemption 4, 247, 305, 349–350, 352–353; post-mortem 21
Relationship Argument 14, 142, 151–154, 156
religion: African 7; Buddhism 7, 85, 376; Chinese 7; Christian xii–xiii, 2, 5–7, 9, 13, 15–16, 21–23, 33, 37, 40–41, 43, 46, 50, 52, 57, 63, 65, 70, 97, 100–105, 107, 116–117, 120–121, 123, 127–128, 130–134. 163, 167, 172–174, 183, 191, 195–197, 199–200, 202, 213, 230, 241–245, 254, 256, 259, 265–266, 277–279, 283–284, 286, 288, 293–294, 296, 300, 305, 308, 316–317, 328–331, 352, 354, 357, 360, 365–366, 368–374, 376, 378–388; Hinduism 7, 183; Islam 7, 37, 41–43, 45, 256; Judaism 7, 10, 13, 36, 37, 38, 41, 42, 43, 47, 94, 97, 101, 102, 105, 121, 125–127, 131–137, 197, 256, 288, 305, 346, 368, 370; non-Christian 7, 370, 387; non-theistic approaches to 7
religious authority 14, 142, 151–154, 156
religious experience *see* experience, religious
religious racial formation theory 21, 366, 368, 374; *see also* racial formation theory
religious studies xii, 3, 5–6, 366, 368, 374, 380
resurrection 213–215
revealed text *see* scripture
Richardson, Louise 99–100
Rolin, Kristina 49
Rowe, William 193–194, 297
Russell, Bertrand 56–59, 67, 72
Rusticus the Deacon 264, 283–285

savior 16, 23, 197
Schellenberg, John 3–4
Schilbrack, Kevin 5, 7, 33
scripture 97, 102, 103, 141, 215, 351; Bible 5, 97, 102–104, 117, 259n30, 294; *The Doctrine and Covenants* 315; Hebrew 13, 97, 102, 116n1, 120–124, 126–130, 132, 134, 135n1, 135n2, 135n6, 136n12
seeing as 12, 98, 113, 115
sense perception *see* perception, sense
sentience 142

Severus of Antioch 280–281, 283
sex xiii, 10, 19, 20, 236n43, 255, 259n29, 291, 315, 318, 321–324, 326n4, 329, 337–339, 341, 344, 368; male xiii, 6, 8, 10, 20, 28n10, 32–33, 43–44, 50–52, 56, 60, 70, 72, 197, 315–316, 318, 320–324, 328, 334, 338, 341, 345; female 19–20, 33–34, 43–44, 255, 315–318, 320–324, 328, 337–339, 341, 345n18; *see also* acts; procreation; sexual activity
sexual activity 293–300, 302–307
sexual ethics 13, 129–131, 133
sexual harassment 64, 72, 79, 82
sexuality 13, 51, 56, 121, 127–128, 130, 133, 295, 321, 323, 365
sexual orientation 33, 66, 130, 222, 313, 325
Seyfarth, Robert 169–170, 176–177
shared attention 111
Shared Power Presumption 189–190
Simmons, J. Aaron 7–9
sin 21, 48, 69, 128, 199, 213, 215, 243, 247, 303–304, 347, 249–265
Singer, Peter 62, 148–149, 274
skeptical theism 145–146
smell *see* religious experience, olfaction
Smuts, Barbara 171, 177
social intelligence hypothesis 170
social ontology *see* ontology, social
social structures 245, 313, 338, 342, 382
Social Trinitarianism 18, 191, 286; *see also* trinity
sociology of race *see* race, sociology of
solidarity, divine 16, 197, 199, 204n18
speciesism 274
spiritual perception *see* perception, spiritual
standpoint epistemology 44, 49–50, 56, 319, 324
standpoint theory 312–315
Stokes, Dustin 112–113
Stoljar, Natalie 329, 341
strong objectivity 314
Stump, Eleonore 8, 14, 21, 23, 117n4, 165–168, 174, 176, 179n3, 217, 231n9, 232n18, 233nn.24–25, 233n26, 233n30, 234n31, 236n47, 247, 253, 332, 347, 358n5, 359n22, 24

suffering 14–16, 46–47, 57, 59, 67, 103, 141–143, 154–156, 178–179, 191, 193, 196, 199–201, 203n16, 17, 204n18, 219–220, 223, 229, 233n24, 28, 235n40, 243, 247, 252–254, 299, 305, 318, 332
Swinburne, Richard 66, 197–198, 214, 252–253; Swinburnegate 66

Taylor, Paul 366–373
Teresa of Ávila 33 and beyond the mystical veil
testimonial injustice 11, 50, 74n9, 79–82, 86–91, 94n10, 334
testimonial quieting 42–43, 65–67, 69
testimonial silencing 42, 50, 63, 66–67, 70
testimonial smothering 43, 51, 65–69
testimony 6, 11–12, 37, 41–43, 56, 62, 64–72, 79, 81, 83–85, 87–88, 93n4, 95n17, 221, 354
theodicy 24, 253–254
theodicy argument 142–143
theology xii, 1, 3–4, 5–7, 16, 18, 20–21, 46–47, 60–61, 65, 83, 97, 100, 104, 117n4, 173; evangelical (*see* evangelicalism); Mormon 19–20, 38, 47, 312–313, 315–326; perfect being 15, 16, 136n15, 183, 184–185, 241–243, 251, 256n2, 259n30, 265–266, 278, 286, 288, 312, 315, 317, 370, 372, 374, 378, 384; philosophical xiii, 1, 3, 10, 13, 15, 19, 21–22, 22n6, 134, 183, 223; speculative 241–242
theory of mind 149, 175–177
Thiessen, Matthew 370, 373
Timpe, Kevin 17, 21–22, 243, 250, 309n17, 347–352, 354–355, 357
Torrance, Alan 6
Toscano, Margaret 312, 321–322
Toy, Mitchell 211
Trakakis, Nick 2–3
transfeminism 318
Transformation View 16, 199–200, 226–228
transformative experience 59, 79, 85
transgender 63, 73, 312–313, 315, 318–321
transmisogyny 315
Transmormon 318
trauma 55, 60, 73; religious 60, 64, 67–68
Tremain, Shelley Lynn 243

trinity 191, 247, 265, 278–279, 285–286, 288

underrepresentation 10; *see also* minorities; women, underrepresentation of
Unequal Power Presumption 188, 193
universalism 153; animal 14, 142–143, 146, 149–152, 154–155, 157, 200; star 160n1

Valentini, Laura 385–386
van Inwagen, Peter 179, 230n6, 330
Van Wagenen, Joel 330, 343n1
'view from nowhere' 10–11, 31, 49–50, 56–57, 59–61, 63–63, 67, 70–71
Vargas, Manuel 248

Wainwright, William 108–110, 114
Warren, Mary Anne 18, 264–265, 267–272, 276–279, 285–287
well-being 14, 17, 147–149, 151–152, 158, 215–216, 233n23, 297–299; animal 143, 148, 153, 179
Westphal, Merold 2, 7

whiteness 61, 371–373, 379, 381–382
white supremacy 61, 366–367, 371–373; *see also* racism
Wiebe, Phillip H. 83–85
Wierenga, Edward 191, 203n9
Williams syndrome 248–249, 252
Winant, Howard 366–368
Witt, Charlotte 329–340, 342–343
women, underrepresentation of 37, 44
Wood, Forrest 371–372
Woodward, Holly 228
worship 8, 17, 61, 97, 101–102, 106–107, 184, 201, 252, 304; *see also* liturgy
Wynn, Mark 110, 112

Yong, Amos 17, 242, 246–247, 251, 256, 329, 335–336, 340

Zagzebski, Linda 299, 303, 309n13
Zionism 13, 125, 130; religious 126–128, 133
zoolatry 15, 184, 201
zoomorphism 15, 184, 201
zootheism 15–16, 183–185, 191, 195, 200–202